The Minneapolis Story,

Through My Eyes

By Ron Edwards

As told to Peter Jessen

The Words and Experience Of A Renaissance Black Man In A White Man's World

Beacon On The Hill Press
PMB 258
9220 SW Barbur Blvd - Suite 119
Portland, OR 97219

ISBN: 1-932047-70-0

Table of Contents

Seventeen Chapters On Minneapolis: Past and Present

History	Background	Court System,
Politics	Education	Housing
Construction	Vikings	Local Black Organizations
Redistricting	War On Drugs As War On Young Black Men	

Alternative Futures: Status Quo Vs. Change For The Better

Sixteen Short Historical Interludes Between The Chapters

Conclusion On Future Possibilities For Minneapolis.

As it is impossible to list all of the people I have worked with over the past 40 years, I won't try. But I do need to list a few.

As a storyteller, I first want to thank the legion of African storytellers who have been their village memories, passing the Word from generation to generation. To be thought of in that fashion by those who gave me the idea is thanks enough. In addition, I want to thank the storytellers of the Seminole Indian nation, from which my ancestors also come.

Secondly, I want to thank all the African Americans in Minneapolis. You are every bit as interesting and fascinating and noble as our ancestors, indeed more so. Don't ever forget that.

The railroads were important to my life. My father and grandfather worked on them and I rode them for my trips back to Kansas City. My parents found a way to come together even though they were from different sides of the tracks. I acknowledge my family, without whom I would not be here, and happily honor them in my discussions of Chapter 4.

My paternal grandfather, C.M. Edwards, son of a slave, a porter, a man of many trades, but also a storyteller, who kept the bold and beautiful faith until his death at 96, who told me the stories at his knee when I was a little boy and on through my manhood and our shared adulthood.

My father, Alfred Edwards, who worked as a porter for 40 years (Interlude 9), and then as a waiter for another 20 years, who lived until 1996.

My maternal grandfather, L. Virgil Miller, a physician and attorney, who was active in politics and close to Harry S. Truman, and my grandmother, Katie Miller, a high-society hostess in Kansas City.

I would be remiss if I did not thank two women who are representative of all those who have worked so hard to keep their eye on the prize of freedom and equal opportunity: Nellie Stone Johnson and Natalie Johnson-Lee. Nellie was my mentor (Chapter 4 and Interlude 4). Natalie is our newly elected Council Member from the 5th Ward of Minneapolis, who has been eager to learn about Nellie. It has been an honor for me to pass on Nellie's lessons to Natalie, who has picked up the torch of Nellie Stone Johnson (Chapter 12). They are the role models to whom I point the next generation. Study them, follow them, and let them lead you to the Promised Land.

Others I want to thank and acknowledge include Dr. Thomas Johnson, Frank Alsop, Warren Hagstrom, James Tillman, Leroy Bogar, Erthea Wiley, Dr. Herman Dillard, Burl Grigsby, Larry Blackwell, and Rev. William W. Smith.

Finally, I want to thank Peter Jessen for undertaking the task of helping me put my story in writing. Peter sat through hours and hours of taped conversations with me, and undertook the backup research for me. He was certainly the man for this job. I verbalize orally and he verbalizes in writing. We compliment each other very well. I met Peter two years ago when he was working on the story of Sandy Stephens (discussed in Chapters 3 and 10). Peter lived in Minneapolis for four years in the early 1990s and continues to visit for communications and business development consulting and to visit his son in college here. While he lived here, he taught college courses in American Minorities and Social Inequality. As a young man, he also had a chance to meet such community advocates as Saul Alinsky, under whose methods I trained, and Mohammad Ali, on the South Side of Chicago, the White within miles. And he was in Harlem visiting friends the weekend Malcolm X was assassinated. He also used to meet with Lou Stokes who was later Chairman of the Congressional Black Caucus. And he twice experienced what I am calling *The Minneapolis Story* as well. The first time was when he participated in the Metropolitan Council's "Forum on The Economics of Racism" in December 1992 (posted on his web site, www.PeterJessen-gpa.com). He showed me his response and suggestions for a solution, discussion points, a way to develop a solution/vision, that he submitted, of which two of the four parts were an action program for resolving racism (he also included pages of references and resources). His submission was never acknowledged. His second experience occurred when he submitted to the Vikings, the Twins, downtown businessmen, the legislature, the stadium task force, and the Governor, plans for how to finance and fund new stadiums without raising new taxes (Chapter 15). He even let them know they could easily share his materials with others as they needed, as he put all of it on his web site so they could make it easier for staff and others to gain access to his papers on how to provide new stadiums without new tax dollars. He included his collated list of 16 conflict resolution models and 47 communications models (both are on hisi web site). Again, he never received any response from any of them either, not even from their staffers. Not one. That is the Minneapolis Way: if the powers that be don't want it they ignore it. If you want to know what won't happen, pay attention to what they ignore.

There is another reason why I am glad Peter has taken on this task with me, a sad but pragmatic reason. He is White. One of the sad things I have learned in the community over the past 40 years is that for some of our people, if a White person doesn't also say it, then it is not to be believed. Both Whites and Blacks are guilty of this. With Peter's professional training, scholarship, and personal experience in Minneapolis, he helps affirm and validate *The Minneapolis Story Through My Eyes* for those who need a White voice to go along with my Black one.

Finally, Peter is an excellent researcher, especially in using the Internet. After many discussions and tapings together, not all references are remembered. Other phrases and information have been known so long or used so often their initial source is no longer remembered. Thus missed acknowledgments, though inevitable, are not desired. Any that we become aware of will be cited in future printings. And any person who would like to submit additional stories reflecting any of the topics of the chapters of this book, we welcome your stories for a follow up book dealing with urban America in other cities that we would like to write. Either submit them through the web site for the book, www.TheMinneapolisStory.com or through the publisher www.BeaconOnTheHill.com.

My thanks also to **Beacon on the Hill Press.**

A final product is only as good as the professionals behind the scenes. To obtain the best talent and keep costs down, Beacon on the Hill Press uses a unique group of hand picked independent professionals. We highly recommend their talents to you:

Web page designer for www.TheMinneapolisStory.com and
www.BeaconOnTheHill.com

> Design For Web/Ancil Nance
> 503-225-9957
> www.designforweb.com

Book Cover design:

> Page-By-Page
> 503-225-9957
> www.pagebypage.com

Editing/proof reading

> Jill Kelly, Ph.D.
> 503-235-2019
> editor@aracnet.com

> Mimi Macht
> 541-386-4941
> mimimacht@gorge.net

READER'S NOTES:

Preface

Storytelling As Connecting the Dots:
Africa Style and Ron Edwards Style

Once you eliminate the impossible, whatever remains,
no matter how improbable, must be the truth.
> Sherlock Holmes
> (Sir Arthur Conan Doyle)

Don't believe everything you hear, and only half of what you see.
> Burt Lancaster, *The Crimson Pirate*

The world is not what it appears to be.
Reality is of course, ...until further notice.
> Peter L. Berger

A glass half full is still half empty.
A glass half empty is still half full.
> Ron Edwards

There is a saying in Africa that speaks truth to all of us: When a man dies, a whole library goes with him; hence the need for storytellers. In many societies where stories are passed down orally, to gain his listener's attention, the storyteller must provide them with the perspective that his special hearing and sight gives him. Social scientists talk about the "looking glass self," where we hold up mirrors to each other. The storyteller holds up sounds, as he offers the listener an echo of his or her existence. I'm told that in Guatemala, "echoman" is the label for the wisest storyteller.

But this is not an oral report. It is a written report. As Abraham Lincoln said: "*Writing*, the art of communicating thoughts…is the great invention of the world." And that is what I attempt with this book: to give each of you who hear my story and who read it an echo, a reverberation of my inventive communication to you regarding the life of the city we call Minneapolis. I've been taking her pulse for over 40 years. I delight in echoing her past and present for you, as well as providing a vision for you of her future. I seek to bring clarity to the story. Think of me as a missionary of clarity.

I am an advocate of excellence in community life, which can't be achieved until we have overcome not only the adversity of racism but helped the Whites overcome the fears that propel that racism. Because the latter has not taken place yet, Minneapolis has become a kind of last outpost, a land of the great experiment, where the City demonstrates to the world the success of its experiments in how to keep minorities in their place (the great "secret" that James Baldwin talked about regarding how the machinery of White America is geared to keeping the Black man in his place).

Alex Haley discovered his roots through a storyteller in Africa, who recited the names of everyone going back many generations for several hundred years, until he spoke the name of the relative who was taken to this country as a slave: Kunta Kinte. This led Haley to write his family's biography, including the major events that became the embodiment of the history of his family. He didn't want his family members to forget who they were, where they had come from, and the possibilities of where they could go in the future. In turn, his book became a best-seller and the two *Roots* mini-series made from it became two of the most watched programming events in television history. In my book, I tell stories of people too, including the major events of the people of my city, Minneapolis, Minnesota. And I hold forth every week on my TV show (Public Access Channel 17, MTN, which airs every Sunday at 5:00 p.m. You are welcome to tune in at any time as I explore my city, report my city, and tell my city's story.

When you tune in you will learn. When you tune in you will become educated. I have been gratified to learn from newcomers of their appreciation for a show like this, and by their telling me that I caused them to start going for their dictionaries and to their history books because they wanted to learn more about the topics discussed on the show. That is my hope for your experience with this book.

If you are not from Minneapolis, the story of Minneapolis could nonetheless be the story of your city. Like the story of your city, the Minneapolis story sometimes reads like a cheap detective novel: crooked politicians, deadly women, wealthy playboys and playgirls, professional sports figures, domestic double agents (Blacks selling out other Blacks), political double agents (Democrats selling out Blacks who voted for them), corrupt union officials, lazy newshounds, news stories for sale to the highest bidder, billionaires, millionaires, blackmailers, poor people, homeless people, great schools, lousy schools, wonderful neighborhoods, ghettoized neighborhoods, empowered people, disempowered people, enriched people, impoverished people, enfranchised people, disenfranchised people, people seeking justice and fairness, and others trying to make sure there is no justice and no fairness, Keystone-cops capers and Three Stooges slapstick, conspiracies, innocents, sell-outs, deal makers, planners, intellects with truth and intellects with lies, honor and dishonor, order and confusion, puppets and puppet-masters.

Some of you, as you read my Minneapolis story, will think I'm on the left, a Democrat. Others of you will think I am on the right, a Republican. It was heartening to see in the major speeches of the last Presidential election cycle that **both** Democrats and Republicans focused on what might be called traditional American concerns: poverty, injustice, racism, and children. The **difference** is about the remedies. In this book I reject the traditional remedies of both the Democrats and the Republicans because neither has solved these problems.

Nonetheless, in the interests of full disclosure, I will always be a card carrying member of the party of Nellie Stone Johnson (Interlude 3), the leader of the old "Farmer-Labor" party and founder of the merged party with the Democrats, Minnesota's Democratic-Farmer-Labor Party. That is not the same as today's Democratic Party. Nellie stood for tolerance and diversity, pluralism and anti-racism. So do I. She pushed hard for equal access and equal opportunity in terms of education and jobs. So do I.

When you read the Table of Contents, you read the names of my heroes. We all need heroes, especially the young. The best-known heroes to step forward in the past year were in the Twin Towers of New York City and on a plane in Pennsylvania. We need heroes to lead us in the charge against the terrorism of racism. Whether you, the reader, are Democrat or Republican, Independent or Green, I argue that what I propose in this book as remedies actually will serve whichever party that that adopts them, because in adopting them, good things will happen to them and to society in general and to the cities of our country in particular. And all who adopt them would be heroes.

The chief character here is the City of Minneapolis: This is her story, not mine; this is her autobiography, not mine. The Minneapolis story is for everyone: Black, White, Brown and Yellow in every city in America, and especially those inner cities with large Black populations.

The great storyteller William Faulkner said that we as human beings "will not merely endure" but "will prevail." Faulkner saw us as "immortal," not because we "alone among creatures" have "an inexhaustible voice," but because each of us has "a soul, a spirit capable of compassion and sacrifice and endurance." So come. Endure with me. Prevail with me.

I don't tell everything I know in this book. That would require a dozen volumes. But what I do tell is the truth. I tell human truths, political truths, racial truths, and all kinds of other truths. All that I tell is true. It happened to me or I was there as a witness as it happened to others. I provide dates and places and names and let the reader join with me in connecting the dots. As I complete this writing during the summer of 2002, we hear a lot about connecting the dots to better enable us to predict and prevent terrorism. Thus, since 9/11, this term "connect the dots" has become popular again. It is a good phrase. In this book I will connect the dots so you can see what I see through my eyes: Minneapolis.

About some of what I say you may ask: "If this is true, how come I haven't read about it in the newspaper?" That alone helps prove one of my points: that what you have missed in the *Minneapolis Star Tribune* or in the *St. Paul Pioneer Press*, the mouthpieces of the puppet-masters, has been written about in the *Spokesman-*

Recorder, the Minneapolis Black newspaper. So read on. In Minneapolis, as in many cities, it is the Black newspapers that carry the most truth.

Some readers will be scandalized by what I write: "How dare he," they will say. Others will find some of my comments inflammatory. Others, however, will wonder how it is I have stayed so even-tempered, given the events I report, and will call my remarks not inflammatory but honest reporting.

My intended audience is not only the Blacks of Minneapolis. It is also the Whites of Minneapolis, for this is their story too. Finally, I write for all African-Americans in all cities, as this is their story just as much as it is mine.

My special audience for this book is the African-American readers of Minneapolis and, in particular, the readers of the *Minnesota Spokesman-Recorder,* the only independent news voice in Minneapolis (as it is with Black newspapers in many cities). More than any others, Black newspapers know the importance of not being "asleep at the switch" when it comes to knowing what is going on. It is a matter of survival to always "know what time it is" in terms of what is going on. This book is about what time it is in Minneapolis.

I don't write here to trash Minneapolis but to lift her up. I write not to disparage Minneapolis but to remind her of her past greatness and to urge her to a vision of future greatness, in the hope that she will regain a vision that includes all people and peoples of our community.

I do not consider myself a community activist as much as I consider myself a community advocate, a backbencher, if you will, staying the course, advocating for civil and human rights, regardless of who is in power. I am a daily petitioner for those left out or pushed out. I advocate for all people, Black and White, Brown and Yellow, but especially the poor and even more especially, for poor young Black men. And although my work has been primarily with organizations associated with Blacks in Minneapolis, I have stood up for all people regardless of color, for I stand for justice and fairness.

I also write this book for those Black people who have been left behind in the inner cities, who, for a wide range of reasons, haven't been able to or haven't been allowed to take advantage of the opportunities available to Whites. I have long stood for self-help of the poor in inner city communities against a backdrop of organizations and governments and corporations fighting against their rising up and achieving prosperity.

Racism cuts both ways. On the one hand, it prevents opportunity, as Whites block Black access and opportunity. On the other hand, negative acts, such as any crime that is labeled by Liberals, whether White or Black, as being somehow justified as a lashing out by a "victim" is even more preventive of opportunity taking, as it makes such deeds excusable. Young people in particular need to be empowered both personally and professionally so that they can build character and a sense of community, so that they can be successful in their personal and professional lives, so they will focus, undertake the work required, and learn that perseverance works, and abandon the notion of being victims who can only wait to be helped.

So that is what this book is about: connecting the dots, which I've been doing in Minneapolis for 40 years. Telling the Minneapolis Story *Through My Eyes* is the result of my connecting the dots. I've been mentioned over 7,000 times in the local paper. One reason is because reporters like to hear my take on things because they know I will connect the dots for them when I can and will let them know when I can't (Interlude 1).

Not everyone likes the way I connect these dots. Those in power in the Minneapolis branches of the Urban League and the NAACP, as well as the Minneapolis City Council and the Minnesota State legislature, are often like the U.S. Congress and Federal agencies: they like the way things are. They may not like what's going on outside their organizations, but they like what is going on inside, for as long as they can maintain the status quo, they can maintain their jobs and offices and retirement, which, without any other incentive becomes their only incentive. My connecting the dots makes it more and more difficult for them to maintain the status quo.

My way has been to work peacefully within the system. What finally made me write this book is the unbelievable corruption of White and Black leaders, which has resulted in one of the most onerous examples of gerrymandering that I have ever seen. In addition, this corruption has tried to destroy a new Council Member (who, in my view, is not only mayoral but also gubernatorial material) as well as destroy the ward she represents. She scares the establishment, which likes their way just fine and doesn't want to let in anyone new.

Besides connecting the dots, I'll also point to disconnects. In this book, I'll connect the dots that show the disconnects regarding the courts, education, housing, the prison system, the University, redistricting, and the racism of boss government in Minneapolis.

Here are the dots I will connect for you: a wealthy town, a wealthy state, high taxes and great revenue for governments, a dozen headquarters of Fortune 500 companies, a Federal Reserve Bank (one of only nine in the country), the lead city of the upper Midwest, the headwaters of the Mississippi River, the strong center of the country that some refer to as the "middle coast." That is one set of dots. Yet there is also a disconnect. Minneapolis and Minnesota, which are mostly White and which claim to be liberal, are not inclusive of the poor, whether Black or White. Look at the Black dots: Blacks have the lowest education and job and income levels, and they have been herded into a new district of North Minneapolis stripped of its economic base. In essence, Blacks have been shunted to a ghetto-like Ward. What kind of dots connect to make that? Wealthy White dots. I'll show you how that has been done. And I'll suggest how to undo it.

I will also connect the bureaucratic dots that run the massive welfare bureaucracies, which have been allowed to run the lives of the poor, especially Black poor, and thus ruin many of them. Before these monstrous welfare bureaucracies took over, Blacks had better family values and more intact families than Whites. Those dots have now become disconnected: 70% of African-American children are born out of wedlock (although Whites lag behind, they have the same trend, are in danger of that as well). Look at the divorce rates: White and Blacks seem to be in a race to see how many families they can disrupt and how many children they can abandon. We know that 80%-90% of men in prison, depending on how it's counted, Black *and* White, are men who had no father figure in their lives. And yet we continue the old policies that tear down families and denigrate men.

So when you connect the dots, you see a definition of insanity: doing the same thing over and over and expecting different results. When I connect the dots, as I will explain in this book, I take a more sinister view: that the same thing is done over and over in order to make sure that the results don't change the status quo. The war on drugs, for example, is a war on Black men, especially young Black men (Chapter 9): 76% of drug users are White but 70% of those imprisoned for drugs are Blacks. At the current rate of incarceration, 2/3 of Black men will be in the penal system in some fashion by 2020. The large amounts of money that used to go into education now go into prisons, while the lesser amount that used to go for prisons now goes for education. But those in gated communities don't seem to care. They can afford private schools or can afford to live in the suburbs with good schools. They have police who carry guns to protect them. Indeed, half of gun carrying officers at any one time in America today are on private pay. They think they have connected with safety from society. Instead, all they have done is disconnect from society, and such disconnected dots are not good for America.

I see all this especially when I attend neighborhood, community, City or State meetings in Minneapolis, St. Paul, and Duluth, as well as hear about meetings in other parts of Minnesota. I talk to people in person and to the many who call me during my TV show to discuss issues of the day and to provide more information and insight about what is going on in Minneapolis. I obtain the information and insights that enable me to connect the dots. Sometimes I think I'm the only guy doing this. So be it. I've always worked with the system. I'm sure the story of Minneapolis is the story of other cities as well. But I only know the Minneapolis story. I don't know of anyone else who can tell the story as I can. I hope others in other cities will be moved to tell their city's story as well.

And so, because we do indeed live in a wonderful country, our glass is half full. But, as Frederic Douglass said, we still have "the unfinished business" of obtaining freedom for everyone. And thus our glass is half empty. I have made it my business to work with everyone to help achieve a full glass for everyone, which I define as equal access and equal opportunity in terms of becoming a part of the social, political, and economic mainstreams.

From my volunteer positions in White and Black organizations, I see how to connect the dots. From my TV show and from my other public service, I get more information helping me connect the dots. And so I'll not only connect the dots, I'll predict where they are taking us depending on how we choose to connect the dots in the future. Doing so will not be new for me. The faithful followers of my TV program listen precisely because I not only connect the dots but I listen to their questions, find out answers for them, and report back on my next show. They also tune in because they know I can predict how the dots are going to get connected. Forewarned is forearmed. And this book will also provide forewarning to Minneapolis.

I have only one goal: fairness. I advocate for fairness, for equal access, and equal opportunity for all, for fairness in education, housing and jobs. And so I write about Minneapolis as I see her, a wonderful place for White people and the home of the masters of the great experiment of the last outpost: how to keep and put excess minorities in their place, especially young Black men. I write about Minneapolis as a Minneapolis person of the last 56 years; I have spent the last 40+ years as a community activist here.

Now I am no genius. There are precious few of those. I would even wager that you, dear reader, are not a genius either. But let me tell you what I am. I am an American of African-American and Native-American parents and grandparents and great-grandparents. And that too is part of the Minneapolis story.

I have struggled to get the message out in Minneapolis for over 40 years, and I have met with two types of obstructionists. At first, they were mostly White obstructionists, when Blacks courageously engaged the system in the 50s and 60s, when Black was bold and beautiful. My oh my, did we have much to be proud of! Then two things happened. First, White Liberals lost their nerve. Then the Black "leaders" lost their nerve. This failure of nerve led White Liberals to say, in the final analysis, that Blacks couldn't make it and that they needed government help. This was clever of the Liberals, for it made Blacks dependent on Liberal-backed government largesse, so that the White Liberals could maintain power over Blacks, not share it with them. It allowed Liberals to use Blacks just for their votes for White power. It also enabled Black leaders to become paid "middle managers" between the White bosses and the Black population. This generated the second type of obstructionists: Blacks who battle for the funds set aside for Blacks, which has led to the corruption of many Black leaders. Rather than serve those in the field, these Blacks elected to serve the White boss in the "Big House," where they could at least take care of themselves, even if it was on the backs of those in the field.

These sellouts in turn tell the White Mastuhs that these field hands are just jealous, that they are not real seekers of social justice. And so they make deals with the

Mastuhs' henchmen, usually politicians and government agency managers. And thus, for the excess inner city Negroes, the NAACP has become the National Association for the Advancement of Colored Plantationers. And the Urban League has become the paymaster of liberal government paymasters, just as long as the field hands stay in line.

I am a field hand. I am proud to be a field hand. I plow the same field that Martin Luther King plowed. I invite everyone, Black and White, to work in these fields with me.

When I use the terms *scam* and *fraud* and *corrupt*, I use them in their moral sense, not just the legal sense: that something is illegal and therefore wrong, because some legal things are not always right, as in slavery when it was legal or Jim Crow laws. What I keep seeing causes me even greater anxiety: that because of the ways the laws and regulations are written, defined, and interpreted, these Black leaders have deluded and defrauded Blacks without actually doing anything illegal. The best example is one I'll repeat several times in this book: the $1 billion expended for public housing in Minneapolis that has resulted in only 52 units (Chapter 8). If that doesn't run a chill up and down your spine, nothing will. Here is an appropriate parallel: This is the same reason we have yet to see many arrests or fines in corporate America despite the parade of CEOs caught up in corporate accounting scandals. Much of it was legal. Slavery was legal. Jim Crow was legal. Hence we have social movements, like the Civil Rights Movements, because much of what is legal is not right. And if we continue to allow laws opposing civil rights in education, housing, employment, and economic development to continue, there will be an active revision of the Civil Rights Movement.

Something wonderful happened in Minneapolis in November of 2001. The house Negroes were unable to deliver the vote of the field hands. Natalie Johnson-Lee, a Black field hand, won a City Council seat, beating the White president of the City Council, Jackie Cherryhomes. This was the biggest upset in the history of Minneapolis politics. It was a people's victory.

But when that happened, there was a furious response from the White DFL city Mastuhs, who then turned against both the field hand who had won and the house Negroes who were supposed to prevent it. The DFL cut off the house Negroes and then tried to redistrict the field hand out of any power by permanently disempowering and impoverishing her Ward (Chapters 12 and 13).

No matter how often in history this happens, it eventually sits like ashes in the mouths of the house Negroes, even though at first it looked like a sweet apple. But the DFL, which offered the apple, is a snake. Like too many who are offered the apple, the house Negroes decided, just as Adam and Eve did, to eat of it. We see the same dynamic at work in the film *Mr. Smith Goes To Washington*, where Mr. Smith refuses to be bought. Where are the Mr. Smiths of Minneapolis? The sad thing today is that we no longer have movies where at least one person fights that corruption and then awakens others to do so too. Now the movies not only portray corruption as a given, showing none that are not on the take, but they also make comedies out of it, as if no one believes such ideals are possible anymore and that greed is the main virtue, as if the secret of success and power is to tempt a person's greed and they will sell out. I am not one of those. I still believe in the American ideal, in the American dream of freedom and liberty for all. I have never sold out and never will. And I'm not the only one. Many believe. Many of those in power who didn't believe it found it out after 9/11. 9/11 has been a wake-up call in more ways than one, reminding us that God can make good out of evil. In my view, we are still looking for that wake-up call from 9/11 to happen in Minneapolis.

Some people think I am on a Don Quixote quest charging windmills. I take that as a compliment. As a student of the 1960s and one caught up in the idealism of that period, I have never given up on the dream, as others have. What sets me apart is that I have the courage to stay true to the dream, which itself is true to the ideals of this great country. If more Whites and Blacks held to these ideals, we would be a better country. Indeed, the very fact that I can write and publish such a book bears testimony to the greatness of this country.

I have given myself the freedom to fail. I don't have to be successful in anything other than to know and be true to myself, to follow the discipline necessary to do what I do, and to follow the ideals of our great land. I report to you my experience in doing so. This country, you, me, all of us, are works in progress. So too is Minneapolis. I am here to tell you her story as I see it.

Minnesota is known for being "Minnesota-nice." But as I connect the dots, it is often Minnesota ice: freezing Blacks out, keeping Blacks out in the cold.

Minneapolis is a wonderful city that is too often confused, too seldom moved to make things simple, and too willing to perpetuate the status quo.

My interest is simple: To do everything I can to help all people of Minneapolis achieve equal access and equal opportunity. I keep my eye on the prize: the time when there is equal access and equal opportunity for all. That is what gives my life meaning. And with that meaning, I can endure almost any suffering.

I'm not here to ride on anyone's back and I'm not here to be ridden. I'm not here to raise your consciousness, because that suggests I'm in a superior position, nor would I submit to your trying to raise my consciousness as if you were superior. Rather, I'm here to stand with you, shoulder to shoulder, as we point out the to each other and work together to expand each other's consciousness so that we can see more of what is on the horizon, together, as equals, and in so doing find our common ground.

What I write is not based on some kind of special knowledge because I am Black or because I am part of a minority, as if some kind of Black essence gives me special insights. Not at all. I follow no race-based agenda nor political party. Rather I follow the American Creed of equality, and thus seek equal access and equal opportunity for all. Whether they succeed or fail after that is their business. This is not about equal results or redistribution of the haves to the have-nots. It's about the haves giving the have-nots a chance too.

Also, Blacks have no monopoly on morality, although certainly, in my view, the cause of civil rights has a higher moral authority than does the cause of Jim Crow denial of civil rights. Blacks are not inherently more or less moral than others, despite popular myths to the contrary (some say we are higher, others lower). I found it interesting in September 2002 that Colin Powell, U.S. Secretary of State, a Black man, was loudly booed by other Black men, primarily those of sub-Saharan Africa as well as North African Arabs, for espousing human rights. He was loudly booed for saying:

> In one country in this region, Zimbabwe, the lack of respect for human rights and rule of law has [helped] push millions of people toward the brink of starvation.

> In the face of famine, several governments in Southern Africa have prevented critical U.S. food assistance from being distributed to the hungry by rejecting biotech corn.

Here we again have an example of good intentions causing bad things. The Greens, including the Sierra Club and Green Peace, like the rest of us, want the best for Africa. But their lenses of perception are clouded by outmoded ideology supported by junk science which is going to lead to the death by starvation of over 10 million people in Southern Africa. Two-thirds of American food is genetically modified. The Greens think it is bad for you. So they have convinced Africa not to eat it. Tons of our food therefore rots on their docks. And because Europe wants to maintain its heavily subsidized farm system, they won't allow in our foods, and because they control a lot of what goes to Africa, they won't let it in either. So the deaths of these 10 or more million will be caused by the Greens and the European union, although the U.S. and globalization will get the blame.

It is this same kind ideological following supported by the same kind of junk science that drives many of the policies in America as it relates to education, housing, employment, and race relations. I will briefly discuss some of the more important documents.

So it is not Blackness that guides me. It is Americanness, following the words of the Declaration of Independence and then Lincoln's Gettysburg address that brought the Constitution up-to-date with the Declaration, that "all men are created equal," and that government is to be "of the people, for the people, and by the people."

On the horizon are our collective and individual futures. Let's make it as wide and bright as possible and let's make it for everyone. And that, to me, means that we must also pay attention to public policy and the law in terms of what fosters and encourages the flourishing of every human being, recognizing that the key to this is not only freedom of choice but the recognition that for each of us, our freedom ends where the other person's nose begins.

We need to accurately connect the dots, not only in Minneapolis, but in other cities as well. I invite those of you in New York, Chicago, Los Angeles, Philadelphia, Kansas City, Milwaukee, Atlanta, Newark and Detroit, to do so as well. From a Black man's perspective, considering slavery, Jim Crow days, and the attempts since then to return to Jim Crow, I can ask but can't answer why any Southern state or any Northern city like Minneapolis elevates the scum (any who are racist) of its own people to positions of power to then crush non-White citizens. I can't answer why but I can point out who and what is getting crushed: people and their education, housing, and jobs. I speak as more than an "I"; I also speak as a "we." I invite you to join me in speaking up for yourself, for ourselves, and for others within the framework of freedom and liberty for all while being responsible for all as well. Join with me, now, as we work to connect the dots of the Minneapolis story.

So who am I? The future is important to me and to those close to me, including my family and my neighbors. I am an American man, an American family man, with a son, parents, grandparents, aunts, uncles, nieces and nephews, not to mention friends of all kinds. I live in a community called Minneapolis. Thus, I am also a community man of Minneapolis. My interest is community. In addition to my various vocations (worker in corporate America, radio and TV host), my passion is my avocation: working for the community. I am a community advocate constantly lobbying to get people to work together to achieve equal access and equal opportunity for all Americans, regardless of race or gender, creed or age. I am opposed to any kind of supremacy, but particularly White supremacy and male chauvinist supremacy, which I see as related. That is how I define myself. That is the sum and substance of my existence. How do you define yourself? What is the sum and substance of your existence?

All of the positions I have held in service to Minneapolis, such as on the Civil Rights Commission, the NAACP, and the Urban League, have been unpaid positions. I have never taken money for my community work. This is an important distinction for three reasons. First, some think I have been in paid positions. I have not. I have held these positions as a concerned citizen. Second, there are too many people who don't ask what they can do for the community without first asking how much the bosses or "Mastuhs," call them what you will, will pay them to help keep the community in line for the bosses. Third, I urge you to serve your community in some capacity during your life.

I believe that being an American is very special, and I feel blessed to have been born here. Who having tasted the fruits of America would want to be born where those fruits are lacking, say in Africa, or South America or any Muslim country in the world? Why do immigrants want to come here? Why aren't the boats leaving our shores for elsewhere? Because this is the best place to be. We all know that. That is why we stay too. Now we just have to make our stay better, achieving the last step on the way to the freedom's prize: equal access and equal opportunity in education, housing, and employment. When asked about the conditions in Africa, Mohammad Ali said he was glad his ancestors got on those boats. This is why I don't favor reparations for slavery. But I do favor reparations for all the land and wealth that has been stolen from us since the Civil War (Interlude 8). When the reparations movement heaps abuse on the Founding Fathers, they are beating a dead horse. Neither America nor Americans invented slavery or racism. It was legal worldwide at the time. But these Founding Fathers did create the system that enabled the abolition movement to thrive, that enabled a movement to build to end slavery, a system unlike any other in the world that was able to finally enfranchise not only the female descendants of their wives and daughters but also the descendants of the slaves of those that had them (many outside the South did not have slaves).

The Civil Rights Movement was about moving Black Americans from the status of Jim Crow citizenship to real citizenship, from facing roadblocks to access and opportunity to being allowed on the road to access and opportunity. We've come a long way. But there are those who haven't, those considered "excess," especially young inner city Black men, who are instead put in jail. Those in school are kept from being educated, for they serve as fodder, first to give the teachers and social service professionals steady work (for you see, those students unable to read and write are captives who cannot qualify for or afford private schools). Even some Liberals have their sense of quotas and feel there are already enough educated Blacks, so that no more need to be educated and allowed in.

America is an exceptional place. Its recipe is striving for freedom, liberty, and justice for all, under a constitution, rule of law, and right of private property. But that did not include Blacks in the beginning and still excludes too many, on a *de facto* basis, not to mention the *de jure* exclusion as promulgated by such actions as the redistricting of Minneapolis in 2002 (Chapters 12 and 13). Nonetheless, America is good, and it is the good of America that is my foundation. America has its ideals and its flaws. My work is on the flaws of America. It is America's good that protects me while I work on those flaws.

There have been those who say it was the non-violent philosophy of Gandhi that helped free India from England and helped end the Jim Crow laws in America. This is true, to a point. But why hasn't non-violence worked elsewhere in the world? It is because when England was faced with having to slaughter Indians to retain colonial control, the response of its citizens was: "we are not like that." It was their moral basis that caused them to end their violence and leave India. The same is true of the

Jim Crow South. Television brought to the rest of America the South's Jim Crow means as well as its record of violence, cross burnings, murders, and lynchings. When people in the United States saw Bull Connors and his dogs and fire hoses and his officers wielding night sticks on the heads of people peacefully marching, America said: "That is not us. We don't do that." And so regardless of the racism and the desire for a homogenous society, Americans' ideals won't let them go there. That is our greatest strength, our most powerful weapon.

America doesn't have as many flaws as other countries, but if you are one of those being hurt or held back by those flaws, it doesn't matter how few there are. The greatest plank in the foundation of America is freedom. Others use the word "liberty." No other country in the history of the world has advocated freedom as America has or delivered as much liberty as America has. That is why boats and planes are carrying immigrants here, and why few leave.

My job, as I see it, is to work toward helping those hurt and held back by America's flaws by working with our institutions and individuals, to bring them together, so that all might benefit from the opportunity America offers. We all need, together, to seek out higher answers, to exercise our minds and the talents buried within us. We all need to learn what is going on and help make this country even greater, by working to include all in the liberty and freedom to be, to succeed as well as to fail and to try again.

I have other identities also, identities given to me by my ancestors. These are identities of background, the kind of identities that built America and made it exceptional, identities that others are often not aware of. You see, I am also a Missourian. One of my grandfathers was both a lawyer and a doctor in Kansas City. He was a Black man who worked with Harry Truman before Harry became President. And my grandmother was one of the city's great hostesses. My other grandfather was a railroad porter. So I had grandparents who came from different sides of the railroad tracks.

I am also a Minnesotan. I went to grade school and junior and senior high school here and have lived here all of my adult life. That makes me a man of the upper mid-West. Thus, I'm not an Easterner nor a Southerner nor a Northwesterner nor a Californian. I am a mid-Western American, who lives in a city that straddles the Mississippi, which runs from the northern-most part of Minnesota to the southern-most part of Louisiana in the Gulf of Mexico in the delta at New Orleans. Because of the West Coast and East Coast, some call the cities along the Mississippi line The Middle Coast.

And I have still other identities. I am a Seminole Indian. I am a descendent of a once-proud people who have long been denied equal access and equal opportunity. I maintain that pride. I seek equal access and opportunity for them too. It is my belief that they not only should have that equal access and equal opportunity, but that everyone else's freedom and liberty is tarnished if we don't work toward universal access and opportunity.

I am also a Black man. My ancestors were slaves. They had absolutely no access and no opportunities, as we would define those terms. Many Blacks have since obtained that opportunity, but others have not. And for those who have not, it is often because of corrupt leaders, both White and Black, which I'll discuss in this book as well. I believe that those who are denied should also have equal access and equal opportunity. It is imperative for the soul of America. Indeed, it is my fervent belief that until all Blacks in America have equal access and equal opportunity, we cannot put true capital letters to "f"reedom and to "l"iberty. And, for those who pursue the idiocy of the one drop rule, I am also a White man, as somewhere in that foggy past of my ancestors, there is at least one drop of White blood of some kind.

Equal access and equal opportunity, in my view, refer to education, housing, and what some call economic development, which I define as jobs, living wage, and entrepreneurial growth across racial and gender lines.

So I am a Black Missourian-Minnesotan-Native American-Community Advocate-American Man. For short, just call me an American. Do I have a preference? Yes, I do. My preference is for the poor and disadvantaged who have been either denied or hindered in obtaining equal access and equal opportunity to be fully participating Americans, regardless of their color. My work has focused primarily on the poor people of color, but it applies to all who are poor.

I believe it is long past time for Blacks to be uppity and deign to think for themselves. Letting the Democrats and Republicans do the thinking hasn't helped win the final prize: freedom for all Blacks and minorities. It is time for us to do something other than wait for the White Mastuhs. As for me, I'll keep doing what I describe in this book in addition to writing this book. I will continue to document and expose discrimination and racism, whether by White or Black, as I do in this book. And no matter how long it takes, my attitude is very simple: My joy comes each day from knowing that I'm in the right struggle at the right place at the right time after the right prize: Freedom for everyone. What is important to me is not in whose lifetime the battle is finally won, but that each day the battle was fought.
Fight on.

Chapter 1

Introduction: To Be A Beacon On The Hill

"For years we studied the history of what racial segregation and slavery has done to the emotions and psychology of Black people, but we haven't really looked at what it has done to the emotional and psychological health of White people."

                                        Toni Morrison

Large numbers of the population are excluded from participating fully in society. Democracy and the justice associated with democracy, in this country and around the world, is an aspiration. What are the implications of this? We have segregated housing patterns and segregated schools. We have people isolated from health insurance and we have communities ravaged by unemployment. What are the implications for the entire society?

                                        Isaac Peterson III

W.E.B. Dubois said that we've traded democracy and justice for white supremacy. The whole society has been crippled by this. The struggle, I think, is about the soul of America and about the future of democracy. So in some ways, it's a much larger struggle than what most people acknowledge. And I would go further and say that even when we deal with it in practical terms, like racial profiling and schools and health care, ultimately it's also rooted in a sense of spiritual being. We increasingly recognize our that relationship to earth matters, how we abuse the earth and our trust. We still have to realize that in relation to each other. So part of it is to sort of rethink how do we not just change lives but how we dream again. How do we make those dreams real? How do we dream of a society as a loving community, where we all recognize that we really share a common destiny, that we are a family?

                                        john a. powell

There is but one way to know the truth, and that is not a golden one. It is fraught with toil and sacrifice and perhaps ridicule. The seeker of the truth must be fearless, he must not be afraid to enter the innermost holies of holies, and to tear down the veils of superstition that hang about any human and so-called divine institution. It is the truth that makes men free. If the truth tears down every church and government under the sun, let the truth be known and this truth only will be known when men cease to swallow the

capsules of ancient doctors of divinities and politics; and when men begin to
seek the truth in the records of history, politics, religion, and science.

                                                              Charles Austin Beard, 1898

This has been another season of our discontent. There was the slavery season. There
was the season of Jim Crow. There was the Civil Rights Movement. Now we have a
new season of Jim Crow, more clever and better disguised, that is a counter-
movement to return to the Civil Rights Movement. That is now happening in
Minneapolis with a vengeance. Hence, I write this book. My dream is that we can
finally achieve a season of content. That is my dream. It was the dream of Martin
Luther King, Jr. I know that you, the reader, have a dream. Above, I quote john a.
powell on our capacity to dream. But before we can dream the best for Minneapolis,
we have to step back and be dispassionate about what has prevented our dreams.
Then we can be passionate about achieving our dream of justice and fairness and
equal access and opportunity for all. We need to find the truth of the past in order to
build an honest future. It will take a lot of connecting the dots to do so. We need to
understand the chessboard of Minneapolis and how no matter what move we make,
the powers make two, constantly pursuing their goal of putting us under checkmate.

Not much has changed from the description given by the National Commission on
Civil Disorders in 1968, called the Kerner Report:

> Segregation and poverty have created in the racial ghetto a destructive
> environment totally unknown to most white Americans. What white
> Americans have never fully understood - but what the Negro can never
> forget - is that white society is deeply implicated in the ghetto. White
> institutions created it, white institutions maintain it, and white society
> condones it.

And that is what I do: I am a connector of dots. I am an American seeking the truth
about the past while working toward building an honest future for everyone. We all
need to be Americans together. This is not my story. This is the story of
Minneapolis, as seen through my eyes. This book tells my story only in so far as my
story helps to tell the Minneapolis story, a story as seen through my eyes, the eyes of
a community advocate, the eyes of a Black man. This book is my contribution to
those thousand points of light in the community trying to make our community a
better place. My goal for the book is that it stands like a beacon on a hill and provide
light to illuminate the path to our content.

This is also not an attempt to guilt-trip Americans. All peoples have suffered at one
time or another in history. And all colors, somewhere in the world, are doing
unloving, un-neighborly things to others. No one alive today is responsible for what
happened 300 years ago nor suffered what happened 300 years ago. But we do exist

today. We are responsible for today. And if we now, knowing what we do about the past, stand by and don't work together to achieve the dream of justice for all now, today, then we *are* guilty from this day forward, and if we stand by and do nothing as others block that dream for people today, then we *are* manifestly guilty by association. I am saddened by the stories of the past that have caused so much pain and suffering for others. I am saddened that so many Blacks had their lives stolen from them. But I am also excited about the positive possibilities we can all bring together to make happen today and in the future, as we help those purposefully kept behind catch up. We've missed chances before. *The Minneapolis Story Through My Eyes* is about some of those missed opportunities. It is also about the glorious possibilities for the future.

The Minneapolis story is the story of a city that has offered and not offered, attempted and not attempted, encouraged and prevented, equal access and equal opportunity in education, housing, and economic development for both the Black and White poor in general and Blacks in particular. My hope for this book is the same hope I have for my community advocacy work: to foster in Whites and Blacks alike the acceptance of and the desire to foster equal access and equal opportunity for all. The Minneapolis story is also about how to get to a post-plantation, high-education-demand world. I know it can be done. I know we can do it.

I have heard of the telling exchange in a debate between conservative pundit Robert Novak and liberal pundit Mark Shields during a political campaign that helps illustrate this: Novak launched into a tirade against the poor of Appalachia, who are mostly White, saying that they were poor because they were losers that didn't have the ambition to do well that comes from exercising the American competitive spirit. He blamed them. What a put-down. Shields immediately stopped Novak by saying to him: "Stop that. You're a better person than that." And I say to Minneapolis: "You're better than that." I say to Minneapolis that you have been better than you are now, and you can be better in the future.

My hope is to stir hearts and minds in such a way that a decision is made to act and be better sooner than later in Minneapolis. We need to do more than just heal. We need to reconcile the differences between Blacks and Whites. We need to break the inertia of the Jim-Crow status quo mentality and emulate not the long history of apartheid attempts of the South but the abolitionist history of acceptance of Blacks, compassion for what has/is being done to them, and advocacy of freedom for all, including Blacks. We must stand tall in favor of the democratic capitalism that has brought so much to so many but not at the expense of forgetting the needs of the poorest and most disadvantaged, whose greatest help is not just some ongoing relief but the education that leads to jobs and housing and opportunities to join the mainstream of American economic and social life.

In Chapter 1, I will set the stage with my **Introduction** *The Minneapolis Story Through My Eyes*, and sketch some of the broader themes.

In Interlude 1, I outline the <u>history of my</u> overlapping, <u>non-paid, leadership positions</u> over the past nearly 40 years, including overlapping leadership positions with the Civil Rights Commission (16 years), the Urban League (17 years), and the NAACP (16 years), which is why I am <u>one of the most quoted persons in the *Star Tribune*</u>. I am known for knowing what is happening. And after you read this book, you will know what is happening too.

In Chapter 2, I discuss **my path to Minnesota,** my racial and ethnic background, my education, and how racist policies tried to force me out of a good education, out of good housing, and out of economic opportunity. Today I fight to keep that from happening to others.

In Interlude 2, I discuss and define my understanding of <u>racism, Part I</u>. This is based on the long journalism series in 1990 by the *Minneapolis Star Tribune* on racism. Let it suffice here to say that I am not speaking in code. I am not winking at the Black reader with "the Whites just don't get it" routine, that any time a Black feels misunderstood, the failure of the White to understand is racism (what is it, then, when a Black doesn't understand when a White feels misunderstood?). I believe all of us, White and Black, Yellow and Brown, fall under certain universal standards of evaluation that have nothing to do with race. Maybe this is why we rarely hear W.E.B. DuBois talked about or quoted anymore, as he was opposed to Blacks playing the racist victim game. And although I too oppose playing the racist victim game, this book shows how, nonetheless, Whites in this country have victimized us because of our race. I write in terms of race, therefore, in terms of Blacks and Whites, because that is what Whites have thrust on us. However, aside from that, my basic theme about equal access and equal opportunity, of fairness, is based on not only my belief but also the scientifically sound understanding that all of us, Black, White, Brown, Yellow, are fellow human beings. I thus do not speak Black truths in this book, nor White truths, but rather *human* truths. And when we can all see the value of talking in human terms, racism will end and most wars will end. But until that happy moment, I must speak my human truths within the context of those in power that prefer to speak of race truths, as they subordinate the truth to them. I reject the thinking and the actions of such subordination. And if you think that way, dear reader, I invite you to rethink your position and open yourself up to a more fuller existence by no longer thinking in that way.

I will return to this theme of racism again in Interlude 10. For those who think I am being extreme about racism, I refer you to the report of CBS News.com on August 22, 2002, which reported that "racism [is] on the rise worldwide." Certainly who better to tell their story of racism than Jews, Arabs after September 11, and many of the Blacks and Browns in the Southern Hemisphere?   On the same day on www.blackheadlines.com, these stories also appeared, among others, also taken from CBS News.com: "Racism's Roots Run Deep," "Racism and Power in the South," and "Study: Racism Kills Black Men."

In Chapter 3, I will tell a story of **the courts** that greatly underscores a basic problem in Minneapolis: the constant battle over the definition of "is," as in "what is the Truth" and as in "is that what really happened?"   I tell the story of how a judge purposefully had 173 pages of court transcript deleted in an attempt to prevent me from appealing my case. She failed. But if the courts are willing to play this loose with the definition of reality, of "what is," as was done to me, to how many others has this been done?   In every chapter we see the battle between the definition of reality between those in power and those out, between Whites and Blacks, between "House Negroes" (those working for the bosses to get goods for themselves at the expense of the rest) and the "Field Hands" (those Blacks not on any one's payoff payroll, trying to make a living and get by). My focus is on those left behind in the inner city in general and, in particular, young Black men for whom it appears that the solution is not to enable them to rise up out of their circumstances but to plummet them down into incarceration (see the end of Chapter 8).

In Interlude 3, I discuss one of my mentors, the well-known and known and nationally admired Nellie Stone Johnson, the driving force behind the Farmer-Labor Party, the one who negotiated the creation of the DFL: Democratic-Farmer-Labor Party and was then later betrayed by the DFL.

In Chapter 4, I will discuss the paradox behind my **"anywhere but here" philosophy**. There are things that happen that I don't want to happen, I want them to happen "anywhere but here." But I don't really want them anywhere and so I discuss how I don't want them, as in **"not here, there, or anywhere."** But I live here, so that is my emphasis. And at other times it means that we as citizens and neighbors would rather be anywhere but here. So my goal is to help Minneapolis no longer be a place where people say "anywhere but here" or, as one corporate friend called it years ago, "Minnie-a-no-place" but rather a good place where things that go on that we enjoy, and thus we say they should be "here, there, and everywhere."

In Interlude 4, I discuss those I consider to be among the greatest trios and the greatest quartets in American history and the guidance they offer us for the future, a White trio and a Black quartet. The White trio consists of "I won't be King" George Washington, "All will be free" Abraham Lincoln, and "All were created equal" Thomas Jefferson. The Black quartet consists of "We can make it on our own" George Washington Carver, "But let's make it happen now" W.E.B. DuBois, "I have a dream for all" Martin Luther King, Jr., and "We will make the law serve everyone" Thurgood Marshall.

In Chapter 5, I will deal more directly with the questions of **equal access and equal opportunity** from the standpoint of justice and fairness. I believe the solution is for all of us, Blacks and Whites, to come to an agreement on the common ground we share, in the form of the things we all say YES to and the things we all say NO to. If we can agree on these, we will have smooth sailing in the future. I provide a beginning set of lists for discussions of what, from my perspective, should be on the YES list and what should be on the NO list.

In Interlude 5, I discuss Part I of "The Good News About Race" from the 2000 Census (Part II is in Interlude 7), to show how much has been achieved in order to better focus on what we have yet to do, so that we can see that it is not hopeless, that we can prevail, that we can overcome.

In Chapter 6, I outline the **"identifying characteristics" of Minneapolis** and her Bosses, as I discuss what makes Minneapolis Minneapolis. Chapter 6 also begins the discussion of a byproduct of those characteristics, the role of Minneapolis Black organizations in the Minneapolis story and how they went from being part of the solution to being part of the problem. This is also discussed in more detail in Chapter 14.

In Interlude 6 I discuss the Dred Scott case, which helped extend our official slave status in this country in the 19th century and which has been seen as a factor in bringing about the Civil War. The case started when Scott was arrested as a runaway slave at our own Fort Snelling in Minneapolis. Those same dynamics have been repeated during the recent redistricting fiasco (Chapters 12-13).

Chapter 7 begins a series of specific discussions: this one on **Education**, which is used to give Whites a helping hand up and inner city Blacks an unhelpful push back down.

Interlude 7 brings us Part II of the "Good News About Race" from the 2000 Census, and discusses the relationship between Education, Jobs, and Prosperity.

Chapter 8 discusses **housing** in general and Minneapolis the Hollman project in particular, and the gentrification activities geared to turning the city back over to Whites after the white flight of the 60s and 70s. It also discusses the one billion dollars spent to provide 52 units of housing for minorities, as the city's campaign continues for pushing Blacks out and bringing Whites back into the city.

Interlude 8 discusses the <u>**great wealth and land takings from Blacks**</u> in the 19th and 20th centuries, and makes a case for reparation not for slavery but for what has been taken in terms of land and wealth, in this country, from Blacks, since the end of slavery.

Chapter 9 discusses the corrupt and racist <u>**construction contract system,**</u> the substitution of jails for jobs for young Black men, and <u>**the war on drugs as a war on Black men**</u>.

Interlude 9 discusses the film <u>*10,000 Men Named George*</u> and how <u>A. Phillip Randolph</u> was able to stand up to The Pullman Company, the railroad car maker, one of the most powerful companies in the country at that time, and establish a union, wages, and health-care benefits for the workers. Randolph is the model we should be holding up to our young Black men, not celebrity entertainers and athletes, to show that indeed, one man can make a difference.

Chapter 10 focuses on <u>the University of Minnesota and the scapegoating of Luther Darville</u> in the Athletic Department scandal as another example of how Minneapolis keeps Blacks in their place.

Interlude 10 is a second discussion on <u>racism, Part II</u>, this time from articles in the *Mlps.StPaul* magazine of 1990 and 2001. Racism existed then and it exists now, with much of it still in the closet.

Chapter 11 discusses my understanding of how the DFL dumped its own Black DFL mayor as a demonstration of the corrupt, racist nature of the Minneapolis city government, which was shamefully done in collusion with the Urban League and NAACP. Politics does indeed make for strange bedfellows.

Interlude 11 discusses one of the most powerful Black men of the 20th century, <u>Adam Clayton Powell, Jr.</u>, as shown in the Showtime movie, <u>*Keep the Faith, Baby.*</u> Here is another model for today's young Black men. One person can make a difference, which is what the Minneapolis Mastuhs fear the most.

Chapter 12 discusses the recent **redistricting** attempt to further crush Blacks in Minneapolis and some of the steps taken to fight it.

Interlude 12 discusses <u>gerrymandering,</u> one of the games played to distort redistricting into an unfair and unjust process, and how it is being used to disenfranchise, disempower, impoverish, and ghettoize inner city-Blacks in Minneapolis.

Chapter 13 summarizes my ideas and remedies regarding this governmental travesty.

Interlude 13 recounts the story of the slaughter of Blacks during the Tulsa Race Riots, as told to me by my Grandfather, in another successful act by Whites to burn down and destroy the affluent Black town of Greenwood, near Tulsa (The same strategy was used in Rosewood, Florida, as if their motto was: if you can't beat them, burn them).

Chapter 14 discusses my battles with the two organizations that have turned their backs on the inner city Blacks of Minneapolis, the local branches of the Urban League and the NAACP, and how they have hurt, not helped, the cause of fighting for equal access and equal opportunity over the past decade.

Interlude 14 reminds us all, lest we forget, that **we all have slavery in our background.**

Chapter 15 discusses the reality of how our beloved Minnesota Vikings are being run out of town. Say Goodbye to the Vikings; they are leaving. Say Goodbye to the Vikings; they are lost.

Interlude 15 discusses how far north the Mason Dixon line has gone, as it recounts the lynching in Duluth in 1921, as well as my remembrance of the assassination of Martin Luther King, Jr.

In **Chapter 16**, I ask if August- September 2002 is Preview of the future for Minneapolis. If the future is going to be the same ol' same ol,' then the disturbances, melees, riots, call them what you will (the local newspapers call them differently too), will continue as the price Minneapolis (and other cities) is willing to pay to keep Blacks in their place. This chapter deals with the shootings and ensuing "melees" (as the local newspapers labeled them) of August 2002 of citizens of the inner city of Minneapolis, their hope and request for a Federal mediator to help straighten things out between the neighborhoods and the police, and the Minneapolis City Council's demonstrated contempt for the inner city neighborhoods and refusal to engage in any kind of objective mediation.

Interlude 16 provides a brief on how to caculate the future differently, using a calculus of meaning (good, positive things, the YESes to foster of Chapters 5 and 17) and a calculus of pain (bad, negative things, the NOs to stop or prevent of Chapters 5 and 17). Here I provide a parable for calculating actions and laws for their real pain and meaning to people, not just their intentions, so real equal access and real equal opportunity can take place.

In **Chapter 17** I lay out "Future Positive Possibilities for the Minneapolis Story," if we take seriously the existence of a list of YESes and NOs on which we can agree and on which we can accordingly act.

In my **Conclusion,** I recite why and how the negatives can be turned to positives, and provide my vision, my dream, and my prayer of hope for Minneapolis. I envision a dream and encourage us all to work together to sustain our dreams to stand tall and free.

The Interludes between each chapter are brief, one to two pages, which address specific historic topics and personages. Most include history many have forgotten or never heard about, and include references to books, videos, and cable TV programs, which can provide greater detail for the reader wanting to learn more.   These concrete resources can be used by Blacks, Whites, Blacks and Whites together, and especially by and for young Black men, to study the past and learn from its mistakes in order to better prepare for and navigate the future.

For those who can't wait for the details, please feel free to jump to the other Chapters and Interludes of your interest. What I will do for the remainder of this introductory chapter is provide a broader understanding against which to place our discussion of the American and Minnesota backdrop.

But I am a positive man. I'll also include connecting the dots to the kind of future everyone can accept and enjoy (Chapters 5 and 17), White or Black, rich or poor, a future all can agree on and work toward, a future which holds that human and civil rights include equal access and equal opportunity for all, Black or White or Brown or Yellow, male or female, young or old. That is my goal. I hope it is yours, and if it is not, I invite you to make it yours.

For the movers and shakers on top of the hill who don't want to share: Despite all that they have, even sharing access and opportunity is untenable. They behave with what could be called "lifeboat ethics," as if the ship has sunk and there are not enough lifeboats so they pass out hatchets to those in the boats to chop off the hands of those in the water trying to get in. But the ship won't sink and the water is far away. We stand on firm ground. They just call it sinking because they don't want to share. Whether it be rich folks passing zoning laws requiring 5-acre lots (Princeton,

NJ in the 1970s) or environmentalists getting injunctions against others using land they use (resulting in many of the massive fires in Western forrests in the summer of 2002), the result is the same. People greedy for money or for seclusion seek special treatment to freeze others out. The purpose of this book is to help bring a thaw to such freezes.

To have equal access and equal opportunity, everything has to be opened up. I stand for opening up our society to everyone. But the political far left and the political far right have ganged up against Natalie Johnson-Lee, a field hand that the White DFL puppet-masters are trying to destroy.

If nothing is done to change the trend, we are stuck with only two interpretations: Those in charge are either stupid and should be replaced (both bureaucrats and the legislators who have oversight over them) or those in charge want it this way. If the latter, my view is that they should still be replaced as this means that they are morally corrupt. I can think of no other interpretations when you connect these dots.

Blacks have been made the excess of an unspoken quota system of Whites who fear educated, articulate Blacks. This was particularly true in the redistricting action of early 2002, which failed in its attempt to put Natalie Johnson-Lee out of her district and then defeat her in a special election. It appears again in the same redistricting action that makes Minneapolis' 5th Ward a disenfranchised ghetto stripped of its economic development grants and stripped of the economy of Downtown as Downtown is made into a separate district unto itself (Chapters 12 and 13). These are dots the power brokers don't want people to connect. I connect them in this book. It is why I have written this book. Enough is enough.

This summer of 2002, the governor of Minnesota led the largest trade mission of business leaders to ever go to China, what he has called "the mother of all trade missions." Getting into the Chinese market would be great for Minnesota, great for Minnesota companies, great for Minnesota employees, great for creating jobs. It would be a boon to Northwest Airlines, which flies there, and for all the Carlson companies, including their travel agencies, not to mention to the Mall of America, which would getting tourists from China, tourists who would also attend Twins games at the Metrodome. But where are the Black business leaders on the governor's trip? Where are those with an interest to see that equal access and equal opportunity be for Blacks as well? When we connect the dots, we see why they have left out Blacks and minorities. So I congratulate them on their mission but condemn them for not making it for all. I write this book as a reminder that we Blacks are here and are to be included as well.

Most who come to America want to be Americans. I am not an Afro-American or an African-American or a Black-American, although it seems to some to be more politically correct to use those hyphens. Whites dropped their hyphens long ago. Blacks need to drop their hyphens. Indeed, it is precisely because of the hyphens that people are fighting each other around the world. Hyphens prevent the finding of the common ground (Chapter 5) needed to be a free nation with a free people. What is needed is for Blacks to stop using the hyphen that gives Whites the chance to continue to do the "they-are-different" thing because we purposefully hold ourselves separate. We need to work together to write a new story of commonality and acceptance. Not that there isn't room for African-American, for it makes a wonderful slogan for companies and products to put African-American first. But I am not a slogan and I am not a product. I am a man, an American man.

The Minneapolis story is not about the culture wars, the battle between the Left and Right as they carry on about such topics as abortion, gun control, homosexuality, the death penalty, multiculturalism, and eliminating religion in public areas (like prayer in schools). Nor is it about entitlements of other kinds: gender rights, affirmative action, sexual orientation rights, physically challenged (handicapped rights), although elements of these are involved. To me those are frivolous topics compared to survival through equal access and equal opportunity and integration into the economic mainstream of all people, regardless of color. Those trivial topics are the topics not of manual laborers, although they affect them, but of white-collar people with non-calloused hands in non-manual labor, dressed in suits or polo shirts, most often government or non-profit bureaucrats who wield pens, not shovels or hammers, regardless of whether or not they are practical or impractical, helpful to society or hurtful to society, whose jobs seem to be safe, whose paychecks seem to be secure, and those retirements seem to be assured. They can afford to follow their ideologies in air-conditioned comfort while real workers sweat.

Again, I'm talking about fairness, access, and opportunity, period. And if these were addressed, those culture war issues listed would be taken care of as well. But they are used as a smoke screen for the extremes of American politics, of people interested in their own welfare and the welfare of their ideas but not the welfare of the poor, the orphaned, the deserted, the abandoned, the abused.

The Minneapolis story is about the lack of universal fairness, access, and opportunity in many different areas, but four stand out: education, housing, political participation and entrepreneurial growth. Is Minneapolis open to all or only to specialized groups or groups with special grievances, where the leadership makes money by leading the grievance parade, but the masses make nothing? How has Minneapolis measured up? How has it approached fairness, access, and opportunity? Has it offered equal access and opportunity in education, housing, political participation, and entrepreneurial growth? If not, why not? What can be done about it? That is what I invite you to consider with me. And as I discuss things that have happened to me, we'll have to confront this question. If it happened to me, how many others did it happen to and how was it covered up?

One of the great achievements of America is that it has truly been a melting pot, where people from every country, like fans at a Vikings or Twins game, have joined together to become one fantastic group, with joy and celebration. Even the children of former slaves stand there and sing *God Bless America*, and the National Anthem, *The Star Spangled Banner*, together before ball games.

But not everyone wants that. Many want to differentiate who they are as separate Americans, or not as Americans at all, and maintain who they are as separate people, on the street as well as at home, making their identify as American secondary to their ideology or country of origin. This has been sponsored by the politically correct Left who seem uncomfortable being Americans, who therefore urge others who come here to also not be Americans, hiding behind the skirts of culture to say that immigrants have a right to remain who they are. No country can survive that way, and certainly not a country that is striving, however haltingly at times, for tolerance and integration. This was one of the arguments of slavery by the masters. Now the masters of the PC Left are using it. Allowing all to be separate, to follow different cultures under the divisive and destructive name of diversity, prevents finding the common ground, pits groups against each other, and essentially becomes the dynamic to destroy the country, for their children are raised not as Americans but as _____ [fill in the blank] who just happen to live here. They want rights not as Americans, nor even as hyphenated Americans, but as who they claim to be to the left of the hyphen. And for most of these groups, exclusion is the process they live by. Blacks, as you'll see in the statistics on education, housing, political participation, and entrepreneurial growth, are purposefully excluded while they attempt to be included. Those who feel it is hopeless join the Nation of Islam, just as others during the 70s joined The Black Panthers.

Those wearing the narrow blinders of diversity don't see a common ground. They don't see Americans. They see hyphens. Today we are caught between moral relativists of the political and religious Left and Right, not only in this country but abroad, especially as seen in acts of terrorism, such as from Islamic extremists, where blowing up children and young people at schools and synagogues and parties is defined as glory to God (or Allah, call him/her/it what you will) and as the brave work of "freedom fighters." Those who don't define the deliberate killing of children as murder and terrorism have truly lost their way, for if children are fair game, we are all fair game. This is how Negroes in the Antebellum South and the post-Civil War Jim Crow South were treated. We need to remember what is on some of our coins: *E pluribus Unum*: out of many, one.

Do you like music, dear reader? I find that music often provides the gospels of America, with many verses of a common Bible of music wisdom (I have listed some of our anthems on my web site, www.TheMinneapolisStory.com).   For instance, in 1967, guitarist Jimi Hendrix cut an album called *Axis: Bold as Love*. There are many kinds of axes. To Jimi Hendrix, love was to be the axis of the future. But today, at the beginning of a worldwide terrorist attack on modern, non-Muslim life, the axis is evil. And isn't that the choice we all have to make? Which axis we will choose? The axis of love or the axis of evil? Slavery, Jim Crow laws, segregation, denial of access and opportunity, are on the axis of evil.

And just what is an axis? An axis, whether of good or evil, refers to three lines that cross at a common point, hence, a partnership or alliance. Hence, the three of WWII (Germany, Japan, Italy), and the three highlighted today (Iraq, Iran, North Korea). I prefer four other sets of three, **(1)** the axis of love, which includes the three of service, sacrifice, and constant reconciliation, and to which we can apply three other sets of threes: **(2)** education, housing, and jobs, and **(3)** being brought into participation in the social, economic, and political mainstream, with **(4)** equal access, equal opportunity, and equal entrepreneurial incentives. To put four threes into one word: we are to be equal in the eyes of each other just as we are seen as equal, as our *Declaration of Independence* says, in the eyes of our Creator. The three sets of three above all have one thing in mind: the total sovereignty of the state over the individual. The Minneapolis story is also the story of state and city sovereignty, adopting what Southern states mean by states' rights: the right of the state to keep out the Federal government so the state can squash the rights of Blacks. In my view, that is not what the founders meant by separation of powers.

You can see why I say I am an activist, an advocate, a facilitator, but not a militant agitator. You can either call me a throwback to the 60s or a pioneer for a new century, one who has stepped out into the unknown. In that, I am, again, very American. Aren't we taught that it is the pioneer spirit that made America, the spirit of people unafraid to brave the unknown in pursuit of their dreams? Of course, most of those pioneers who left the East and crossed to the plains of the Middle West and those who went on to the Southwest or pursued the Oregon Trail to the Northwest, were what people today, with a different mindset, might call losers. Who could possibly entertain the notion of crossing an unknown continent except those for whom the status quo didn't work, who were left out, who had no access and no opportunity in their local societies on America's East Coast? Many were so poor and out of the mainstream that they had no choice but to move on if they were to succeed. But no continent waits, no geographic frontier extends before us. What extends before us is our minds. We now have to cross the frontier of our differences so that we can all be one with our differences.

Thus, the choice is not to "love it **or** leave it" but to "love it **and** make it better" <u>for all.</u> I call America the best because I compare America to the rest of the world, not to the ideal, and yet still set my sights on doing what I can to close the gap between what is real and what we hold as our ideal.

We "talk the walk" about reconciling White and Black versions of liberty and affirming a path to liberty for both, but we don't yet "walk the talk." I work to make that happen in Minneapolis. There is much work to be done. A lot has been accomplished. I see my task as working to make sure we don't rest on our laurels, but instead we strive to achieve our shared ideals. We need to stop taking steps backward, as in the redistricting (Chapters 12 and 13), in education (Chapter 7), housing (Chapter 8), or jobs (Chapter 9), or denying objective mediation when problems develop in the communities, such as with the police (Chapter 16). It's time to move forward again.

Too many Blacks and too many Whites, both liberal and conservative, hold on to the relics of the 50s and 60s. As a preview, we can look again at the Brown vs. Board of Education decision of the Supreme Court and see that it was a probably an unavoidable Faustian bargain with the devil made by Blacks and Liberals, not in terms of the goal but in terms of the rationale for the goal. The goal was integration, equal access, and equal opportunity. I agree with those. However, they chose to overcome it by challenging the constitutional notion of "separate but equal" education. The Liberals couldn't let go of the notion that it had to be done by the Federal government to make it happen, and Blacks, given the notorious history of the South, didn't see good things happening through the states.

There are five reports that help us understand the underlying question: are Blacks bright enough to be given equal access and equal opportunity:

1. Paul Lazerfeld's pre-Civil Rights Movement statement that, based on social science research surveys, race relations in America were resolved.
2. Gunnar Myrdal's 1944 *An American Dilemma,* which influenced Brown vs. Board of Education, which stated that Blacks and Whites are equal.
3. James Coleman's report that led to bussing as the answer to school inequality.
4. 1960's *Kerner Commission Report* which stated Blacks can't make it on their own and need government support.
5. 1998's *Bell Curve*, which suggests Blacks have the lowest intelligence, after Asians, Whites, and Browns, and thus need government support.

The sociologist Paul Lazerfeld had written an article saying race relations were no longer a problem in America. Needless to say, he wrote from a narrow perspective using specific numbers. He went with the numbers from surveys without ever visiting the communities they were supposed to represent. Today when you read this you might laugh. But it helps explain why it took so long to get people in this country to accept that this was not true. As Nellie Stone Johnson (Interlude 3) used to say, it is difficult when everyone is also trying to make a living to keep up with everything that is going on. And of course, the media coverage we have today didn't exist in those days.

Therefore, it fell to two other studies to inform the Supreme Court in its deliberations and decision. The first was the 1944 report of the Swedish Sociologist, Gunnar Myrdal, the second was a study of education by sociologist James Coleman.

Myrdal's book, *An American Dilemma: The Negro Problem and Modern Democracy* (Harper and Row, New York, 1944: see also http://www.africa2000.com/indx/myrdal.htm) was the first to really lay it on the line for Americans. It recognized the American dual spirit and the tensions between the ideals it espoused and the shortcomings in meeting those ideals. The book was important for doing three things that impact today on our deliberations: **(1)** the poor economic and social conditions under which Americans of African descent lived during the first half of the twentieth century, **(2)** the first detailed description of what today we might call their "life style" in terms of family structure and lifestyle, political awareness, communal institutions, and religion, **(3)** the first time the enormous variety issues related to American "discrimination" and "bigotry," the words used then ("racism" is used today) was documented, including how it impacted Blacks in being kept from equal access and equal opportunity, **(4)** providing academic and political leaders useful and truthful evidence that the end of the Civil War didn't end the subservience and subordination of Blacks, as Myrdal's study showed the facts and evidence of the enduring effects on Blacks both of slavery and contemporary racism of whites, providing the first real verification of the impact of systematic discrimination in the United States that even intellectuals up to that time did not accept, **(5)** the tension between the personal views of a "virtually-universal genocidal intent" wanting to either send them away, back to Africa, or reduce their birth rate, and the tension of the American ideals that any such action be done by "approved means." The fact that there are none has greatly contributed to the difficulties, **(6)** that for many Whites the problem was not that they held Blacks to be inferior but rather that they looked so much more different that Whites, so that, in Myrdal's words, it is " the desire of the politically dominant white population to get rid of the Negroes," and **(7)** the final statement of tension:

> This is a goal difficult to reach by approved means, and the desire has never been translated into action directly, and probably never will be. All the most obvious means go strongly against the American Creed. The Negroes cannot be killed off. Compulsory deportation would infringe upon personal liberty

in such a radical fashion that it is excluded. Voluntary exportation of Negroes could not be carried on extensively because of unwillingness on the part of recipient nations as well as on the part of the American Negroes themselves, who usually do not want to leave the country but prefer to stay and fight it out here.

And so, I have continued to be among those who have chosen to stay and fight it out.

The major premise of Myrdal's work on which the great debate has hung has been this statement:

> White prejudice and discrimination keep the Negro low in standards of living, health, education, manners and morals. This, in its turn, gives support to white prejudice. White prejudice and Negro standards thus mutually "cause" each other."

An opposite view was published as recently as April 1996, in *American Renaissance,* by Jared Taylor, in an article called "Sowing the Seeds of Destruction: Gunnar Myrdal's Assault on America" (http://www.pat2k.com/civil_rights/gunmyr.html). The view here is that Myrdal's view depends on whether or not Blacks are inferior or not. Taylor holds his negative view of Myrdal because he insists that Blacks *are* inferior to Whites, and rejects the "egalitarian" view of the races. In Jared's view, it is not discrimination that causes Black poverty but the lower intelligence of Blacks. Where Myrdal rejects "beliefs among whites concerning Negro racial inferiority," Taylor accepts it. It is my contention that it is this Taylor view by the Minneapolis City Council and DFL that have led to the redistricting resulting in ghettoizing the Blacks of the inner city of Minneapolis. Taylor and his ilk still accept the notion of "racial differences" beyond that of color. Indeed, to prove his point, he quotes Myrdal's description of Blacks, descriptions that would be called racist today. It is as if Myrdal believed them, yet believed Blacks could be "fixed" via social engineering.

So there you have it. If you believe that the races are equal, you have no choice but to accept that there is a moral lag which is what Myrdal calls the "American Dilemma." The injustice is treating Blacks as inferior when they are actually equal. It is an injustice, Myrdal would say, as it goes against "The American Creed" of equality. Taylor rejects this.

If you accept Taylor, then you will have to say that my book is just another exercise in exposing white wickedness to explain Black failure. Clearly, I do not do that. Indeed, I show that the problem is Black elites working with White elites to maintain the state of affairs, as clearly explained in Chapter 14. I report the use of this book because of its clear, wide influence. As even Taylor summarizes:

Meanwhile *An American Dilemma* was helping change the United States. Myrdal was a personal friend of Supreme Court Justice Felix Frankfurter, and his book was cited in the *Brown v. Board of Education* decision. When President Truman established a presidential commission on civil rights, its members used *An American Dilemma* as their central text. In 1947 the commission issued a report, "To Secure These Rights," which followed Myrdal's recommendations. Truman implemented the report in his 1948 civil rights program that abolished segregation in the armed forces, set up a civil rights division in the Justice Department, and promoted national legislation to combat racism. During the first sit-in demonstration, in Greensboro, North Carolina, blacks cited Myrdal as an important influence.

From his study of 500,000 students, James Coleman concluded that Blacks did better in schools while sitting next to Whites. The problem then became how that was defined. "Separate but equal" was defined as wrong because Blacks were not sitting with Whites, that is, were not integrated. So bussing was invented to achieve a *de facto* integration of schools, leaving communities, neighborhoods, and economic zones as segregated as before, doing little for education. It was an integrator in schools, not an educator in schools. Had they stayed with the truth and said that the independent variable was **not** Black students sitting next to White students but green money sitting next to any students, Black or White, they could have still called it what it was: separate and unequal, but come up with a different conclusion: not bussing but paying. In other words, it was NEVER separate AND equal and was never intended to be. Not believing Whites would give money to Blacks only, they invented the White-Black student issue, in the hope that it would expose Black students to more money.

But the result was to say no Black could be adequately educated except with Whites. Period. Thus, the whole liberal bussing plan was based on the racist notion Blacks are actually inferior, and can't be educated without sitting next to Whites.

And as White liberals distrusted the corporations that made the jobs that pay the people who pay the taxes that sustain their liberal education and foundation jobs, the solution, to them, could only be by sovereign government and its key soldiers, the judges, who turned the schools and their monster budgets over to the Liberals. But to say so they would have to say Blacks are inferior.

This is also why opposing school vouchers, as a separation of church and state issue, is just another skirt liberals hide behind, because vouchers would once again allow schools to be run by and for Blacks and take the control of their monster budgets away from Whites. And the best voucher programs today have been exactly those:

those run by Blacks for Blacks. And that is what Whites, even liberal Whites, fear, not religion in the schools but Blacks running the schools, meaning the legions of White education bosses would lose their jobs. So instead they hide behind the notion that vouchers mean paying money to church schools.

Having education in the hands of governments and unions led by Whites became a greater priority than actual education. And now, 50 years later, we are right back where we started: poor inner city Black kids in poor Black schools getting a poor education. In the meantime, look at the thousands and thousands of Whites who have made a living off this. This is, pure and simple, White Liberal Plantationism. When we lost the notion that Blacks could educate themselves, it perpetuated the notion of Black inferiority and White supremacy, turning over the education of our Black children to Whites and their constantly changing bizarre education theories, theories always with one thing in common: together, they keep the minorities in the inner cities uneducated. And if you can't read and write, you can't make it out of the inner city into the modern world. During slave days it was a capital offense to teach reading to Blacks, for then they could follow the road signs out. In the inner cities, White education is making sure young Black men can't get educated enough to find their way out of the inner cities. How this is done in Minneapolis is covered in Chapter 7. It is interesting to note that this argument does not take place with Black colleges, nor does the objection of Federal money to students attending church related institutions exist at the college level. Only in regards to public schools do Blacks get this full treatment.

The most recent major statement is in *The Bell Curve*, which states that because Blacks are not as intelligent, the government has to take care of them. This occurs in a very short chapter of a much longer book on intelligence, a book which has been roundly criticized for its conclusions. If the conclusions are correct, there is nothing to criticize and nothing to apologize for. However, the studies are askew as many tested represent the cream of the crop of their country who have come here much to our benefit but causing a brain drain in their countries of origin. Blacks in this country, coming from centuries of bad education and wretched poverty, both of which impact negatively on the development of both the brain as an organ and intelligence as a function of that organ, thus score lower. This can be reversed with nutrition and good schools.

But even if you grant that Blacks are in fourth place, which I don't, but for the sake of argument I'm willing to grant, then why not allow them equal access to a good education and let the results speak for themselves. Or as Jawanza Kunjufu (Chapter 5) said in Minneapolis on November 1, 2001, at Pilot City Neighborhood Center, if Blacks are so inferior, there is not reason to discriminate. Fear is usually reserved for those who are superior. So why do Whites fear Blacks if not for the fact that they fear that if they are "turned loose" and given equal access and equal opportunity, they will surpass Whites?

Housing projects were originally created as starter places for poor Whites, not poor Blacks. It was only later that Blacks were included, and then only because of the advocacy and interference of Eleanor Roosevelt. And today, when Black projects are demolished, Blacks are dispersed, while the replacement housing is reserved mainly for White gentrification, as you will see with the Hollman fiasco in Minneapolis (Chapter 8). The taking of government monies like this makes Enron's actions look like kid stuff. No corporation, as we shall see, has matched the corruption and taking of billions as have government workers/bureaucrats and, with them, legislators for campaign contributions. One example of many that I will discuss: in five years, the Minneapolis Community Development Agency received $856.5 million dollars from the Federal, state and city governments, for affordable housing units. The result: the bulldozing of thousands of homes of Blacks and the building of only 52 replacement units. Repeat that: $856.5 million for 52 replacement units. Combined with monies spent on the same project by other agencies, that's nearly a billion dollars. The records of the Ward Council Member/Council President Jackie Cherryhomes disappeared from her office along with her when Natalie Johnson-Lee defeated her. The response of the establishment was not to seek justice, but to seek a reaffirmation of the status quo through redistricting Blacks out of contention (Chapters 12-13), out of participation, out of being citizens, and out of access and opportunity.

As for prosperity and entrepreneurial growth, the 1968 Report of the National Advisory Commission on Civil Disorders, known simply as The Kerner Commission Report, said that the United States was heading toward become two nations, one Black and one White. It got the overall situation correct:

> Segregation and poverty have created in the racial ghetto a destructive environment totally unknown to most white Americans. What white Americans have never fully understood—but what the Negro can never forget—is that white society is deeply implicated in the ghetto. White institutions created it, white institutions maintain it, and white society condones it.

But it got the meaning wrong (that American is heading toward becoming two nations, one White, one Black), and it got the situation wrong (that because the times were different, unlike immigrants, Blacks couldn't bootstrap to prosperity and thus could not attain self-sufficiency), and it got the solution wrong (that Blacks would therefore have to become wards of the state).

The Liberals and the Democratic Party (with close assistance from the Republicans) said this was the direction of the nation. And instead of fighting it, or even asking for better evidence, they used it as the vehicle to put us in our place and make it happen faster, especially in the inner cities.

What is remarkable is how many Blacks have made it despite having one hand tied behind their backs by liberal, racist policies (Interludes 5 and 7). Now update the 1998 Kerner Commission Report with the 1998 book *Bell Curve*, which comes to the same conclusion: Blacks have to be wards of the state. The book, despite its great work in discussing the efficacy of IQ tests, states, in one small chapter, that Blacks are too dumb to make it, that they are intellectually inferior to the Asians, Whites, and Browns, in that order, and thus they need the government to take care of them. That leaves those of us who are Black with the chilling reality that both Conservatives and Liberals, both right of center and left of center, both Democrats and Republicans agree, for different reasons, that Blacks can't make it on their own, and, as they would say at a Twins game, whiff, whiff, whiff, three strikes, and Blacks are out. So why "waste" money on us for education and housing and jobs?

The liberal 1968 *Kerner Commission Report* and "it's-too-late-for-Blacks-to-make it" idea and the 1998 *Bell Curve* idea that Blacks-are-too-dumb-to-make it both share the same solution: Blacks have to be wards of the state. This has led to too many Black volunteers being paid as foremen to keep the rest of the Blacks in line. They are wrong. I've spent 40 years trying to prove them wrong (just as Interludes 5 and 7 prove them wrong). And I'll spend the next 40 years continuing to do so until we get this turned around.

Indeed, "keeping us in our place" is what James Baldwin called "the machinery of our country's operations." My goal is to help us all see that it is in everyone's best interest to be in the same place, a place I outline in Chapter 5.

Now I ask you, how is that any less racist than the plantation days of slavery? When you tell generations that they don't have it, can't have it, and won't have it, and then take away their access and opportunity, offer up policies that weaken if not tear apart families, you kill ambition and energy and the spark needed to climb the mountains of life. What is so remarkable are not the statistics on young Black men, on poor, uneducated, out-of-work Black men. What is remarkable are not those who are kept ghettoized by public policy, but rather how many Blacks have made it despite the mastering by Minneapolis of ghettoizing Blacks (Chapter 3). And when ghettoizing in a place like North Minneapolis doesn't work, they use the ultimate ghetto: the prison (Chapter 9).

I present to you *The Minneapolis Story Through My Eyes* as a reality check. **First,** the January 1990 issue of the *Mpls.St.Paul* Magazine cover story headlined: "I'm

Not Racist, But....", which was answered by the subhead " 'Nice' Minnesotans don't talk about it, but the ugly fact is that racism is alive—*and growing*—in the Twin Cities" (Interlude 1). **Second,** the June 10-24, 1990 series in the *Minneapolis Star Tribune* detailed the racism (Interlude 10)? In other words: Racism exists in large enough amounts to create a bad situation for many, including Minneapolis as a whole. The question is: is it now more so or less so? Has there been a change? Both sources, in the 21st century, say no. Racism denies Minneapolis the contributions of those who could contribute but don't because they are purposefully forced out when they are denied equal access, equal opportunity, and equal entrepreneurial growth. For those of you who might say I am playing the race card, I ask only this: Read the book, read the statistics, read about what has happened, and then ask yourself if this is an anomaly or is there purposeful public policy and private action regarding Blacks? Am I playing the race card or is the race card being continuously played by Whites and their house Negroes?

Despite the Far Left and its insistence on an impossible utopia it would create and then freeze (conserve) into place or the Far Right and its insistence on re-creating a non-existent golden age from the past and freezing (conserve) it into place, history doesn't work that way. It never freezes (even geology doesn't). But history does have a sense of humor and is always in motion, almost as if it too were subject to the dynamic of Newton's theory of action and reaction. Certainly there are reciprocal actions between the leaders and the led, the victors and the vanquished, and between the simple interactions of everyday living between everyday people living everyday lives. *The Minneapolis Story Through My Eyes* explores how Whites leave Blacks out in an attempt to thwart the historic nature of these reciprocal actions and how knowing that this historic nature exists offers hope for getting inside the system to make it work for all.

As we explore the Minneapolis story, we will probe the desired end question: Do we want to be a nation of two parts, one Black and one White, or an integrated nation that says no to racism as it once said no to slavery and balances the opportunity for economic integration for all? Or is that also to be anywhere but here?

Throughout this book, I will explore the trends using stinging statistics, using my own experiences with them, and ask why is this so in Minneapolis?

My role is that of a walking library, of a community storyteller, like a wandering Renaissance minstrel retelling the stories of past generations so that the current generation can tell their sons and daughters and keep their history and legacy alive. That way, all will not only want to live here but thrive here. They will be proud of being here and proud of being from here, and be proud of all the others who are here.

The U.S. economic pie continues to grow but not for all. All must have a chance. Good business sense compels corporations to look beyond diversity legislation for purely business reasons: growth and profits, which means including all. Some have said that we won WW II because we fully mobilized and used everyone, men and women. In Germany and Japan, two very chauvinistic and exclusionary societies, the women stayed home, causing many men to remain behind doing work women could have done in order to free them for battle. The US economic pie is great. But it can grow greater, especially if we free all to fail or succeed, free all to engage in commerce, free all to find their niche, to be free to make it or lose it, but either way to be free to try.

Thus, although I am a Black man, I do not write about the culture wars, *per se*. I invite you, dear reader, to transcend those issues to focus on issues that are more important: fairness, access, and opportunity. The Minneapolis story is about the partial progress that has been made in universal fairness, access, and opportunity (the glass half full) and the progress that is still to be made (the glass half empty).

Minneapolis is one-third Black, and yet it only has one African-American on the City Council, a woman the Minneapolis power structure tried to throw out through the crassness of gerrymandering her out of her district and then calling for new elections (Interlude 12 and discussed in Chapters 12 and 13). The puppet masters and their Black and White dupes claim they did this to give minorities more opportunities when they knew it would do the opposite. Why do they continue to ghettoize Blacks in 2002? Because they can. Will you let them continue, dear reader? Your answer will be reflected by who you vote for in the next elections.

In 2002, the power people of Minneapolis are closer than ever to reaching their goal of making Minneapolis the last outpost of the last experiment to show the rest of the country how to put minorities in their place and keep them there. The record shows Minneapolis offering itself up as a model, just as the South did with the Missouri Compromise (Interlude 6). My goal is to expose this desire on their part and to demonstrate how foolhardy it is to even attempt.

What makes this possible are the so-called Black leaders, especially of the Urban League and the NAACP, these equivalents of house Negroes, who are sell-outs accepting scraps from deal-makers (Chapter 14). As background, I will share with you information that declares that Minneapolis stands against equal access, equal opportunity, and fair treatment for all (Chapters 5-13). As Americans, we are promised the right to pursue life, liberty and happiness. As Minneapolis wistfully looks back to a time that probably didn't exist, I will collide head-on with her to tell a story about a city whose leaders nostalgically look forward through the rear view mirror.

You will learn some startling statistics in this book and you will learn that most of the blocking of Black progress is technically legal. And because it is also immoral, unjust, and unfair, it clashes with other values (remember, slavery and Jim Crow laws were once legal too). When we look at various statistics, including high school graduation rates, the number of Black men in prison, and other statistics regarding education and housing and political participation and minority entrepreneurial growth, you will better understand why I call the statistics startling and stinging.

Now, dear reader, you might say to me: Look, what's all the fuss? That would be a Minneapolis answer. You could ask me, as people have: Why do you keep on? After all, the welfare rolls have been cut in half, child poverty statistics have dropped, overall poverty is down, work statistics are up." And maybe you could say that I am unreasonable, that I want 99% positive answers for all of these statistics.

But let me ask you this: Would you settle for 99% in things? 99% still leaves a lot of pain. For instance, at 99%, there would be 200,000 wrong prescriptions written each year. More than 30,000 newborn babies would be accidentally dropped by doctors or nurses each year at birth. Drinking water would be unsafe almost 4 days each year. Electricity, water, and heat would not be available for about 15 minutes each day. And out of 300 million people, 99% above the poverty line still leaves 3 million below. That is a lot of poor people in a society where it is not necessary to have any. In that one percent many babies would die, those using machines would be endangered, not to mention those in hospitals, and those four unsafe water days could make the entire population sick. No, my friends, 99% is not good enough.

I am arguing for 100% equal access and equal opportunity. Effort, or lack of effort, will take over from there. Thus, I am not arguing for 100% equal results. That is impossible for any group, Black or White. All I am arguing for is equal access, equal opportunity, and equal inclusion in the mainstream, for the same opportunity to succeed as well as fail as the next person. I'm not looking for percentages or quotas or preferences or 99% success. I'm looking for just two things and two things only: fairness and justice, which I translate as equal access and equal opportunity, meaning fair treatment in both. Poverty is not the issue. It's whether people have an opportunity to get out of it or not. There are more poor Whites in this country than all the Blacks put together. But no one is holding them back because they are White. There is no residue of "Whites need not apply" or "no Whites allowed at the lunch counter" or "no Whites allowed to vote." You see, dear reader, ending poverty requires prosperity that all have access to, and prosperity, as we witness in history and today around the world is fairly simple: it depends on a market economy that encourages private enterprise where all engage with the same rules and same exercise of the law, including the right to private property. The market economy, or capitalism, has brought more people out of poverty than any other system. What I am asking for is to open up that system to everyone.

Have you ever seen the statue of Walt Disney in Disneyland? He is proud to be an American, standing with his customers, dreaming about making every family feel good about themselves and putting a smile on the faces of their children with Mickey Mouse. I was a teenager when Disneyland opened. This book is my Ron Edwardsland. I too want do put a smile on the face of every person in Minneapolis. In Minneapolis we have a different version of Walt Disney. He's called Kurt Carlson. His statue is not Mickey Mouse. His statue is a naked boy flying on his own beside a flying horse, with the plaque noting that the boy's ability to jump off the horse and fly on his own is a tribute to man's genius to overcome difficulty. My concern is not the single exceptional person able to fly on his own but the thought that anyone can do it and the failure to credit the wind under his wings that enables him to fly in the first place, a wind composed of his customers and clients. He takes the credit, but he couldn't do it without all the others (his clients and customers). We need to get away from the Carlson notion of individuals making it on their own and remember Lincoln's words about unity over division. A society of individuals with no ties to others is the house divided that Lincoln said can't stand.

Disney actually achieved his goal and made it possible for everyone to smile. Carlson, on the other hand, made it possible to smile only for those in his in-crowd, who shared his Scandinavian roots and entrepreneurial success, and who were born or married into his family. I don't begrudge Kurt his success. He earned it. But he didn't do anything for the poor person in rags, only the dream-boy jumping off his horse and flying by himself without any help. And you could find similar examples with the other so-called great families of Minneapolis: the Bingers, the Cowleses, the Cargills, the Dyers, the Junts, the Maases, the McKays, the McMillans, the Pohlads, the Taylors, the Whitneys. Whether great or not, they are wealthy. They have given to themselves but not to the masses. They have given to the arts and music and theatre and high cultural philanthropy of their own interests, which is their right, but have given far less to anything that would enable the minorities in the inner city to leap off their ghettoized horses and fly on their own. And indeed, they are about to do one of their worst collective take aways: sending the city's beloved Vikings out of state (Chapter 15). That will be the final bit of proof of just how selfish and uncaring about the rest of Minneapolis and Minnesota these so-called upstanding families really are, a legacy that will forever follow their families' names after the Vikings leave.

There is a difference between being legally correct and being morally correct. The correctness of my story has stood the test of time and has shown to be true, not only in the events that I report where I was at the center as a participant or observer, but also in the Interludes reporting the events of history. In ancient Rome, there was no debate about corporal punishment or spanking. If a son disobeyed, the father had the legal right to kill him. And who can forget slavery, an institution that was legal around the world throughout history well into the 19th century. And think about "separate but equal" apartheid in South Africa, our own Jim Crow apartheid in the South after the Civil War until the 1950s and 1960s, and current attempts to thwart or reverse Black progress. Simply put, what is legal is what the law says it is, and the law is made by the rulers. Laws reflect the morality of the time. To know what people's morals are, see what laws they favor and oppose. Our laws are the least offensive of any on planet earth. But if those that are most offensive are aimed at you, the fact that we have the least offensive of the laws on earth is small comfort other than knowing we are free to fight them openly. And so I continue to fight any and all that favor Jim Crow. I urge all of my readers, Black and White, to join me in that battle.

I hope, dear reader, that you realize where I'm coming from: Not from a Black agenda, and not from any minority or Black thing, but rather, from the simple highest ideal of the America agenda: equal liberty and equal justice for all. The attention of such an effort is needed most in America's poverty pockets that have been purposefully disempowered and disenfranchised, like inner cities, not to mention places like poor White Appalachia.

My story is a gift to all people, whether Black or White, Brown or Yellow. It is my gift to all in Minneapolis and Minnesota, and to all trying to make a better story out of their cities too, wherever in this great land of America they reside.

I hope after reading about the Minneapolis story you will say: "Hey, I knew that," and then join with others to do something positive about it. My hope is that you have many an "aha!" experience that will cause you to pay more attention to the political process, and, when you can, to join in that process and do something about it with your votes and advocacy actions, so that we close the gap in equal access, equal opportunity, and equal entrepreneurial opportunity for all in education, housing, political participation, and economic development.

What was said about women is still being said about too many Blacks: keep them down on the farm, keep them barefoot and pregnant so they won't run away (for men, just barefoot), and don't let any of them read. Combined, these will keep them in their place. We need to work until that is no longer applied to anyone, regardless of color.

To not allow and indeed to work against equal access and equal opportunity is discrimination and intolerance at its worst. Some exercise their intolerance in the name of political ideology (think of Lenin, Stalin, Mao, Kim Il Sung, Pol Pot, Castro,

Hitler, Mussolini) or religion (think of the Crusades, Inquisition, Islam's beginning and continued evangelizing, Islam's concept of Taqlid that no truth exists outside the Koran, or its terrorist jihads today), or ethnicity (think of the Chinese burning their ocean-going vessels, which were five times bigger than those of Columbus, 50 years before Columbus sailed West, as they saw nothing worthy beyond their Celestial Kingdom), or of Spain kicking out their business class, the Jews, the same year Columbus sailed, leaving Spain with little expertise in converting the discovered gold into business investments and growth.

Always ask who benefits from programs and laws that are enacted. For instance, when, as noted, the 1968 *Kerner Commission Report* declared that Blacks could not make it on their own and thus needed government assistance, the beneficiary was the party who had always had that Plantation mentality: the Democratic Party, because Blacks then lined up for government help. And even though this contributed to the weakening of many families, with the cash in hand, they have continued to vote for Democrats in overwhelming numbers.

Is it any wonder that Blacks who recognize the racist intolerance of the thinking behind the *Kerner Commission Report* and *The Bell Curve* are now turning to other political parties like the Green Party (the Republicans have yet to prove themselves, and thus few Blacks join them)? Turning to the Green party are especially young Blacks who recognize that the senior Blacks work to protect their power, influence, and material benefits gained from doing so, and thus are condemning the younger generation rather than help it.

There are those, especially Liberals, who like to say more people have died in the name of God (meaning the Christian God) than any other. This, of course, is false. Only tens of thousands died in those attributed to the Christian God. Many more wre killed by Genghis Khan, Attila the Hun, and Islam as it swept across Northern Africa and attempted to sweep across Europe. And even these combined with the Christians pale by comparison to the tens of millions who died in the name of the godless ideas of the 20th century. In the 20th century alone, in the name of political ideologies that were attached to no god, tens of millions perished, not in battle but at the hand of their own leaders. Most 20th century wars were not about God but about power, begun by forces of intolerance and absolutism that were finally turned back by forces of tolerance and democracy. The defeated ones, to keep their power internally, slaughtered their own, the examples for which are Lenin, Stalin, Mao, Kim Il Sung, Pol Pot, Castro, and Hitler, none of whom represented a religion.

The series on racism that ran in 1990 by the *Minneapolis Star Tribune* (Interlude 1), and by the *MplsSt.Paul Magazine* issue that same year (Interlude 10) were devoted to the study of racism in Minneapolis. They made it clear that many people cannot see their own racism. It is too hard to admit. They literally cannot do it.

Therefore, I ask you to consider a different question: are you tolerant? Or do you believe in absolutist views that allow you to exclude others (Chapter 4)?

Look at the data. Are Blacks more excluded than Whites (and ask the same question regarding Browns and Yellows as well as poor Whites)? Do equal access, equal opportunity, democracy, and honor exist for Blacks as it does for Whites? If the answer is yes to the first question and no the second, it would appear, at least to me, that you are either a racist or an intolerant absolutist. To me there is no difference. How would you judge? And one more question: How would you react if you were the subject of the historical anecdotes in the Interludes? Jews may be God's chosen people, but Blacks in America and South Africa have proven to be the only ones able to consistently turn the other cheek while striving for justice and equality. Had any of this happened to you, would you have turned your cheek and kept working for equality (Chapter 5)?

It is interesting to me that there are more non-White Christians in the world than White Christians. A recent report from the November/December 2001 *Books and Culture,* quoted in *Context,* noted that more believers attend church in China than in all of so-called Christian Europe, and that more Anglicans attend church in the African nations of Kenya, South Africa, Tanzania, and Uganda than do Anglicans in Britain and the United States combined. It reported that more Presbyterians were in church in Ghana than in Scotland and more of them were in church in South Africa than in the United States. Finally, it reported that mostly Black congregations in England and France had the largest attendance in church that White congregations had in England and France.

These statistics are important. As more and more non-Whites become Christian, the one great common ground they share is Christianity, a religion that, like the U.S. constitution, also says that all are equal in the sight of God, and that all are to love and serve one another. Given the history of their treatment, some of the worst of which is covered in the Interludes, Blacks seem better at keeping their eye on the prize of freedom and not getting distracted by the kind of violence and constant oppression exercised by Whites, especially in inner-cities. And this religious interest to me is good, not bad. Peace advocates are essentially grounded in the spiritual practices of some transcendent sense. Islam has its Sufis, Christianity its mystics, and Judaism its Hassidics. All urge kindness, courtesy, and consideration of others. All promote spiritual practices for achieving this (see www.spiritualityhealth.com).

Consider the following from these Black writers quoted in the May 2001 issue of *Context* (Martin E. Marty on Religion and Culture):

Hatred which could destroy so much, never failed to destroy the man who hated, and this was an immutable law....I imagine that one of the reasons that people cling to their hates so stubbornly is because they sense, once hate is gone, that they will be forced to deal with the pain."

James Baldwin

To be a poor man is hard, but to be a poor race in a land of dollars is the very bottom of hardship.

W.E.B. DuBois

The great thing about serving the poor is that there is no competition.

Eugene Rivers

If it's wrong for 13-year old inner city girls to have babies without the benefit of marriage, it's wrong for rich celebrities, and we ought to stop putting them on the cover of *People* magazine.

Marian Wright Edelman

We all need to come together. Hear this about and from scholar K. Anthony Appiah, the son of a Ghanaian father and an English mother, from *In My Father's House: Africa in the Philosophy of Culture,* as reported by Danny Postel in *Context*:

But the idea of race isn't merely bad science, Mr. Appiah argues; it is also morally dangerous. And it isn't only people of European provenance who have bought into the idea of race; many on the receiving end of racial oppression have done so as well....Mr. Appiah argues that [the notion of a racial "essence," a quality or set of qualities supposed to be shared by all Blacks] is just as fraudulent as the 19th-century European notion of a racial hierarchy, with Whites at the top.

For all of his intellectual accomplishments and his passion for the life of the mind, Mr. Appiah believes there is a vital need to do more than just theorize and argue. "We cannot change the world," he writes, "simply by evidence and reasoning. "And yet," he adds, "we can surely not change it without them either."

When a friend of mine heard I was writing this book, he said I sometimes reminded him of Studs Terkel, the longshoreman turned philosopher. Context quoted him quoting George Bernard Shaw about serving in one's community. He told me that when he read this he said to himself, "Hey, this is Ron Edwards." I must admit I resonate deeply with the words, and so I repeat them here for you:

I am of the opinion that my life belongs to the whole community, and as long as I live it is my privilege to do for it what I can. I want to be thoroughly used up when I die, for the harder I work, the more I live. I rejoice in life for its own sake. Life is no brief candle for me. It is sort of a splendid torch that I have got hold of for a moment, and I want to make it burn as brightly as possible before handing it on to future generations.

That we Blacks have endured through so much is why I call us bold, beautiful, and better, not because of some shared essence of Blackness or due to some place on a hierarchy of racial betterment. No. I mean it in the sense of Viktor Frankl in his *Man's Search for Meaning,* when he says he realized, as they stood naked and beaten before their Nazi captors, that they still had the last freedom, the freedom to choose their attitude. And after you have read about the Minneapolis story, let me know whether or not you agree that wrong has and continues to be done to Blacks in Minneapolis, particulary in the inner city. Let me know if you agree with me that, for the most part, given what we have had to take and given what we have not been allowed to do, we have borne it all with dignity just as we continue to push to secure the prize of freedom for ourselves with dignity.   Racism is but one form of intolerance. How many forms do you see? How many do you personally hold? Could you, if you are White, pursue the prize of Freedom with the dignity we have shown if you were also treated as we have been treated?

Martin Luther King, Jr. combined vision and action. Martin Luther King, Jr. said it best: "We Shall Overcome." President Lyndon Johnson surprised the nation by closing his 1968 State of the Union Address, stating that the nation still had much to do to overcome the inequality under which Blacks were still made to suffer. As President Kennedy before him, he tried to enlist Whites in common cause with Blacks to remove the barriers to equal access and equal opportunity, as he promised to work on removing such barriers, closing with these words: "We shall overcome." We live in a great country. That is why I see our glass as half full. But our glass is also half full, for, as Frederic Douglass stated it, we still have the unfinished business of obtaining freedom for everyone.

So we still have lots of work left to do for the Blacks kept segregated and down in the inner city, especially young Black men. Thus, there are those, Black and White, who would change that to "we shall overturn" or "we shall overrun." That would be a mistake. In this book I have documented the outrages but also the progress. We have come this far "turning the other cheek." We will get the rest of the way the same way. Let us not let our voices roar when our power can but whisper. But our minds and our actions, and our use of the legal system for justice and fairness for all, is what needs to be heard and that will enable us to finally overcome for all.

We cannot retain our moral high ground and achieve our ends if we act like the Mastuh. No, my friends, we won't go down to their level to overturn and over run. But we shall overcome.

I promise you this,

- We shall achieve equal access.
- We shall achieve equal opportunity.
- We shall overcome.
- We shall succeed.

And I will continue to add my comments on these topics on the "web log" on my Minneapolis story web site, www.TheMinneapolisStory.com (these also called "Blogs").

Interlude 1

Ron Edwards: One Of The Most Media Covered Citizen Advocates

Someone once did a media review of me because he said it seemed as if I were in the paper every day. This friend figured out that I must have been mentioned in over 7,000 articles in the Minneapolis *Star Tribune* alone.

I discuss this because it is important to an understanding of my telling of my interpretation of the Minneapolis story. Certainly in my own files I have an extensive collection of clippings from the Minneapolis media (not to mention hours of tape from years of both radio and TV shows, including my current role as host and commentator on *Black Focus* on MTN). And I've used many of these articles going back to the 1960s, as well as my memory, my radio and TV work, and a researcher, to write this book.

And yet it still always amuses me when people ask me why the media doesn't talk to them as often as they talk to me. I usually shrug my shoulders and play dumb. But I know why I get so much coverage. It is not hard to understand or to explain.

1. Credibility: Reporters and investigative journalists live or die on the credibility of their sources. They know that I know what I am talking about. If I don't, I say so; I don't make something up for them. I know that you only get to make one mistake in this and you lose your credibility. I've maintained my credibility for over 40 years

2. Trustworthiness: They know that if I promise them a follow-up, I will do so, or if I promise to be quiet about my sources, I will, or if I promise to keep their confidence, I will. I know that you only get to make one mistake in this and you lose their trust. People have trusted me for over 40 years.

3. Knowledge: I'm in the middle of things; I'm on the edge of things. I'm on the ramparts. In some situations, I've been the gavel at the front of the room and in others I'm the fly on the wall. Either way, I've got the scoop. But more than that, I have a valuable understanding and interpretation of the events they are covering.

   In these matters, I have been a part of the three major Minneapolis organizations that have been in the middle of the civil rights and human rights movements in Minneapolis, serving in highly visible, albeit non-paid positions: The Civil Rights Commission for 16 years (long served, as

Chairman, 1979 1983, and as Vice Chairman, 1967-1972). The <u>Urban League</u> (longest serving Chairman, 11 years, 1978-1989. And I've been in the middle of the most recent housing and redistricting controversies with the NAACP in my position on the Executive Committee, 1999-2002. In the movie Ghost Busters, the question is: "Who ya gonna call?" In Minneapolis the answer is easy: call Ron Edwards.

4. <u>Objective subjectiveness</u>. I have my point of view. In the movie *Grand Canyon,* a White man's fancy sports car stalls in the middle of a ghetto street he has used as a shortcut. Five tough Black street youth surround him. A tow truck operator, also Black, interrupts them. He says to their leader, "Man, the world ain't s'pposed to work like this. Maybe you don't know that, but this ain't the way its s'pposed to be. I'm s'pposed to be able to do my job without askin' you if I can. And that dude is s'pposed to be able to wait with his car without you rippin' him off. Everthin's s'posed to be different than what it is here." As a tow truck driver of Minneapolis, I remind people, Black and White, of the way things are supposed to be: peace, justice, fairness, equal access, equal opportunity, mutual respect, goodwill, with deliberate and widespread attention to the public good. That is the way things are s'pposed to be. That is my advocacy every day. It has been my advocacy for 40 years. No wonder they ask me.

Chapter 2

My Path to Minneapolis

[T]here is no doubt that *the overwhelming majority of white Americans desire that there be as few Negroes as possible in America.* If the Negroes could be eliminated from America or greatly decreased in numbers, this would meet the whites' approval -- *provided that it could be accomplished by means which are also approved.* Correspondingly, an increase of the proportion of Negroes in the American population is commonly looked upon as undesirable.

> Gunnar Myrdal, *An American Dilemma: The Negro Problem and Modern Democracy*, 1944
> http://www.africa2000.com/indx/myrdal.htm

I am writing the Minneapolis story, not the Ron Edwards story. I am also writing part of what could be called The Black Man's Story, as all Black people share the same context for their lives: living in a country that has a split viewpoint: enamored by the ideals of democracy, freedom, liberty, democracy, and prosperity while simultaneously enamored with its own White complexion. I bring up Myrdal again (Chapter 1) to remind us that racism exists, on many different levels. The reason we have inner city ghettos is because, as Myrdal points out in his book, there is a virtually universal genocidal intent on the part of whites. Not genocidal in terms of racial cleaning through killing, but in terms of separation, keeping us apart from them. This explains the Southern acceptance of slavery and its universal Jim Crow laws after slavery was ended. And it is still the best definition of a racist: one who tries to either keep Blacks apart and separate, or who goes out of his or her way to avoid them and not include them in their organizations and affairs, both personally and professionally. I maintain Minneapolis still harbors this view. But as Myrdal points out, Americans want to eliminate us but only in approved ways. As they can't find any, we are left with tension between the races. That is the American dilemma.

It is this context that contributes to the authority by which I write and why I write. Interlude 1 gives a good summary of my actions and activities. But there is more. There will be Blacks who will say I write this "of course" because my grandfather was a Black doctor and lawyer will be just as wrong as those Whites who say that as a railroad porter's son, I should know my place, ride in the back of the bus, keep my peace, and write nothing. Like you, dear reader, I am more than my relatives.

Some Blacks, especially those who are self appointed leaders and consider themselves among the Black elite, will ask why the grandson of one of Kansas City's most prominent Black citizens, L. Virgil Miller (a medical doctor and an attorney and a confidant of Harry S. Truman), doesn't take his place with the elite and work *for* White power, not *against* it, and let those dreadful porters and field hands fend for themselves. There will be Whites who say I can write and speak and am intelligent because of the White blood in me, regardless of the fact that the White part of me is a very small percentage. There will be other Whites who will say I can't possibly know much because I am the son of a railroad porter, one of the legions of those called "George" (Interlude 9). Both my grandfather, C.M. Edwards, and my dad, Alfred Edwards, spent many years as porters (my father always had steady employment and supported himself and his family first as a Pullman porter for 40 years and then as a waiter for 20 years at the Mule Bok Hotel). There will also be Blacks who say I can't possibly understand what it is to be a Black man because I am not Black enough. And there will be those who will say that because I am also part Seminole Indian, I need to go back to the reservation where I belong. Needless to say, whether from Whites or Blacks, most of these are racist comments.

Well, to all of them, I say only this: I belong where there is a need for a voice to fight for fairness and justice, for equal access and equal opportunity for all, regardless of race, color, ethnic background, gender, or sexual orientation. I view it as my place, my calling, if you will, to speak out against any group that lays claim to special status and says they are entitled to privileges because of their ancestors (which, in this country, is usually Whites) or because of what happened to their ancestors (which, in this country, is usually Blacks and Browns), at the expense of others. Isn't it interesting that the descendents of slaves make almost the same kind of entitlement speeches that descendents of wealthy people make? Both claim superiority and entitlement because of their ancestors.

Somewhere along the line, we all came from somewhere. Most who have come to this country, originally came from either slaves or outcasts. I have no problem with that. What I have a problem with is when people forget their roots and act as if they have sprung fully realized and powerful and wealthy from the mind of God and therefore can now treat others as slaves and outcasts. To all of them I say: "Shame on you." I also say: "You know better." I also say: "You are better than that." People without shame can commit all manner of indignities upon others, ranging from social slights to atrocities, from the merely rude to the deplorably evil.

When I was a young boy talking with my grandfather, I was talking to someone who knew the former slaves from whom he was descended. And maybe that is one of the reasons why we Blacks have been so gracious in our struggles. What little we have is so much more than our recent ancestors had. The grand struggle for freedom is not yet old for us. We haven't fully won it so we don't have to protect it, to draw up the drawbridges to our castles of freedom. And for me the struggle for freedom is seen in two ways, not only from my slave side but from my Native American side as well.

I have relatives whose ancestors came from Africa and who were raised on slave plantations. I also have relatives who were raised on what can only be called the national plantations of the Federal Government, so-called reservations, which were a different kind of slave quarters. They weren't slaves as in the South. But they were still purposefully left isolated and hopeless, hoping they would have "the decency" to kill themselves off, under the notion that "the only good Indian is a dead Indian."

As you read my take on the Minneapolis story, you will feel its power, the power that the Minnesota story has for people who, no matter how they are treated, still strive to overcome. Its my job to make a difference, to give of myself, to get myself involved, to be honest and to stick to the simple goal of being a community advocate for fairness and justice, an advocate for equal access and equal opportunity. The battle I joined 40 years ago continues. But first let's look at how I came to Minneapolis.

I first came to Minneapolis at the age of 7, in 1945 with my dad. I can't say I came, I saw, I conquered, but I can say I came, I saw, and I was captivated. It might not have been the city by the bay, or the city of strong shoulders, or the city of lights or even of stars. These were not its rivals. It was just the Twin Cities at the beginning of the Mississippi. The rival towns were Mississippi towns: Milwaukee, Kansas City, Omaha, and St. Louis.

My mother came from high society. Her dad, L. Virgil Miller, a double-degreed Black gentleman (doctor, attorney) did not approve of my mom marrying a street-wise man. L. Virgil had them separated (in another Romeo and Juliet kind of tragedy of parents not accepting their child's choices, my mother never remarried). I got my golden tongue and smooth style from the cultured ways of my mom's side of the family, my toughness and street smarts from my dad's side. My maternal grandfather, L. Virgil Miller, was a friend of Harry S. Truman, and in my trips to visit my mom in Kansas City, I would hear the stories about him and President Truman. It helped develop in me a life-long interest in the political process.

To give my mom an opportunity to develop her potential, my dad brought me with him to Minneapolis, where he lived, at age 7. I grew up on the north side of Minneapolis, in what was and is called the Negro area. I had a wonderful time.

Despite my social pedigree, I was one of the clubbed baby seals I talk about in Chapter 7, on education. Despite my lofty ambitions to go to college, to follow in the footsteps of L. Virgil Miller, my guidance counselor saw that I was Black and told me: "Oh you can't do that," laughed, and slotted me to a non-academic track. This was not based on my grades or my schoolwork, but on my race and my color. That was an attitude of racism followed by an act of racism.

The pivotal academic experience of my life, accompanied by hands-on experience in community advocacy, community organizing, and community development, came during the year I studied at the University of Syracuse, in upstate New York. I had been selected in 1965 to join the program at Syracuse led by the era's greatest community organizer and advocate, Saul Alinsky. After a year in that program, I received my certificate of completion and returned to Minneapolis.

My dream then, as now, was to make a difference, to advocate the American dream for all: truth, justice, fairness, and economic integration into the economic, political, and social mainstream by all people of poverty.

My developing role as the conscience of Minneapolis combined with my belief that each of us only comes this way but once and must make the most of it for others too. The biggest waste is to live and do nothing. My goal has kept me going for over 40 years. I reach out to touch lives and to be helpful.

I have thus become the Minneapolis Marathon Man of community activism and advocacy. The key to my overcoming adversity and achieving goals has been my use of "self talk" and visualization to energize my subconscious to lead my conscious self to achieve, to think things into being. My greatest joy has come from helping others achieve their goals.

I have had three paying jobs in my life. My first job, for three and a half years, was as a janitor at the World Theatre at a dollar an hour. My second was with the gas company for two and a half years. My third and last job was also my longest, for 21 years, with Northern States Power (NSP) Company (now Xcell Energy Company).

I have never worked for a social agency, although I have sat in on many meetings dealing with them. I say this because one of the destructive rumors used against me was that I was being paid for my work at the Urban League and Civil Rights Commission and at the NAACP. Those were all non-paid, appointive positions. It is sad that so many know so little about how things work. People used to think that as President of the Urban League, the title in those days, now its Chairman of the Board, and that as Chairman of the Civil Rights Commission that I was getting big salaries. Not at all. I was getting no pay of any kind for this work.

So people would say: Hey, Ron Edwards is making big money; he's at NSP, paid at the Commission and Urban League. People didn't know the difference. They also didn't know the difference between the Civil Rights Commission and the Civil

Rights Department. And that's also sad because it significantly undermined my credibility and dedication, as people would say: He ain't really doing anything because he's being paid to do that. And the bosses were shrewd with their system. I saw it early on. They played it like a violin. And so these arguments would go on about me, and folks would say: I hear what you're sayin', man, but you know, you've got it good, you're makin' good, gettin' paid at the Urban League, at the Commission, at NSP. You're livin' good. I write this to set the record straight.

Today I do what I've done for over 40 years, continue my work in community advocacy. One of my favorite activities is my TV show (*Black Focus*, on MTN-TV, Channel 17, Sundays, at 5:00 p.m.), as I am able to bring the word to the community in a way they can't get through the mainstream media. And I do some consulting. At 64 I'm not retired and don't plan to retire. I have my community mission in life, part of which is my current TV show, which follows from my earlier career on radio. I didn't get paid for that and I don't get paid for my current TV show,

In 1978, I started my radio show, *Black Focus and Street Talk,* on KMOJ, a 10-watt station with a 30-block range, operating out of a public housing unit. In 1988, we grew to 100 watts and in 1990-91 to 1,000 watts. It had started earlier as an Urban League program, *Urban Views*, which I left when forced out by the Urban League because of our differing views. Many of my disagreements with the NAACP and the Urban League (Chapter 7) came from the fact that I never sold out. For me, the community and individuals come first. For them, too often, the organization and their collusion with the DFL and collecting pay-offs have been more important (which means they have sown the seeds of their own destruction). It is important that we don't forget where we came from, what was done to us. I will not turn my back on others to whom it is happening. My loyalty is to them, not to the organizations. I have fought for economic self-sufficiency for everyone. They manipulate the system to serve just themselves. They are what I call "sell-outs."

I remember what it was like being a Black youth in White Minneapolis in the 1950s. As a young man, I shared my friends' love for sports, especially football. There were only 12 African-American males out of over 1,600 students at our downtown Minneapolis Vocational High School. Nine of us were on the football team. But the policy on the North side in those days was that only one Negro could start per team, which is why we decided to go to Minneapolis Vocational High School, where we could all start on the football team. Richard Green was there; he was one of our heroes. We were all proud later when this fine Black man whom we all looked up to became School Superintendent. Minneapolis had the premier football conference in those days (today the best programs are in the suburbs).

We loved playing football. I believe I was one of the first Negro quarterback starters for a Minnesota high school. We played out of a "T" formation using the first-all Negro backfield. I showed I had the skill and intelligence to be a quarterback, something most Whites felt was impossible, but then, how did all of those Negro football teams at Negro colleges do so well with Negro quarterbacks? Unfortunately, our coach, Jerry Cady, was also a racist. He had his assistant coach, Dick Chambers, work with the "Coloreds." Despite our hard play, our coach still called us "Ni**ers," "Jungle Bunnies," and "Jigaboos."

His racism killed our next season. He favored Whites over "Coloreds," even when we were the best. We had 8 Negro starters, 2 White starters, and one Native-American starter, Ron Roy, who was 6'4" and weighed 300 pounds. We started the season with high expectations. In an early game, we went to half time ahead 14-0. Now understand that our racist coach, Jerry Cady, was 6'6" and 270 pounds, so he felt he could do anything he wanted to anyone. He didn't like something about the first half. So he grabbed Ron Roy by his shoulder pads and slammed him into a locker, humiliating and embarrassing him. This was the final straw for Ron, who said, "F**k you" to Coach Cady and walked out. We lost 27-14. We called Ron over the weekend, but he still refused to come to Monday practice. We lost him. Ron knew if he came back Cady would be worse. He wasn't going to give him the satisfaction. In retrospect, maybe we should all have quit. But then they held all the cards. It would have kept us out of college. We were in a no-win situation. Cady replaced Ron Roy with a white Ukrainian immigrant who was 6'2" and 215 pounds but who couldn't block. The season went belly-up. And we remained bitter. But it helped to steel me in my resolve to work for a time when that would not happen any more. I've been working at that now for over 40 years. Lots of progress. Lots to go.

As high school seniors, the guidance counselor directed us to the post office or the railroad or the packinghouse, which was killer work surrounded by blood and disease. Think of the social implications of that, telling Black kids that they only had these three options. It would be unrealistic to call them choices when the selections were made for you.

My good friend and fellow teammate Leroy Bogar, one of our finest multi-sport athletes, thought of going to Augsburg College. But in the fall of 1957, they had only one scholarship for a Negro. One of us would have had to walk on without a scholarship. We stood up to that. The University of North Dakota and North Dakota State were beginning to play Negroes, but not many. Most schools were still mostly white, including the University of Minnesota.

So we turned to fast street action, hustling, shooting pool, gambling. But most of us stayed away from the needle. We wanted no part of heroin. The options were either jobs we didn't want, or going to college through sports (except that most scholarships were for Whites), or doing the street action. So I hustled to survive while working as a janitor at the theater. This work only required three hours of my time, but I was paid for eight, so that gave me time to sleep and more time to hustle after work.

The turning point for me came two years later in 1959, when I was 22, when I came under the stewardship of Dr. Thomas Johnson and Frank Alsop. These Renaissance men were very good to me and to other young Black men. They helped forge my identity as a dedicated community advocate.

Frank was a Black man with a fair complexion. He was born deaf, in Alabama, but had taught himself to read lips. He was a brilliant labor organizer who helped organize Negro meat packers in Nebraska in 1930. He had also been a Captain in the Army. But Negro organizers were not wanted. He was shot at in 1933, in Chicago, in an organized assassination attempt.   And although he served the AFL-CIO headquarters in the East as a low-level vice president, he was run out of the AFL-CIO for preaching too much Blackness. He came to Minnesota and hooked up with Thomas Johnson, M.D.

These two men put together a program for young Black men. We met with them 2-3 hours every Sunday, in a classroom, where we reflected on and discussed the issues of the day. They then started PEP: **P**eople **E**mploying **P**eople, to help battle the employment discrimination against Negroes. We learned early that low-level bosses could invite Negroes to lunch, but NOT at the Minneapolis Athletic Club. PEP forced policy changes, took over the Urban League in 1970, and moved on the NAACP in 1962. We moved on the Urban League because we didn't think they were being advocates for the poor and dispossessed. The Urban League has returned to that, which is one of the reasons they ousted me (Chapter 14).

Another influence on me was Nellie Stone Johnson (Interlude 3), who died this year at the age of 96. She remains one of my biggest heroes. She was a mentor. Before her death, she was considered by many to be the most revered civil rights activist in Minnesota.   She was not only known as a key catalyst for political change in America, she was a catalyst to many of us young Black men eager to make a positive difference in our community. Her influence in the areas of labor relations and politics and public policy directions went way beyond Minneapolis and Minnesota. She strongly influenced three major Minnesota political figures on the national stage: Hubert H. Humphrey, Walter Mondale, and Eugene McCarthy. She was also a major influence on Thurgood Marshall, the first Black Supreme Court Justice (Interlude 2). Nellie helped all of us crystallize our goals and language of tolerance and diversity, pluralism and anti-racism. She was a community-oriented person who helped us keep from being distracted from our mission: the community.

Other influences on me were Erthea Wiley and his brother, Dr. Herman Dillard. Both were brilliant. Erthea had one of the greatest minds you could hope to meet. Because Herman was the oldest, a White family convinced their mother to let Herman live with them and be educated at Wayzata High School. Erthea didn't get that opportunity. His size, 6'3" and 320 pounds, scared White folks.

Even though Herman graduated first in his class at the School of Medicine of the University of Minnesota, the doors to existing doctors' offices and clinics were closed to him, so he opened his own office. He fought AMA (American Medical Association) residency policies and what he called the Plantation mentality of the school board and its sitting by while the Black minds of students were being "raped" (his term). He figuratively terrorized the schools and the city with what he stood for, and then he literally terrorized them when he showed up at Lincoln High School in 1967, with an automatic rifle, two pistols, and a bandolier of ammunition. He was killed later by an overdose in Washington, D.C., during the March on Washington. No one knows who administered it. Some say it was Blacks working with Whites to keep the Blacks in their place. Regardless, Herman inspired and galvanized us. And his work of community advocacy and trying to get the schools to teach Blacks as well as they taught Whites was continued by Erthea. I consider myself a person picking up that dropped community advocacy baton as well.

When Vernon Jordan, then head of the national Urban League in the 1970s, came out to Minneapolis and saw what we were doing, he too became a believer. He was trying to get beyond the separatist and strident rhetoric and radical posturing and move toward working with the real political and economic world of the time, especially emphasizing economic self-sufficiency for Blacks in general, not just special ones. He advocated Black small business, home ownership, and jobs paying decent wages, what today we call living wages.

Jordan saw that we took control, that we were not into empty rhetoric. We took action. We made advocacy for the people our theme, our goal, our object of action. How much the Urban League has changed since then is seen even though I later held the office of President (later called Chairman) of the Minneapolis Urban League. There was no recognition of that fact when they held their 75th anniversary in 2000.

The last major influence on me that I want to talk about was my training at the University of Syracuse in 1965. After a year of training, I received a Community Action Training Certification. My influences there at the center founded by Saul Alinsky were his teachings and those of Warren Hagstrom, James Tillman, Frank Alsop, and Leroy Bogar. Some called us: 60s toughies let loose in the world. As I have sat through thousands of hearings over the last 40 years, listening to many more arguments for doing something this way or that, those theories keep coming to mind.

But after all the words and statistics, there is really only one bottom line: Something either is or isn't getting done. In the case of Minneapolis, it is really very simple. We either are or are not educating all the kids, we either are or are not enabling housing for all, we either are or are not allowing everyone to participate in the economic and political processes, we either are or are not working toward full equal access and full equal opportunity in education, housing, and economic development.

And how could young "toughies" like us not be drawn to a guy like Saul Alinsky, who spoke out in defense of community? He was for civil rights, but, like us, he saw the shortcomings of the movement. He was for a Federal war on poverty but he saw deficiencies there as well. Good goals pursued by bad programs didn't make sense to him. And making sense was important to him just as it became important to us.

And how could you not, as a young man, be drawn to a guy who said "Call me rebel" and who could put his theories and other beliefs into books with such catchy titles as *Reveille For Radicals*, which was written in 1946 and which we studied, as well as *Rules for Radicals*, which he codified in his 1971 book of that title.

In *Reveille*, he provided more than just his political philosophy; he included his practical methodology of how to achieve it as well. We were taught to engage in community action and in rational political discourse. He was famous for being someone who could not be bought, who could not be intimidated. I have patterned my work after these ideals. And although he is rarely discussed today, he was considered one of the giants in his own day.

In *Rules*, Alinsky's key point was that groups had to obtain power to succeed in achieving their goals. What appealed most to us was his firmly held belief in the possibility of attaining social justice for ordinary people through the processes of American democracy. He wanted to empower people, especially those left out, those politically weak, those unorganized. He had an incredible flair for not only helping to found the community self-help movement but for using different means of protest to bring attention to the goals. We were all taught these "tricks of the trade."

It was Alinsky's work that successfully enabled the success of the "back of the yards" movement in the mostly Black South Side of Chicago. But once the group successfully obtained power and development, they wouldn't help others get theirs. Alinsky's philosophy was great and his methods do work; however, missing is a way of enabling groups to achieve their goals without having to do so at the expense of others and feeling that to keep theirs they can't help others. When he would occasionally visit the University to make presentations to our classes and engage us in dialogue, we would argue this point with him. He said yes, but at least they got theirs. He hadn't figured out how to get everyone theirs, although different groups were using his methods. What I have wanted to achieve is for everyone to have the opportunity to get theirs, and as they do, in turn help those who still haven't.

These influences are at work throughout this book, as they have influenced me for 40 years, as I work to make a difference, to advocate the American dream for all. For over 40 years, I have never strayed from this vision. I have tasted defeat and I have tasted reform. But always, the goal was the thing. The goal was always bigger than I was, bigger than others. Some people took it the other way; that the goal was they and their organization first, not the people. People recognize that because I never had a part in any of the economic development deals, was never in anyone's pocket, I came to be seen by many as being the conscience of Minneapolis. They have tried to knock me out, but that won't happen, because the goal is what matters, not me.

What makes me sad about this is that the NAACP and the Urban League should be the conscience of the community rather than the lap dogs of the DFL. We should all act as the consciences of our communities. If we could all recognize that each of us only comes this way but once and must make the most of it for others too, how different things would be. As the Negro College Fund says: "A mind is a terrible thing to waste," and the statistics on education and opportunity and income and housing and jobs, that I discuss later, show just how many minds are being wasted.

My grandmother, a very learned woman, was very disappointed because she had wanted me to go to either law school or medical school. But you see, the passion of the civil rights movement had caught me to the extent that I wasn't really interested in more schooling. My interest was the Civil Rights Movement. It is that same interest that has compelled me to write *The Minneapolis Story Through My Eyes*.

My attitude as an adult is always positive. I see life as a continuing struggle of joy and celebration in order to stay focused on overcoming adversity, not only mine but helping others overcome theirs as well.

One of my proudest accomplishments, achieved with many others in the community, was to support and elect Natalie Johnson-Lee in 2001, when she beat the incumbent, Jackie Cherryhomes, who was City Council President, in what some have called the biggest upset in Minneapolis political history (Chapters 11 and 12). It was the culmination of many years of working in and for the community.

My goal is to do whatever I can to help preserve that win and to once again bring to the fore the need to return to the common ground needed for all in Minneapolis: equal access and equal opportunity, justice and fairness for all. Unfortunately, the DFL establishment is attempting to crush Council Member Johnson-Lee, even though she is the only non-White on the Council. So my work continues.

Interlude 2

RACISM I: *Minneapolis Star Tribune* Series, 1990

The truth about racism in Minneapolis can be seen in the devastating headlines used in the series in the *Minneapolis Star Tribune,* which states that Minneapolis is "reflecting malice, insensitivity, closet racism." Racism is both an attitude and an action.

Most define racism as the 1950s Bull Connor with fire hoses, attack dogs, and beating people with nightsticks. As Minnesotans don't do these things, they don't consider themselves racist. But true racism is exclusion, the willingness to turn Blacks away and keep as many as possible "on the inner city reservation." Allowing black students to rot in lousy schools can only be called racism. Active Plantation racism of the Left (1968 *Kerner Commission Report*) and the Right (1998 *The Bell Curve*) both conclude that Blacks can only make it if they are cared for by the government. Shelby Steele calls it what he titled his book: *A Dream Deferred: The Second Betrayal of Black Freedom in America.*

Racism is something Minneapolis does not like to talk about or admit. Not much has changed since two major pieces in 1990, first in the *Star Tribune*, which ran its "Issues of Race" series, June 10-24, 1990. This followed the *Mpls.StPaul* magazine cover story, "I'm Not Racist, But...," in January 1990 with the subhead of: "Nice" Minnesotans don't talk about it, but the ugly fact is that racism is alive—and growing—in the Twin Cities" (Interlude 10)

Webster's Ninth New Collegiate Dictionary defines **racism** as **"1:** a belief that race is the primary determinant of human traits and capacities and that racial differences produce an inherent superiority of a particular race. **2:** racial prejudice or discrimination." A person who practices racism is a racist. Sample headlines from the *Minneapolis Star Tribune* series showed active racism:

- "Birth to death: race sets our agenda for life." (p. 1)

- "Students learn, teach lessons on prejudice." (p. 3)

- "Stresses, injustices add up for people of color." (p. 6)

- "Neighborhoods' clout tied to color." (p. 7); "Advocates not hopeful about clout." (p. 34)

- "Race is not an issue to many, but minorities view situation differently." (p. 13)

- "Freedom from the prison of racism by learning, working, playing together." (p. 25)

- "Dark skin perceived as a crime waiting to happen." (p. 28)

- "Minority police still scarce in Minneapolis, St. Paul." (p. 30)

- "Despite denials, race became issue in classroom at 'U.'" (p. 31)

- "Few people of color shape policy in state." (p. 33)

- "Racial friction surfaces in the land of liberals." (p. 35)

- "For minorities, career ladder leads down." (p. 38)

- "Despite laws & targets, '80s were a lost decade for affirmative action programs." (p. 41)

- "Minority neighborhoods get fewer home loans." (p. 43)

- "Sports teams are slow to reach out to minority fans." (p. 49)

- "Books, schools offer few positive images for black children." (p. 49)

- "On race, local media deserves euthanasia." (p. 60)

- "Some angry, some fearful about future of Twin Cities race relations." (p. 63)

Chapter 3

The Minneapolis <u>Courts</u>:
Whose Rule by Law? The Peoples' or the Judges'?
What to do when "legal" trumps "moral"?

> But let justice roll on like a river, righteousness like a never failing stream.
>   Amos 5: 21-24
>   Martin Luther King, Jr.

> What does the Lord require of you but to do justice, and to love kindness,
> and to walk humbly with your God?
>   Micah 6:8

In this chapter, I discuss the Minneapolis courts: they can be and sometimes are rigged. That it seldom happens doesn't excuse the times it does. In the case I discuss, the supreme law appeared to be the Law of the Supremes, until I, as a citizen, defended myself with the same law they sought to use to defeat me. This same drama, including the misuse of the law by officials and the challenge of such by citizens is still going on in the case of the disappearing city files (Chapter 12) and the disenfranchisement, disempowerment, and impoverishment attempted through redistricting (Chapters 12 and 13). In the case discussed in here, I had to challenge the court over its purposeful deletion of 173 pages of testimony so it could not be challenged on appeal. I challenged anyway and won. All of this leaves the haunting question of how many others have they done this to and gotten away with it?

This case is about two things: first, the corruption of the Court system, second a subset of that corruption, the racist treatment of a Black man before the court.

I have been taken to court six times. Six times I have represented myself. And six times I have won. How many others, unable to represent themselves, or without the ability to defend themselves, have been done in by the legal system? My court experience is documented in the written, court-recorded reality of the truths of my story and forms the foundation of the questions I raise in this book. It happened to me. How many others did it happen to also?

Many could write about Minneapolis as they see it. However, a big problem with many of the movers and shakers who could do so is that they might feel compelled to do the Charles De Gaulle thing: when De Gaulle wrote his memoirs, his first sentence was "I am France!" Too many of the wealthy families honestly believe they *are* Minneapolis. The difference between them and me is that I know I'm not. And they are not. They just haven't learned that yet. They look in the mirror and say: "I am Minneapolis." I stand and ask: "Why won't Minneapolis let my people go?" Now that last sentence was said with a wink. I've always wanted to say that line. It seemed very appropriate to do so here, as I haven't forgotten the goal: equal access and equal opportunity based on ability and not on color or gender or creed.

One of the most beautiful women in the world in my eyes is Justice, as she stands boldly, strongly, holding her scales, blindfolded, letting all know that in America, Justice is as blind to outside influences as it is to the personal peccadilloes of one's mind. That is the ideal we all hold to.

Unfortunately, that is not the Justice I see standing before the courthouse in Minneapolis. That is not the Justice of the Minneapolis story. Minneapolis is a place where Justice has a different kind of blindness: an unwillingness to see, a purposeful denial, the desire for personal power over the ideal of liberty and justice for all, a darkness of the soul, and an absence of light in the mind. My task here is to shed light on many situations in Minneapolis where the beautiful lady Justice has been purposefully blinded even without the blindfold, making her eyes like the corpse, closed wide shut, in order to deny justice. Hence my line, "let my people go." In times like these, someone needs to return sight to Justice by telling the Truth.

The most notorious of my six cases went to the Minnesota Supreme Court. I beat the bosses, and they lost. But the bosses protected themselves. When you read what they did, ask yourself this: How many others, Black or White, were sacrificed to protect their privilege and cover up their incompetence, malfeasance, and pure and simple law breaking?

Here is the bottom line on the stories I will tell:

- A judge who tampers with a court transcript, having 173 pages purposefully deleted from my transcript (the equivalent of shredding) in order to prevent a successful appeal to a wrongful conviction (Chapter 3).
- A Council President is defeated and then removes most of her files to cover up the deals cut with developers, agencies, and the sell-out Black leadership (Chapter 12).
- The disenfranchisement/disempowerment/impoverishment of Blacks through gerrymandered redistricting with the help of the same sell-out Blacks (Chapters 12-13)
- Examples outside Minneapolis of this same dynamic: making legal that which is unjust and unfair as slavery was once legal.

Justice as the Golden Rule, Not Justice as Gold Rules

This tampering with my testimony occurred 30 years ago, when I was 32. It reminds me of the different levels of ethics that people live by. The most superficial level is that of events and facts that we note without interpretation. A friend who teaches literature likes to talk about the allegorical level: when we interpret events and facts as guiding myths with heroes to emulate to guide our own actions. I consider the heroes in Interludes 3, 4, 9, 11, and the end of 15 as some of the <u>real</u> heroes. We don't need allegorical ones to follow. I know that there are many others you the reader could add to the list.

I see a moral level of interpretation in news reports in the papers and on TV. As any Black man, I am very much aware that for most, morality is a reflection of social customs or laws or regulations that have been established by society and encoded in law. This is why Southern Christians could justify slavery with passages from the Bible just as Muslims today use passages in the Koran to justify waging religious war. Most think that morals are beyond question. No Black man would think that way. How could he? We have had to live with moral interpretations that said slavery and then Jim Crow laws were not only moral but also just and right. Too many twist their views into morals, as they play the Charles De Gaulle "I am" role.

But there is a dimension of morals that is harder to twist and that instead should give us pause, as it is about morals on a transcendent or spiritual level. I consider myself a spiritual man although not a religious man (I don't follow a specific creed). This may be one of the reasons why I reject the notion that everything works out by God's plan, for how can slavery or Jim Crow laws or the events I write of in this book be considered a part of God's plan? That is a racist view as it leaves it unchanged and unremedied, as if it is part of God's plan. No, dear readers, whoever holds that view has a pretty puny view of God. The transcendent, as I understand it, refers to what God intends us to do regardless of how we interpret from our perspective what we think he wants us to do. Slavery and Jim Crow have certainly been part and parcel of custom and laws and myths for providing minorities with lousy education, housing, and jobs, not to mention the recent redistricting in Minneapolis and other events written about in this book. But do you really think that is the intent of God? Remember the "peoples of the book" are Jews, Christians, and Moslems. After creating the world and human beings, the Bible says that God looked on his creation, including humans, and said that it was good. Therefore, very simply, any who would not do good to other humans is not doing what God would want, which is why every major religion has this one common role for all: the Golden Rule.

In terms of worth and value then, we have to conclude that are created equal. The Golden Rule is a reminder that each person has worth and value. What too many rulers want, however, is not the Golden Rule but the Gold Rule: he who has the gold (or power) rules. To bring it to our time, I am reminded of this by the saying of former President Gerald Ford who, when he was the Minority Leader in the U.S. House of Representatives, when asked what the Constitution and the laws mean, answered whatever the Supreme Court or Congress meant at the time. This is why, in its time, slavery could be called legal and moral, as were Jim Crow laws, and a whole host of other laws, passed to keep Blacks in their place (not to mention not allowing women to vote until the early 20th century).

It is at the transcendent level where I see Justice as beautiful and untarnished. It is what separates the Golden Rule from the Gold Rule.

I believe that God, however you define God, wants us all to treat each other well, which is why what is called the Golden Rule is a part of every major religion and philosophy. It helps us to better understand the transcendent level and it helps us understand the "American Dilemma" in dealing with Blacks: as fellow creature of God are we different somehow and therefore should we be separate? Here is what leading religions and philosophers have said, which I list alphabetically:

Religious perspectives

- American Indian: Live in harmony, for we are all related.
- Buddhist: Hurt not others with that which pains yourself.
- Christian/Jesus: Do unto others as you would have them do unto you.
- Hindu: This is the sum of duty: do naught to others which, if done to thee, would cause thee pain.
- Jewish: What is hateful to you, do not do to your fellow men. That is the entire Law; all the rest is commentary.
- Islam: No one of you is a believer until he desires for his brother that which he desires for himself.

The problem with these is that is possible to interpret them narrowly to one's own group and thus leave out the rest of human kind. Here are two philosophical versions that attempt to close that potential loophole:

Philosophical perspectives

- Etzioni: Respect and uphold society's moral order as you would have society respect and uphold your autonomy to live a full life.
- Kant: Do unto others as you would have everyone do unto everybody.

In its treatment of minorities, and especially of Blacks in its inner city, Minneapolis sidesteps the Golden Rule in favor of Gold Rules.

President John F. Kennedy showed how tough this concept of the Golden Rule is and how difficult it is to get people to follow it, especially in terms of how to treat Blacks and bring them into the mainstream. In 1963, President Kennedy attempted to get White people to treat Black people better. In an anti-segregation speech, he called on the use of the Golden Rule, back at the time of the first enrollment of a Black student at the University of Alabama. He asked Whites to consider what it would be like to be treated as second-class citizens because of their skin color. He asked them to imagine themselves as Black, to imagine being told that they couldn't vote, or go to the best public schools, or eat at most restaurants, or sit in the front of the bus. He said that: "the heart of the question is whether we are going to treat our fellow Americans as we want to be treated." He asked them if they would like be treated that way. The mystery remains: They would not like to be treated that way although that is how they too often treated Blacks. Given the evidence since 1963, his exhortation and question are still relevant. They still need to be widely heeded. The same Golden Rule President Kennedy asked for is still lacking in Minneapolis for many inner city Blacks.

I leave it to you, dear reader, to interpret, in this chapter and in the chapters that follow which rule is being followed, the Golden Rule or the Gold Rule. Whether you are Black or White, always ask yourself: Do I want to be treated in the same way others are being treated, and, more close to home, do I want to be treated as I am treating others? If people treated others as they would like to be treated, we would certainly need fewer courts. But people don't.

I cannot say it often enough: legal is what *they* say it is. Human beings have sought shortcuts for millennia. What stops them is our system of checks and balances. Our Constitution, Bill of Rights, and Amendments are what has given us the chance to continue to fight the good fight and pursue the American Dream even in the presence of those who would prevent us from doing so. The separation of powers that is our checks and balances prevents any power elite from gaining full control, although at times it seems as if the enemy is not outside interests but the partnership between entrenched legislators and special interests that write laws and allow the kind of gerrymandering and redistricting to thwart competitive elections. But time is on our side. And as long as we don't become like them, we shall overcome. We may not live as luxuriously as they do, but our legacies will endure as positives while theirs will eventually endure as negatives. Clearly, human nature has not changed for millennia. Therefore what has changed is the body of laws and regulations. It is this legal infrastructure and the lack of enforcement that allows judges and corporations and government bureaucrats to act in ways that are not in the best interest of the average American.   This is what needs to be changed. We need more checks and balances in Minneapolis. Which brings us back to my case, when 173 pages were removed from the transcript of my trial.

A judge tampering with a court transcript, deleting 173 pages of testimony

The bottom line in my case: To prevent me from being able to appeal, the judge had 173 pages removed from the official court stenographer's transcript. This was a purposeful choice, as the judge chose the Gold Rule over the Golden Rule.

I was in court because I had been arrested for interfering with a police decoy operation. I had interfered intentionally. I was opposed to this policy because I felt it was dangerous to the Black community, which later proved to be true when young Blacks were killed by police during these decoy operations.

Too long has it been legal to discriminate against Blacks. Too long has Minneapolis carried on its own low-key Apartheid against "excess" Blacks, especially young Black men. I tell this story because it obviously reflects others. Others have told me it was done to them. They have told me that their transcripts were altered. But without proof, nothing can be done. In my case, it is all in the records of my case. And if you are now asking in how many other cases does Lady Justice doff her scales and blindfold for a green eye shade, a cigar, and a smoke-filled backroom to cut deals of injustice and unfairness, then we are on the same page.

The judge was Sheryl Ramstad Hvass (currently the Commissioner of Corrections, appointed by Governor Jesse Ventura), the sister-in-law of Jim Ramstad (Congressman from the 3rd Ward, 3rd Congressional district) and the daughter of a powerful man, one of the top airline liability attorneys. Rather than take these connections as a great gift unavailable to others, a gift to use responsibly, she used it irresponsibly. My sense was that she felt she had a dumb Black Boy before her and could treat me the way she saw the men in her family treat Blacks. She was wrong. She just wasn't as good at it as they were. I'm a very seasoned individual in many respects. I am comfortable in court. I am not afraid of the Gold Rules set, because no matter what they may try to do, they'll never get close to my mind and spirit. And that is my great strength. The judge made a terrible mistake in thinking she could twist the law with Ron Edwards.

The trial lasted two and a half days. That's a lot of pages of transcript. Who would miss a few pages or even know? The key is that I saw this trick coming from a mile away. You see, I used no notes. I had no legal pads. I have a wonderful memory. The judge obviously didn't believe a Black man could get through without notes. She had to be thinking she could do what she wanted. She saw a guy representing himself, without professional counsel, without notes, without even taking notes. She thought she had a real rube, a country bumpkin, a dumb Black Sambo. She was wrong.

The arresting officer testifying against me in this jury trial was David Neber, who at first seemed to be amicable. During the various testimonies, Judge Sheryl Hvass treated me with disdain and condescension, which I noticed was beginning to affect the jury, not a good sign. But I was watching. Realizing what was going on, I began to do what any smart attorney does, especially if the Judge is being partial; that is, I proceeded to conduct my case in such a way as to set up an appeal if I lost. This common strategy is to set the judge up by saying and doing things to demonstrate her bias and lack of impartiality that can then be used later on appeal. Too many judges think that we are not one nation under law or one nation under God but are instead one nation under judges.

I watched for an opening. It came when Officer Neber purposefully said that he had arrested me before, for a DUI (driving under the influence), an obvious attempt to further sway the jury against me, trying to paint me as an old darkie town drunk. His statement was false on two counts. First, he had never arrested me for a DUI (nor had anyone else). Secondly, I decided in my early 20s not to drink, that my mind and being would be better off without alcohol. So he accused a guy who didn't drink. When he made this charge, I immediately objected. Judge Sheryl Hvass overruled me. So I asked to approach the bench. I told her that the testimony of Officer Neber to the prosecutor, Mr. Tumbley, was absolutely untrue.

She was obviously annoyed because I was defending myself without using an attorney. I responded that the record needed to be set straight. She looked at me and then with a scornful tone let me know that she was running the trial. I agreed. She then directed both Tumbley and me to research this in the court's office to determine if the DUI arrest had happened. At the recess, we went back to the clerk's office, reviewed the microfiche files, and found out that, of course, as I had said, Officer Neber had never arrested me for a DUI. Nor had anyone else.

Recognizing that we could clearly impugn Officer Neber's testimony, we returned to the court. We joined Judge Hvass in her chambers with a court stenographer. Tumbley informed her that I was correct. I, of course, gave that "you know" Black person's stupid smile. White people always interpret it as meaning that we are stupid, ignorant, and just don't know what is going on. I sensed that that was how she viewed me. She then interrupted the stenographer while we were speaking and told her to get her robe, which the stenographer did while we continued talking. I told the Judge that this information pretty much satisfied the issue at hand and that I was now in the position to impugn Officer Neber's testimony. I then asked, "Officer Neber will correct his testimony, right?" And she gave a non-answer: "Yes, we will certainly work it out," yet all the while the stenographer was not yet back to take it all down. As you can probably guess, saying we will work it out doesn't mean anything, not in a court of law. They either do or do not, will or will not.

To me, her tone, her posture, and her attitude clearly revealed her racism. It was if she was thinking who does this damn Black fool think he is, this Black sonofabitch trying to act as if he were a lawyer in my courtroom. This entire conversation was not recorded because the stenographer was away from her dictating machine. It appeared to me as if Judge Hvass had purposefully had this last exchange occur when it could not be recorded.

We then returned to the courtroom.

Tumbly returned to his examination of Officer Neber. All of a sudden, Neber went back to the DUI charge. I again objected. Judge Hvass overruled me, and I asked to approach. She said she'd already heard me and that she'd already warned me. You can imagine how I was now looking to the jury. I then said: "Exception," something that's very rarely used in a Minnesota court. Now it was clear that there was more than a normal objection. Her face got red as a beet and you could see the how dare you written all over it. So, I said okay.

Then it was my turn, and I proceeded to question Neber. I kept him on the stand for 4 hours. The judge was angry and Neber's face was turning red. All of a sudden Judge Hvass cut me off and did something absolutely outrageous. She said, "Just a minute Mr. Edwards." She then turned to Neber and said: "Officer, would you like a drink of water?"

Now you are never supposed to do that. This was on my time. I was cross-examining this man. We were dealing with the issue of possible perjury, but Judge Hvass poured him a cup of water and handed it to him. So I turned and looked at the jury. I could only assume they were thinking, "Oh, here's a nice White officer. He is just a nice young man with a boy's face and this pushy Negro over here isn't treating him nicely, and even the judge sees that." In my view, by their actions and words, the judge and the officer were able to bias the jury, which then found me guilty.

So I retained Joe Peterson to handle my appeal. Joe is both an attorney and a law professor. When he asked me the basis of the appeal, I told him it would be their tampering with the transcript. Now, Peterson had known me for a long time and respected me, and yet even he was taken aback by my allegation, an allegation that goes to the very heart of the integrity of the court system. I then explained it to him.

I wasn't being cynical. As a civil rights and human rights advocate and social change agent, I had already heard it all. But hearing it and proving it are two different things. I have had Black men tell me that earlier court transcripts read back to them also had key portions deleted. But they were unable to prove it. And so they were defeated before they started. In my case, I was able to prove it.

Neber was the key officer, the decoy officer in the alley who said he allegedly overheard me tell two Black men standing 60 feet away that they needed to come on out of that alley to avoid problems. Later on, the Supreme Court of Minnesota ruled that I had in no way violated the statute. Neber's testimony was that he could hear this conversation, but I was too far away for him to hear anything. I was standing right next to these men and was not talking loudly.

At that time, I had been Chairman of the Urban League for almost three years, and I had maintained that these decoy operations were going to get innocent Black citizens killed. There had already been some beatings. Then a year later, Neber and five other officers blew off the top of a Black man's head in a similar decoy operation. And it happened to others. It was a lousy program. It is no longer used. I'm glad I stood up against it and bested them. And now they were going to try to best me in court after having arrested me.

So we made notification of appeal. The normal procedure always is to order a transcript and pay for it when you pick it up. In my case, they made an exception: They demanded a $1,400 payment in advance. Peterson didn't like that, but we paid it up front. After another delay, the transcript was delivered to me. I read through it, and sure enough, it had been tampered with. I walked Peterson through that transcript and I showed him where that specific exchange between Judge Hvass, me and Tumbley was gone, as well as additional testimony. I said it was cute the way she did it by asking her to get the robe. I could see from the expression on the young lady's face that that had troubled her, but this was the Judge, her boss. I then showed Joe Petersen where parts of my cross examination of Officer Neber were deleted. Judge Hvass had definitely directed the stenographer to delete pages. So Peterson moved into high gear. He filed a petition that went beyond the appeal. Joe Petersen presented a motion and a demand for inquiry that dealt with impropriety by the trial judge herself, causing both a gap in the transcribing by not having it taken down and deleting actual pages that had been part of the court record. Tampering with a court transcript goes to the heart of the integrity of the court itself.

What the Supreme Court does in a situation like this is to appoint a special master who convenes a hearing. As this was a legal matter for attorneys and judges only, and I wasn't an attorney, I couldn't be there, which was all right with me, and probably best as this way it would only be between members of the club: all professional attorneys and judges. Peterson told me later what happened.

The key moment came when he questioned the stenographer; because I had detailed everything for him, he was able to ask her all the right questions. I knew she was going to be key. He later told me that she had told the group that I was one of the finest lawyers she had ever seen and that my closing argument was one of the best she had ever heard. This was a very, very heavy setting that included all kinds of implications. Peterson asked her if, after Tumbley and I came into the judge's chambers, whether or not she transcribed the whole time or whether she got up to get the judge's robe. She asked, "Who told you that?" and she was told that I did. She said I must have an incredible memory, as what was described was correct in every detail. Then she broke down and started to cry, asking what she was supposed to do, as she didn't want to lose her career.

At that point, I was told that the room began to get very tense. The observer from the Supreme Court was looking at the master and the master was looking at him. The stenographer was assured that her career was safe. And then she spoke the blockbuster, going beyond just not taking down transcription. She said Judge Hvass had called her into her chambers and told her to delete 173 pages of the transcript. Peterson told me that the observer and the master became visibly upset. She was then asked if the particular part of my statement that I claimed was excluded was indeed part of what she deleted. She said yes. Then she said something unusual, in that she was not an attorney. She said that these were definitely issues that I would win on appeal. That ended it. It was over. Needless to say, I later won my appeal.

But what about the judge? They were stuck, yet they protected their own. A report went back to the State Supreme Court, which then ordered the Appellate Court to reverse the decision and overturn my conviction, but the rationale on my reversal sheet was a technicality having nothing to do with what I had raised. The Supreme Court covered up by having their reversal sheet go all the way back to the beginning of the case and used a judge by the name of Sedlin to maintain that when I made my first appearance, the audio tape that was allegedly kept in the courtroom had malfunctioned and there was no clear record of whether I had been advised of my rights. For that reason the decision was reversed. They completely ignored what Judge Hvass had done. By going back to the beginning, everything that came after didn't count, so, technically, she didn't do anything wrong. In other words, to the Court, it is acceptable if it violates our constitutional rights.

Rigging the system against Blacks: The fix is in.

My second example deals with covering up a whole lot of rigging or fixes by the outgoing Minneapolis City Council President, Jackie Cherryhomes, who stole and then hid or destroyed most of the documents in her office covering 12 years, leaving no record of her deals for her successor (Chapter 12). I would wager anything that some of the scandals that I discuss in Chapters 7-13 would be exposed in those files, which is why I believe they were taken.

It is my opinion that these missing files will identify the sell-out Blacks in the NAACP and especially in the Urban League who went along with Cherryhomes' deals during her years in office. What did Cherryhomes take? In all probability, all of the files dealing with economic development and especially the Hollman case. The story received very little coverage in the local *Minneapolis Star Tribune* because that paper has long had its own definition of what is "fit to print," and that means either anything favorable to it and its cronies or anything negative about those the paper doesn't like. *The Minnesota Spokesman-Recorder* was the only media outlet to give the story of the missing files major coverage (it even put a picture showing the wall of empty file cabinets on its front page), but that is a Black newspaper, so who will pay attention to that? And so nearly a year after the files disappeared (stolen? Hidden? Shredded ?), neither the newly elected Mayor nor the City Attorney nor any other public official, city or state, has honored the request of Cherryhomes' successor, Natalie Johnson-Lee, to investigate the taking of the missing files.

The rigging/fixing of redistricting

My third example of how the DFL political puppet masters rig the process to disempower, disenfranchise, and ghettoize Minneapolis Blacks is their legal gerrymandering in the unjust and unfair redistricting of the city's wards after the 2000 census, done immediately after Cherryhomes lost to Johnson-Lee. Is this coincidence? I don't think so. See more detail in Chapters 11-13. The key is to remember as you read those chapters that so much of this is legal. So was slavery. Making it legal doesn't make it right and it certainly doesn't make it just or fair.

Other examples, other cities

You, dear reader, have heard the airways and headlines filled during this past year with examples of corporate accounting deeds that we all probably agree are abhorrent. If you are like me, you were then horrified further to find out that much of what they did was legal. Government regulations gave them the loopholes. A lack of checks and balances enabled them to drive truck loads of money through those loop holes. My point is that the law is the sum total of what is agreed to be legal. My argument is this: We must turn the law into more than what is allowed by those who can manipulate it, and thus have laws that are just and fair. Thus, I purposely repeat myself:

Legal does not mean moral; legal does not mean fair and just. Legal just means whatever those who made the law or are designated to interpret it says it means. In a word, legal means you can do whatever is declared legal and not go to jail or be fined.

What occurred in my case was legal: the Supremes could go back to the Miranda rule (reading a person his or her rights before anything else is said or done to him or her) and use it to cover up what the Judge did. Was that legal? Yes indeed. Was it moral? Yes or no, depending on your view. From my point of view it was not moral. Was it corrupt? Again, if you said yes that it was moral then you would not conclude that it was corrupt even though, in my view, it was. Regardless, I contend that the reason the Judge did what she did was because of the racism. I was a high profile Black head of a high profile organization that the police felt was interfering with their work. To them, being Black was a sign of a crime waiting to happen (Interlude 2). And although I appreciate their concern regarding what they considered my interference, their interference in the lives of Minneapolis Blacks has far outweighed anything that I have done (Interludes 2 and 10, Chapters 7-13).

So the Minneapolis story is also about rigging the system with fixes, legal fixes, fixes made legal by laws and by judges. It has happened to me. The headlines tell us it has happened to others. How many lives have been ruined or hurt by falling through the trap doors of fixes when Lady Justice was sent to stand and face the corner without her blindfold, without her scales, and without her light, not to mention when this is done in the nation beyond Minneapolis.

Justice is not always wanted in this country. For those who followed the Microsoft trial with confusion regarding how a company could be allowed to squash the competition, fix prices, and extort cooperation from other companies, all one has to do is look at the competing definitions of justice. The July 2002 *Upside* Magazine cover story, "In Microsoft We Trust" notes that for Microsoft to lose, the first thing that has to happen is "to overcome the judges trained to disregard the law." We have all read that Microsoft broke Sherman Antitrust Act laws and others, 12 different ways all told, and yet is, as of this writing, getting away with it. Why? Because the prevailing view among judges is that monopolies are OK (just as they once said slavery was OK). Here is the blood-curdling, spine-chilling evidence: the attempt "to take justice out of the federal judiciary," a movement led by the Law & Economics Center (LEC) at George Mason University School of Law in Virginia and supported by such well-known judges as Richard A. Posner, Robert Bork, and Phillip Areeda. While teaching a law class, former circuit judge and former chief judge for the 7th U.S. Circuit Court of Appeals in Chicago, Richard A. Posner, "once wrote 'justice' on the blackboard while teaching a law class. He then told his students he didn't want to hear that word in his class" (Upside article, p. 23).

Now here is the rub: where "many believe moral philosophy must underlie a system of justice, Posner says 'I hate the moral-philosophy stuff'" (p. 23).

Now here is how this relates to the Minneapolis story and to Minneapolis race relations, especially in North Minneapolis. Justice is, to me, justice. You either have it or you don't. If these judges can allow Microsoft to break the law because they don't like the law, and pay judges to come to their seminars explaining their view, isn't this same as when, in the South, judges would hear cases of Whites murdering Blacks and then either dismiss the cases or provide such light sentencing, suspended sentences, probation or small fines, that even murder was allowed because it was only Blacks that they murdered. I believe there is a link here.

I also believe that at some point someone is going to find a link between the legal philosophy of Judge Posner and all of the corporate accounting scandals: if it is OK to allow unfair methods of competition, unfair contracts, the restraint of trade, and monopolization, a kind of corporate state's rights that Southern states call for in their treatment of Blacks, why would the U.S. system of justice combat unfairness in terms of shareholders or employee pension funds?
As Arsenio Hall used to say, "Hmmmmmmmm."

October 2002 Postscript

For those of you, dear readers, who want to learn more about the Jim Crow laws, which continued the burden of segregation, injustice and violence borne by Blacks during that 91 year period between the Emancipation Proclamation and the U.S. Supreme Court ruling of Brown vs. Board of Education, consider getting the video tape of the PBS four part documentary, "The Rise and Fall of Jim Crow," that aired for the first time October 1st. I'm sure they'll have a companion book as well. Here is what the New York Times says in its October 1, 2002 review about the Jim Crow story "When Heroes Faced Down Injustice and Terror":

- An indictment
- A narrative of broken promises
- A narrative of stolen hopes

Given how the world is responding today to those who have chosen terror as their way of seeking social change as well as preventing social change, what this series says is important and needs to be heard: that the U.S. also has its history of **terror** use.

So that you don't think I'm going off the deep end, I quote from the article. The bold emphases are mine:

> Not long after the Civil War, he hopes of the freed slaves for better lives were largely dashed. "The way White supremacists made sure ex-slaves would fall back into place, or nearly back into place, was terror" the Princeton historian Neil Painter says, emphasizing the last word as **"ter-roar."**

> The four hours include chilling descriptions and unbearable pictures of lynchings, some well into the 20th century. A third-generation Klansman recalled one he attended as a child, describing the hanging as matter-of-factly as if it had been a football game. To Vernon Jarrett, a journalist, ritualized lynching of Blacks had "religious and patriotic connotations," a worship of segregation.

And yet, hear the soaring spirit of the Black man that I celebrate in this book singing even under Jim Crow. The series quotes W.W. Law, a historian and civil rights leader who died at the age of 79 this year. He is but one of the impassioned witnesses this series portrays. Law said:

> I'm not ashamed of the segregated and Jim Crow experience because we were able to devise techniques for survival. That permitted us to bid our time and to wait until change comes.

And so, as I demonstrate in the Minneapolis story, we continue to work for our freedom, as we bide our time for what we know will come. The article concludes this way, quoting Charles Hamilton Houston, the NAACP lawyer who helped develop the strategies that led, after his death, to the Brown decision. He said:

> The fight has just begun," Hamilton said after one of his legal victories. "Shout if you want, but don't shout too soon.

> "The Rise and Fall of Jim Crow" does not shout, nor does it exult. It pays homage to sacrifice and achievement, and it leaves the door open to hope. Now run and tell that.

And that is what I am trying to do with the Minneapolis story: to run and tell everyone the story of hope as well as perhaps some helpful suggestions regarding how to realize that hope.

And after you have read this book, I invite you too to run and tell the story, the Minneapolis story as it has been, and the Minneapolis story as it could be.

Interlude 3

NELLIE STONE JOHNSON, 1906 – 2002

Community Advocate
Civil Rights Activist

Nellie was one of my mentors. She had enormous influence on some of the most significant politicians of the century in Minnesota. For example, she had enormous influence with Governor Olson, whom I consider to be the greatest Minnesota governor before Rudy Perpich. Nellie was instrumental in forming the Democratic-Farmer-Labor Party. In the 1930s, the Democrats were third in Minnesota, behind the Republicans and the Farmer-Labor party. Nellie was a key leader of the Farmer-Labor Party, and she negotiated with Hubert H. Humphrey in 1944 to merge her Farmer Labor Party with the Democratic Party, making sure they kept the name: Democrat-Farmer-Labor party (DFL). What a combination! But once merged, the Democrats betrayed her. But she always kept her eye on the prize. And she knew she had to be able to support herself, so she never gave up her job as a seamstress. Just imagine: a woman with this intellect and drive and fire, who builds a political party bigger than the Democrats and yet is betrayed by them, spends her life as a seamstress, just in case, as she continued her work to foster civil rights for everyone, farmers, workers, minorities.

Nellie was a true community advocate. She was born in Lakeville, Minnesota. Her father was the second Negro ever elected to a Minnesota office. Forty years later, in 1944, she became the third Negro person ever elected to a public office in Minnesota, when she was elected to the Library Board. She was elected along with another young man, from South Dakota, Hubert H. Humphrey. And while a student at the University of Minnesota in the 1920s, she met and befriended future Governor Floyd B. Olson and Dr. Thomas Johnson.

Nellie is rightly given credit for being one of the pillars that made Minnesota a liberal state and an influence on such Liberal Democratic politicians on the national stage as Humphrey, Walter Mondale, and Eugene McCarthy, as they expanded Minnesota's influence nationwide. She was not well understood by angry conservatives who called the state "The People's Republic of Minnesota." Nonetheless, Nellie was instrumental in bringing to the forefront of political dialogue in Minnesota and nationwide the language of tolerance and diversity, pluralism and anti-racism.

But she was also a community-oriented person, and this is what eventually led to her being betrayed by the Liberals, as they saw the vehicle of deliverance a state-centered liberalism, a state political party in control. They wanted to control everything because they believed their utopian ideas were best for everyone (Chapters 7, 12-14). Nellie's issues were not state control but people in community with equal access and equal opportunity to work and learn and do good in their own communities. She believed in freedom and property rights. Her issues were education, jobs, and health care.

She was a great supporter and gifted person of ideas for Floyd B. Olson when he was Governor. And Rudy Perpich, when he was Governor, worshiped the ground she walked on. When the Urban League kicked her and me out, Governor Perpich said that he had no time for any organization that did not include Nellie Stone Johnson and Ron Edwards.

Nellie earned her political wings at the University of Minnesota and considered herself briefly, in the early years, a socialist, which is why others later falsely branded her a communist.

Throughout all of her activism, she earned her way as a seamstress, doing so into her 90s. She lived life fully, normally, she said. But she was in for the long haul. Nellie is quoted in the Epilog of the new book, *Making Minnesota Liberal,* by Jennifer A. Delton:

> *"Somebody asked me...what I thought was going to happen when we founded the DFL Party. I said I thought by now we would have taken over the whole country. At the time, I thought our politics were so good, so pure, so equality-minded that it didn't make any difference where we went, people would flock to us. That hasn't been the case."*

And this is still the case today. Not enough have flocked to her cause of being equality-minded, meaning equal access and equal opportunity for all. She fought for it her whole life and helped many move in that direction. I invite all of you readers to find a way to join in Nellie's cause to make sure everyone has a chance.
For those who want to learn more about Nellie:

- *Nellie Stone Johnson: The Life of an Activist* by Nellie Stone Johnson and as told to David Brauer (royalties go to the Nellie Stone Johnson Scholarship Fund).

- *Making Minnesota Liberal: Civil Rights and the Transformation of the Democratic Party* by Jennifer A. Delton, University of Minnesota Press.

Chapter 4

My Philosophical Paradox:
From "Anywhere But Here"
To "Not Here, Not There, Not Anywhere"

There is more in us than we know. If we can be made to see it, perhaps,
for the rest of our lives, we will be unwilling to settle for less.
Kurt Hahn, 1886-1974
Founder, Outward Bound

Someone once asked me if I had a substantive theme or motto or title for a book, and I replied that as far as I was concerned, my theme, my motto is: "Anywhere but here." In other words, I wanted racism and unfairness "anywhere but here"; discrimination in education, housing, and economic development "anywhere but here"; racism in government "anywhere but here"; I saw my "anywhere but here" as not unlike the Jewish rabbi's blessing in *Fiddler on the Roof* for the Tsar in the days of the pogroms (persecution) of the Jews: "May God bless the Tsar, far away from here."

That same person who asked me if I had a title for a book encouraged me to put my thoughts down on paper. I replied: Yeah one of these days I'm going to write a book. And we moved on. But I remember when his book came out and I remember reading it. I had begun to think about a book years ago, back when I was in my 30s and in fact, I had initially entitled it *The Invisible Cage*, although I also thought of it in terms of plural, *The Invisible Cages.* And it had to do with the cages that we Blacks are put in, cages in society, that have invisible boundaries which we Blacks can't cross, boundaries put there by White society, boundaries which, if we Blacks try to cross we run into walls of policy and rules, written and unwritten, that are like invisible bars that keep us within the White-prescribed cages.

Our first cage was slavery. Our second cage was the post-Reconstruction period of Jim Crow laws. The third cage was the period after the heyday of the Civil Rights Movement. Wonderful progress has been made (Interludes 5 and 7), but Blacks in the inner city are still treated as if they were best left in a cage, and the new redistricting in Minneapolis has created new bars for the inner city cage (Chapters 12 and 13). I realized I didn't just want cages anywhere but here, I didn't want them anywhere. We still have a great deal of work to do in the inner cities. That was my thinking 30 years ago. We still do. As I have watched activity and life evolve since then, particularly after different groups, Black and White, tried to ruin me because of my community advocacy and because I stood up for those no one else would stand up for, I began to think of writing a book again. Then came the recent efforts to turn the clock back with the redistricting conspiracy between the DFL and the local Black organizations (Chapter 14), and I decided it was time to write the Minneapolis story as I experienced it. I wanted to tell the story of community advocacy in Minneapolis, a story showing how both White and Black elites have worked against those in the Black community.

I wanted to tell the story of not giving up. I wanted to continue to work to change the complexion of Minneapolis race relations. But as my thinking expanded to the country and the world, as I tried to make sense of Minneapolis, I realized that "anywhere but here" didn't go far enough, and so I changed "anywhere but here" to a sort of Dr. Seuss rhythm: "not here, not there, not anywhere." In terms of denying equal access and opportunity in education, housing, and entrepreneurial growth, I knew my response had to be not here, not there, not anywhere.

When people start to talk about conditions or situations that I don't like, I now like to say: "not here, not there, not anywhere." Especially if they make what I consider to be ill thought-out suggestions: "anywhere but here." And that brings us to the question of capitalism and of democratic capitalism. Straight capitalism and free market capitalism have provided their share of poverty and oppression, as the history particularly of South America and the American South shows with their different versions of apartheid. Nonetheless, capitalism has brought more people out of poverty than any other system. Of course, those who have done it amazingly well and who stand at the top of that spectrum are the democratic capitalist states. Those are the facts. You may not like them, and they may not fit into what you think should be, especially if you still pine nostalgically for socialism or for some form of supremacy, but those are, pure and simple, the facts. So that brings us not to the question of Left or Right but to the question of inclusion, of equal access and to equal opportunity. Not equal results, but equal opportunity, regardless of whether one succeeds or not. The more people who are included in the political and economic life of our society, the more prosperous and peaceful we will all be. And that is why Blacks and all people need to be included here, there, and everywhere.

It goes without saying that I don't like racism, poverty, and unfairness, whether it's practiced on me or someone else. And so about racism, poverty and unfairness I reply not here, not there, not anywhere.

We used to have a wonderful phrase, Black is beautiful, as well as Black is bold and beautiful. Given what we are up against, and how well we do in spite of it, when we as Black people do our best, then I like to also say Black is best.

How many White folks do you know would be as gracious about it as we have been, working through legal slavery to legal discrimination, to illegal-but -allowed prejudice and discrimination? And so my boyhood, my public schooling, the jobs I've had, the advocacy and activism of which I have been a part, have all provided negative experiences related to prejudice and racism. But I don't dwell there. It doesn't get me anywhere and it certainly isn't any fun. So about such things I say not here, not there, not anywhere. I've had to go up against the system at work, on my radio and on TV programs. I have, several times, been bossed off the stage of equal access and equal opportunity, but I have never given up, never lost sight of the dream; I have kept my eye on the prize and thus have always continued as an advocate pushing for equal access and equal opportunity for all, here, there, and everywhere.

But by saying Black is bold, beautiful, and best, I do not mean to imply there is a difference between Blacks and Whites, even though Whites might think so. The notion of the superiority of Blacks or Whites is just as false as the notion of race itself. The notion of race is morally dangerous because it is at the heart of why so many Whites don't see anything wrong in not allowing equal access and equal opportunity. As long as basic qualities like intelligence and worthiness are tied to superficial issues such as color or false constructs such as race, we will be stuck with the negative consequences of racism. We can't make colorblindness a reality until we make equal access and equal opportunity a reality. Regional differences, yes. Socio-economic differences, yes. Racial differences, no. Should there be racial preferences? No. Should there be preferences for those suffering deprivation, be it cultural or economic? Yes, at least to start.

The war on poverty was to provide that start, but it was derailed when it was made race-based and a program of entitlements instead of a bridge to the future. It is those with these attitudes who now run the NAACP and the Urban League (Chapter 14). As it is hard to show progress against poverty and easier to show color, race is used to bring in money without having to demonstrate any accountability for the use of that money or to demonstrate achievement. That needs to be reversed. This is why I maintain that schools and government agencies and all who deal with the poor and minorities should show their budgets, show test results, and provide other data regarding the monies received in order to gauge the effectiveness of their programs beyond demonstrating that they are going to Blacks or to another minority. The real problem is unemployment and poverty. Race becomes a problem when it is used by one race to discriminate against another race or to prevent their employment and thus continue their poverty. It also becomes a problem when one race uses it to claim victimhood rather than for start-up assistance.

Victimhood and hate, whether by Blacks or Whites, is evil. We all need to get beyond that, together. We need to evaluate facts with values, which brings us to my litany of not here, not there, not anywhere, in terms of education (liberal education causing inner city children to remain uneducated), housing (Minneapolis eliminating Black housing and replacing it with White housing), jobs (Minneapolis, a city that is 30% Black, has giant construction projects that don't include Black contractors and very few if any Black workers).

By now, dear reader, you must have the sense that I will not divide the world in any fashion, whether by race or religion or gender or by status and wealth. I prefer the absolute religious genius of Jesus, who utterly refused all notions of behavior as demonstrated by the group called the Zealots, who demanded 1,000 laws and codes of behavior for purity, even while they treated people badly. This is not unlike the over 2,400 varieties of Protestant churches (or the several competing visions inside the Roman Catholic Church, not to mention the different strains of Judaism, Islam, Buddhism, etc.) who, in his name demand the same while still treating people badly. Jesus didn't avoid sinners, and he refused to divide the world into the pure and the impure, much to the chagrin of almost everybody, then and now. For if we do that, we can easily label the rest impure and ourselves pure, which lets us justify keeping what we have and not sharing it.

This is one of he reasons I am intrigued by the man Jesus. He brought people hope with his acceptance of them, his obvious love for them, and his directive to "go and sin no more." That too should be here, there, and everywhere. Here was a man who was not exclusionary. He is never portrayed as being shocked by sinners. Rather, he was shocked by how few will forgive and reconcile after he had demonstrated that that is the path to paradise. He was very clear that everyone was to be included, as he demonstrated in his own life and in the parable of the Good Samaritan. What shocked Jesus, if we can say such a thing, was anyone who did not and could not see himself as a sinner. For us, Black or White, once we can't see our own hatred and our own evil, and thus we feel no remorse for our own actions or policies that enslave or impoverish or diminish others in any way (Interludes 2, 6, 8-11, 13-15) there is no way to get to shared, common ground. That kind of blindness should not be here, there, or anywhere.

Exclusion, expulsion, turning away from others, all signal that a person sees no common ground with the others. That is the great sin. And that brings us back to the crossroads: what will we choose? The axis of evil or the axis of love? To increase the power and efficiency of evil or diminish it by admitting our part in it and working to remove it from ourselves and our communities, here, there, and everywhere? Fairness and justice are what is required. Fairness and justice for all is what I ask, here, there, and everywhere.

Now before I go too much further, let me return to my statement that when Blacks do their best, Black is best. I don't mean to sound racist or put down Whites when I say that. But let's look at it for a moment. This has been said about South African Blacks. It has been said about American Blacks. Both of us have experienced legislatively approved apartheid as well as informally approved apartheid. Both of us have had to endure it. Now, dear reader, if you are White, let me ask you this: How would you have responded as a slave, if the Civil War to free slaves still left you segregated and a third-class citizen (poor Whites were second-class)? How would you respond to such prejudice today? How would you respond if you are from Minneapolis to the apartheid that continues in a benign way even today? How would you respond if the stories and facts laid out about Education (chapter 7), housing (chapter 8), development (Chapter 9), being scapegoated (10), and government and redistricting (chapters 11-13) were about you or your relatives or your friends or some combination?

Some might think that I advocate violence or would justify violence given the treatment that Blacks have endured. I most decidedly do not. We Blacks are better than that, which is what I mean by Black is best. I would never advocate taking such a low road as the Whites have in treating Blacks (Interludes 2, 6, 8-15). We are beautiful, bold, and better. We can endure all things, and will endure all things; and so, in the end, no matter how many cages, no matter how many roadblocks we encounter, we will indeed overcome. Whose lifetime it takes place in is not as important as the fact that we endure beautiful, bold, and better in advocating the kind of inclusion that the Whites have denied us with their American apartheid.

There are wonderful examples of this. In his book <u>Man's Search for Meaning</u>, about his four years in four concentration camps of Nazi Germany during World War II, Victor Frankl says that in the final analysis, all of us still have control over our attitudes. He said that even as the Nazis stripped them naked and beat them, the choice of attitude was still theirs. This is this history of Blacks in America, acting with wonderful attitudes, despite it all. You can see it in our music which we have used to help keep ourselves from responding with bitterness to the way we were treated. Angry yes, bitter and vengeful, no. This is quite remarkable given the racist partisanship thrown at us, as, for the most part, we have responded with a generosity of spirit inspired by our music.

The history of Blacks is the history of a noble people not giving into the impulse to be as bad as their oppressors but to rise above them, to stay on the high road of offering the best that humanity has to offer, even when roadblocks were thrown at us to bring us down to their level, to destroy our communities and families. We have always sung *We shall overcome*, and we will. The two greatest examples of this are

Blacks in America and Blacks in South Africa during and after the Apartheid of each, as each practice the positive approach here, there, and everywhere.

When you read the stories of South Africa, and I commend to you the excellent book by the White South African evangelist, Michael Cassidy, The Passing Summer: A South African's Response to White Fear, Black Anger, and the Politics of Love, written before the end of Apartheid in South Africa, you get a wonderful example of what I mean. Here I will use his words for my own purpose, to demonstrate a way in which this approach is best, for Blacks and Whites, here, there and everywhere, although, mercy, mercy, I am open to anyone who can prove me wrong. Here are this White man's words about sitting with Black leaders in meetings with the government's White Apartheid leaders, meetings in which the Black man would always suggest and then open with prayer:

> Listening [to them], I grasped afresh that South African Blacks, especially Black Christians, are in many ways incredible. Their capacity to bear pain, to tolerate indignity, to forgive, to dredge up new goodwill from who knows where and still be gracious never ceases to amaze me.

As Blacks, we have continually dredged up new goodwill. Now some readers may not be old enough to remember the Sidney Poitier movies, the Denzel Washington movies, *Roots I and II*, or seen the pictures of Bull Connor's attack dogs and fire hoses, Blacks beaten on the Selma bridge, assassinations, the U.S. Army creating a protective line so kids could go to school, Southern governors (all Democrats) standing at the schoolhouse doors yelling: "Segregation forever," the taking of Black land and wealth, the lynchings (which also took place in Minnesota), the blowing up of innocent little girls in Sunday School, cross burnings on lawns, poor schools, and being prevented from learning to read and then given literacy tests and prevented from voting, and being kept from public facilities as well as from private facilities. How would Whites have responded? With love, as in this story of South Africa, or in the stories of Martin Luther King, Booker T. Washington, Thurgood Marshall, and others?

Lets listen in again to the Black South African and get a clue as to why I say we are Beautiful, Bold, and Best, and how this is what I want to see here in Minneapolis, and there and everywhere. And as you read, White reader or Black reader, ask yourself this: Would this describe you? These are the words of a Black man who, like Nelson Mandela, had been imprisoned for his political view, but unlike Mandela, who was imprisoned for 28 years and then became the first elected President of the post-Apartheid South Africa, this Black man was *only* imprisoned for three years. Let us listen in as Cassidy, "taking verbatim notes," enlightens us as he enlightened himself. Note again that this meeting took place before Mandela was released, while Apartheid in South Africa was still going strong. My goal has likewise been to act the same way, treat others the same way. If my behavior as a man is not laudatory, how can I obtain the same for my ideas, for equal access and opportunity for all, black and White, rich and poor? Listen in to how Cassidy describes this man, Mmutlanyane Mogoba:

> ...a truly authentic, credible South African Black. Yet here, in the presence of this man who in Black eyes was behind all the abominated detentions, he could with gentle dignity and quiet assurance open his comments saying, "Mr. Minister, thank you for letting us see you tonight. We are concerned for you as a person working under so much pressure. So we have felt the need to come and agonize with you and affirm you as a human being with your great responsibilities.

> But we are also deeply concerned and really worried over South Africa and its future. In fact we are baffled by the statements made by the authorities and by their actions. As far as the police go, the situation is even more worrying because their behavior is very unbecoming and they are now seen by our people as the enemy.

> However, there is a wider problem, one that must be seen as part of that larger context. You see, Mr. Minister, because of what your Government has done, our people have lost hope in the future. Your Government has brought some reforms, for which we have been grateful. But the timing is all wrong. Little reforms coming too late and bit-by-bit, piecemeal, don't help.

> The people do not perceive the Government as seriously caring for them as people or as understanding them and their feelings in any way.

> These present actions are very complicating. They jeopardize the whole future. They put Blacks and Whites into a trap of confrontation. The result is that unless something very major happens now, it will not be possible to talk in the future."

This man was speaking what religious people might call the prophetic word, yet doing so with a "gentle firmness." He then explained what his religious faith did for him:

> Jesus took away all my bitterness to Whites, which had been consuming me. I can now be angry with Whites but never bitter. Experiences like this therefore give me hope.

Powerful stuff.

As Martin Luther King, Jr., said:

> In the process of gaining our rightful place we must not be guilty of wrongful deeds. Let us not seek to satisfy our thirst for freedom by drinking from the cup of bitterness and hatred.
>
> We must forever conduct our struggle on the high plane of dignity and discipline. We must not allow our creative protest to degenerate into physical violence. Again and again we must rise to the majestic heights of meeting physical force with soul force.

You see, dear reader, I believe we have the same attitude situation here: sincerity on the parts of Whites and Blacks yet often neither is able to see their own hypocrisy. May this book help open all of our eyes and move us to gracious action together.

Another example of Black steady determination to not take the eye off the prize, and maintain a positive attitude, can be seen in Sam Fuller's 1951 movie The Helmet, about a squad of soldiers during the Korean War, trapped in a small Buddhist temple. The film clearly makes the point that we are a melting pot of Americans. They capture a North Korean Major who was well educated in America and speaks excellent English (note the parallel with many of educated *jihadi* opposed to America today). He plays the race card first on Thompson, a Black medic, played by James Edwards, and then on Sgt. Tanaka, an American Nisei, played by Richard Loo. In the first scene, James Edwards, playing the medic, is bandaging up the North Korean Major's wound.

M: I don't understand you. You can't eat with them unless there is a war. And even then it's difficult. Isn't that so?

JE: That's right.

M: You'll pay for a ticket, but you even have to sit in the back of a public bus. Isn't that so.

JE: That's right. A hundred years ago I couldn't even ride a bus. At least now I can sit in the back. Maybe in 50 years, sit in the middle. Some day, even, up front. There are some things you just can't rush, Buster.

M: You are a stupid man.

JE: You're the stupid, Joe. Why don't you get wise, Buster.

M: [Spits on him]

JE: [Rips off a layer of dressing] You're ruining my dressing. [Puts another layer on]

End of scene.

Later that night, prior to the next morning when the Major is to be returned for questioning:

M:	You've got the same kind of eyes I have.
RL:	Huh?
M:	You've got the same kind of eyes I have
RL:	I heard you. So what.
M:	They hate us because of our eyes.
RL:	Major, you have a long hike ahead of you in the morning. Better get some shut-eye.
M:	Doesn't it make you feel like a traitor?
RL:	For a little guy with a lot of combat time, Major, you surprise me. Don't you guys know when you're licked?
M:	I surprise you? They threw Japanese-Americans into prison camps in the last war, didn't they? Perhaps even your parents. Perhaps even you.
RL:	You rang the bell that time. They did.
M:	And some of you had to pass as Filipinos to get a job. I know.
M:	You Nisei are incredible. You make no sense.
RL:	If I wasn't in the Army and you weren't a PW, I'd, ahhhh, in our country, we have rules, even about war.
M:	[Laughs] Were you one of those idiots who fought in Europe, for your country?
RL:	42nd combat team. And you know what? Over 3,000 of us idiots got the Purple Heart. You can't figure that out, Major, can you?
M:	No! That's what I don't understand. They call you dirty Jap rats, and yet you fight for them. Why?
RL:	I've got some hot infantry news for you. I'm not a dirty Jap rat. I'm an American. And if we get pushed around back home, well, that's our business. But we don't like it when we get pushed around [pauses].... Ahhhhhh, knock it off before I forget the articles of war and slap those rabbit teeth of yours one at a time.

Real unrest is in people's hearts. Laws, police, dogs, fire hoses, etc., cannot still this unrest. We need political solutions, not solutions of force, or drugs, or prison. This is why I also say that the system itself needs to be changed.

There has been a wonderful move afoot to do so. In the 2000 elections, Ward people of Minneapolis turned out in strength to vote, peacefully, hopefully, joyfully, only to have the DFL party attempt in 2001 to take away what the people had spoken for. But the saddest part is that this attempt to strip them of their voice was aided and abetted by two organizations that should know better, that are supposed to work with this charitable manner we have just read about to achieve the integration of Blacks into the mainstream of Minneapolis, the local NAACP and the Urban League (see chapter 14).

But whether the local branches of the Minneapolis Urban League or the NAACP are with us or not, we shall not stop until we overcome. Recall these words expressed earlier of Dr. Martin Luther King, Jr., that appear in the next Interlude:

> It would be fatal for the nation to overlook the urgency of the moment and to underestimate the determination of the Negro. This sweltering summer of the Negro's legitimate discontent will not pass until there is an invigorating autumn of freedom and equality.

Interlude 4

The Greatest Trio and the Greatest Quartet:

18th and 19th Centuries:
George Washington, Thomas Jefferson, Abraham Lincoln
20th Century:
Booker T. Washington & W.E.B. DuBois,
Martin Luther King, Jr. & Thurgood Marshall
21st Century:
Who will step up: ?   ?   ?

These seven men, a White trio and a Black quartet, were men who offer us a great understanding, both in terms of self and in terms of leading others. The White trio set the stage; the Black Quartet opened it to all. What White and Black men and women now continue their work?

George Washington. "I will not be king." He gave us his example in both word and deed. He stayed with the ideal: no kings, no one was to hold others in subjugation. His stepping down after two terms was astonishing in a world where that was not done. Rulers or men in charge held on till death. He set the tone for the peaceful transition of power: the man with the most power would simply step aside when his elective turn was over. George Washington never gave up. He could have marched his Army on the squabbling, uncooperative Continental Congress during the war, but did not. He waited for law and obeyed the law. He didn't win all his battles in war, but he won the one that counted, the final one that won the war. He again set the example for others to not be kings over others, when, in his will, he freed his slaves. For everyone, he set the example for personal honesty, fealty to duty, responsibility for one's own action, and planning for future generations.

Thomas Jefferson. "All men are created equal." This was a radical idea, introduced as the foundation stone of a people for the first time in history. No nation or group or tribe, whether in Europe, Africa, Asia, or Latin America ever proposed equality for their people before. Jefferson gave us the example of words even if he couldn't fully in deed. He was the scribe for the group that developed the Declaration of Independence, filled with words that thrill all who read them and who believe in and fight for liberty. He also reflects human weakness. As a young man, he fought for freeing slaves. When he lost that battle he never tried again. Eighty slaves were needed to run his home at Monticello. None of his great work could have been done without them. He created the University of Virginia, a goal for all. But in the final moments, he could not relent; he could not, as George Washington did, free his slaves, even after death, a sober reminder to us all. "All created equal" Tom couldn't free the 80 slaves who made the work of his ideals possible. On the other hand, he was ahead of his time with his slave Sally Hemming. On her deathbed, Tom's wife made him promise not to remarry. Nonetheless, he had a wonderful, loving relationship with his slave Sally, with whom, the DNA tests show, he established another bloodline. W.E.B. DuBois would later say that: "the problem of the Twentieth Century is the problem of the color-line." Jefferson was willing to cross the color line. It is part of what Myrdal meant in what he called "An American Dilemma" (Chapters 1 & 5), which called for equality but then couldn't accept it for the Negro race in general and not at all in terms of inter-racial marriage. Despite the continuing tension on this issue in people's minds, the reality is that tens of millions of Americans have various percentages of other races in them. Add to that all of the religious and ethnic group mixed-marriages (which some oppose more fiercely than inter-racial marriage; it was not that long ago when Swedish dads didn't want their daughters marrying Norwegians), and one might say that today, America is the inter-marriage capital of the world, that in all probability, over half of Americans are in some kind of inter-racial/ethnic/religious marriage (which means the multiculturalism of the left and the monoculturalism of the right are gone). In other words, there are few pure bloodlines in America today. In whatever fashion, it is time for all of us, in one way or another, to intellectually and emotionally cross the color line as well.

Abraham Lincoln. "Slave emancipator." He gave us both words and actions. He settled the question that "all men are created equal," as in those few short words he had the Constitution catch up with the Declaration of Independence. He lost all his electoral races but the one that truly counted, the Presidency. He understood the value of union and the sacrifice needed to retain it. He lived the ideal we need to reaffirm, "with malice toward none, charity for all, ... to bind up the nation's wounds ... to do all which may achieve and cherish a just and a lasting peace among ourselves, and with all nations," gathered in a Republic, a "government of the people. . .by the people. . .for the people. . . [that] shall not perish from the earth.

Booker T. Washington. "Pragmatist." Born in slavery in 1856, he set out to enable Black men to achieve and succeed despite the White man's yoke (wrote Up From Slavery). Booker T. Washington was an educator, reformer and the most influential black leader of his time (1856-1915). He preached a philosophy of self-help, racial solidarity and accommodation. His preferential option was for the poor, and to turn the unqualified but qualifiable into the qualified. In his book, Booker T. Washington observes, "Among a large class [of Blacks] there seemed to be a dependence upon the Government for every conceivable thing. The members of this class had little ambition to create a position for themselves, but wanted the Federal officials to create one for them." This is continued today by the Urban League and the NAACP. Booker T. Washington urged Blacks to "cast down your buckets" and acquire the skills and capital needed to start at the bottom instead of looking to government for help. We need to develop Black small businesses to help revitalize North Minneapolis. Blacks need to invest savings to build wealth for their children and their own retirement. Booker T. Washington shows the vision for which we must set goals and set objectives to bring about successful projects. It resonated so well with Whites that he became the most respected Black among Whites and the first Black invited to the White House for dinner (by Theodore Roosevelt). Having watched the party of Lincoln cast aside the Negro in 1876, trading their freedom for the Presidency, taking it in exchange for ending reconstruction and allowing Southern states to enact "states rights" decisions that disenfranchised Blacks and all that they had built up since the end of the war, he decided Blacks would have to wait, accommodate, and get everyone educated first.

Washington was born a slave. Had Congress listened to that other great slave writer, Frederic Douglass, who warned in 1866 of the need of a civil rights act to affirm the equality of blacks and whites in the United States in order to prevent the re-enslavement of Blacks in the South, Washington would not have suggested his approach. But Washington had watched the party of Lincoln cast off the Negro in the historic compromise with Southern leaders that enabled Rutherford B. Hayes to be elected in 1876. The price of this steal of a national election was a removal of occupying federal troops and an end to the radical reconstruction that had been imposed after Lincoln's assassination. This deal had left the future of the newly freed, largely uneducated Negro to states rights decisions. This led Washington to feel gradualism was the best approach, and he thus accepted segregation. He is famous for his speech at the Atlanta Exposition in 1895, where, at his key paragraph, he held up both arms, the fingers of each hand spread wide, and said, "In all things that are purely social we can be as separate as the fingers, yet as the hand" -- and here Washington quickly clinched each hand – "in all things essential to mutual progress." Whites interpreted this as "separate but equal."

W.E.B. DuBois, "civil rights activist." Born a freeman in Boston, in 1868, and died in 1963, was a passionate fighter for full civil rights and equality of citizenship for the Negro. He had helped found the NAACP but had broken with it in 1948 because of its timidity. So you can see my concern with the NAACP and Urban League, as I discuss in Chapter 14, is not a new one. He was not for gradualism at all. DuBois dreamed of creating a "talented tenth" that would supply the leadership necessary to winning rights and full equality for the Negro. He wanted to fill "the central problem of training men for life," which Washington wanted as well. I maintain that it is precisely for this reason that Whites have sabotaged Black education (Chapter 7) so they would not attain full rights and equality (Chapters 8-9). Both men were giants of their time and greatly admired each other, yet proposed different approaches. We need diversity of thought. Some have referred to their debate as "The Two Nations of Black America," not unlike the Kerner Commission would later use the term for Blacks and Whites, showing that they advocated Booker T.'s approach, Blacks to wait long suffering some more, rather than the W.E.B approach, which was for action to manifest equality right away. But the time has come for those Blacks and Whites who still hold to gradualism and separatism to let it go while holding on to Booker T's mission, shared with W.E.B. DuBois, to see all Blacks educated. W.E.B. DuBois, a towering black intellectual, scholar and political thinker (1868-1963) said no to Washington's strategy on the basis that he felt it would serve only to perpetuate white oppression. DuBois advocated political action and a civil rights agenda, and was another foundation on which King and Marshall would build.

For more on Booker T. Washington and W.E.B. DuBois, go to:

- http://www.pbs.org/wgbh/pages/frontline/shows/race/etc/road.html
- http://www.theatlantic.com/unbound/flashbks/black/mcgillbh.htm

Martin Luther King. "I have a dream." He was the megaphone preaching justice from the pulpits and getting action from the people in the streets, who dreamed the dream, and who lived and died to set men free. A preacher who taught the moral high ground, he lived where people lived, he spent time in jail, as St. Paul did, and he helped turn the dream into a reality. His dream is still the dream of all good people. The question remains how to achieve the dream. We need to remind ourselves of his dream, read it, make it our own, and figure out how to make it come true. His 1963 speech, with excerpts below, are as relevant today as they were 40 years ago.

Thurgood Marshall. "Defender of the oppressed." He was the gavel announcing justice and getting legal action in the halls of justice. He argued before the Supreme Court the legal case for making the dream legal, striking the *de facto* slave laws and instituting the *de jure* freedom laws. He later served on the Supreme Court, contributing to keeping the dream alive. "Equal means," he said, "getting the same thing, at the same time and in the same place." LBJ said, on appointing Marshall to the Supreme Court (1967), that it was "the right thing to do, the right time to do it, the right man and the right place." In a famous 63 page dissent, after the court held, 5-4, that the Constitution's guarantee of equal protection was not violated by the property tax system used in Texas and most other states to finance public education, Marshall accused the majority of "unsupportable acquiescence in a system which deprives children in their earliest years of the chance to reach their full potential as citizens." To our dismay, this continues today (Chapter 7).

Excerpts from Martin Luther King's "I Have A Dream" speech:
August 28, 1963, on the steps at the Lincoln Memorial in Washington D.C.

Five score years ago, a great American, in whose symbolic shadow we stand signed the Emancipation Proclamation. This momentous decree came as a great beacon light of hope to millions of Negro slaves who had been seared in the flames of withering injustice. It came as a joyous daybreak to end the long night of captivity. But one hundred years later, we must face the tragic fact that the Negro is still not free.

One hundred years later, the life of the Negro is still sadly crippled by the manacles of segregation and the chains of discrimination. One hundred years later, the Negro lives on a lonely island of poverty in the midst of a vast ocean of material prosperity. One hundred years later, the Negro is still languishing in the corners of American society and finds himself an exile in his own land.

So we have come here today to dramatize an appalling condition. In a sense we have come to our nation's capital to cash a check. When the architects of our republic wrote the magnificent words of the Constitution and the Declaration of Independence, they were signing a promissory note to which every American was to fall heir.

This note was a promise that all men would be guaranteed the inalienable rights of life, liberty, and the pursuit of happiness. It is obvious today that America has defaulted on this promissory note insofar as her citizens of color are concerned. Instead of honoring this sacred obligation, America has given the Negro people a bad check, which has come back marked "insufficient funds." But we refuse to believe that the bank of justice is bankrupt. We refuse to believe that there are insufficient funds in the great vaults of opportunity of this nation.

So we have come to cash this check -- a check that will give us upon demand the riches of freedom and the security of justice. We have also come to this hallowed spot to remind America of the fierce urgency of now. This is no time to engage in the luxury of cooling off or to take the tranquilizing drug of gradualism. Now is the time to rise from the dark and desolate valley of segregation to the sunlit path of racial justice. Now is the time to open the doors of opportunity to all of God's children. Now is the time to lift our nation from the quicksands of racial injustice to the solid rock of brotherhood.

It would be fatal for the nation to overlook the urgency of the moment and to underestimate the determination of the Negro. This sweltering summer of the Negro's legitimate discontent will not pass until there is an invigorating autumn of freedom and equality. Nineteen sixty-three is not an end, but a beginning. Those who hope that the Negro needed to blow off steam and will now be content will have a rude awakening if the nation returns to business as usual. There will be neither rest nor tranquility in America until the Negro is granted his citizenship rights.

The whirlwinds of revolt will continue to shake the foundations of our nation until the bright day of justice emerges. But there is something that I must say to my people who stand on the warm threshold, which leads into the palace of justice. In the process of gaining our rightful place we must not be guilty of wrongful deeds. Let us not seek to satisfy our thirst for freedom by drinking from the cup of bitterness and hatred.

We must forever conduct our struggle on the high plane of dignity and discipline. We must not allow our creative protest to degenerate into physical violence. Again and again we must rise to the majestic heights of meeting physical force with soul force.

The marvelous new militancy which has engulfed the Negro community must not lead us to distrust of all white people, for many of our white brothers, as evidenced by their presence here today, have come to realize that their destiny is tied up with our destiny and their freedom is inextricably bound to our freedom.

We cannot walk alone. And as we walk, we must make the pledge that we shall march ahead. We cannot turn back. There are those who are asking the devotees of civil rights, "When will you be satisfied?" we can never be satisfied as long as our bodies, heavy with the fatigue of travel, cannot gain lodging in the motels of the highways and the hotels of the cities. We cannot be satisfied as long as the Negro's basic mobility is from a smaller ghetto to a larger one. We can never be satisfied as long as a Negro in Mississippi cannot vote and a Negro in New York believes he has nothing for which to vote. No, no, we are not satisfied, and we will not be satisfied until justice rolls down like waters and righteousness like a mighty stream.

I am not unmindful that some of you have come here out of great trials and tribulations. Some of you have come fresh from narrow cells. Some of you have come from areas where your quest for freedom left you battered by the storms of persecution and staggered by the winds of police brutality. You have been the veterans of creative suffering. Continue to work with the faith that unearned suffering is redemptive.

Go back to Mississippi, go back to Alabama, go back to Georgia, go back to Louisiana, go back to the slums and ghettos of our northern cities, knowing that somehow this situation can and will be changed. Let us not wallow in the valley of despair. I say to you today, my friends, that in spite of the difficulties and frustrations of the moment, I still have a dream. It is a dream deeply rooted in the American dream.

I have a dream that one day this nation will rise up and live out the true meaning of its creed: "We hold these truths to be self-evident: that all men are created equal." I have a dream that one day on the red hills of Georgia the sons of former slaves and the sons of former slave owners will be able to sit down together at a table of brotherhood. I have a dream that one day even the state of Mississippi, a desert state, sweltering with the heat of injustice and oppression, will be transformed into an oasis of freedom and justice. I have a dream that my four children will one day live in a nation where they will not be judged by the color of their skin but by the content of their character. I have a dream today.

I have a dream that one day the state of Alabama, whose governor's lips are presently dripping with the words of interposition and nullification, will be transformed into a situation where little black boys and black girls will be able to join hands with little white boys and white girls and walk together as sisters and brothers. I have a dream today. I have a dream that one day every valley shall be exalted, every hill and mountain shall be made low, the rough places will be made plain, and the crooked places will be made straight, and the glory of the Lord shall be revealed, and all flesh shall see it together. This is our hope. This is the faith with which I return to the South. With this faith we will be able to hew out of the mountain of despair a stone of hope. With this faith we will be able to transform the jangling discords of our nation into a beautiful symphony of brotherhood. With this faith we will be able to work together, to pray together, to struggle together, to go to jail together, to stand up for freedom together, knowing that we will be free one day.

This will be the day when all of God's children will be able to sing with a new meaning, "My country, 'tis of thee, sweet land of liberty, of thee I sing. Land where my fathers died, land of the pilgrim's pride, from every mountainside, let freedom ring." And if America is to be a great nation, this must become true. So let freedom ring from the prodigious hilltops of New Hampshire. Let freedom ring from the mighty mountains of New York. Let freedom ring from the heightening Alleghenies of Pennsylvania! Let freedom ring from the snowcapped Rockies of Colorado! Let freedom ring from the curvaceous peaks of California! But not only that; let freedom ring from Stone Mountain of Georgia! Let freedom ring from Lookout Mountain of Tennessee! Let freedom ring from every hill and every molehill of Mississippi. From every mountainside, let freedom ring.

When we let freedom ring, when we let it ring from every village and every hamlet, from every state and every city, we will be able to speed up that day when all of God's children, black men and white men, Jews and Gentiles, Protestants and Catholics, will be able to join hands and sing in the words of the old Negro spiritual, "Free at last! Free at last! Thank God Almighty, we are free at last!"

<u>Favorite verses</u>

Genesis 41:15

I have had a dream.

Genesis 37:9

I have had another dream.

Judges 7:13: I

I had a dream.

Proverbs 29:18

"Where there is no vision, the people perish.

Proverbs 23:7

For as [a man] thinketh in his heart, so is he.

Joel 2:28-29; Acts 14:17-18

Then afterward I will pour out my spirit in all flesh; your sons and your daughters shall prophesy, your old men shall dream dreams, and your men shall see visions. Even on the male and female slaves, in those days, I will pour out my spirit.

Proverbs 23:7

For as a man thinketh in his heart, so is he.

Philippians 3:13

Forgetting those things which are behind, and reaching forth unto those things which are before I press toward the mark for the **prize**

<u>A verse from a favorite hymn</u>
(by Manley, 1940: *Spirit: Spirit of Gentleness*

You call from tomorrow, you break ancient schemes. From the bondage of sorrow all the captives dream dreams; our women see visions, our men clear their eyes, with bold new decisions your people arise.

Chorus: Spirit, spirit of gentleness

"Nothing happens unless first a dream."

-- Carl Sandburg

Chapter 5

Justice and Fairness:
The Question Of Equal Access And Equal Opportunity

The issue is a simple one. Will Minneapolis work to be fair or not in education, housing, and economic development (including jobs, living wages, and Black entrepreneurial growth. How will Minneapolis answer the question: To be fair or not to be fair? Racists would answer: not to be fair. Do the math. The record of Minneapolis in Education, Housing, and Jail Instead of Jobs, is clear: It is a racist record of injustice and unfairness, which I document in these chapters.

The question will not go away for Minneapolis or any other city: to be fair or not to be fair. It is all a matter of choice. What choice will the city make? This choice will determine the kind of justice that will be prevail, as discussed in Chapter 2.

To answer "be fair" will require a shift from the idea that it is the state that is the mechanism for groups to gain power to the idea that the state is the referee (checks and balances) for individuals, groups, and organizations in the search for fairness. If the mechanism is the state, democracy cannot last. And without democracy, even Whites will lose.

This is not an easy question. But if we are going to deal with it openly, we need to face the truth about racism in America in general and in particular in Minneapolis. As noted in Chapter 1, accepted best study for its time, 1944, was Gunnar Myrdal's *An American Dilemma: The Negro Problem and Modern Democracy*. Let us recall the dilemma then that exists today: how do Americans, who don't want the Negro, get rid of the Negro in an acceptable manner? This book heavily influenced the Supreme Court's 1954 anti-segregation decision. Any discussion must start with the bedrock of what Myrdal documented: that in the U.S., there was a virtual genocidal intent on the part of Whites. He had no solution to the problem other than advocating reducing their birth rate and openly advocating removing as many from the country as possible. Myrdal also documented how it was that liberal White Americans came to rationalize the notion that there would be less prejudice if the Black population could be reduced. We can see this rationalization at work in Minneapolis as attempts are made to depopulate Blacks from the city. And this, of course, is the same dilemma Myrdal wrote about. Americans are decent, law abiding citizens who believe in democracy and liberty. The dilemma: how to appropriately meet their goal of "of removing black people from the country "under those ideals? Or, as he phrased it (emphasis is his):

> [T]here is no doubt that *the overwhelming majority of white Americans desire that there be as few Negroes as possible in America*. If the Negroes could be eliminated from America or greatly decreased in numbers, this would meet the whites' approval -- *provided that it could be accomplished by means which are also approved.*

Or, as I like to put it, how can a nice guy be a bad guy too? That is a contradiction in terms. So the White man in America has botched being nice and botched being bad. But there is a solution: the universal brotherhood of man. The word Philadelphia means "City of Brotherly Love." I believe 21st Century America is ready to move on, to let go of the genocidal notion, and accept integration. That must be the goal. My hope is that my book might show some ways for doing so.

And the obvious first place to begin is unemployment, the most basic and fundamental area of unfairness and injustice practiced against the poor. Solve it here and it will be solved virtually everywhere. But it can't be solved in employment until we get we stop following failed economic dogma.

Recall that although the average unemployment today hovers around 4-5%, it was 25% during the Great Depression. In the 1970s it often reached 10%. We are still plagued by the economic theory of the 1970s, which said that it was good that many stay unemployed, so there would always be a surplus of workers for companies when they needed them. Hubert Humphrey tried to temper this idea when he was in the Senate, with what was called the Humphrey Hawkins Full Employment Act, which sought to set a ceiling for unemployment at 7%. If it rose beyond that, the Federal government would step in and become the employer of last resort, just as it was with the WPA and similar programs during the Great Depression.

I remember hearing that in the 1970s. As a Black man, I knew that we made up a lot of that 10%. It was an average number, but for Whites it was in single digits and for Blacks it was in double digits. I am still amazed that so-called liberals could still condone 7% unemployed as OK. Remember what I said earlier: much of this is about law. If the law is such and the government works to enforce whatever it is, it is legal. And if legal, moral Not fair, but legal and moral. Not just, but legal (hence my repeated example of slavery and the Jim Crow laws in the South which, in their day were legal and moral and which, today, some states, as we shall see in this book, are trying to bring back). The theory of the day said there needed to be surplus workers for companies to dip into during expansion time who could be dismissed when not needed.

Some of us used to joke that as the Black man was the key to the success of the economy, providing this labor pool for Whites to draw from, Blacks should be paid for carrying this important function. Not everyone thought we were funny.

And yet just think of the economic energy that would be freed up if we enabled rather than blocked Black entrepreneurs, if we hired Black contractors and service companies and used Black workers. During the 1990's, more than 80% of the net gain in new jobs was not from corporate giants but from small companies involved in a wide range of businesses (far broader than the dot-coms). We have allowed Whites to manage the corporate and government contracting by engaging White companies and workers, but have not required to be in compliance regarding hiring minorities as well.

Small businesses are where most people get started, as this is where most of the new jobs are created. In 2000, nearly half the work force in the United States was employed in small businesses. It was small business that actually powered the record economic growth of the 1990's. Yet less than 8% are Black. We need to establish policies that will provide micro-loans that actually go to Black company startups (many now go to women as minorities; there is nothing wrong with that as long as they are in addition to, not instead of those to Blacks). If we make a concerted effort to facilitate such loans for Blacks, not only will they have an opportunity to improve their lives but they will become active stakeholders in society also. Micro-lending nurtures the fundamental values of democracy and helps them take root. Therefore, recommendations by the current Administration to cut SBA in half are counter to the values of the real America and counter to progressive plans for helping Blacks raise themselves up.

Businesses based on jobs and profit are the real foundation of American capitalism, **not** stock market speculation play money or re-regulations that invite wholesale stealing (calling it accounting fraud is way too tame) or all of those working to promote the gambles of the stock market, which, when played properly, can benefit any player (since 1926, it has a yearly average of 10% return).

During the 1980s, Milton Friedman's theories were popular with the Federal government. Friedman believed it was immoral to pay a person more than $1.25/hour if you could find someone who would work for that amount or less. It is always strange how Christians can apply the law of supply and demand to human beings, for it makes commodities out of them. In reality, it says what people really think of poor people: not much, just commodities, to be used or not used, bought and sold in the labor market if needed or not needed. Fortunately, on this issue, Friedman's ideas are no longer listened to. The Republicans lost their moral high ground with his positions. The jury is still out whether they will regain the moral high ground back on George W. Bush's compassionate conservative label. Labels don't count, only action counts, and the action in this case is what is recommended to be law as compassionate: will it be a "living wage" or not, or what some call a family wage, the amount needed for a family of four to succeed in America.

This gets to the heart of the structural problems in the debate. An economic system which institutionalizes work structures that allows wages to be less than what is required to support a family needs to be changed. There is no moral high ground there. The attitude that nothing can be done about it, and that Friedman's Fantasy (which I also like to call Milton's madness) is really reasonable, shows how far we still have to go in terms of fairness, let alone justice.

All major religions ask their adherents to serve each other, to love one another, and to take care of each other. Indeed, the famous Biblical questions, "Who is my neighbor?" and "Am I my brother's keeper?" are answered by the story of "The Good Samaritan." In this parable by Jesus, who George W. Bush says is his favorite philosopher, the concept of neighbor is not defined by geography or blood or ethnicity or race, but rather by need. By this account, compassionate conservatism should provide a floor below which the poor do not fall (Interestingly enough, the Republican President Richard Nixon proposed this but the Democrats defeated it: It would have given Southern Blacks economic opportunity, which in turn would have made it difficult to keep them in their place). There is a need for a threshold below which no one should have to fall in this society, in this economy. And here I am talking strictly about people working full time, not those not at work. I might add that there is already a mechanism to use to transition to employers paying more and that is the Earned Income Credit (EIC). For the corporate pirates we have discussed, treating corporations and governments as piggy banks, we have been treated to what these leaders accept as the ceiling: the sky's the limit. Now we need to see them contribute to a floor.

The good news is that the percent of Americans earning minimum wage has dropped from 9% in 1980 to 1% in 2001. It is still bad news for those earning a minimum wage of $5.15 to $6.64, who number about 12 million workers all told (*Wall Street Journal*, July 19, 2001, p. A1 and A10), which is still below the poverty line for a family of four. 12 million workers is still a HUGE number and it needs to be addressed. And the obvious: Among Blacks, the percentages are starker. These are both moral and economic issues. How will Minneapolis address them?

I ask you, dear reader, to do the numbers with me and ask yourself: What is fair? *The New York Times* (June 23, 2002, p. BU4), states that those in the 90th percentile earn $1,440 a week (that's $74,880 a year). That means that 10% of the population earns more and a whopping 90% earn less. How much less? The same article states that the middle carn wages averaging $646/week, which is $33,592. The low end earns an average of $307/week, or $15,964. Which, dear reader, can you live on?

Nickel and Dimed On (Not) Getting By in America by Barbara Ehrenreich provides her account of spending several months in different cities attempting to live on jobs paying the minimum wage, including Minneapolis. What she found in Minneapolis in terms of jobs, housing, and a living wage was not good. And she dealt mostly with poor Whites. Read her book. Think Minneapolis. You may be offended, dear reader, by this question, although I do believe you will understand the question, which is: "Is what is happening in Minneapolis as she reports fair for those workers?" Your answer will tell more about who you are as a person and what your view of society is than almost any other question.

We might also venture into something some readers may feel is far afield for this book, and that is this: that CEO's and other top executives should only receive rewards above their salaries based on the performance of the companies under their stewardship, rather than on the performance of the stock that can be manipulated to look good even when the company is doing poorly. Additional rewards, whatever form they take, should only be awarded when the company is actually profitable in real terms and not in creative accounting terms. Think of the opportunities for success in other areas corporations could achieve if this money underwrote that kind of potential growth activity rather than the growth merely of the pirates commanding the corporate ship. Whether real or imaginary, whether Blackbeard or Captain Hook, a pirate is a pirate. When pirates command the economic fleet, be they in corporations or the legislatures, plunder is their game and impoverishing us is their name.

Without equal access and equal opportunity, beginning with education, there can be no life, liberty, and the pursuit of happiness for all; there can be no one nation, indivisible, with liberty and justice for all. It is OK for those at the top of the opportunity ladder to enrich themselves as long as it is done fairly, which means it is also fair that those at the bottom of the opportunity ladder **not** be impoverished by the process that enriches the top.

Fairness and justice are more than cheap slogans in empty patriotic rituals. How we define these terms defines our self-understanding as a society regarding the age-old questions that are at the heart of all societies and their internal and foreign conflicts: Who are we? And how are we to live together? It can only work if we agree to at least a basic common ground on which we can all stand and from which we can work to integrate the negotiations necessary to include everyone. To do that, we need a sense of *both* individual and group solidarity and sacrifice. I find this missing in Minneapolis. We need a common morality more than we need a common set of bureaucratic rules for standard operating procedures. When all goes well, the latter may work, but when things do not go well, they won't unless we have the sense of individual and group solidarity.

At this point in any discussion of fairness in Minneapolis, we must remind ourselves of the story of the Good Samaritan and of the Golden Rule discussed in Chapter 2: President George W. Bush's favorite philosopher, Jesus' "Do unto others as you would have them do unto you", or, as Immanuel Kant put it, "do unto others as you would have everyone do unto everybody." Certainly this is what the Good Samaritan followed and which the others in the story did not do, including the clergy. It's an excellent rule. It defines the phrase "preferential option for the poor." And because the Golden Rule is based on need, not geography or race or creed, we have a better idea of what is meant by those who say preferential option for the poor. So you can imagine how we as young men at Syracuse were wanting to delve more deeply into the concept, especially young Black men trying to figure out why we were not treated with the Golden Rule by Whites, just the Gold Rules. So you can imagine how we likes Kant's super golden rule much better. I still do. Jesus' version could conceivably permit exclusion and expulsion. Kant's can't be misinterpreted that way. All must be included. It is a more perfect rule. I commend it to Minneapolis. As we shall see, too often the rule is do unto us as we command you while we will do unto you as we desire. That I cannot accept.

The three main issues raised for Minneapolis are these: **First**: To be fair or not to be fair, especially in education, housing, and economic development (including jobs, living wages, and Black entrepreneurial growth). **Second**: To determine what the "do" is that we want everyone to do unto everyone else. **Third**: Are we willing to practice this individually and collectively? In other words, are we willing to treat others in education, housing, jobs, wages, entrepreneurial activity, the way we want to be treated?

If we followed this super Golden Rule, we would not need affirmative action or the Voting Rights Act. That we need these things shows the unfairness that is not only tolerated but also is purposely attempted. Following the Civil War, the 13th, 14th and 15th Amendments were supposed to settle this fairness question. The 13th ended slavery. The 14th guaranteed African Americans equal rights under the law, and the 15th granted the right of all citizens to vote regardless of race color, or previous condition of servitude. However, with full approval of the courts, the South enacted the Jim Crow laws, which created conditions and procedures that essentially subverted these amendments. Again, what is legal reflects the morals of the day. And it was considered then to be moral to block the rights and votes of Blacks. Nowhere is this seen more clearly than in the comment of the infamous South Carolina Senator "Pitchfork" Ben Tillman, who led the South in its racist ingenuity, proudly captured by Tillman's comment about the black disenfranchisement campaign:

""We have done our level best. We have scratched our heads to find out how we could eliminate every last one of them. We stuffed ballot boxes. We shot them. We are not ashamed of it."

Under Presidents Harding, Coolidge and Hoover, a whole lot of peculiar things took place: shootings at the polling places, the charge of a tax to vote (which poor Blacks didn't have), and the infamous voting test: reciting verbatim the Constitution of the United States, something the White obstructionists couldn't even do. And one of the events would have a very chilling effect on Blacks: following a lynching in Marion, Indiana, there was the march in Indianapolis of over 100,000 Ku Klux Klansmen, the favorite group of White Supremacists. All three of these Presidents were Republicans. This is another explanation as to why Blacks then gravitated to Hoover's successor, Franklin D. Roosevelt.

That chill stayed that way until the Voting Rights Act of 1965 made such taxes and tests illegal and backed with the force of the Federal government. Minneapolis, through its recent redistricting plan (Chapters 12 and 13) returns us to that way of thinking, as the inner city Blacks of Minneapolis are herded into districts in order to disenfranchise, disempower, and impoverish them. "Pitchfork" Ben Tillman would have been proud.

The web site **http://www.aclu.org/issues/racial/racevote.html** provides more detail, as it outlines how the Southern states, with the complicity of the Federal courts (which is why who is on the bench at every level matters), rewrote their state constitutions to legitimize a host of Jim Crow laws and regulations designed to keep Blacks out of the voting booth and out of government, subverting the 14th and 15th Amendments. Denying Blacks the vote is being attempted again by subverting the Voting Rights Act of 1965 (renewed in 1982), which was passed guaranteeing that votes of Blacks meant something by removing those Jim Crow laws. Whites need to get beyond the attempts to exile us internally. Blacks need to get beyond the notion of working to be accommodated. Both Blacks and Whites need to work on fairness in education, housing, jobs, and wages, and let race be incidental, not primary.

The redistricting in Minneapolis (Chapters 13 and 14) is another example of the attempt to dilute, degrade, and render Black votes useless. We have won battles, but the war is not yet won. There are other means to disenfranchise Blacks, which we need to be on the look-out for, so that these methods don't get used on us too. One in particular is the at-large voting trick to replace district voting.

The goal is to continue the trend away from racism and toward integration, to improve beyond the damaging data and statistics of (1) the long, *Star Tribune* series

(Interlude 1) on racism that ran from June 10-June 24, 1990, a racism that continues today, and (2) the cover story in the *Mpls.StPaul* magazine of January, 1990, "I'm Not Racist, But...." (Interlude 10). The pace has been slow. It needs to move post-haste.

The Minneapolis economic pie continues to grow but not for all, and certainly not for North Minneapolis. All must have a chance. Good business sense compels corporations to look beyond diversity for pure business reasons: growth and profits, which a wider, and more diverse approach to the market can help.

It is said that one should not complain unless one has a solution to offer. There is still much to be discussed. But let me here offer some solutions in three key areas to show that I still have hope, that I still dream the dream. More importantly, I hope that you the reader can see that what is being asked is not that much, but that it will resolve the problems. I include them here to provide an optimistic backdrop to the negative things I will discuss in more detail in the following chapters on education, housing, development, and government.

We can tell which policies to follow by developing a calculus on what we want and don't want. Put simply put, let's agree to policies which support, which say YES to, policies resulting in positive outcomes regarding education, children, and families:

- YES to a better quality of life for ALL citizens
- YES to a better quality education for all students and higher graduation rates for all schools
- YES to first-rate health care
- YES to wider home ownership

Let's agree to say YES to policies resulting in positive outcomes regarding transportation, energy, and the environment:

- YES to abundant natural resources: clean water and clean air
- YES to highways that keep up with the increase in cars
- YES to energy policies that prevent establishing a California in Minnesota

Let's agree to say YES to policies resulting in positive outcomes regarding the economy, jobs, wages, and business:

- YES to low unemployment and wages that let full-time workers support their families
- YES to contractors doing business with the government hiring minority workers

- YES to a business-friendly environment
- YES to world class corporate research and world class university research
- YES to rural-metro partnerships, not needless competition
- YES to tax breaks (fair and just) for individuals and for companies
- YES to a respect for property and laws and access to both for all
- YES to equality of opportunity for all races, especially in terms of education and job training
- YES to keeping Fortune 500 Companies headquarters
- YES to once again earning the Most Livable State award

Those are the YESes. What about the NOs? Let's agree to say NO to policies resulting in these negative outcomes regarding education, children, and families:

- NO to only 17% of our African-American male high school students graduating
- NO to 25% of 4th graders today being unable to read at 4th-grade level (the percentage rises to over 50% for Hispanics and over 60% for Blacks)
- NO to minority students being kept in school systems where they are provided far fewer resources and score much lower than White students. They are our friends and our neighbors, and they too will join us as part of tomorrow's work force. They should have the same opportunities.
- NO to hunger and children living in garbage

Let's agree to say NO to policies resulting in these negative outcomes for transportation, energy, and the environment:

- NO to highway construction that does not keep up with the increase in cars
- NO to an energy policy that is not adequate for the future

Let's agree to say NO to policies resulting in these negative outcomes for the economy, jobs, wages, and business:

- NO to having people work full time for wages that won't support their families
- NO to 25% of our citizens not being able to afford to own their own homes
- NO to companies contracting to government agencies who don't hire minorities
- NO to maintaining a conflict between rural and metro areas; instead, forming partnerships
- NO to our taxes becoming too high for the return we get in services
- NO to terror and totalitarianism

- NO to not being willing to evaluate programs for their true consequences so that we can be prepared to change policies that result in high pain and low meaning, whether for individuals, schools, or companies

Now let's look at these YESes and NOs through the lens of young Black men. It is my contention that the redistricting of Chapters 12 and 13 works against the YESes and favors the NOs. It is also my contention that these YESes and NOs will work best for everyone, especially the young Black men who are hemmed in by what I have called the invisible cage in which Minneapolis has put them.

Minneapolis is in Hennepin County. Have you seen the figures on the number of African-American young men arrested in Hennepin County? It is close to 50%. This is outrageous. It is part of the war on young Black men (see end of Chapter 9).

On the other hand, look at the environment the Black organizations and the White power structure have created for these young Black men. All around them they see their housing razed and not replaced, promised jobs that don't come through, and wages that are purposefully too low. These young Black men are coming to realize that they won't get hired anyway, so why prepare for work? In taking care of themselves, the adults have sacrificed the next generation, causing the young to lose respect for them. Too many are left with only the alternative of the street.

When a generation loses respect for its elders, the elders can't do much for them. Which is too bad as these same adults can certainly provide a wide range of adults in the criminal justice and social worker areas to help them deal with their problems

These young men don't have confidence in the system because it has failed them, beginning with education in Kindergarten or 1st grade and continuing on for a dozen years. That is a lot of negative reinforcement. In the process, they haven't learned and developed a work ethic, as they have been denied the education and training they needed. You can't succeed when you can't stand up for yourself, and you can't stand up for yourself if you think you are inferior. Minneapolis has become a place that is very discouraging for young Black men.

In the final analysis, though, this is not a matter of tradition, as some conservatives might think, nor a matter of morality, as some Liberals might think, but a matter of law, of legislation, which determines or reflects, depending upon your point of view, both tradition and morality. What will be or what won't be will be because of legislation. Legislators have enough money to live and retire on because they have made that a matter of law, at taxpayer expense. The came cannot be said about the rest of us.

And that is what is needed in Minneapolis. A change in laws. Minneapolis has done this with its new redistricting, only for the worse, making laws that favor the powerful and wealthy and disempower those without any power or wealth. It continues to try to do in Minneapolis what the South has continued to attempt: to reverse the intent of the Civil Rights laws by changing the ward boundaries of Minneapolis in order to purposefully impoverish, disempower, and disenfranchise Blacks in Minneapolis, all for the same reason as in the South: to preserve the Mastuhs of the plantation, who, in this case, are the rulers of the DFL. Masking as liberals, they are really tyrants. I have watched this for 40 years and lay it all out in the chapters ahead.

October postscript: Who Won The Civil War?

The **September 30, 2002** *U.S. News and World Report,* asks this question on the cover. The inside heading was:

> The Better Angels: We are still fighting over who was right and who was wrong in the Civil War.

I found this cover question stunning, and had an "aha!" experience. The antebellum and pre-civil war South knew how to keep Blacks "in their place:" as slaves. The abolitionist North said their place was as any other human being: at society's table as equals, as free men and women, although they had no plan for how.

I had heard of the German argument that there are Gemrans who deny that the Hollocaust in Germany during World War II ever took place, that yes a few Jews were killed, but it wasn't many and there certainy wasn't a systematic plan to exterminate all of them. Now dear reader, I know that you, like me, have seen the pictures, photographs and film of the concentration camp liberation scenes. Like me I am sure that you have read at least an article if not a book or two about it. We know it happened.

So now I receive great insight from the *U.S. News and World Report* article: many in America today, including in Minneapolis, are in denial about the Civil War. Talk to college kids today and they will tell you slavery was tacked on at the end, that it was really about economics and trade. I've long wondered how this could be. Now I know. Even the liberals of the left in the universities are in denial.

Even our park bureaus which tend the Civil War battlefield parks have been neutral up until lately, concentrating on the valor and heroics, tactics and strategies, as if these were merely like Sunday afternoon professional football games. Even Colonial

Williamsburg was long sanitized, showing no existence of slaves at all, and the few
Blacks in costume were shown as servants, not slaves.

This is important. If all that counts is valor and heroics and tactics and strategies,
then any and all fighting is good, any and all war is cool, and that in the current War
on Terrorism we should just all sit back and relasx and enjoy the heroics and valor
and chess board moves of the combatants of each side, and think nothing more of it.

But it is not the fight that counts. It is what is fought for that counts. As we shall see
in Interlude 16, what quite often happens is that the result of the battles fought by
opposing sides is often nothing like what they fought for.

Let me be as clear as I can: the Civil War was about **slavery** in general and about
freeing **Blacks** from slavery in particular. All who fought for the South and defend
the South today essentially still believe Blacks should be put in their place at the
back of the bus, bottom of the stairs, on the straw mats on the dirt floor in the
servants' quarters. The Germans have had to deal with their Nazi past. Whites need
to deal with their slave past. Saying "I never owned slaves nor did my family" is not
enough. What we need to hear is: lets end all Jim Crowism, invite Blacks to the
table, and provide equal access and equal opportunity to end the vestiges of the Civil
War and the antebellum South once and for all: by delivering freedom to the inner
city residents and following the YESes and NOs of Chapters 5 and 17.

One side felt slaves were a part of the natural order, especially if they were Black,
and therefore should be so for life. The other side said slavery was wrong and should
be ended but had no plan and had no given thought to Blacks then actually moving to
where they were. So one side fought for a physical, material way of life in which it
road the saddle on the backs of slaves, and the other side fought for the idea that it
was wrong to ride on other's backs but still haven't figured out how to remove the
saddle from the backs of the slaves and let them roam the plains free with everyone
else. Now is the time to do that.

The famous Confederate General John Mosby, of "Gray Ghost" guerilla warfare
fame, said this:

> We went to war on account of the thing we quarrelled with the North about.
> I never heard of any other cause of quarrel than slavery.

> Men fight from sentiment. After the fight is over they invent some fanciful
> theory on which they imagine that they fought for.

The huge casualties on both sides created a bitterness Blacks are still paying for.
Its time for a new Reconstruction for inner city America.

Interlude 5

The Good News on Race, Part I:
From the 2000 Census: General Advances

> A glass half full is still half empty.
> A glass half empty is still half full.
> Ron Edwards

Given the odds and the roadblocks thrown up in the path of minorities, the news from the 2000 census is good. The general upward progress of minorities has taken place despite the roadblocks, which makes it nothing short of spectacular. What makes it all the more notable for Blacks is that they have achieved these advances despite being continually told that they can't do it on their own, by themselves. And yet: we still have.

Not that the 2000 Census means that we can lie down and say the battle is over. Far from it. But as we work to clear the roadblocks, especially for inner city Blacks, let us pause to review how far we have come and to encourage everyone to stay the course, especially for all of those left behind in North Minneapolis.

This Interlude counters those professional victimizers, those Federal-program-fund ambulance chasers, who dismiss Black achievement. Yes, there are shortcomings, but we also need to see the progress.

In general, for Blacks, 2000 poverty rates were down and employment rates went up. The Black middle class has come into its own. Here are some of the more exciting numbers, which give us something to celebrate as well as goals to aim for:

- 1980: Black poverty rate 36%
- 2000: Black poverty rate 22%
- 1980: Black household median income $10,000
- 2000: Black household median income $30,000
- Black rise in household income, 1967-1997: 31%
- White rise in household income, 1967-1997: 18%
- 2000: 51% of Blacks report their economic situation has improved over past year (an historic first).
- 2000: 32% of Whites report their economic situation has improved over past year.
- 2000: 9% of Blacks said they were worse off.

- 2000: 17% of Whites said they were worse off.
- 2000: 25% of Blacks earn $75,000/year or more. BUT 33% are still below poverty line.
- Blacks own more homes than before.
- Blacks occupy less-segregated communities in more prosperous parts of the country.
- Of 291 metropolitan areas, all but 19 are more integrated than in 1990.

BUT:

- Racial gaps continue in most categories; a glass half full is still half empty.
- If inner city poverty is not resolved, these good numbers will turn bad.
- We still need to concentrate on education, jobs, housing, and economic participation.
- These numbers will frighten those who don't want progress and make them more hardened against further progress. Thus, the battle must continue for all.

Much progress has been made. 25% of Blacks earn $75,000/year or more. But the system still has 33% of Blacks below the poverty line, including those with jobs making only minimum or lower wages. And thus Minneapolis and the state of Minnesota still have a lot of explaining to do when it comes to minorities. **http://www.state.mn.us/aam/aamp1-6.html#skyblue,** Minnesota's own web page, demonstrates that Whites overwhelmingly outnumber minorities. Minnesota's population is 4,919,479. This is how it breaks down: *

    a. **State rank in population:** 21st
    b. **White:** 4,400,282 **(89.4%)**
    c. **Black or African-American:** 171,731 **(3.5%)**
    d. **Hispanic or Latino:** 1 43,382 **(2.9%)**
    e. **Asian:** 141,968 **(2.8%)**
    f. **Two or more races:** 82,742 **(1.7%)**
    g. **Some other race:** 65,810 **(1.3%)**
    h. **American Indian and Alaska Native:** 54,967 **(1.1%)**
    i. **Native Hawaiian and Other Pacific Islander:** 1,979 **(.04%)**

       2000 Census Information

Remember the goals, the prize: equal access, equal opportunity, fairness and justice.

In America today, there are two million minority-owned firms generating in excess of $205 billion annually. The U.S. Census Bureau middle series shows that the minority of the U.S. population is projected to increase from 29% in 2000 to 46% in 2045 and to over 50% by 2060. This means that there will be an increase in minority disposable income spending of $3 trillion over the next 45 years. But there are those who don't want to see this happen. They fight it behind the scenes.

As Benjamin Barber put it in his delightful phrase (July 29, 2002, "A Failure of Democracy, Not Capitalism"), it is "not that [we] may have been complicit in the vices of capitalism, but that [we] are today insufficiently complicit in the virtues of democracy." You can read more about his view about "strong democracy" in

And please, dear reader, understand this is not a rant to discredit corporations or capitalism or even of governmennt. Far from it. It is a rant objecting to wealth-taking by pirates. Government does it too. Indeed, no one cooks the books better than government, for unlike corporations, who can be deserted by investors tired of their poor performance, legislators just pass more tax laws. Notice this: There are no laws or penalties for Federal bookkeepers. If program budgets get busted, they raise taxes instead of busting the heads of the programs. And when Congress outspends itself and needs more, it just passes a law to raise the debt ceiling and then just keeps on spending, disguising their new spending levels as "for the people" when they are, in fact, for their buddies and campaign contributors. And can you remember the last time a government admitted a mistake and cancelled a program? Neither can I.

Bureaucracies primarily do what legislators tell them to do. Our problem is not of democracy, nor its institutions, but rather how some are misusing them. We have strong capitalism. We must make sure we also have strong democracy (see these books by Benjamin Barber:

- *Strong Democracy: Participatory Politics for a New Age*
- *A Place for Us: How to Make Society Civil and Democracy Strong*
- *An Aristocracy for Everyone: The Politics of Education and the Future of America).*

We can have both strong democracy and strong capitalism. Each needs its own set of checks and balances. But it is individuals and political parties that set up how it is to be done. Look not at government, an idea, but at the parties who are the actors involved, the human actors. Humans will always be susceptible to temptation. And as we have the strongest economy in the world, we have strong capitalism we also have strong temptations.

So how far did we get after collectively as a city community reading the Star Tribune series on racism. Here is what the papers said in 1992:

Here are the words of the *Star Tribune* Publisher in 1992:

- "social justice, a global rather than isolationist perspective, good government, and the obligation of businesses to make the community better."
- "diversity, openness, empowerment, and win/win solutions."
- "not form...views by counting votes, but surely should listen and learn and change."

Here are the words of the *Pioneer Press* Editorial Page Editor in 1992:

- "talking about what must be done to stem growing poverty, social isolation and racial tension in the Twin Cities"
- "what is important is a recognition that serious problems are spreading...the will to do something about them"
- "we ignore these messages at our own peril"
- "improve life for those in poverty and to avoid confining poverty in core communities

This shows again how good Minneapolis is at talking the walk. My book, nonetheless demonstrates its unwillingness to actually walk the talk.

To discuss these issues across the board, from a higher plane of reference, freedom ar liberty, see also the essay now considered a classic, "The Culture of Liberty: An Agenda Peter L. Berger, 35th Anniversary Issue of *Society,* Vo. 35, No. 2, January-February 199: pp. 407-415. See also *Sociology Reinterpreted: AnEssay On Method and Vocation,* Pete L. Berger, with Hansfried Kellner (Anchor Press/Doubleday, Garden City, NY, 1981).

Chapter 6

What makes Minneapolis Minneapolis?
Identifying characteristics of the Bosses of Minnesota,
Or: Life on the Mississippi's Grandest Liberal Plantation

Minneapolis is like the last outpost of a great experiment in how to be a model to the rest of the country on how to keep Black people in their place (remember that was what James Baldwin said was the "big secret" that all Black people knew: that "the machinery of the country's operations were to keep the Ni**er in his place"). Minneapolis has mastered the art of doing so. Baldwin also said that if you really want to know what the White power structure really wanted for Blacks, just look at what they did to Indians.   Too many White folks in Minneapolis, as well as nationwide, accept this. That makes it easier for them to go along with the exclusion of non-Whites from education, housing, and ecronomic development.

One of things Martin Luther King, Jr. said that he discovered was that the boss mentality of the South didn't stop at the Mason-Dixon line: It extended all the way to the Canadian border.

There is an old saying of Freud that men often quote in exasperation about women, "My God, what do they want?" But it's really not a mystery. They want what everyone wants: sovereignty, which means dignity and control over their lives as partners with men in their shared biographies, rather than as subjects in biographies written by men. This is what Blacks want too: control over their lives as partners with Whites in their shared biographies, rather than as subjects in biographies written by Whites.

If we were to lump everyone together and ask what they wanted, we would find that people want three things: their interests (however they define them, often in economic, political and personal terms), dignity (receiving respect for who they are and for what they do), and recognition (not just pats on the back but to be seen as existing and participating in the community, not as invisible people to be slapped at periodically like so many tiny insects whenever they swarm together and appear visible when it is time to vote for Democrats).

Interests, dignity, recognition. This has been the history of this great land ever since those first immigrants that came to this country in the 17th century in search of a place where they could worship and live as they saw fit, fulfilling their interests, living in dignity, and receiving recognition from the rest of the community. Many who are immigrating to this country, or who are trying to, are doing so because they seek our freedoms that don't exist anywhere else in the world the way they do here.

Even though the War for Independence was for freedom from England, and the War Between the States was for keeping the union together and to provide freedom for slaves, White folks don't want to hear about slavery. They won't accept the fact that Blacks would stop talking about slavery if White folks would stop romanticizing it and stop trying to return to Jim Crow laws. Until Whites, from both North and South, come out and clearly state that slavery and discrimination and exclusion of any kind of people are **neither** political choices **nor** cultural ways of life, but rather reflect pure, unadulterated evil, the conflict will continue.

Blacks don't seek equal results. Blacks are far more hard-working and dignified than that. We want equal access and equal opportunity. We just want to be in the race. We want on the track. Hell, we want in the stadium. Many are already in the stadium. I'm talking about the inner city Blacks who have not yet been allowed in. And I am also talking about those that are in that some are trying to kick back out.

You have two perspectives in conflict, each, in its own way, correct. One perspective, usually from Blacks, is that the slaves wanted to be free and have sovereignty. The other side, usually White, who were never slaves, has long been free, and can't grasp what the big deal is, as, after all, the Civil War is long over and the Confederacy is gone. But the idea of superiority over the descendants of slaves is not gone. Blacks who have been left behind in the inner city, Blacks who are still seeking their freedom and sovereignty, won't obtain it until they too have equal access and equal opportunity. The third view, of the antebellum South and the 20th century Jim Crow South, is the notion that Blacks were better off as slaves cared for by Whites.

Minneapolis could be so much more. And that is what I am fighting for. The notion of many that we can have this peaceful coexistence means that they don't mind being under the same influence and power of an idea that tore this country apart in the 1860s. The notion that a group of fellow human beings is inferior and therefore can be treated in demeaning ways is a pornographic notion, an evil notion, a destructive notion, and one that cannot be erased even by smooth-tongued hypocrisy.

When some people think of the Old South, they think of the Mississippi River era of barges and showboats. Well, the Mississippi River begins in Minnesota. Attitudes of the State of Mississippi work all the way back to the headwaters of the river. When people think of plantations, they think of bosses. Given Minnesota's claim to be liberal, and given its political history compared to the racism that still abides, it is fair to say we in Minneapolis live on a grand Liberal Plantation. The Minneapolis *Star Tribune* and the *Mlps.StPaul* magazine both wrote major pieces in 1990 on the racism here (Interludes 2 and 10). Over a decade later, it is still here, as a follow-up article in 2001 maintains (Interlude 10). And so, dear reader, I invite you to join me in ending it, in helping write a new and different Minneapolis story.

The East Coast and the West Coast are sometimes referred to politically by some as the Right Coast and Left Coast. Well, Minneapolis is on the Middle Coast. Common to all three is water, two oceans and a river. Minneapolis is one of many river towns along the Mississippi. I don't know much about the other river towns, except for Kansas City, but I do know about Minneapolis.

I trust, dear reader, that you realize then, that this is not about culture wars, the battle between the Left and Right on such topics as abortion, gun control, the death penalty, gender, and sexual orientation. Those are primarily the frivolous topics of white-collar, non-manual labor professionals. For them these are fun topics. But compared to those of survival and compared to the dignity and recognition needed to be able to pursue one's interests, they take a back seat.

When dignity and recognition and equal access and equal opportunity are denied, the pursuit of interests is also denied. And thus we are back once again to talking about the fairness of equal access and opportunity. When the Democrats can get Blacks to sign onto the culture war topics as a distraction from what is *not* going on for them in education, housing, and economic development, they are not helping us with our best interests. They have merely enlisted us in their culture war. That is not my interest. I'll not join that war until we have won the equal access and equal opportunity in education, housing, and job wars.

So, from my perspective, the Minneapolis story is the story of a systematic and successful attempt to deny universal fairness, access, and opportunity to minorities. It could be a different story. My hope is that the minority in favor of taking the action necessary to make Minneapolis open to all will become a majority and take over the writing of the Minneapolis story and move it in that direction.

Even more intriguing to me is the fact that many Whites also have happening to them what has happened to Blacks but can't bring themselves to admit it. So, dear reader, especially those of you who are White, see if your your story is here as well, not just the story of Blacks and other minorities, but the stories of anyone Minneapolis has not served as well as it could and should, in terms of equal access and equal opportunity.

So what makes Minneapolis Minneapolis? What are some of the identifying characteristics? Some are unique. Others are common to other cities as well. Here are some of the words that best describe Minneapolis: control; wealthy, tribal, parochial; big-league pretensions; denial of family succession; second- and third-generation timidity; racial exclusion; payback mentality; belief in the myth of homogeneous community; not a clutch city; has a tortoise-and-hare process, the former for the masses, the latter for the elite; and narrow-minded regarding its professional athletic teams.

The wealthy families on their plantation porches appear to want to control everything. The bosses feel they can do what they want. The results discussed in Chapters 2, and 7-13 suggest that they remained unconcerned unless something affects them. They don't seem to mind negative effects as long as they are happening only to the little guy. They have an inability to face mortality, acting as if they will live forever. There appears to be a denial of succession by these fathers of the 1950's, so that their sons have no loyalty to anything but the myths of the fathers.

Few of the wealthy families seem able to prepare their next generation. How is it that Carl Pohlad, billionaire owner of the Minnesota Twins, feeble and old, still holds on to everything even in his mid-80s, just as the travel and hospitality empire billionaire Kurt Carlson did, right up to the day he died? Why don't they trust their sons and daughters? Why don't their sons and daughters stand up for themselves? How will the next generation of these families act and behave, as they intermarry and eventually take over when their fathers die? Why have these of the second and third generation, who have been given so much (being born on 3rd base is an apt analogy), become so timid and ungenerous and unwilling to truly use the stewardship of their inheritance for the good of the current community, including the inner city? Why do they pursue the previous generations' interests of the past and not their own of the future ?

Will they continue to treat Minneapolis as their plantation, where they can do as they will, or will they treat Minneapolis as their partner, grateful for what it did for their parents and grandparents who in turn left so much for them? Will the leading families of wealth, Cargill, Carlson, Jundt, Biner, McKnight, Whitney, McMillan and other Minneapolis families serve the community or will they continue to want to be served, especially in terms of being served by the minorities? What negative effects will this holding on to death by the fathers have on the next generation? How will the dark fear of the second, third, and later generations who are viewed as not deserving play out? Will they show gratitude and give of themselves to fairness as a gift to the city that made their families rich, or will they attempt to show that they do indeed deserve it by wielding the power of their wealth so others may see what they can do, even if doing so has negative and deleterious effects on Minneapolis? And as so many of them have little or no contact with minorities, and especially with Blacks, will they continue to further push back and push down the non-Whites?

And how can the city claim to remain "big league" when it has the financial and political clout and muscle of local billionaires and millionaires to retain professional teams but won't lift a finger—or a dollar—to help keep what Minnesotans are so passionate about: their Vikings? And so the "The Stadium Game" continues. Even though the wealthy could purchase the teams and build each one a new stadium or arena, they refuse, as they nostalgically remember the glory days of being involved with Branch Rickey and expect others to make it happen. Fans follow suit despite the evidence of how much and how often baseball and the bosses continue to fleece them, and laugh at them, at the same time conspiring to kick out of town their favorite team, the Vikings NFL football team (Chapter 15).

Racial exclusion is another characteristic of Minneapolis. Check out this statistic: how is it that a city that is 35% Black had the potential in 2001, for an al-White city council, ending up after the elections with just one Black, and that an "accident"? How is it that non-Whites and poor Whites, despite their numbers, are excluded from opportunities to join the social, economic, and political mainstream?

Another characteristic is the payback mentality. When Hubert Humphrey lost the U.S. Presidency in 1968, he blamed Blacks and the riots that took place after Martin Luther King's assassination, as Walter Mondale would later blame them when he lost in 1984. When current Senator Paul Wellstone ran afoul of Walter Mondale over the nomination of judges that Wellstone wanted over those favored by Mondale, Mondale and the Democrats withdrew a lot of their support for Wellstone. They'll make him pay, even if it means losing his Senate seat, and even if it means risking turning the Senate back over to the Republicans. Payback winning in Minneapolis is often more important that winning elections.

Just like clutch athletes, clutch cities are dynamic and do what is necessary to come through in the clutch. Think New York City after 9/11, or San Francisco after the World Series earthquake, or Los Angeles after various riots. These are the proverbial the-tough-get-going-when-the-going-gets-tough cities. That is not Minneapolis. Minneapolis too often plays the little city that could but then decides not to, and then becomes the little city that could but won't. It continues to be out of step.

In the past decade, nearly 20% of the Fortune 500 companies headquartered here have left. The city has lost population to the suburbs. Minorities, despite being 30% of the population, are purposefully blocked, resulting in their continued under-representation in key positions. The wealthy families in charge can't see what is coming over the horizon, as the beautiful hedges they have grown up in their gated properties keep them from having to look at the real world, as they look out only at their lakes. They are unprepared for the future although they are meticulously prepared for the past. But they have their money. It is everyone else who will pay the price.

Think of how the city responds in two speeds, like a hare for the elites, like a tortoise for everyone else. By the time complaints are researched, processed, filed and refiled, what was complained about is completed and the perpetrators have moved on. Justice at tortoise pace loses the race. Decisions in favor of the bosses occur at the snap of their fingers. They win. If you, dear reader, are not sure of your place in Minneapolis, just ask yourself this one question: do you get the hare or the tortoise response?

Minneapolis wants to be the biggest and best, but only in what the bosses want it to be biggest and best in. Thus we have the largest university, the largest private company, the largest shopping mall, and still have a dozen of the top Fortune 500, and four major professional sports franchises (which will be three once the Vikings are finally run out of town). But "best" cannot be applied to our neighborhoods and community organizations of the inner city.

Under the chill of Minnesota Nice, which some of us refer to as Minnesota Ice, there is an amazing thin skinnedness of people who can dish it out but can't take it, and a stultifying air of political correctness that, in my view, is just a cover-up for not dealing with issues the powers that be don't want to discuss, like poor education for poor people, excluding Blacks, and dislocating Blacks and other poor from their housing, and denying them jobs and economic opportunity.

Now here is something, dear reader, that I don't understand. Why do so many activists expend so much energy trying to save the environment and animals, but don't expend energy to bring relief for poor kids, especially the Black ones, in terms of education, housing, jobs, and the ability of parents to earn enough in a 40 hour work week to put enough food on the table for their families? It seems to me that they are being fooled just as much as Democrats are. They see the DFL as the environmental party and the party of minorities, so they go along for the ride without realizing that the DFL is not serving their needs any more than they are serving the needs of Blacks.

Minneapolis has gone from wheat millers to wafer microchips. Both have been good for the overall economic growth of the city. Now I want us to go from unequal access and opportunity to equal access and opportunity. Even the *Minneapolis Star Tribune* has run a series ("Will Minnesota keep up?") about the energy and leadership of 40 years ago that has now dissipated into a vacuum without leadership. The series outlined how it was great then but not now. But if the parents won't let go and pass the baton of leadership to their children, their children won't learn and they won't be able to lead. That is why Black people must raise up our own community leaders, which we did in the election of Natalie Johnson-Lee.

As the *Minneapolis Star Tribune* series said, Minneapolis is a place with great resources that are not being leveraged because the city is stuck in the 70s and in denial about it. The city is in denial about a lot of things, including about being in denial. The *Star Tribune* series reported that we have gone from one of the best to one of the decliners. Why? Because the leadership with the financial muscle rests on recliners.

Please do not think, dear reader, that I'm being harsh. Despite the statements about being biggest and best as I note above, let's look at what even the Minneapolis *Star Tribune* has reported which verifies what I am saying. When we look at its March 22, 2002, report that Minnesota ranks as #1 state in terms of knowledge, the empirical reports earlier in the *Star Tribune* painted a different picture. Here are the facts taken from these two *Star Tribune* reports:

- Trend line is down: June US Commerce Dept study: Minnesota is **9th** in current economic outcomes, **12th** in intensity of technology base, **15th** on human resources, **17th** in capital investment, **27th** in per capita technology

- payroll, **29th** in funding.

- Other downtrends: **5th** in adults completing HS, **11th** in personal income, **9th** in companies engaged in high tech, **19th** in college grads (as share of the population, aged 18-24), **20th** in science and engineering graduate students (as share of population 18-24), **15th** in R&D spending per $1,000 of gross state product, and **20th** in technology employment, the percent of employment in tech-intensive industries.

- Still more downtrends: **27th** on the list of states for new business growth (1990-1997), **28th** on the list of states for postgraduate degrees, and **32nd** of top metro areas for high-tech industry.

- Minnesota, which once called itself "The Brainpower State," now ranks **23rd** in spending on higher education.

- 25% of the current work force is not sufficiently educated to be qualified for jobs that would pay enough to sustain the middle-class life.

- 20% of Minnesota kids live in poverty, according to statistics on the state web site.

Bottom line: Minnesota ranks **5th to 32nd** in key indicators, which means Minnesota is far from first.

Interlude 6

Dred Scott at Fort Snelling:
The Kind of "Being First" We Don't Want

Dred Scott is a name that will live forever whenever and wherever Constitutional interpretations are discussed. It is part of the history of why some fear the judiciary and others love it. As you will see in Chapters 13 and 14, the law has allowed redistricting in Minneapolis in such a way that it reminds us of Dred Scott and treating Blacks as being non-citizens. Can Dred Scott happen in Minneapolis? It just did, in Ward 5.

The Supreme Court used Dred Scott as the first major sustainer of slavery. It later overruled its own Dred Scott decision.   Hopefully, the corrupt Minneapolis redistricting (see Chapters 12 and 13), a new kind of first in turning back the clock on race relations, will also be thrown out with its same "no-citizenship-for-Blacks" view as the Supreme Court in 1859. When Scott fled the slave state of Missouri, he came to Minnesota. Slave bounty hunters took him back, having captured him here in Minneapolis at Fort Snelling. A lot of people in Minnesota tend to forget that Dred Scott was arrested here. It started here. We could have been the first to fight it. But we didn't. We need to fight the redistricting now. Maybe people in Minneapolis didn't want to be reminded that Blacks can be free. Certainly those doing the redistricting don't want to be reminded.

In 1846, Dred Scott, with the help of abolitionist attorneys, filed suit for his freedom in the St. Louis, Missouri Circuit Court. He had been born a slave in 1799, in Virginia, into the Peter Blow family. He spent his life as a slave and was not allowed to learn to read and write. In 1820, after much fierce debate, Missouri was admitted to the Union as a slave state, under what was called the Missouri Compromise, maintaining the balance of slave and free states: Missouri entered as a slave state simultaneously with the free state of Maine. In 1830, the Blow family moved to St. Louis. Scott was sold to a military surgeon, John Emerson, who took Scott to his various posts, including in Illinois and the Wisconsin territory, where the Compromise prohibited slavery in both. Returning to St. Louis, Dr. Emerson died. Scott filed suit for his freedom, based on his seven years in a free state and free territory. Mrs. Emerson didn't want to lose such valuable property, and fought it. The court ruled in her favor. Scott and his attorneys appealed, and the court ruled for Scott. Mrs. Emerson appealed and won. The Missouri Supreme Court returned him to her as a slave. The case was then appealed before the U.S. Supreme Court, which ruled that Scott should remain a slave, that as a slave he was not a citizen of the U.S., and thus not eligible to bring suit in a federal court, that as a slave he was personal property and thus had never been free. Dred Scott died in 1858, still a slave, never having been allowed to be a citizen.

In what many feel helped lead to the Civil War, the U.S. Supreme Court also ruled as a part of its Dred Scott decision, that the provision in the Missouri Compromise that permitted Congress to prohibit slavery in the territories was unconstitutional. This was huge. America was pushing west, and new territories were opening up. They all wanted to become states. But as free states or slave states?

This was the great battle between the abolitionists and the antebellum (pre-Civil War) South. For Northerners who had remained silent about slavery, the Dred Scott decision made them realize that if territories could be slave and Negroes could not be citizens, it might not be long before free states would also have to allow slavery too. As Abraham Lincoln commented on the abominable and base Dred Scott Decision and the "shocks and throes and convulsions" it caused in his famous "House Divided" speech:

- " house divided against itself cannot stand. . . .

- "This government cannot endure, permanently half slave and half free."

The "shocks and throes and convulsions" felt then about the Dred Scott case regarding slavery are felt now in the Minneapolis Black community in the redistricting case. We will not accept being treated as Dred Scotts.

Chapter 7

The Corrupt and Racist Education System:

Poor Schools for Poor Kids To Keep Them Poor: Clubbing the Cubs Into Inferiority and Helplessness: Stop the Clubbing and Teach Skills, Optimism, and Hope

Patience, and shuffle the cards.
James Baldwin

As a school system goes, so goes a city. Cities rise and fall on the quality of the education they provide their future workers. That education is determined by how the government shuffles the cards of resources. And for those in the inner city who get dealt out of the game, we must create our own cards to win with while we continue to work for the big deck of cards to be shuffled yet again, and for everyone, including inner city Blacks.

I interpret the recent plan to carve out a separate corporate island downtown, which I discuss later in Chapter 12, a further indication that the people in power, both behind the scenes and out front, have decided to isolate the neighborhoods further, sacrificing them and their schools in the hopes that circling the wagons around their precious downtown buildings will save the city by then relying on suburban schools and workers. The reality is that **only** education on one end **and** jobs on the other end can save the city, something which is not accepted nor appreciated by either the City or the schools' controlling body, the teacher unions, based on how they have allowed education to go downhill for minorities in the inner city, just as they have allowed it to uphill in terms of pay, benefits, and retirement in the suburbs.

All groups, and especially minority groups, need an asset base. No group or person can succeed without human, financial, and physical capital. All of this is now being denied the Minneapolis inner city wards where minorities are concentrated.

The struggle for schools to succeed is not about who is in charge but about loosening poverty's grip on the wards where the schools are. Schools in poor areas have fewer resources and a higher turnover of students, making improvement in their test scores more difficult. Add problems at home and you have the need to completely change the model used to instruct. Using a suburban model in the inner city is doomed to fail. Without providing all three groups—students, parents, teachers—with the appropriate resources, student lives won't improve nor will their education.

I've experienced this the hard way. My own big turning point in high school came when I went to my Guidance Counselor to talk about college, who turned out to be a Shove Counselor. When I told him I wanted to go to college, he just laughed at me and said: "You want to do what?" And he laughed some more. He told me: "You'll do vocational, Boy, that's what you were made for." In other words, no college. Not for my race of people. He shoved me off the higher education track..

Now we come to my favorite question: If this was said to me, to how many more was it also said? And to how many today is it still being said, followed by laughter in the kid's face, pointing a finger down, meaning lower goals. Indeed, White friends have told me that even their kids, if the counselor thought there was a problem, either with grades or behavior, laughed and said no, and shoved them in a non-college direction as well, telling them they were lucky that they were allowed to stay in school. In a phrase, this is how we club our baby seals, clubbing them into a sense of inferiority and helplessness. Of course, this helps keep them in their place.

I was lucky. Although my dad and his dad were railroad porters, my mother's father, as I've said, was a doctor and attorney. I was bound to study more, and I did. But how many did not because of being shoved out to keep them in their place: "You'll do vocational, Boy, that's what you were made for."

Is there any wonder why we are amazed when those who can escape do so? Is it any wonder that in Minneapolis, only 70% go to public schools, whereas South of City only 50% go, and that only 17% of the Black males of Minneapolis graduate?

But to get a true flavor of this, lets first be a fly on the wall in New York. If this doesn't make you a true believer, nothing will. This is a mirror of Minneapolis (and of how many other cities as well). Let's listen in to The New York Supreme Court's Appellate Division in Manhattan. Did you read or hear about the June 2002 ruling regarding funding for New York City students and their education?

The lower court had said that the state failed to provide "a sound, basic education" for the students, as required by the New York State Constitution. The appellate court overruled that ruling. And here is where see the power of words in defining reality. The definition of the situation by one court was the exact opposite of how reality was perceived by the other court. And it was not a close vote, as it was 4-1. Here is what they ruled, which should make your blood boil: that the State of New York is obligated *only* to provide a "minimally adequate opportunity." This is certainly not an equal opportunity. And how does this court of justice, the wearer of the blindfold of justice, define "minimum opportunity?" Very low, as you might assume: an eighth-grade education. And get this. The court said that that was already being provided. This means that the kids can waste the last four years in school and learn nothing. The state court finds nothing wrong with that. And isn't that one of the question of Chapter 3, whose Rule of Law, the people's or the judges?

The one dissenting judge wrote, quite profoundly, that this meant that the state had

no meaningful obligation to provide any high school education at all.

And is it me or are you also scandalized that only one judge dissented?

This lone dissenting judge noted the common thread in studies that show that to succeed in today's society and earn a decent income, a high school diploma is no longer enough; one needs a college diploma. He then went on to write that:

chronic underfunding, although interspersed with some years of greater funding, has also led to deterioration of school buildings, overcrowding, inadequacy of textbooks, library materials, laboratory supplies and basic classroom supplies, and, in some schools, even an insufficient number of desks and chairs.

Change "New York City" to "Minneapolis" and the same description applies.

The appellate panel in New York legitimized what one author called the state of education in his *Death at an Early Age*. This is what I mean by the clubbing of baby seals. Just like in Minneapolis, the state of New York will continue funding the polar bears, the wealthy suburbs, while it continues to club the baby seals of the city's public schools. In other words, the long tradition of the wealthy suburbs robbing the funds and thus the opportunities of the poor city schools may continue, legally.

This means that the New York State appellate court in Manhattan, all male, all White, has a different definition of fairness and of justice regarding who has to meet the state constitutional requirements and who does not, who the state has to be fair to and who it does not have to be fair to. For these judges, the schools serve the wealthy, not the poor. And now, in education, it is no longer 2002, as the schools revert to 1702, or 1802, or 1902, when few were educated and the rest were considered either uneducable or not worth educating. This is **not** how I define fairness or justice.

In Chapter 9, I discuss the concept of "minimum wage" vs. "living wage." Here we get a new concept: **minimum education**. It has been proven that workers cannot support a family of four on the minimum wage, although the pretext of both private and public employers has been that they can. But with education, we see New York ripping off its mask in a naked declaration not only of power but in a demonstration of how they will keep minorities in their place: with minimal education sufficient for the lowest forms and lowest paid labor, but no more. They will make sure there is no chance for them to climb the ladder of social mobility.

This also means that they are arbitrarily denying college education. Just like on the Plantation. All that the schools need do is prepare students for the lowest-level, lowest-paying jobs. That is all. As the three majority justices wrote

> Society needs workers in all levels of jobs, the majority of which may very well be low level.

Majority? Pure and simple, this is using education to provide *de facto* apartheid: no access, no opportunity, and no hope. As their schools are more than 70% of a city's schools are Black and Hispanic, then these judicial experts have singled out the Blacks and Hispanics, by race, to be the maids and gardeners and service sector servants for the Whites, as, by the definition of these judicial experts, Blacks and Hispanics are not worthy of a decent education, as they are of little value. So club them. This is racism at its most blatant and most vicious. And it resides in Minneapolis education too.

The litmus test for such judges should be sending **their** kids **and** grandkids to these schools. Indeed, even many of the teachers don't send their kids to the schools in the districts where they teach. And so, we have now come full circle with Brown Vs. Board of Education. Only now, the Board of Education is served, not the kids. Now, as it was then, education is for Whites. Blacks who get educated do so in spite of the school systems.

With a straight face, the Minneapolis school system calls the poor inner city schools, as reported with pride in the newspapers, the "Beat-the-odds" schools, as if the game is for a few winners, as in a casino, rather than for everyone who walks in. It is another sign of the travesty being perpetrated upon innocent children. In casinos, the games are set so that the house always wins something, no matter how much is won by the few. But always, the majority of bettors lose. That is NOT supposed to be what happens in the schools, but it is. When the Minneapolis School District says these kids "beat the odds," the district is saying they only expect a few to do well in their schools and are surprised when they do. How do they deal with it? By giving them a nickname: 'Beat-the-odds." In these beat-the-odds schools, over 90% are kids of color, and most of those are Black. Many affluent parents, Black and White, send their kids to suburban or private schools. Minneapolis schools are 90% minority, where 9 of 10 kids are eligible for free or reduced lunches. Although Minneapolis school personnel would say differently, given the results, I must conclude that these kids get clubbed by the adults who are supposed to be looking after them, and by "adult" I refer to those in the school buildings, those in the legislature, those in the teachers' unions, and those Whites in their voting booths. The Minneapolis district's expectations are so low that if a kid makes it, they say he or she "beat the odds." That is a travesty. In my view, leaving minority kids in public schools that graduate only a few minorities, compared to Whites who are truly able to read and write and do numbers, is a form of child abuse.

We have in Minneapolis, plain and simple, segregated schools. But worse, as it is accepted policy and is the result of policy, I have to call it apartheid. The press says we accept segregation. Yes, that true, just as we accepted slavery. Minneapolis liberals postured with great piety against South Africa and demanded that anyone holding stock in companies doing business there divest themselves of that stock. And yet, in our own backyard, our own city, we do the opposite; we divest ourselves of the kids themselves, of our seed corn for the future.

It never ceases to amaze me how few outside the Black community complain about this. We divest ourselves of our kids, club them, and then wonder why they wind up on drugs, in prison, or hanging out on the street corners, not only unemployed but unemployable. We have contributed to the short-circuiting of their development and then we blame them, when the blame is clear and shared by Whites, Blacks, and students alike.

And although there is plenty of blame to go around, Black and White, I am more concerned about what Blacks are doing to sustain poor education by supporting the DFL's education policies. How many young Black men are dead or in prison who could have avoided that fate had we fought for education for kids rather than just more salary for teachers who had either already given up on our kids or never believed in them in the first place? What is in it for Blacks when Whites understand how the rigging of education is to work against their Black students? And those Whites who protest my comments here and yet refuse to look at the statistical variations and not conclude it is the education, are just as bad, no matter how naive or well meaning they are, as they too blame kids and parents for to them they are too noble and pure to ever have it be their particular system or approach. For these, blame is never for the schools. What other organization do you know, dear reader, that gets away with this kind of thinking? Well, OK, the state legislature and City Council do, none of whom have to meet a payroll, as it's always paid for by the tax payer, where in a normal business they would be fired for these results.

What we have participated in is horrible. Poor schools for poor kids. Divesting ourselves of our kids. That is what the education system is: a place to club the cubs. That means that the system has destroyed many kids who are young and defenseless before they have a chance. It starts with the system clubbing them. The statistics I cite should both alarm and shame you, dear reader. They should alarm you because kids are the seed corn of the future and our abandonding them is the same as a farmer eating his seed corn rather than plant it. And the statistics should shame you because you have either bought into an abusive system that clubs kids or, even if you don't buy into it, have done nothing to change it. The cubs can't defend themselves and so get clubbed. The kids have no power. Those with power wield clubs. Where you have poor kids in Minneapolis, you have poor schools. Minneapolis has good schools for good economic areas, poor schools for poor economic areas. What more proof do you need?

Rather than address this situation and change the status quo, the NAACP and Urban League are too busy prancing for being the first significant civil-rights groups and are too busy upholding this miserable status quo of education by providing support for it, simply because they are Democrats.

How much longer will Minneapolis allow the schools to be consumed by politics and controlled by special interests that don't put the kids first? Why did parents once think of Minneapolis schools as the best in the country whereas today's parents are fleeing them? Because White flight has left the schools primarily Black and poor.

The National Assessment of Education Progress reported in June 2001, that "a third of America's fourth graders are illiterate." **BUT**, the average disguises stunning divisions: for **Hispanic** fourth graders, for whom the figure rises to **58%** and for **African Americans,** for whom the figure rises **to 63%**. *This is not simply failure. This is mass fraud.* And in an economy that increasingly puts a premium on skills, the system is condemning too many of these children to second-class citizenship in the American Dream. The problem is that the *soft bigotry of low expectations* is by no means confined to the teachers' unions and school systems; it also implicates politicians and parents. The reading advocates at Achieve Minneapolis, the Minneapolis Public Schools Title I department, note that in 2002, 70% of 6th graders at a North Minneapolis school came in reading at the 3rd grade level.

Note again the disparity between Black and White. Note again that **only 17% of Black males** graduate from High School in Minneapolis.

A person's success or lack of success in life parallels his or success or lack of success in school. The high drop-out rate needs to be condemned, not accepted, with a goal set of reducing it each year in 5% increments until the average is 5% or less, and then keep on working to keep on reducing it. School leaders who cannot achieve these goals must be fired. Start by telling administrators and teachers that we have changed the deal: all kids get taught how to read and write well, not just Whites. If they don't follow suit, start firing those same administrators and teachers and then watch how fast their replacements get the statistics to change. And because the education chain is 12 years long, K-12, with the upper grades inheriting the teacher failures of the lower grades, allow more flexibility, and over a three year period. In the first year, give the primary grades, K-3, one semester to show progress and 4-12 one school year. In the second year, give K-3 one quarter, 4-6 two quarters, and 7-12 one school year. Finally, in the 3rd year, all get just one quarter. With any who don't make it work, let the firing and the replacement begin.

Now some may say how this could be done with a teacher shortage. And yet there are as many certified for teaching who are not teaching, as there are those who are teaching, as our colleges turn out more than there are positions for. With the right incentives, high pay for high performance and being fired for low performance, the incentive would then raise teachers to do their best.

Now you might bring up the statistic that in 1902, one in ten U.S. adults (10%) could not read or write, and that only 6% of Americans were high school graduates. But that was 1902. Universal education didn't exist. And the numbers fit everyone, Whites included. Today's numbers show the great disparity, the still very separate and very unequal education provided to young Blacks.

Good education benefits everyone. It enables workers to read and write and contribute and be better citizens. For this reason, all need to be involved in education, including the private sector. The huge discrepancies noted above between Black and White (25% overall illiteracy tests for 4th graders, which further breaks down to 63% Black and 58% Hispanic) shows that both White and Black leaders, and especially the teachers unions and DFL party, are more concerned about their power and their pensions than they are about their students and learning. The statistics speak for themselves, clearly showing who is getting the best education and who is not.

Michael Cassidy made a great observation in writing about post-Apartheid Africa:

> As a result of the past, they have a lot of catching up to do in terms of education, training, learning, and how to function in a modern society as a whole, and as part of the majority.

The same applies to our own educational apartheid system. It cannot be solved in one generation, but it won't get done if we don't start now. And education is more than school learning. It is also about learning how to relate to others in their private lives as well as participating in the public life of government, beginning with voting. But how can kids develop that sense if they are being clubbed?

Martin Luther King, Jr. acknowledged as much when he talked about Blacks not being qualified but that they were qualifiable, through education and training. The key is to get Blacks, especially young Black men, qualified by whatever training is necessary. And throughout history, people have sought dignity, respect, and recognition just as much as they sought survival, food, clothing, shelter, and safe communities. The poor education provided by Minneapolis takes this opportunity away, on purpose. It is way past time to change the purpose.

In summary:

1. In America today, education is a disaster in the inner-cities, all across the country.

2. The education system in Minneapolis is even worse.

3. The education system in Minneapolis is a deliberate attempt to keep inner city kids poor and uneducated and not competitive with the kids in the suburban schools.

4. The education system in Minneapolis clubs the baby cubs and prevents them from becoming respectful and responsible American citizens.

This is the truth, and every one knows it. The question is this: will we continue to lead the nation in showing how to club our Black kids or will we lead the nation to demonstrate how to give them as good an education as the suburban schools?

Interlude 7

**The Good News on Race: Part II: From the 2000 Census:
The relationship between Education, Jobs, Housing, and Poverty
and Income and Prosperity**

A glass half full is still half empty.
A glass half empty is still half full.
Ron Edwards

To repeat what I said in Interlude 5, Census Good News Part I: the news for Blacks in 2000 is good. Given the odds and the roadblocks thrown up in our way, the news from the 2000 census is tremendous. The general advance of Blacks has been nothing short of spectacular. But there is still tremendous work to do, especially for young Black men. It will require work and effort, along with a willingness of the older generation of Blacks to stand up for values that can help young Black men achieve and ascend.

In general, for Blacks as for Whites, there is a connection between education (schooling), poverty (income), and housing (prosperity). And when you consider that we are only one to two generations removed from Jim Crow laws, these numbers are all the more exciting, giving us something to celebrate as well as goals still to aim for in America:

- Economic ascension correlates directly with educational achievement.

- Education is a far better indicator of socioeconomic status than race.

- Desegregated Blacks are more likely to prosper.

- The more diverse the community the better the public resources (schools, law enforcement, political representation, etc.) are.

- 1980: 50% of Blacks held a high school diploma.

- 2000: 80% of Blacks hold a high school diploma (this is an aggregate figure; when only inner cities are included the number is only 20%).

- 2000: 86% of Blacks, 25-29, hold a high school diploma, the same as for Whites.

- 1980-2000: the number of Black college graduates has doubled.

- 1990: 19% of Blacks lived in suburbs.

- 2000: 27% of Blacks lived in suburbs.

- Many Blacks are returning to the South, to suburban areas.

- 1990: 16 million Blacks lived in the South.

- 2000: 19 million Blacks lived in the South.

- 2000: Southern segregation is 15-20 % less than in 1980.

BUT:

- Too many inner city kids are still being left behind.

- 68% of Black 4th graders can't read at grade level.

- Only 17% of Black males are graduating from High School

- If inner city education problems are not resolved, these good numbers will turn bad.

- Racial residential segregation, the last hurdle, must still be overcome.

- Segregation remains acute in Minneapolis, especially North Minneapolis

Chapter 8

The Corrupt and Racist Housing System:
The Hollman Project: A Project To Exclude Blacks
Gentrification as a Return to Plantation Bosses:
Razing Black Homes and Then Raising White Homes in Their Place

The neighborhood revitalization program misses those most in need:

When the Minnesota Legislature created the Neighborhood Revitalization Program (NRP) for the City of Minneapolis in 1990, the goal was to provide an economic-development tool that would democratize decision-making at the grassroots level and concentrate on the needs of lower-income residents. But evidence compiled by the Tenant Issues Working Group, a coalition of eight tenants'-rights groups within the city, demonstrates that resources for the $20 million program were disproportionately spent on white homeowners.

Using data collected by independent evaluators commissioned by the NRP, the tenants' group found that from 1993 to 2000, 88 percent of those receiving grants and loans from the program were white, even as the white population in the city was declining from 78% percent to 65%.

Britt Robson, "The White Flight," www.Citypages.com, August 14, 2002

This history of Minneapolis is a history of immigrants moving in and moving up, with the first wave Germans and Norwegians coming in the late 19th century of, then followed by a second wave, this time by Swedes, Finns, Serbs, eastern European Jews, and Blacks, and finally, the last wave, the recent arrival of southeast Asians and those from Central and South America (known to most Whites as Hispanics or Latinos, terms that only a few of them actually use). Most move in and then move on. I find it interesting, then, that the recently proposed heritage walk for the new Heritage Park replaces four housing projects. From my perspective, what we have here is a nostalgic reminder of a past all shared but a reminder to me of the present and future: providing far more tax money for housing for Whites even though they are a declining percentage of the population. Whatever the intent, and White Minnesota-Nice Minneapolis always has good intent on paper, the reality is that Whites are returning to the city at the expense of Blacks.

Housing is one of the Big Three of education, housing, and jobs/economic development. I seek equal access and equal opportunity for all. To repeat: To be self-reliant, people need an asset base. Without human, financial or physical capital, they cannot prosper. It starts with education (Chapter 7). It is manifested in housing (this chapter). It is enabled by jobs (Chapter 9). Minneapolis has and continues to systematically deny these to its inner city poor, especially the Black inner city poor.

The Minneapolis story is also about the lack of universal fairness in the form of equal access and equal opportunity in housing. Is Minneapolis housing open to all or only to specialized groups? How has Minneapolis housing measured up for different groups, especially Black and White? How has it approached fairness and access? This chapter discusses the Minneapolis story in terms of housing, with its sordid stories of scandals and cover-ups.

When I say "through my eyes," that is particularly apt for housing. To my knowledge, I am the only one, until recently, besides the coverage in the *Spokesman-Recorder*, who has continually hammered away on the fraud surrounding the Hollman Housing Project. I have done so from the perspective of my position on the Minneapolis NAACP executive committee and as the Chairman of the Minneapolis Branch NAACP Housing Committee.

In 1990, the NAACP was maneuvered by Legal Aid to get involved in confronting the issue of concentrated poverty in Minneapolis. Legal Aid and the NAACP got 14 to 17 citizens together from a cross section of mostly Blacks and Hmongs. One of those was Lucy Hollman, who became the lead plaintiff. That's why it became The Hollman Lawsuit." Initially they sued Jack Kemp, Reagan's Secretary of HUD. They were suing about the living conditions and the toxic gasses (as the project, as so many in this country, was built on old brown fields, whether known by all involved or not; a brown field is land contaminated with toxins), seeking the dual goal of getting the toxic land cleaned up and getting new housing.

As the Hollman project was about HUD housing, every time there was a new HUD Secretary, the details on what to do would change. By the time they got to the negotiation stage in the mid-1990s, Henry Cisneros was HUD Secretary, under President Clinton. So it became Hollman vs. Cisneros. But the original lawsuit was Hollman vs. Kemp. On April 20, 1995, Federal Judge James Rosenbaum brought the parties (NAACP, HUD) together. They signed the consent decree known as Hollman vs. Cisneros. All kinds of wonderful things were in it. It started out with the judge ordering $117 million to be set aside for new housing and relocating 770 families. But then nothing actually happened. It is a great scandal this town doesn't want to admit, as it was all part of the national agenda of keeping Blacks in their place.

The Hollman project is not unlike what many minority areas became: a podium for grandstanding by political candidates, be these candidates presidential or gubernatorial, mayoral or city council. The North Side remains just that: a podium for political promises and payola. And the half-baked projects have been failures frozen in time, like Potemkin villages or Hollywood back lots of façades with no substance behind them for minorities.

As a result of the Hollman settlement, the four housing projects were demolished. They were supposed to be replaced with what are called replacement units for public-housing residents, to be built in Minneapolis and the suburbs. Nine hundred mixed-income housing units were to be built on the Hollman site, 300 for public-housing residents and 100 for the elderly poor.

Housing is important, especially for homeless children. Yet the NAACP and the Urban League colluded with the City (Chapter 14) in not following through on Hollman, including the impact of redistricting on it (Chapter 12). And because I protested, in my role as Chair of the Minneapolis NAACP Housing Committee, the Minneapolis NAACP relieved me of my position.

But now we have the big headline at the end of June 2002 about the McKinsey report that finally talks about public housing, but not in terms of fraud, but in terms of "oh by the way," meaning, pure and simple: cover up. Until recently, you would never know there had been any fraud. And the McKinsey Report disguises that fraud. So I am here to report to you that it is fraud.

The report issued by the giant consulting firm, McKinsey, is about Downtown and Minneapolis citywide. It reports that the Minneapolis Community Development Agency (MCDA), the Neighborhood Revitalization Program (NRP), and the Planning Department, spent just under **$1 billion** on housing. From this, the city has gained a net of **only 52 housing units.** That is the equivalent of $19,230,767 per unit. Let me repeat that: the equivalent of spending over $19 million per unit. The report also says that Minneapolis is 8,300 units short of its immediate affordable housing needs. Did the McKinsey report comment on either the costs or the fraud issue? No. And although the McKinsey reports notes that the money has already been spent, it does not address how those missing housing units should be funded?

Nor does the McKinsey Report discuss the missing files of Jackie Cherryhomes' office. The development files for all of this were kept in the office of Jackie Cherryhomes. When Natalie Johnson-Lee defeated her, Cherryhomes took the files and all of the evidence, except for a handful of files. The report also missed the fact that in all probability even these few homes would not have been built except for the fact that it became necessary to make it look like something was happening before the November 2001 elections. The McKinsey report also did not address communities of color or tackle poverty, which was part of the reason for these housing projects in the first place.

The McKinsey Report essentially said that the $1 billion for 52 units was costly because of the overlap of agencies, so it recommended the creation of a super agency to handle all of the tasks of five separate agencies, creating an office of Community Planning and Economic Development (CPED), which would have 400-600 city workers. Again, Minneapolis would continue its system of payola. It certainly doesn't take 400-600 people to plan for 52 housing units. This super agency would accompany the super downtown district. Astonishingly, no one is asking how five agencies could spend $1 billion and come up with just 52 units. Why just me?

To call this "organizational inefficiency" plus simple "cost overruns" is a cover-up of astonishing proportions, all based on a technicality (and people think only the Enrons and WorldComs engage in creative accounting and spending). And they would, of course, technically be correct. In this context fairness and justice are words that some don't want to hear, due to this kind of purposeful cost overruns which some would call fraud which, in a sense, it is. It is also what I call system of payoffs and payola to a wide range of developers and community people paid to keep everyone in line. Sadly, it is actually legal. So, if it is legal, then, technically, it is also not fraud. But any reader knows by now that legal and justice, legal and fair, do not have to go together, especially when it comes to making oneself rich, whether it be by cooking the corporate books or cooking the government books. And even if declared legal, can anyone honestly, in their heart of hearts, call it fair?

Some may think I'm being a crank, but wouldn't you be cranky if it cost $1 billion of taxpayer dollars (some local, some federal) to provide 52 units? Someone might think that Minneapolis is leading the way in showing the nation to use tax dollars to keep Blacks in their place by spending money designated for them on Whites instead, including the administration (White jobs) of taking care of Blacks. But in reality Minneapolis is just doing what other cities do. The July 2000 issue of the *Journal of The American Planning Association*, reported a study of 258 different projects around the country that showed how such cost overruns have been the norm for the 20th century (1910-1998). The average overage is 28%, with transportation projects being a gigantic 45% over in costs. Now this happens for two reasons. Developers and city planners both want to get the projects approved and save their jobs and they want to have opportunities to make significant extra money by doing this with selected developers and community leaders who can keep the neighborhoods docile.

The planners behind the public projects know this but like it as more projects equals more power, safer jobs). Most people (voters, tax payers) are not aware of such cost overruns. And because it doesn't make them look good, city officials and planners don't want to discuss it. As many of these projects enhance the political standing of elected officials, they aren't gong to blow the whistle either.

Now remember, planners always have the backup paymaster: the fleeced taxpayer. The planners and economists and transportation experts and promoters consistently underestimate costs to get projects started. But finishing has taken hundreds of billions more nationwide in taxpayer dollars for these projects. So a billion dollars for 52 units in Minneapolis is hardly seen as fraud. It is just doing business as usual. But, dear readers, if it looks like a duck, waddles like a duck, and quacks like a duck, it is a duck. And this duck, clearly, from the way I see it, is a massive *fraud.*

And so the cover-up continues. No outrage at the loss of funds. After all, it's *only* taxpayer dollars. To give the reader a sense of the amount, consider this: that same billion dollars, added to what the teams and their leagues would have contributed towards new stadiums, would have picked up the remaining tab for a new stadium each for the Twins, the Vikings, and the Gophers. Instead, it has bought 52 low-income houses at over $19 million each.

Second, it is my belief that the files purposely taken by Cherryhomes could answer a lot of these questions. I believe they were either shredded like Enron did or squirreled away for later use to keep track of who was promised what and who owes whom what political favor. We won't know until we see the files. And so far, neither the mayor, city attorney, or local media seem to care, as since November 2001, it has been only the *Minnesota Spokesman-Recorder*, newly elected Council Member Natalie Johnson-Lee, and I who have called for their return and for an investigation into their taking and their content.

Look at it another way: the McKinsey report says that there have been four attempts made in 20 years to reform Minneapolis city government. All four have failed. What can we conclude from that? In my view, we can conclude that the powers don't want it to happen, and have just gone through the motions to make people think something was happening, whenever they got restless, knowing the bureaucracy would kill whatever they wanted killed. And left out, again, are the minorities, especially the Blacks, in any reorganization efforts except to be squeezed.

I'm still having a hard time wrapping my mind around that number. Let's try again: a billion dollars for 52 housing units. Think about what has to be going on, and how, finally, we are back to the *real* goal of public housing: providing it for Whites.

Remember that it wasn't until 1935 that programs for good, nice, clean, livable housing began, for Whites only, when the Roosevelt Administration started talking about getting rid of dilapidated housing and bringing in new housing called Projects. In Minnesota, the discussion for such housing began with a group of Negroes (what we were called and what we called ourselves then) with Nellie Stone Johnson at the center, working with young students at the University of Minnesota. They raised the question of whether Negroes would be included in public housing, and they lobbied for their inclusion. During two years of meetings, they raised some very interesting questions and offered some very interesting opinions about what should happen, how it should happen, and who should live there. Sure enough, after construction started in 1939, and after the first units were opened, they were segregated, like everything else. And again: at first: Whites only.

Negroes were not allowed in until 1941, and that only happened because Nellie Stone Johnson and the League of Negro Women solicited the support of Mary McCloud Bethune, a great African-American activist of her day, who was a good and close friend of Eleanor Roosevelt.

Nellie also involved the Negro League with the Negro League of Women. These are some of the many organizations that have existed that have been lost to history. So they got Mary McCloud Bethune to facilitate a meeting sometime around late 1940 with Eleanor Roosevelt and told her what was happening. There were a lot of these WPA projects going up around the country. Cecil Newman (activist and founder of the *Minnesota Spokesman-Recorder*) was asked to be involved. Eleanor Roosevelt saw immediately what was going on. She applied pressure on Federal officials, resulting, in 1941, the first Negro family being invited into public housing. These were the housing development we always referred to as The Projects.

For their time, they were more than adequate and provided people with a sense of good housing and dignity. There were gas stoves, refrigerators, laundry rooms, etc. However, people did not realize that these houses were built on the tops of brown fields, environmentally toxic areas, ecological volcanos with radon gas.

In Minneapolis, by 1946 or 1947, buildings in Projects at the north end of Summerfield were beginning to develop massive cracks. I remember visiting friends who would take me down to the basement and show me all these faults and cracks in the walls, from the mist and the gases. This is why we believe so many people came out of public housing projects with cancer. Young men whom I knew who lived in The Projects died of cancer.

With all of that, you can imagine how that $1 billion could have been used to clean up. And yet the facts remain: nothing much has been done other than to spend $1 billion to bring 52 housing units on line, the latter done hastily before the last election, with most of the money going as payola to bureaucrats, developers, and so-called community leaders.

There is not enough safe affordable housing in Minneapolis, especially for lower income people. The high real-estate tax is unfair. Minneapolis needs to engage with the state to set meaningful, **measurable** goals for developing housing policy with fair housing goals including the kind of tax breaks other developments get, so that developers and others can provide decent, safe, affordable housing at a profit.

But you see, dear reader, that was not the real goal. The real goal was to clear out poor Black housing in order to allow for White gentrification. The handmaiden of gentrification has been corruption. You can read more about this phenomenon as this web site: http://www.sinica.edu.tw/as/survey/srda/english/subject/e87003.htm:

> The change of an urban structure depends mainly on its social-economic conditions. The development of cities, in the past, can be divided roughly into four phases, that is urbanization, suburbanization [that was the White flight of the 60s], counterurbanization, and gentrification– a new tendency that began in the 70s of urban development, which is defined briefly as the widespread emergence of middle-and upper middle-class enclaves in formerly deteriorated inner city neighborhoods [i.e., Whites replacing Blacks].

The bottom line: To achieve this development for inner city neighborhoods, you have to get rid of the minority residents in order to make way for middle and upper middle-class Whites.

Gentrification has really become just another word for neighborhood racial cleansing. Now I know, dear reader, you are going to say I am being harsh. But what else is there to call a practice that destroys the homes of Blacks, and then builds few replacement units until the Whites can gather up what is there? To add insult to injury, when the move-back process started, the Blacks who lived there before, who were promised they could come back, received notice that they were not qualified and thus could not move back.

Gentrification is clear-cut; it is also a way to make lots of money (and if $1 billion to build 52 units doesn't underscore that, I don't know what does). The Hollman scam was simple: Move out the Blacks, move in the Whites, and make a ton of money in the process. And hide the files that prove it is a scam. So what is the Hollman project? It is really a White developer's and White bureaucrat's redistribution of what was for Blacks to Whites, using taxpayer dollars?

Yes it is, which is why the Hollman project and housing are tied into the redistricting that creates a Downtown Ward separate from the neighborhoods of the Wards that once shared it (Chapters 12 and 13). The redistricting gambit takes away what was Black and makes it White. And the reason it will be all White and not integrated is because Minneapolis isn't integrated. So if it is going to go to the middle and upper class, it will go to the White middle and upper class, because that is the way Minneapolis works. And that is the plan.

One of the reasons there has been such opposition to Natalie Johnson-Lee is her interfering with the Hollman fraud. She ran her campaign on honesty and a call to have the Hollman project dealt with honestly. The biggest problem for her opponents is their worry that their days of not being watched may now be over. That is why they tried to gerrymander Natalie Johnson-Lee out of her district and have another election so she would be off the Council entirely. The powers are worried about her and any community group that supports her. It has been some time since Minneapolis has had a person like Johnson-Lee win who didn't first ask permission to run, and then apologize for doing so, let alone not apologizing for winning. She stands in their way.

The Hollman project bottom line is simple:

1. The pushing out of a significant number of low-income Blacks from North Minneapolis and replacing them with middle income Whites.
2. Tearing down projects BEFORE building replacement housing.
3. Saying at first that all who want to may return and then later labeling the displaced residents as ineligible to return.
4. Building 52 units, with most of the $1 billion pocketed by developers, bureaucrats, with so-called civil rights activists representatives acting in obedience to the Mastuhs.

You may wonder how I know. As Housing Chairman of the NAACP, I sat in on the meetings and followed it more closely than anyone else. This is why the NAACP wants me out as they are part of it as well (Chapter 14). You see, there were two maps laying out the details of the development for the Hollman project. The City's intent was for the public to see one map and then submit their real plans to the Federal government. Then one set of bureaucrats would fleece another set. You see, the Minneapolis folks relied on the fact that as the HUD folks are not a part of Minneapolis, they wouldn't know the difference when they made the map switch.

This came to a head in May 2000. The city went after Project Hope money for rehabbing in the city, assuming that this money would create jobs. The Hope 6 package was for $30 million. Council President Jackie Cherryhomes represented the city and had St. Louis contractor McCormack Barron start the project. But McCormick Barron didn't spend any money on housing. The purpose of Hope 6 was to help people of color and the poor. A key was to be job training. Talking about construction and jobs and training allowed Cherryhomes to counter my statements that it was a farce and a dead project. She talked about progress. I talked about what they were actually doing, but I was dismissed. As the game is played in Minneapolis, the public face is always about the ideal, not the real fraud going on behind the scenes. The ideal serves as a Hollywood street façade, hiding the fact that no real housing is going on behind the façade.

In my opinion, Minneapolis used an out-of-town firm, St. Louis-based McCormick Barron, to better enable kick-backs. McCormick Barron is notorious for being part of this scam. The map showed the public had everything in place, but the map in the book sent to HUD for Hope 6 showed the **real** shape, which was far less than what was shown in Minneapolis. The bureaucrats got $6-7 million of the referenced $30 million just to do their jobs. What a deal. And, as we have seen, all kinds of others have obviously gotten big chunks of that $1 billion reported by McKinsey.

On May 16, 2000, formal presentations on the Hollman project were made at a meeting at the North Side community facility of Pilot City. The map showed a purging of the buildings that were to be used by African-American organizations. Chuck Lutz, who is White, was replaced by Darrel Washington, who is Black, in order to give cover. Whites like to substitute to save White agent *provocateurs*. To get rid of Black housing, they put in charge those who are incompetent or dishonest. I exposed Hollman for what it was: to remove Blacks and replace them with Whites. In June 2000, Chuck Lutz handed out the book. I switched books with him, with his notes, and had the book with the real maps, so I could study it further.

And when I exposed this scam, what did the local NAACP and other Black leaders on the take say? Did they stand up for the displaced poor? Of course not. They called me the Black Rasputin. Isn't it ironic that it is I who believes in the system and not they? No one was raising questions. Cherryhomes did a beautiful job. She used her wiles and position to control the City Council and to control the male-dominated Black leadership.

This is but one example of how the powers that have destroyed so much of what was Black in terms of development economics, enterprise, and community. Today there are few Black businesses. There were more Black businesses between the 1920s and the early 40s than there are today. One of the top enterprise zones was displaced, relocated, putting two Black businesses out of business. The secret is that the Black areas and people are not relocated, like Indians on reservations, but just removed to fend for themselves. By not allowing Black construction (Chapter 9), everything is left to Whites, reducing Black businesses and housing.

This was the control scenario of Jackie Cherryhomes and her agent *provocateurs* who, until she was defeated in November 2001, carried the day. From 1995-2000, Jackie and the City captured the housing issue while working hard to *appear* as an enlightened center. They were comfortable with their level of corruption, because the whole city was. They were not concerned, for after all, weren't they getting rid of the Blacks? What is so telling is that not only were few amazed, but that most just sat back, smiled, and watched. Only recently has anyone tried to do something about it besides Natalie Johnson-Lee, the *Spokesman-Recorder,* and I.

Because too many self-appointed African-American leaders are corrupted, it is dangerous to Blacks and frightening for the future. Drugs and corruption are used as opiates. In the 1960s and 1970s, drugs were allowed to enter the city in greater number. There have been many stories regarding how it happened. Was it just criminals from other cities expanding their territory? Was it with the help of the CIA selling drugs to finance its operations in South America, as numerous sources have contended, or was it just a coincidence that it was a control mechanism to keep the Blacks in their place? Regardless, the bottom line is the same: Drugs flourish and the powers either can't stop them or are not interested and won't. Either way, Minneapolis minorities lose.

Minneapolis has the method down pat for compromising a community. The Whites were able to rule in South Africa because of Black informants and snitches. The same is true in Minneapolis. In return, they get to be in on the take, which can be as minimal as a guaranteed job to the more lucrative of being in on payoffs. In the meantime, poor Blacks have their housing taken from them, are dispersed from their neighborhoods, and their neighborhoods get taken over by Whites in the gentrification process. It is too bad that the Black community houses so many turncoats in the Urban League, NAACP, and church pulpits.

And now, there is another special interest group taking over in housing, and that is the mostly White GLBT (gay, lesbian, bi-sexual, transgendered) group, who so far are taking advantage of city housing dollars to regentrify the South Side and buy, refurbish, and set up numerous housing properties for themselves. Or as one woman wrote in a September 2002 issue of the Northside Information Exchange, "the DFL endorsement" and "help for officeholders and office honchos" is from a DFL "political machine" that is "drawing on the trinity of feminists, gays and lesbians, and neighborhood/nonprofit types." She quotes an analyst who says "It's the old labor side versus what I'd call the feminist and gay/lesbian/transgender side. And right now, the feminists dominate." My point remains: these are issues that should be secondary to completing what Frederic Douglass called "the unfinished business" of obtaining freedom for everyone.

The DFL is caught in a time warp. In the November 2001 elections, they supported all five openly gay candidates for the City Council but ran only one African-American candidate, despite the fact that the city is one-third Black. The new group for the DFL agenda is White and gay. The DFL is caught in their ongoing and obvious racism.

This distorted view of the DFL has led to more access and opportunity for the GLBT group and less for Blacks, as it continually promotes special interest and self-described White victim groups.   Each such group takes more away from equal opportunity and equal access for Blacks.   That tradition continues to this day with three openly gay council members, and two of the most influential members of the state, the chief of staff for the governor and the newly created position of Minneapolis deputy mayor being gay as is the City Council President.   Together, they are quietly taking over housing with City funds.

And how has this new special interest group used their newfound power?   By voting nearly as a block for the DFL.   They get the favored treatment the Blacks expect but don't get from the DFL even though they also vote DFL.   These gay City Council Members obtain city monies to buy homes, fix them up, and then rent them to fellow gays, particularly on the South side.   Thus, we now have another group whose leaders get city money to continue steering their members to the DFL.   This is not meant to say anything disparaging about gays.   It is merely to point out a DFL pattern of making sure the victim groups get their monies so the DFL can get their votes.   The gay group, mostly White, are now doing better in terms of housing than are Blacks, as Blacks are taken for granted in terms of their voting for the DFL.

Here I add the proposition that with the rising cost of homes, there may well be a place for using the concept of manufactured homes in order to provide affordable housing that could be used in both the city and the suburbs.   Certainly, given all of the different circumstances, it is only fair to offset market rate housing for the poor. The so-called affordable housing crisis has obviously had a sharper impact on minorities and helps to perpetuate segregation.   Either way, Blacks lose.   Of course the Feds have tried to get compliance and have tied $75 million in federal transportation funding into how cities and counties perform on affordable-housing issues.   But who will stop them when they don't comply, if so many, at all levels, are in on the various scams to divert those funds?   There is nothing wrong with the wealthy suburbs.   But there is something wrong when policy and money only seem to support the wealthy suburbs.

To put this in financial perspective, let's return to our discussion of minimum (living) wage and relate it to housing and our concept of fairness.   There is a wonderful web site of the National Low Income Housing Coalition (www.nlihc.org), which shows the statistics of the money needed to afford housing in different communities across the country.   The average minimum wage is $5.15/hour, but this is not enough to afford fair market rent.   Here is the clincher: The average American, to afford a two-bedroom house or apartment, needs to earn $13.87/hour.   At minimum wage, that means a worker would have to work 84 hours a week to be able to afford affordable housing. Thus, in a very real sense, government housing does not just subsidize low-income workers, it subsidizes employers who won't pay a living wage.

And let's not forget the report last year by the University of Minnesota's Center for Urban and Regional Affairs discussing how affordable housing has been abandoned for the more profitable market-rate housing, despite the availability of Federal funds through the 1976 Land Use Planning Act, which is not being used. The result is *de facto* discrimination against the poor in general and the Black poor in particular. In a study of 25 cities, the report found that **only** six of every 100 acres designated by cities for affordable, high-density housing actually got affordable units. Sure sounds like legal fraud to me. The Feds put up the money and the cities and developers use it for themselves, not for the low and moderate-income residents as designated.

For now, it is clear that the entitlement system is running amok, and now it benefits Whites more than Blacks. And those Whites are using city monies to displace Black project housing for gentrification of Whites, particularly on the South Side of Minneapolis. Why does the DFL run roughshod over the Blacks in favor of these White groups? Three reasons. First, Blacks will vote DFL anyway, so why bother with them except on Election Day? Secondly, these other interest groups are White. And thirdly, in terms of gays, they provide yet another group of volunteers to work the door-to-door campaigns set up to get out the vote for the DFL.

Finally, all of this is just the tip of the iceberg. The law suit recently brought against the regional Metropolitan Council chaired by Ted Mondale and against the City of Eagan by three housing groups may finally break the log jam of feet dragging preventing the following of the 1976 Land Use Planning Act that calls for providing affordable housing for people with limited income as part of any community's goals. The lawsuit is being filed as a human rights complaint. I think you would agree, dear reader, that 26 years is long enough. More than enough. Now, combine this action with the Hollman lawsuit, and tremendous movement becomes possible, as it will deal with thousands, not just the hundreds of Hollman.

And although the Metropolitan Council says it prefers its methods, it can't get away from the fact that its own figures show that they are only providing 10% of what they acknowledge is needed. But, if they can do the delay thing a little while longer, then the land still available for development will be used up and there will be no room left, a traditional stall tactic for the purpose of making sure the intent of the law does not happen. Indeed, even a study covering the last 25 years by the University of Minnesota calls the council's action "a missed opportunity of huge proportions."

It is time to get real. It is time to step up and use legal tools like this lawsuit to force compliance. If the Jim Crow laws were used to legally take away our freedoms, it is time we once again used the law to take them back.

Interlude 8:

"Torn From The Land"

A Newspaper Series on How Blacks Lost (legally stolen) Their Land and Wealth Since Reconstruction
Making the Case for Reparations For Stolen Land/Wealth, Not for Slavery: The Rediscovery of Black Capability and Black Capitalism

> This land is my land, this land is your land.
> Woody Guthrie

> Some will rob you with a six-gun
> And some with a fountain pen.
> Woody Guthrie

> In a sense we have come to our nation's capitol to cash a check. When the architects of our republic wrote the magnificent words of the Constitution and the Declaration of Independence, they were signing a promissory note to which every American was to fall heir. ... America has defaulted on this promissory note. ... America has given the Negro people a bad check.... But we refuse to believe that the bank of justice is bankrupt. We refuse to believe that there are insufficient funds in the great vaults of opportunity of this nation.
> Martin Luther King, Jr.

In the 1940s and in the 1950s, the African-American community in Minneapolis had a stronger economic base than they do now. It is important for the young to know how well Minneapolis did. It was harder and tougher then, and we were stronger. Too many have since bought into the notion we can't do it on our own. Before the turn of the 20th century, there developed, around 55th/56th and Humboldt Streets in now North Minneapolis, the important community of Humboldt Heights. The residents were doing well and wanted to incorporate as a town. The White Liberals blocked their doing so. The Jews had tried unsuccessfully to do the same along what is now Olson Highway, Hwy 55.

There is only so much that White liberals in a mostly White state will allow the non-White.

This Interlude will demonstrate three things:

(1) That there were **more** significant well-off Black communities in this country before the Civil Rights Movement;

(2) Secondly, jealous Whites destroyed them before the Civil Rights Movement; and

(3) We can build prosperous communities again.

Today Whites don't have to use torches, guns and ropes to defeat us. They have their laws do it for them as they have writ the South large by creating in every city a Liberal Plantation of Black workers. They do it in every state with the law, with the stroke of a pen signed by the President or Governor or Mayor, either on a legislatively voted bill or a singular executive order. Blacks, especially young Black men, need to know that Blacks have been just as entrepreneurial and just as wealth producing as Whites, sometimes more so, and that we need to get back into that mind set.

Much of this Interlude is taken from the three part newspaper series of December 2001, by the Associated Press, *Torn From the Land.* The subheading for the first piece was *"Black Americans' Farmland Taken Through Cheating, Intimidation, Even Murder."* Reparations should be paid to them. The three-part series was accompanied by numerous sidebars, graphics, and photographs, a multimedia presentation appearing on the AP Web site, The Wire. APTN, the AP's television service, produced a video report.

I'm glad this series exists so that (1) I can refer you to it, dear reader, because although the taking of Black land and wealth was first brought to my attention in an early 1970s series that reported the theft of 13 million acres, I have been unable to find the reference. *Torn From the Land* is an admirable replacement; (2) Without it many would not believe it, (3) it provides a tangible, historical, defendable case for reparations, a case far easier to make than the one regarding reparations for slavery.

A related incident appears in the movie *Rosewood* about Rosewood, Florida, a town that was more prosperous than the White communities surrounding it. The mostly Black population owned most of the land and businesses. The Blacks enjoyed more prosperity than their White neighbors in the shantytown of Sumner, who just couldn't stand that. So, in the first week of 1923, a mob of Whites massacred Rosewood's inhabitants and burned the town to the ground. The ever-growing white mob acted like mass murder was no different from baseball, to be enjoyed by children and grown-ups alike. In one scene shown in the film, recreating actual events, families are seen not only enjoying a picnic, the men gathering together in front of a burned Black man's body to take a picture meant to commemorate the day. Brutalized bodies hang from tree branches in the background. Their descendents should receive reparations.

The same thing happened in the same decade in the prosperous Black town of Greenwood, Oklahoma, outside Tulsa, Oklahoma, where the Blacks prospered more than the Whites, and the Whites couldn't stand their success either. Whites burned Greenwood to the ground as well (Interlude 13). Their descendents should receive reparations.

After the Democrats traded the Presidency to the Republicans in 1876 in exchange for the pull-out of all Federal troops, allowing for Jim Crow laws and the Ku Klux Klan, the Southern Democrats stripped Blacks of their offices, land, and wealth. Blacks were office holders in the states and counties and cities and towns. They were stripped of these offices. They had owned land and begun businesses. These were taken away, especially across the South.

After Reconstruction was repealed, whole generations of Blacks had their land, education, housing, and jobs stolen from them. Here again is where I see the case for reparations. And if the Democrats really want to prove that today they are as pro-Black as they claim, then they should offer an apology for their ancestors and lead the movement for such reparations, wherever they should be paid anywhere in America, whether by private or governments sources, depending upon each claim.

The key to wealth is land. For most in America, that means home ownership. This has been denied Blacks during most of their history in America, just as it is denied now to inner city Blacks in Minneapolis (Chapter 8). Rosewood and Greenwood, discussed above, are merely the more spectacular examples.

Slavery was legal worldwide until the second half of the 19th century, and is still legal in some parts of the world today. Not much room for the reparations argument there, but the theft of land and property was not legal.

Here is the case for reparations. In many cases, government officials approved the land-takings; in others, they took part in them and in yet others took the land for themselves. In others, the land was confiscated by the Federal Government itself, without payment, for its own projects. Some was taken for homeland defense needs during World War II but not returned afterwards. These, again, are examples that help make the case for reparations.

And by the way, we'll know our American leaders are truly against slavery when they stand up against slavery in other parts of the world, no matter what resources those countries happen to export (for example, oil from the North African Arab countries or West African Black countries). We'll know that key corporations, especially the giants of Minnesota, are also against slavery here when we see them stand up against slavery in the countries in which they do business. What better way to show the United Nations they mean business? The political Left's insistence on diversity and multiculturalism allows for slavery (today they would have had to condemn the North for attacking the South in our Civil War). The political Right is perfectly willing to allow the political Left to carry that spear so there is no interruption in their business in those countries. Both parties walk hand in hand.

This theft of land and wealth took place over a 200-year period. Pouring over records throughout the South, the AP reporters who wrote *Torn from the Land* were able to trace the land as it exchanged hands. Some of their findings were more onerous than others: one plot of land taken from a Black family and is now a racially exclusive country club in Virginia; other formerly Black land includes a profitable oil field in Mississippi and a major league baseball training facility in Florida. One of the formulas for success in America is one generation making something, even if just the homes they live in or the land they work, and passing it on to their children and grandchildren. Whites did this routinely, at the expense of Blacks and their kids and grandkids. Intergenerational wealth development has been systematically denied in ways ranging from the spectacular, as in Rosewood and Greenwood, to the simple, a sheriff with a fake tax notice, or somewhere in between, at gunpoint or using other intimidation techniques.

When you steal a family's property, you steal their future. The findings of the *Torn from the Land* series suggests that their examples are just the tip of the iceberg in one of the biggest, on-going crimes in this country's history. After reviewing tens of thousands of public records, the reporters documented land-takings in 13 Southern and border states, covering black landowners who lost tens of thousands of acres of farm and timberland plus smaller properties, including stores and city lots. And this is only what they can prove. Valued at tens of millions of dollars, virtually all of this property is now owned by Whites, both individuals and corporations. This too is part of a case for reparations. A national commission hearing from Black family records as well as going through more court houses, could develop what could be called a list for reparations reconciliation. Even more startling, as noted below, is that the takings of Black land has been far greater since the Civil Rights Movement heyday of the 1950s than before.

An interesting and very ugly side bar, according to the NAACP, is that most of the 3,000 documented lynchings (Interlude 15), were property owners. Fisk University's

Race Relations Institute says if you are looking for stolen property: "just follow the lynching trail." Again: a case for reparations is here.

Progress? Hardly. The title of the 3rd part of the series says it all: *In recent years, Black families have continued to lose land* as the takings continue, resulting in a 91-year decline in black landownership in America. This *really* helps the case for reparations. For example, in 1910, Black Americans owned at least 15 million acres of farmland, nearly all of it in the South, according to the U.S. Agricultural Census. Today, Blacks own only 1.1 million acres of farmland and are only part owners of another 1.07 million acres. This too helps the case for reparations.

Obviously, one big problem was that Blacks were powerless to prevent the takings in the decades between Reconstruction and the Civil-Rights struggle and even today. One example of the types of cover-up rendered was the torching of courthouses and their records.

The series quotes a person whose ancestors lost their land: "how Virginia's courts acted goes against everything America stands for." I make the same claim about North Minneapolis: how the Whites are treating the inner city Blacks of North Minneapolis goes against everything America stands for. It is time for the Whites of Minnesota, especially the young generations of the great families of wealth of Minneapolis and Minnesota, to show that they are true Americans and thus stand up for America by standing up for the Blacks of the inner city of Minneapolis. As the *Torn from the Land* series notes, lawyers and real estate traders are still stripping Black Americans of their ancestral land today, simply by following the law, which favors Whites over Blacks.

Since 1969, the decline has been particularly steep. Black Americans have lost 80 percent of the 5.5 million acres of farmland they owned in the South 32 years ago, according to the U.S. Agricultural Census. The law is what the states want it to be. As one put it: "All of the legal procedures of Louisiana law were followed." This too helps the case for reparations.

To me, this is a clear cut case for the need for reparations to help level the playing field made uneven by all of these events over these many decades, including those cases recounted in the Interludes.

There are two reparations arguments in America today, one centering on reparations for all Blacks because of slavery, and mine, articulated here, to provide reparations for the takings of land and wealth. Slavery was legal until the middle of the second half of the 19th century, world wide, and only a tiny minority of Whites in the South actually owned slaves (most Whites in the South were poor dirt farmers). Many

White Americans worked against slavery and many, many Whites died in the war to
end it.

As we Blacks in America have a per capita income 20-50 times those of Blacks
living in African nations, reparations for slavery means we would benefit from the
servitude of our ancestors. With that attitude we would be as morally corrupt as the
White plunderers.

However, given the actions noted in the Interludes, a very real case can be made for
reparations for the wealth and land stolen from Blacks in this country, that continues
today when inner city Blacks are shut out of a good education, jobs, and housing.
Many Blacks have made it. We need reparations for those who have been prevented
from making it by these takings of land and wealth. A National Commission of
Reconciliation and Reparations should be established to investigate and work out the
payments that would be involved.

Chapter 9

The Corrupt and Racist Construction Contract System, Resulting in Jail not Jobs: The War on Drugs as
A War on Black Men: Blacks as Inmates not as Contractors or Workers

Another Example of Black Corruption Selling Out to White Corruption

This chapter explores the relationship between jobs and jail and the war on drugs as a war on Black men. This is not the integration Blacks have in mind: jobs for Whites building jails for Black inmates. Jails have become construction jobs for Whites and residential facilities for Blacks. This is very wrong. This chapter also explores the question of why Blacks, either as contractors or workers, despite making up one-third of the population of Minneapolis, are practically non-existent at any of the construction sites building or rebuilding Minneapolis and St. Paul.

As stated before, self-reliance requires an asset base, like education, housing, and jobs. Oppression cannot be lifted without human, financial or physical capital. Minneapolis denies these to its inner city Blacks.

In one sense, this is the simplest of my topics. The data suggests, without fear of contradiction, that the war on drugs is also a war on the Black man, especially the young Black man, which is where this chain reaction begins. It then ends with prison contracts excluding Blacks in the construction of prisons but including them as inmates.

The construction contract system was meant to include Black contractors. It did not, with the exception of Black fronts of White investors and White workers, what could be called "Oreo cookie companies" (Black as titular head, a few Black secretaries and gophers, and inbetween them: White professionals in the office and field). It is also meant to enrich White contractors. The new jail cost $108 million. But it only added 96 beds. That over a million dollars a bed (do you see the parallel with the spending in housing (Chapter 7)?

But the war on the Black man didn't start with drugs; it started with slavery prior to the founding of the nation and continued after its founding under the Democrats. We won that battle, but the war continued. Reconstruction halted the war against the Black man. We won that battle too, but the war continued again when the Democrats traded the Presidency in 1876 so they could begin the war against the Black man all over again, which they did with a vengeance as soon as the Federal troops were withdrawn, the Jim Crow laws were enacted, and the Ku Klux Klan was established and turned loose, using lynching as one of the ways to take wealth from Blacks (Interludes 8 and 15), all done to keep us in our place.

Martin Luther King, Jr., discovered that the Mason-Dixon line extended all the way to the Canadian border. The battle against the Black man continued with the Civil Rights days of the 60s, which became another battle that we won, this time with the help of Northern Democrats, but the war still continued. In the first 350 years of this country's history, we were needed in the fields, and in the second half of the 20th century we were needed in the factories. Now we are perceived as not being needed since the Boss can't picture us as anything but field hands; he really doesn't want us in the house, so he really doesn't want us. Again, Minneapolis is an Upper Midwest outpost of the great experiment of how to keep Black people in their place. Keep them uneducated, destroy their housing and kick them out, ghettoize those in the 5th Ward who have no other place to go, reduce its size so it makes sure it has nothing to offer its residents, take away its economically viable portion that was part of Downtown, enable drug use, arrest us and move all of who are considered excess baggage off to prison or jail.

As minority firms in almost any city can confirm, age-long discrimination and economic road blocks for racial minorities and women have long been embedded in the process. The only way to level the playing fields for minority contractors is to sustain equality of opportunity. And the few who get a chance are kept from the real goal of all contractors: graduating from small time to prime time. The moral compass in need of movement is not only that of White contractors, but of government agencies as well, which have the oversight and the power to give contracts, that nonetheless do not follow their own rules for leveling the playing field. The only conclusion one can draw is that these DFL directed agencies aren't supposed to.

This is why I have concluded that the only association that seems to be desired for Blacks is to occupy the jails built by the White contractors. It is why I see the war on drugs as a war on young Black men, especially the poor of the inner city. Everyone's spirit soars when they work on what they enjoy working on. When society purposefully not only prevents, but also withholds opportunities for decent education, jobs and incomes through policies that allow discrimination and exclusion, it is the same as making war on them.

Gated communities are being created because those who have assured their place in society fear and despise those on whose backs they have made it, those whom they have saddled and spurred. We make inner city minorities poor, prevent good education, and then blame them for not being able to overcome the obstacles that have been put in their path.

And although it is not spoken of in the White community, the Black community sees the war on drugs as another battle in the war on Black men. Prisons are a growth industry. But Blacks are excluded here too, except as inmates. White contractors use White laborers, reserving Black involvement for the finished product as inmates.

1981 was a pivotal year in the war on drugs as a war on Black men. Let's look at it from a Black person's perspective. 1981 was when crack cocaine was first introduced into the poor Black communities of America. California's Democratic Congresswoman Maxine Waters has demonstrated a tie between the CIA wars in Latin America with their involvement in introducing drugs from Latin American drug lords into our cities. Why? Because the CIA needed money to fight the war in El Salvador through the Contras, a war that Congress would not fund. So the CIA got money by selling these drugs on the streets of America's inner cities. And as long as the drugs stayed in the Black ghetto, everyone won: the CIA got its money, the Contras got their weapons, Latin America dealers got their sales, and the Blacks were kept "down on the farm" in the ghetto, drugged up, robbing and killing each other or getting jailed. And if the babies were born crack addicted, that only meant that they were guaranteed to never grow up to amount to anything.

Note: This is not new. The British started the opium trade for the same dual reason: to keep the Chinese docile but also to become a huge market for the opium the British were selling. At one point, over 25% of Chinese were opium addicted. Mao's solution was to execute all who would not or could not go cold turkey to get off drugs. He killed millions. We are more humane. We flood the ghetto with drugs, turn its residents into addicts, and then just put them in jail. Either way, its racial cleansing. The greatest boon to Black revival in America would be for Blacks to go cold turkey on drugs and put all the energy into education, housing, jobs and economic development.

Let's look at the numbers. In 1980, in the United States, there were only 100,000 African Americans in jail. By the year 2001 it was 1.3 million. At this rate, by the year 2020, 2/3 of all young Black men will be in jail. Again, dear reader, we have to turn to statistics to help make the case: **76% of all users of illegal drugs are White, yet 70% of drug convictions are Black** In seven states, Blacks make up 80-90% of all drug offenders sent to prison. In 15 states, Black men are committed to state prisons across this country at a rate ranging from 20-57 times the rate of White men, depending on the state. In the United States in 2001, 52,000 people were arrested in the U.S. and jailed for smoking marijuana in public, up from 720 in 1992. Lots of jailing options there.

Now here is a mind-boggling number: the Substance Abuse and Mental Health Administration has shown that 12-17 year old **White youths are one third more**

likely to have sold drugs than Black youth, yet it is Black youth who get arrested. So even though Blacks make up only 13% of drug users, they are 35% of those arrested for drug possession, 55% of those convicted, and 74% of those sent to prison. What is the difference? The value attributed to the individuals. Blacks and Browns are set to prison while privileged Whites get rehabilitation programs. It's that simple. It's that racist. It's that unjust. It's that unfair. One need not dwell long on these statistics to realize we have turned our backs on our commitment to fairness, justice, and racial equality. We get it from both Republicans and Democrats. Is it any wonder Blacks are reaching out to the Green Party and evaluating other political options?

Clearly, this reflects a justice system that is racist, and that applies that racism to fostering Black poverty by providing a steady flow of drugs in order to provide a steady flow of inmates for a growth industry needing inmates to justify the expense of building jails and prisons. This in turn allows for a steady outflow of Blacks from cities to the prisons so that cities can be emptied of Blacks and regained by the Whites who left them during the fearful White-flight days of the 1960s and 1970s.

This is all part of the racial cleansing of neighborhoods I discussed in the previous chapter. If Blacks are gone, they are gone, making it easier for Whites to regentrify.

This is also why privatizing prisons is a terrible idea. Privatizing prisons means they have to make a profit. To make a profit, they have to be full to capacity. What happens if there is a drop in crime and arrests? These prisons fail to make money for their stockholders. If public, they could be shuttered until needed. If private, they need always be full, constantly and forever or they go bankrupt. Where best to get a supply of inmates to make sure they are profitable, than the young Black men of the inner city? Note: This too is not new. Ships in the 18th and 19th centuries, especially in California ports, used to "Shanghai" men, usually by drugging them, in order to have shipmate workers on board for long sea voyages.

Visit http://www.nytimes.com/2002/07/18/opinion/18HERB.html?todaysheadlines to get a good perspective on the craziness, stupidity and destructiveness of many drug laws; the godfather of many of them was Nelson Rockefeller trying to show how tough he was when he was a Governor wanting to be President. The Rockefeller legacy, pushed through the New York State Legislature, is still as wrongheaded an approach to crime and drug addiction as you can get, albeit a simple approach: jail them, and often for life. They thought it would scare people straight. Remember, 70% of drug users in America are White but 70% of those sent to jail are Black, and in New York, the figure is higher: 94 percent of the people doing time for drug offenses in the state of New York are Black or Hispanic. The system of sentencing is so corrupt that nonviolent low-level drug offenders are sentenced to prison terms that are longer than those served by some killers and rapists. Consider this: compare

New York's college and incarceration numbers for young Black and Hispanic/Latino men: more become inmates each year than become college graduates. And although I am not for legalizing drugs, I am for decriminalizing them, treating them as worthy of fines as we do for underage smokers and drinkers or for those who get drunk.

Lets face it; marijuana was not always the boogeyman. Before the end of Prohibition, Congress heard testimony from the American Medical Association regarding the medicinal value of marijuana. Then Prohibition ended and Congress got a different story. From John Anslinger, the head of the government's prohibition "G" men. His most famous subordinate was Elliot Ness, of *Untouchables* fame. But with Prohibition over, what was Anslinger going to do with all of his Prohibition agents? And his empire? Answer: go after another substance besides alcohol. A Mexican in Texas got into a fight outside a bar and killed his opponent. They found marijuana in his pocket. With this, Anslinger turned it into "the devil weed" and testified to Congress that unless his agents went after marijuana users, America's youth were doomed. Congress appropriated money and once again a bureaucrat kept his empire, turning all of his booze barrel breaking agents into narcotics agents. At first, it was primarily a fun war against those from South of the border. After the 60s, narcotics agents went after counter-culture Whites on drugs and Blacks. And in the 80s the inner cities were introduced to crack cocaine for the first time and the assembly line to fill the jails and empty the inner city ghettos began.

It gets worse: to achieve this policy of keeping Blacks in line, the Black families had to first be destroyed. The welfare policies that achieved this were developed by Democrats who put more faith in the State than in its individual citizens or in communities and their neighborhoods. Fathers are the backbones of families. 91% of those in jail had no dads at home when they were growing up. In 1920, 90% of Black fathers were at home; in 1960, the figure was 80%. By 2001, the number had fallen to a staggering 32%. No dads, no discipline. But feminists of the Left still support these denigrating, anti-male social welfare policies. Pregnancies, suicides, and most other negative variables are the result of no dads being at home, providing perfect fodder for prisons.

Thus, the policy seems to be to give them drugs and guns so they can kill each other, and then we take those left and send them to prison. And what a *great* solution, as once they are released, they will commit crimes, provide work for the vast therapeutic bureaucracy of social workers, who are also tied into the Democrats. Then, as the recidivism rate is over 80%, they return to prison, assuring a high rate of inmates. The true policy is not to solve the problem but to maintain it through containment. There are also reports that religious programs in prisons help reduce this but they are not adopted by politicians on the left due to their obsession with separation of church and state.

Minneapolis needs to know there is only one jail project that counts, and that is the program that helps kids grow up right so they do not become candidates for jail. That means Whites have to give up the notion that Blacks are jailbait and include Black contractors and hire Black workers. But as long as Black organizations such as the NAACP and the Urban League, and so-called Black leaders, including Black pastors and community center individuals, serve the interest of the Mastuhs, and don't work directly to end the discrimination and horrible consequences of racism in education, housing, and construction hiring, the corruption will remain in place and young Black men will remain on track for jail.

The crux of the matter, as with all societies, is how best to harness the energies of young men. Reports show that girls are doing much better than the boys. Right now, we feed the disdain of young men for education. Instead of educating our young men, we import educated immigrants from India, Pakistan, Indonesia, Taiwan, Hong Kong, and certain countries in Africa and South America. We don't want to work with *our* colored but we'll bring *other* coloreds in from around the world who are already trained. Of course, they are free. Their countries trained them and paid for their training. So the irony is that we continue to bring in coloreds from other countries, hastening the time when Whites will be the minority in the U.S. If we want to get the best from our own people, we need to educate poor Blacks and Whites as well.

But don't older men in positions of power actually fear young males of any race? Indeed, people believe the stereotypes that we hear that Black and Brown young men are aggressive and macho, whereas Black and Brown young women are sweet and good-natured. Racism and sexism all in one sentence. We alienate our young Black and Brown men academically and shove them over the edge into the economic underclass, while offering a hand to their Black and Brown sisters, who are not considered aggressive and macho. It is as if society is saying that we fear the boys but not the girls. It is time to embrace these young men and make them partners with us, not outcasts.

As Americans, we lead the world in so many things, in so many ways. We must also lead our own, not just those who, although educated, do not have the same allegiance to our country, and who often feel the U.S. is merely a place to take advantage of, not a place to set down roots and become American. In an age of diversity where the emphasis is E Unum pluribus (out of one land many loyalties), not our founding E pluribus Unum (out of many, one), when we salute those not like us and bring them here, even when they wish us ill, we sow the seeds of our own destruction.

The need for Congress to increase the immigration quotas for trained individuals is one of the most damning testimonies to the horrible state of American education and the plantation mentality of inner city education policies of the Democratic Party and their allies in corporate America and in the teachers' unions, who, together, emphasize educating suburban Whites but not the urban Blacks and Browns. And why not? As long as the Blacks and Browns put up with it and continue to vote for their Democratic and teachers' union overlords, where is the incentive for these overlords to educate them, especially when they have declared that Blacks and Browns can't make it on their own anyway, and should just bow and answer "yessah, Mastuh?"

It is time to end the war on Black men, especially young Black men. And the first step is to bring them into the educational mainstream so they can enter the economic mainstream. Anything less is a statement that Blacks are inferior and should stay uneducated and impoverished at the bottom of the economic ladder and fill the empty jail beds to make profits for their shareholders. I categorically reject this. Educating and training young Black men, rather than casting them out, will stop creating new recruits for street crime and help those against them end their irrational and counterproductive fears of the poor, especially Black poor. We solve society's problems by creating ways for all workers to earn enough to raise their families. And we can start that by adding young Black men to those hired, in significant numbers, for the construction jobs in Minneapolis. We need a Jackie Robinson moment in hiring in construction in Minneapolis.

This will not just go away. People are at the end of their rope. A major forum was held in Minneapolis at the Sabathani Community Center on Saturday, August 3, 2002. You can read the full story not, of course in the *Star Tribune* or other White papers, but in the Black *Spokesman-Recorder* of the Thursday, August 8-14, 2002 edition.

If people wonder why Blacks in Minneapolis are hot under the collar, this meeting will stop the wondering. The law is being broken on every construction site, and the city and state are standing by and letting them. 35% of Blacks make up Minneapolis and virtually none work on these multi-million dollar projects. The stories of discrimination, lies, and other obstructions offered up to block participation have obviously pushed people to the breaking point. When you can't get a job in your trade to feed your family just because you are Black, hope is killed and social unrest is fostered. Even Black churches usually hire only White contractors, as that is how their leaders stay in the game.

And yet, despite the turn out of high powered officials, nothing has been done about it by these officials. Those in attendance included Mayor R.T. Rybak, City Council Member Dean Zimmerman, representatives from the offices of Senator Paul Wellstone, the Metropolitan Council, the Minnesota Department of Human Rights, the Minneapolis and St. Paul Urban Leagues, and such faith based groups as MICAH/ISAIAH, Sabathani Life Skills, and the African American Men Project, as well as folks from the trade unions and contractors). Progress? None.

Some people were very eager to gain information to show the projects were not in compliance, i.e., not following Federal, state and city laws regarding including Blacks as workers. That was when it was my turn to offer my suggestions. You see, I don't believe that when the fox is left in charge of the hen house, he will do anything but eat the hens. Any figures eventually received, assuming they are even provided, will be bogus. The Bosses, government and corporate, are in the habit of cooking the numbers. They will certainly cook them on us. I outlined several steps I believe should be taken, and I share them now with you, dear reader, in the hopes that whether you live in Minneapolis or some other city, they will help provide inspiration and specific steps to correct this oppression of Black people in our city:

1. Certainly try to get the numbers, but have them certified; don't take their word for it.
2. Join with those who would unite and demand a Federal grand jury investigation.
3. Present the wealth of information already available to City Hall to let them know you know what you are talking about.
4. Demand, politely or through legal injunction, to get the city to state why they allow projects to continue that are not in compliance.
5. Demand, politely or through legal injunction, to get the city to state why they hire contractors with records of not being in compliance.
6. Continue to hold public forums.
7. Continue to come up with plans of action to foster success.
8. Continue to agree on who will carry out the various steps of the plan and then do so.
9. Stop being patient with practices that have gone on since the 1960s.

And there you have it. Marching and protesting are not enough. They just laugh at us. We need to have the information and we need to demand that the city and state follow the law, and bring the Federal government in to investigate the city and state if they won't follow the laws.

As I told the group, and as I could end every chapter in this book: if we really want to give our children a future, we will make noise now. Jim Crow used the law to take our freedoms. Let us use the law to take them back.

Let us not forget the situation we are in. To use the title of Jawanza Kunjufu's book, we are in a *State of Emergency: We Must Save African American Males.* * Any time you falter in the 9 steps above, use these points from Kunjufu's book (pp. 1-20) to remind you of what is at stake:

- If one of every three White males were involved in the penal system, White America would declare a state of emergency.

- If 80% of the White children in special education classes were male, White America would declare a state of emergency.

- If there were three White females for every one White male on college campuses, White America would declare a state of emergency.

- If White women had the life expectancy of African American males—65 years—White America would declare a state of emergency. White women: 79 years.

- If one of every 12 White males in Washington, D.C. were a victim of homicide, White America would declare a state of emergency.

- If AIDS was the number one killer of White males, White America would declare a state of emergency.

- If Whites were 13% of the population, but comprised 35% of drug arrests, 55% of drug convictions, and 74% of drug prisoners, White America would declare a state of emergency.

- If Whites comprised 17% of drivers on the Maryland state highway, but 70% of drivers were stopped by the police, White America would declare a state of emergency.

- If prosecutors sought the death penalty 70% of the time when a White person killed an African American, but only 19% of the time when it was reversed, White America would declare a state of emergency.

- If 40% of White males were illiterate in America, White America would declare a state of emergency.

- If Whites were 13% of the population, but 50% of those waiting on death row, White America would declare a state of emergency.

- If Whites were 13% of the population, but 67% of the juveniles in adult courts and 77% of the juveniles in adult prisons, White America would declare a state of emergency.
- If only one of very 13 White babies were born out of wedlock in 1965, but seven in every ten in 2001, White America would declare a state of emergency.
- If the life expectancy of White males in Washington, D.C. was only 57 years, and there was no state with a White male life expectancy greater than 70 years, White America would declare a state of emergency.
- If Whites represented 84% of crack cocaine convictions, White America would declare a state of emergency.
- If two of every three White males were projected to be involved in the penal system by 2020, White America would declare a state of emergency.
-

As Kunjufu asks, as all this is true in Black America, are we going to rise up and declare a state of emergency?

State of Emergency: We Must Save African American Males, African American Images Press, Chicago, Illinois, 2001, www.AfricanAmericanImages.com

Postscript of October 3, 2002: Black Men need not apply

To put this chapter in different words: Minneapolis doesn't want to hire Black men. Period. All city and Federal construction projects are supposed to. They don't. Minneapolis is not in compliance because it doesn't believe in compliance. There is no push for it from the city. You destroy a man by not letting him get a job. That is the goal: destroy the Black man. He can't raise a family without a job. Its the price Minneapolis is willing to pay to keep us in our place. For over a year we have been trying to get the city to give us compliance numbers. Natalie Johnson-Lee, when told by the Department that they couldn't provide the numbers, ordered them to come to the meeting of her Health and Human Services Committee, October 3, 2002, and state so publicly and in writing. And that is what happened. On October 3, 2002, the head of the Minneapolis Civil Rights Department admitted she had no information regarding compliance in construction and no information regarding the Civilian Review Authority. The Minneapolis Story just keeps on writing itself new verses to the same old song. And the tune isn't pretty. And compliance in Minneapolis for minorities isn't just about American home grown Blacks, as it now also includes a large contingent of Somalis. If you read only the Star Tribune, you remain ignorant. But if you read the *Spokesman-Recorder* or *The City Pages*, you receive a full reporting of this travesty of boss city government.

Interlude 9

Jobs and the Search for Dignity and Respect:

HBO movie on the Pullman Porters:
10,000 Black Men Named George

Back before social engineering was the rule, Blacks went to work as railroad engineers and workers. Both my grandfather Edwards and my father worked as Pullman porters. The inventor and manufacturer of the Pullman sleeper car was George Pullman. Note his first name: George. For my grandfather, father and 10,000 others, George became the new first name of each Black porter. That it happened is one thing. But that so many passengers from East to West, North to South, all participated in the same denigration is one of the low points in the history and dignity of Americans, low in terms of how Whites acted. It is further evidence of the racism of Whites across the country and their continued efforts to keep us in our place. It was meant to be humiliating. And yet these 10,000 porters maintained their dignity despite being called George. But my father said they never let it put them down. For every "George" they got they just smiled back, and to them each smile meant something like: "You are such an idiot." Among themselves, they were able to develop a triumphant sense of solidarity.

The HBO video *10,000 Men Named George* first aired in 2001. The story focuses on A. (Asa) Philip Randolph and his 12-year struggle to unionize the railway porters in the 1920s and 1930s. This was before the AFL or CIO invited Blacks to join. But Randolph was more than just a labor organizer; he was also a civil rights and social justice activist. Some call him the Godfather of the Civil Rights Movement, as he laid its foundation and taught Martin Luther King. Jr. and Adam Clayton Powell. Randolph fought for a living wage and dignified working conditions for the porters. He also helped persuade President Harry S. Truman to ban racial discrimination in the military and he conceived of the March on Washington for Jobs and Freedom in 1941, to protest discrimination in Federal employment. When FDR signed an executive order banning such discrimination, the march was called off. However, it finally came to fruition in Martin Luther King, Jr.'s march in 1963.

The film can also be seen at as a lesson in how a few powerless but dedicated men can literally move mountains. The Pullman Company was one of the largest employers of Blacks in the United States and one of the most powerful companies in the country. Yet Randolph fought back against tremendous opposition to organize. To him, it was a battle to improve working conditions that he also felt was a civil rights and social justice issue.

This story is an important one, especially for young Black men, many of whom feel defeated. They need to see how one person, A. Phillip Randolph, could leave his imprint, all in the face of daunting power, as the full weight of society pitted against him: violence, bribes, and government efforts to thwart his efforts to organize the Black porters on the nation's passenger trains. He forced the powerful Pullman Company to recognize the union, the Brotherhood of Sleeping Car Porters, the first African-American labor union, in 1937.

What Randolph achieved was historic for another reason: he negotiated the first contract ever given to a group of Black American workers. Pullman is said to have tried to save face, after losing the battle to prevent unionization, even having used thugs to beat up the leaders, when he said: "A man who won't meet his own men halfway is a damn fool!" He was pulled kicking and screaming to that halfway point. To commemorate this great achievement, there is a permanent exhibit at the A. Philip Randolph Pullman Porter Museum and Gallery on South Maryland Street in Chicago. Interestingly enough, *10,000 Black Men Named George* was the last project of Stan Margulies, who decades earlier helped bring Alex Haley's *Roots* to TV in that epic series.

Chapter 10

The University of Minnesota: Burying the Truth and Losing Its Soul: The Case of Luther Darville: Scapegoat

The University of Minnesota looms large in Minneapolis and in the state. It is an 800-pound guerilla that sits anywhere it wants. Most of the powers in business and politics in Minneapolis are graduates of the University of Minnesota. The University is like Lola in the musical *Damn Yankees*: Whatever the University wants, the University gets. The only competition the University has is in football attendance with the Minnesota Vikings. The University is the only Big 10 team that has to contend with an NFL team. But soon the Vikings will be gone (Chapter 15), and the last attendance competitor will be gone, and the University will finally get its own campus football stadium, at taxpayer expense.

The University of Minnesota does not even realize that it has lost its soul. I became aware of it when it never treated Sandy Stephens fairly (Stephens died in June 2000, God rest his soul). Sandy was a hero to all of us. He led the University to a national championship in 1961, and a Rose Bowl victory in 1962. He was the first Black All-American First Team Quarterback in history. He excelled in five positions (quarterback, punter, punt returns, kick-off returns, defensive back). He played both offense and defense. He is on the University of Minnesota All Century Team, is one of the Star Tribune's 100 All Century Top Sports Figures, and is on the Rose Bowl's Hall of Fame Team.

In the 1950s, when University of Minnesota Head Football Coach Murray Warmath got tired of losing to teams with top Black players, he went against the grain at the University and went after top Black athletes himself. When Warmath brought Black players on campus, he was hung in effigy and had his car and home pelted with nasty things. His Black players were also treated horribly. But the team went from its worst year to its best year. Warmath, who was revered by his Black players, and Stephens helped build a full Black-White partnership in the University community. Sandy played with guys like Mike Wright, Judge Dickson, Bill Munsey, and others. But after Warmath and Stephens, the University slipped back, and it has not returned.

Sandy received a total of 59 scholarship offers, including eight from the Big 10 schools. In 1961, he was the Most Valuable Player in the Big 10, 4th runner up for the Heissman Trophy, and Outstanding Opponent – All Sports – University of Oregon. And he was on the following All-American First Teams: CONSENSUS, LOOK, API, UPI, NEA, *Sports Illustrated*. In 1962, he was the Most Valuable Player at the Rose Bowl; played in the All-American Game; and in the Hula Bowl.

Sandy's personal theme was "head bloodied, but still unbowed." After an automobile accident three years after college, Sandy was told he would never walk again. But he followed his personal theme, Head Bloodied But Still Unbowed. He recovered. He turned out for the NFL, but the NFL wasn't ready for a Black signal caller who called his own plays (Johnny Unitas had done so, but he was White; the idea that a Black could was incomprehensible to the NFL of that day).

My point about Sandy is a simple one: after all he brought to this state, when he fell on hard times later in life, the city and state would give back little to him. If Minneapolis could do that to Sandy, their star, what about the rest of us Blacks who are unknown and not filling stadiums? The different Interludes tell us.

All of this serves as prelude to the story of Luther Darville. As we shall see, the University continues to accept Blacks for what they can do for them in athletics but not as people. There is an overrepresentation of Blacks in athletics but not in the general student body. Boosters bolster Black athletes with money under the table for games but not jobs afterwards for life. The plantation racism against players on a liberal campus is the temporary good life provided to Black students as long as they play.

The Luther Darville story could not have happened had the University not lost its soul. We saw the same dynamic in the story of that other scapegoat, Clem Haskins, the Head Basketball Coach. Good people like Clem and Luther are sacrificed. Because many of the Black athletes felt alone and marginalized on this overwhelmingly White campus, they often talked to me about their problems. I talked to them, and I talked with others in the Minneapolis community who could work with them and help them. Many were poor, unable to afford going home for holidays or family emergencies. In these situations, Luther provided them with money to do so.

Luther Darville's problem, as we shall see, came as a result of his work with the football team. But he worked for both the Football and Basketball coaches. Like Darville, who worked for the University from 1984-1988, Clem Haskins, who was Basketball Coach from 1986-1999, was Black. Haskins went from a highly respected coach and person some thought could run for governor, to cast out. And yet he had achieved far more than any basketball coach before him. Clem took the University of Minnesota basketball program to another level of national prominence. His ability enabled players to succeed in the NBA when they might not have without his coaching and tutelage. So why was he let go? First because he was Black. It was only incidentally because he tried to help players stay in school when Big Ten policies made it impossible for some students to play and be students. Some of the boosters of the Golden Dunkers (most if whom are White) were livid when Paul Giel, the Athletic Director, hired Clem as basketball coach. Why livid? Because Haskins was Black. They led him to believe they loved him. Indeed, he asked when he first came in 1986 what the procedures were to make sure his players were taken care of and they told him they had it all under control. They all knew they had to act under questionable Big Ten understandings and even more questionable NCAA rules and regulations. This was routine. Then they used that to leak rumors of irregularities about Haskins to the NCAA.

As we have seen throughout our discussion of the Minneapolis story, the law is what those in power say it is. The boosters made Haskins a violator of NCAA rules that favor Whites but not inner city Blacks who come from inferior schools with an inferior education. And they realized that they could use the NCAA rules against someone without getting caught. They got away with it with Luther Darville. I'm sure that made them think that they could get away with it in terms of Clem Haskins as well. And, of course, they did.

I view these NCAA rules as hypocritical and self-serving, as the last vestiges of a plantation system that makes billions of dollars nation-wide every year off the backs of the indentured servants they call athletes, both Black and White. The big college football scene requires athletes to stay in shape year-round, begin practice in the summer, and play several games before school even starts. They are approaching schedules like the NFL but are not being paid appropriately when you consider how much money they bring into their schools. Do I think athletes should be helped out as Darville helped them? Of course. And so did he boosters. And so did the University. But there is a different standard for Whites.

And so when athletes need more time for studies but it isn't available, they get help, just as wealthy students hire tutors for themselves. Clem Haskins got them help for their studies and help for writing papers. But the racism of the boosters led them to do what I believe eventually will be seen as cutting off their collective nose to spite their face. They wanted to get rid of Clem, but he was too great a coach to get him for bad coaching. So they got him for NCAA rules irregularities. He became their scapegoat, including for the violations of Lou Holtz when he coached football at the University of Minnesota. Black Clem Haskins and Black Luther Darville were the scapegoats, while White Holtz got off free.

And so the question used so often comes to mind when we ask what did the University know and when did they know it. They knew, of course, in 1996, during the NCAA investigation. And before that, in 1988, and in the early 1990s the person who helped the athletes with their papers told her story in the Minneapolis *Star Tribune*. So why a trial for Luther and not for Coach Haskins? Because to put Clem on trial would have revealed the truth as the administrators would have had to testify under oath. This is why the Regents had Clem's case sent to arbitration to work out a settlement with Clem. In this fashion, they dodged the testimony that could kill their program, and although it cost them a lot, it was far cheaper than the losses they would have sustained with an NCAA suspension, not to mention their collective jobs. But they didn't have to testify at Luther's trial. They let the students' testimony hang him, making him the lone scapegoat, the only one to be tried and go to jail.

Much of the information here comes from my own direct participation with many of those involved. Indeed, I often met with Don Yaeger and Douglass S. Looney, who also tell the story of Luther Darville as part of their larger story about Notre Dame and Lou Holtz' involvement in both Notre Dame and the University of Minnesota. They write their story in the 1993 book *Under The Tarnished Dome: How Notre Dame Betrayed Its Ideals for Football Glory* (Simon & Schuster, 1993). Although this is a book about Notre Dame football, it includes the NCAA case against the University of Minnesota where Lou Holtz was head football coach becoming head football coach at Notre Dame. Two of the chapters, "Minnesota: Winning Has Its Price" and "Haunted by the Past," includes extensive coverage of interviews with me, as well as with others who I know personally were involved in the case. I can verify to the truth of many of the interviews conducted by Yaeger and Looney. So, for greater details, go to their book.

Football is important to most major universities, not only as a rallying point for school pride but also as a source of tremendous revenue. And at Notre Dame, football is everything, where in the early 1990s it brought in $10 million a year. Indeed, without football, as noted by Yaeger and Looney, Notre Dame would just be "a small Catholic institution with a great chemistry department in a small northern Indiana town with lousy weather". The same could be said about many a geographically isolated state college campus. Football brings life to communities all over America. Baseball may claim to be the national pastime, but clearly our real national pastime, in terms of sports, is football. More, football is our national passion. On Friday nights, every town in America celebrates, with many attending their local high school football games or listening to it on the radio. On Saturdays all across America, people are either in the stands or watching their favorite college teams on TV or listening to the games on radio. The same is true of Sundays and the NFL (and don't forget Monday Night NFL Football and its Thanksgiving and Christmas games). Football means a lot to schools, students, and fans.

NCAA rules are archaic. These college players are really professionals. The rules need to be changed. The rules make liars and cheats out of everyone. What is right or wrong is whatever it is by definition. Little in the NCAA rules makes sense to anyone outside the NCAA. The rules were made when only genteel White boys from affluent homes played sports and hence the fetish for unpaid amateurs was the central point. But ever since poor Whites (think coal miners' sons) and poor Blacks have become the stalwarts of teams, these rules make less and less sense. What the NCAA should be looking at is how players are treated. The NCAA should be looking at racism, and at graduation rates, and leave the ten and hundred dollar bill episodes alone. The NCAA doesn't mind if you are racist or if your players don't graduate, but by golly, don't give them $10 for a meal or $40 for a bus ticket home for the holidays, or find them a tutor or get them help writing papers. The NCAA rules fit affluent Whites, not poor Blacks and Whites.

Even our esteemed governor the former wrestler thinks the whole thing is silly, as he said, when told infractions were reported to the NCAA: "Awwww, why'd they have to report this?" The bottom line: we have this incredible system of perpetrators, like Darville and his superiors who had him help the athletes, as well as the boosters and other enablers, such as the fans and everyone outside the NCAA, turning everyone into a perpetrator and enabler, with University officials waxing eloquently about the integrity and purity and honor of the game, all of which I accept, yet all the while they are also providing the substance and authority of providing for players the way Darville did. All of this diminishes the games and the sports. This system requires some kind of compensation to players for all that they return to their schools. They too deserve the equivalent of a "living wage," a "living scholarship," especially those from poor homes, as studies and football leave no time for a regular type of job.

Stephens, Haskins, and Darville, took it on the chin. They are Black. Holtz got off. He is White. When you understand that "racist" is the word used to describe the football program under Holtz's predecessor, Joe Salem, these events become easier to understand. Under Salem things broke down along Black-White lines. It was clearly and simply racist. Player revolts were common under Salem as was the complaint that White players were being prepared for life after football with summer jobs and internships at Pillsbury and General Mills, whereas Blacks were given jobs in highway construction or in a box factory or work in Harvey Mackay's envelope company. MacKay is a super booster, played a role in the hiring of Lou Holtz, is a best selling motivational book author, envelope factory owner, and was instrumental in getting the NFL's Super Bowl played in Minneapolis in 1992. The Black players may have had a different skin color but inside their heads they had the same gray matter as Whites. They saw clearly, as one of the Black players said, that "there is still that plantation mentality" and that the White see "that Black folks are built just to do manual labor." As one Black athlete put it: "No one gives a sh*t about the black athlete after football is done and over with." Not that this ended when Salem left. As some of his players remarked to Yaeger and Loooney, Holtz was also racist, with the plantation mentality, who didn't care for his Black players as much as he did for his White players, always sending Black players who needed help to Luther Darville. Luther himself said in *Under The Tarnished Dome*:

> My observation of the problem was [that it was] one of a racial nature, and the coaches were reinforcing that. The coaches were doing nothing to compliment or to encourage the black players in particular. ... But if White players were bad-mouthed, it was probably because of their lack of talent or lack of speed. But when [they] dealt with the Black players, it was "ni**er." Use of that word was not uncommon at the time Salem was there.

Darville is a short, 5'8" Black man from the Bahamas, well-educated, well-spoken. He first came to this country and to the University to help keep basketball superstar Mychal Thompson comfortable. Mychal was from the Bahamas. When Thompson left, Luther was asked to stay on to help with students who got into trouble. He was on a campus that had few minorities. He became the Director of the Office of Minority and Special Student Affairs. It was his understanding that he had the authority to spend money to help the athletes who needed help.

Holtz was astonishingly good at playing the PR game, right in front of people, and being praised rather than punished. He was like a carnival barker running a game of 3-card Monte; truth was in whatever card he decided to turn up. He even told an interviewer before the season started, that "it's not easy to win in big-time football without breaking the rules, but we'll do it." But remember, as *Under the Tarnished Dome* clearly points out, Holtz is a consummate and entertaining liar who says what he has to for any given situation. While Holtz was Head Football Coach at the University of Minnesota, cheating on NCAA rules was rampant. Tens of thousands of dollars were paid to players under the table by the boosters. Cars as well as women were provided by boosters. Darville saw that they also got help with studies and writing papers. Holtz was in the middle of it. And he walked away Scot-free, as did all of the administrators and boosters involved. The only one to go to jail was the little Black guy, Luther Darville. For those Holtz fans reading this, all I can say is go read *Under the Tarnished Dome*. This chapter is not about Holtz. It is about the University and Luther Darville. But certainly Holtz played his own nefarious role, the loveable rogue, the delightful scamp, the Wee Willie Wonka White coach.

Indeed, left out of any discussions, except in *Under the Tarnished Dome*, is the work of boosters, none of whom were singled out in the Luther Darville trial nor given one of their own. These boosters gave players cars, cash, and women. And although that wasn't always the case, promises were made and expectations were there. And while some White players were provided with 280Zs, Mercedes, and BMWs, Black players got used cars. Where did poor Black kids without any money, as well as White college boys, get the money to drive their cars? Obviously it came from boosters and it came from Darville. But only Darville was punished. And the Boosters gave out plenty more than Luther did.

But before we can go any further, we have to ask the simple question, was Luther Darville guilty? If that question means did he give money, help, and enticements to University of Minnesota athletes, the answer is yes, if it means did he pocket all the money, the answer is no.

Now ask the another question: if knowing about it or advocating it or authorizing it makes you guilty, who else is guilty? Answer: everyone. As one player said in *Under the Tarnished Dome*: "Lou Holtz and his whole staff knew about Darville," So did the Athletic Director and his staff, and you'd have to be naive as anything to believe that the President didn't know (all NCAA school Presidents know). But the NCAA rules as well as the University's rules are like the laws we read about in Chapter 3: they mean what those who administer them want them to mean on the given day they are talking about them, and they apply to whoever they want them to apply to on any given day. In this situation of the University of Minnesota, they were made to apply only to Luther Darville.

Why, you ask, did the NCAA go along with this if they knew? Because knowing is no longer enough. Correlations don't count. Only smoking guns. And everyone kept quiet in front of the NCAA investigators. The NCAA lives in the same crazy world of hypocrisy as the players and coaches. They have to provide the appearance of an amateur sport while still allowing the schools to do what they must to attract and keep top players. And as long as everyone lies to himself or winks at it as nonsense, they are stuck with lies, for if there are no truth-tellers, it is difficult to find evidence. If they went after everyone, University presidents, administrators, and whole athletic departments would have to stand trial. But the arcane rules of evidence prevent it even when everyone knows, except in the most egregious cases that can't be ignored or, as in the cases of Haskins and Darville, you use them as scapegoats because they are Black.

Certainly everyone agrees that the whole system is stupid. Look how long we refused to play our best basketball players in the Olympics, until they finally lost to the professionals of other countries. We still wrestle with the blurred line between amateur and professional. And until we finally deal with it honestly, these false morality plays will be played out in the grandest of hypocritical form, as with the case of Luther Darville, with the University playing innocent while it not only condoned but authorized what Darville did.

Few would stand up to defend this amateur-pro system today, including myself. So instead it was used as a weapon against Clem and Luther as some schools use it to tell on a rival. The beauty of a Luther Darville is that he was a Black Bahaman, not a White one, and thus he was one who could take all the heat, letting everyone else gets off. You can see this in the CEO scandals. I prefer to call these CEO scandals as opposed to corporate scandals, as they have little to do with corporations or the vast thousands of honest people working for them. Very few of these CEOs will go to jail. Even fewer will pay fines. Why? Because most of what they did was legal. But they too will have their scapegoats, to take the blame away from where it belongs: the Congress that passed the laws that allowed the thievery to take place, which they do to get fat campaign contributions. They'll get them on technicalities, the hubbub will die down, and it will be back to business as usual: corporate heads being allowed to act like pirates so they can share their loot with Congressmen by way of campaign contributions.

The University's rampant rule-breaking was well known, even ordered. And the guy whose job it was to break those rules was Luther Darville. Everyone knows there are a lot or rules in any organization or even games that are idiotic. Nonetheless, if caught, the consequences can be costly in fines or suspensions or jail for individuals, or in rulings that the team can't participate in league play and bowl games. When the latter happens, the real loss is the millions in ticket sales and TV revenues, especially in the post-season. So it all has to be kept quiet and, if discovered, lied about and covered up. This is, in my view, the daily routine for NCAA schools all across the country, including the University of Minnesota (as attested to by the students interviewed in *Under the Tarnished Dome).* The solution is not to punish the schools and players but to change the rules. So at the University of Minnesota, the coach and the administrators knew this was going on. The guy from the Bahamas understood the wink-winks and nods. He was the guy hired to make sure life went well for the Mychal Thompsons and others of the programs. And now he could take the hit, be the designated fall guy and be the scapegoat for everyone else.

Lou Holtz was entertaining. He was also a liar, but a very entertaining liar. He repeated his routine over and over like a cookie cutter, offering up the same jokes and statements everywhere he went. He was a great coach, a superlative coach, no question, which is why he was allowed to get away with what he did. But he served only Lou Holtz. Three days before he resigned from the University to go to Notre Dame, he said at a press conference: "I'm not interested in leaving Minnesota. I'm not planning to leave Minnesota." Earlier he had said he wouldn't leave Minnesota unless he "died or went to the Rose Bowl." Of course, later, he denied saying any of it. And during the NCAA investigation, as reported in *Under the Tarnished Dome,* Holtz told players if they said anything to the NCAA, he would deny it. As expressed in a scene from the old comedy, when asked what to do when you are caught cheating on your wife: "Deny, deny, deny."

In the early 1980s, Paul Giel was the University's Athletic Department. But it was two rich boosters, Bill Maddux and Harvey Mackay, who hired Lou Holtz to be Head Football Coach, while Giel recovered in the hospital from a heart attack. Holtz was like a snake oil salesman: he made promises and he got people to believe. The boosters arranged financing for the building of a $5-million indoor practice facility. More season tickets were sold for the first time since the days of Sandy Stephens. And people continued to believe, even though Holtz's 2-year record was only 10-12.

All of this came to a head when the trial of Luther Darville, *The State of Minnesota vs. Luther Darville,* began in November of 1989. It ran for 18 days. In a nutshell, Luther Darville was on trial for swindling $186,000 in school funds. He said 80-90% went to athletes playing football and basketball; the prosecutor claimed he pocketed it. If the former was proved and it was found that he did it under orders, everyone would lose. But if they could prove he was freelancing, giving the money to players without permission, or that he had pocketed the money, only he would lose.

As Luther put it in *Under the Tarnished Dome*:

> The boosters packed the courtroom at my trial. I looked at some of them and just saw in their faces them pleading with me, for the good of the university, not to destroy the Athletic Department. It's all about economics. I was dispensable. A little Black Boy from a third-world country. Get rid of the ni**er. I wasn't even a pawn. Pawns usually get to take somebody off the board.

And so the show trial continued. One by one, the prosecutors brought forth as witnesses football and basketball players to testify how Luther had given them cash, lunches, and dinners; clothes (especially those from the South who didn't have winter clothes), travel tickets (to get home for holidays), and aid in other situations: family emergencies, auto payments, health club visits. They called not one coach or administrator or booster. All in all, 20 former players testified. Only 20. Just enough to set up Luther as the scapegoat. Just enough to be able to say that all the rest of the money was then pocketed, not given to other players. Any more than that and his statement that he gave most of the money to athletes would have been credible. But not with 20. This, of course, was only a small fraction of those he helped. And the Athletic Director Paul Giel, and Frank B. Wilderson, former VP for Student Affairs, and the rest? They maintained the same story: that Darville kept most of the money for himself, and that they and the University and the boosters knew nothing about it and were innocent of any wrongdoing. Authors Yaeger and Looney state in their book that students admitted there was more, that there were other NCAA violations, but because no one asked them they didn't tell, as they were asked only the specific questions of the charges dealing with Luther, which is how the game is played, which is all the investigators are allowed to ask, in order to hobble NCAA investigations.

And what witnesses did his attorney call?   None from the University.   No administrator, no coach, no booster.   The only witness he called was yours truly. Connect the dots with me, dear reader: no witnesses for the defense from the university community, just me, Ron Edwards, a community advocate. Don't you find that at the very least a bit peculiar? They had to call someone for Luther. They didn't want to call any from the University or boosters, as they would run the risk of having to lie and getting caught in perjury. How did this happen? Because to make sure he lost the case, Darville's attorney, in a rigged deal set up with the boosters, didn't call one witness on Luther's behalf, not one official, not one booster, no one except yours truly, Ron Edwards. You see, it's OK to them to lie when they are not under oath. Under oath in court is different. The way to avoid that is to fix it so they don't ask you any questions. By rigging it so no one else was called, none of them had to answer any questions.

Now when an attorney just sits and does nothing and raises no objections, a Judge can ask questions, which signals to the attorney he isn't doing a good job. But in this case, Judge Fitzgerald also just sat there and said nothing. Because I had talked with many of the students and knew Luther, they used this "dumb 'ol Black guy" Ron Edwards, believing they could use me to nail Luther, because I knew he had given money and help to students and would have to say so. But my testimony was that Luther did not take the money for himself but gave it to students. Several times Judge Fitzgerald defamed me before the jury (again, trying to discredit me as the Judge did in Chapter 2). To further try to discredit me, the prosecutor had a large 3-ring binder on his table well within sight of the jury. The binder read, in large letters, RON EDWARDS. What a bunch of cowards and crooks! They were trying to make it look like I had some kind of criminal record in order to destroy my credibility. I had great joy pointing out that it was irregular and inappropriate, forcing the Judge to order the prosecutor to remove the binder from the sight of the jury, but by then the damage had been done.

Now here is the kicker, the kind of thing that makes Minneapolis what it is, and what I would like to see changed. After 90 minutes of deliberation, the jury decided that it really didn't matter who knew of Luther's actions. All that counted was that he did it. How is that for a true white wash (pun intended)? If any of the others knew, the University would be banned from college athletics and Holtz would not keep his Notre Dame job. All would pay heavily, including the University president. But if they could just pin it all on Luther, they would all go scot-free. And so that is what they did. The jury knew this. The jurors were all good Minnesotans. They were

Gopher fans. They didn't even have to be told to do this. They knew what was best for the University. They "knew" what to do (just like Southern White juries always "knew" what to do). No conspiracy. They just knew. It was part of the Minnesota culture. Just like the jurors who freed Whites in the South for lynching Blacks or killing them in other ways.

What Luther didn't realize until too late is that Lawton was paid to essentially blow the case. Not only did he call no other witnesses, but he also never raised any objections to the testimony against Luther, including lies that were told on the stand, especially by students, nor did he appeal Luther's conviction as he promised Luther he would do. There were even grounds for a mistrial. Instead, Luther was just left dangling, and out of the country at that.

Because they were angry with my testimony, another strange, irregular and inappropriate thing happened: Judge Fitzgerald and City Attorney Tom Johnson, the prosecutor, held a press conference and stated they would haul me up on charges of perjury. This, of course, was a violation of accepted judicial conduct by any judge. My response was: terrific: my conscience is clear, I'll test pure, and so I eagerly awaited my day in court. But it didn't come, as they later realized that I would see to it that those who hadn't testified would now have to testify, including athletic department staff and boosters. That meant they would have to lie and risk going to jail for perjury. So nothing came of it.

Luther went to prison, believing that Lou Holtz and others would help him when he got out. Before the trial, they had promised to help him after he got out if he didn't implicate them. After 17 months in prison, he got out but no one helped. Even one of my fellow community activists, Henrietta Adams Falconer, told Luther not to mention Holtz, for if he left Lou out, Lou would help him after he got out of prison. Indeed Holtz asked her to intercede with Luther for him. And so Luther kept the coaches, the staff, and the boosters out of it, while he served 17 months.

Now get this. His sentence was a year, plus 7 months for contempt of court for refusing to tell who the current athletes were to whom he had given money or help. The prosecution had very cleverly not called any current athletes. Only those who had already graduated or moved on. And they knew he wasn't a snitch, that he would take the fall and not implicate the students he cared so much about and who he thought were innocent as all he was doing was his job. He refused to name them and ruin the athletes for doing what everyone else did and for what he firmly believed he was doing: his job as he was instructed to do it. He courageously held his ground in stark contrast to the pack of cowards among the administration and boosters who set him up.

And what happened when he got out? Nothing. For her help to the University and Holtz, Falconer got $10,000 each from Holtz and Mackay for her charity organization (an organization which was only on paper, so she kept the money). Holtz kept his job at Notre Dame. Falconer got money, and Luther got nothing. Henrietta denies this, of course, but she told me, face to face that this was true, and only later denied it. Luther took the fall. And Henrietta lied to him about what would be done for him. Then she took money for it and shared nothing with Luther. Worse, it was fixed so that Luther cannot come back to this country. He was offered a job but couldn't take the position, as he isn't allowed back into the United States.

So the University got off. No death penalty for its teams. The payoffs to players continue today under similar and other guises. Lots of young men were disillusioned (maybe Lou was running the "Holtz Institute for Future Corporate Accountability Avoidance"); this too has consequences. As one of the athletes said, Holtz called to coach him on what to say to the NCAA investigators. As the athlete told, Yaeger and Looney, "Coach Holtz taught me if you always believe in yourself, be truthful to yourself, you can do whatever you want to do. One thing I didn't understand was that he always tried to teach us to tell the truth, be truthful, and then you're asked to lie." Through intermediaries Holtz also asked Luther to lie. He did. And for his reward, Luther was to be kept out of this country so he couldn't be an embarrassment.

All of these shenanigans have a negative effect on recruiting. They consider us Blacks good enough to entertain them and play for them but not to be administrators or coaches. The word is out in the Black community: don't send your kids to the University of Minnesota. So why, when Black athletes can be treated better elsewhere, would they want to go to the University of Minnesota? The word is out about the drive to racially purify Minnesota. There are no Black head coaches or senior administrators in the Athletic Department. And the Black community certainly took notice in the winter of 2002 when the Vikings had their change of administration: of 13 terminated, 12 were Black.

And why would White students want to get involved. Their most recent "great White hope," Chris Humphrey, was touted as being the next George Miken, the next great big White player. But great players want to play in the NBA. When the University gets rid of a coach who can help players develop for that level, which they did when they got rid of the Black Clem Haskins, and bring in lesser White coaches, a good player is going to go elsewhere. He doesn't care about the color of the coach. He cares about winning and being prepared for the NBA. And to say that the White kid Humphrey would help balance the complexion of the team, Blacks heard again the code word for not being welcome, as that means the white complexion. Playing the race card has backfired for the University again. A racist White player doesn't want to play with Blacks. A non-racist player doesn't want to be used to change complexion and feed their racism. As I said, a star only cares about winning, and goes where he feels he can help them win. Until the University of Minnesota does a better job of showing it is only interested in winning, regardless of whether the team is all Black or all White, the great players will go elsewhere. Sandy Stephens' coach Murray Warmath understood that. He got the best players he could find, regardless of color, and won the national championship and the Rose Bowl.

What, with its current racist attitudes and tolerance of coaches with racist attitudes, does the University expect to sign? And how, with that attitude, does it expect to win?

Postscript from An October 2002 *USA Today:* Blacks left out of coaching

The front page story on October 11, 2002 was headlined:

Success fails to open college doors for black football coaches.

The sub-heading is: **Only four hold top job, and the pipeline is empty.** By "empty," it means that of the 117 Division 1-A schools, where 43% of players are Black, there are only 12 Black coordinators (assistant coaches in charge of offensive or defensive units).

Why? The explanation given by USA Today is an example of the rampant racism and the **assumed racism** by the schools of those important to it (alumni, boosters, and contributors. The schools are racist so "naturally" they assume their constituencies are too. So even when Black coaches are successful, they are not hired. The biggest losers: the fans, who get mediocre coaches whose only saving grace is the color of their skin: White. Only a racist would not feel shame at this.

Let's look at key passages from this article that clearly shows not only the racism, but its acceptance and its foundational location as the starting point from which the colleges and university act (the **bold** emphasis I have added):

> USA TODAY found suggestions that colleges and universities—institutions supposedly devoted to racial diversity—have been **reluctant** to pick African-Americans to run their football programs because of their <u>**concern**</u> **about how alumni and other boosters might react** and <u>**doubts**</u> **about whether black coaches would be up to the tasks of fundraising and public relations.**

So there you have it. They talk the walk: diversity, but won't walk the talk. Alumni and boosters might not like it (they contribute the money). Why wouldn't they like it? Because, obviously, they are racist. Just like the colleges and universities. And doubts?? about their ability to engage successfully in fundraising and public relations? In other words Blacks are too dumb. What more racist comment could they make? Well, USA Today (see also their web site, www.usatoday.com to keep up on a daily basis with the news) reports more comments from and about the colleges and universities that are, pure and simple, racist, just like the University of Minnesota, reflecting what I have written about the Luther Darville case. Here are some more damning statistics and comments showing how entrenched the racism is in the football world as opposed to institutions like basketball or the U.S. Army:

- Army: 26.4% African-American; 11.3% of officer corps are Black; 8.3% of generals are Black.
- Basketball, NCAA, Division I: 93 Black head coaches
- Basketball, NBA: 13 of 29 head coaches are minority
- Major League Baseball: 9 minorities were managers
- The six richest conferences (Atlantic Coast, Big East, Big Ten, Big 12, Pacific-10, and Southeastern: only 1 Black head football coach, 20 Black head basketball coaches
- NCAA office staff managers: from 8.7% in 1994 to 20% today
- Football since 1982: 348 head coaching vacancies, only 18 went to Blacks
- Athletic Directors: of 836 colleges, all divisions, only 29 are Black (3.4%)
- It goes beyond X's and O's. We don't think (a minority coach) can fit into our country club.

Follow the story in *USA Today* as the Black Coaches Association (BCA) soon introduce their plan to alter hiring practices. Now ask yourself, can Blacks coach and handle fund raising and public relations? Think four words: Notre Dame. Tyrone Willingham. After a series of white coaches deflated a premier program, what White coach can you think of who could have done what Black Tyrone Willingham has done? Answer: none that I can think of.

Go Tyrone! Go Notre Dame!

Interlude 10

"RACISM" in Minneapolis II:

Mpls.St.Paul Magazine
January 1990 Cover Story On Racism (and 2001)

On the Cover: **I'm Not Racist, But...,**
**"Nice" Minnesotans don't talk about it, but the ugly fact is
that racism is alive—and growing—in the Twin Cities.**

Inside editorial: **"Hating with Subtlety"**

- "We all fear the unknown and, for most of us Minnesotans, minorities are unknown."
- "The chasm between whites and people of color may be deeper than it ever has been.   And it's that gap that leads to discrimination and racism, sometimes overt but oftentimes subtle."
- Cover story writer Brit Robson "...emerged from the search [and interviews] marveling at the ability of so many minorities to bounce back after being victimized by racism."
- "One thing that surprised ...was the resentment toward the media, especially TV and the *Star Tribune*, felt by so many people of color, [who referred] to the *Star Tribune* as *The Johannesburg Times."*
- "[This] report...is not necessarily an optimistic one. But as the Twin Cities approach the day—as many U.S. cities already have—when Whites will be in the minority, racial attitudes become even more critical. And our ability to deal with the subtleties of racism will signal our success or failure as a pluralistic society."

Article: **"Pride and Prejudice"**

- "...I don't want to be a part of a process that reinforces racist attitudes and teaches people to dislike Blacks, and currently that is exactly what television is doing. That may not be our intention, but in this case, the guilt follows the bullet" (p. 45).
- "People make judgments on where they live and work and go to school and socialize with race as one of the considerations. In other words, 'benign exclusion.'"—former U.S. senatorial candidate and Black man, Earl Craig (p. 45).

- "Back in the 60s, they were thrusting outward, seeking justice; it was easier to draw attention to social prescriptions and arouse community concern. Now people in pain are internalizing by killing themselves with drugs and killing their spouses and next-door neighbors. And now there is the feeling that if you keep that self-destructive behavior 'on the reservation,' it will be okay."—T. Williams, Senior Fellow, Hubert H. Humphrey Institute of Public Affairs (p. 47).

- "When you take children who have not experienced the advantages of a White middle-class child and put them in a school setting that further reinforces their lack of success, then you ensure failure for those children."—Elaine Salinas, Urban Coalition (p. 48).

- "It is racism whether you view Blacks as victims or perpetrators" (p 48).

- "More often than not, people of color are put in a pivotal position at some point in their lives where they must either hate or cope with their social inheritance. More often than not, they cope. They learn about tolerance, tenacity, pain, pride, empathy, teamwork, forgiveness and survival. With each passing day, they become more and more qualified to manage, administer, govern and innovate in the increasingly diverse world of the 1990s and the 21st century (p. 134)."

Note: The *Mpls.St.Paul* magazine writer Brit Robson, in **2001**, in another cover article, quoted radio personality Dark Star as saying: **"There are more closet racists here than any place I have ever lived."** So what is racism? As noted before, it is more than Sheriff Bull Connor with his fire hoses and his attack dogs, beating people with nightsticks. Racism is excluding, turning away, keeping Blacks on their inner city reservation and in their place, allowing Black students to rot in poor inner city schools or new jails. Plantation racism of the left (1968 *Kerner Commission Report*) and of the right (1998 *The Bell Curve*) states that Blacks can only make it with government help. In his book of the same title, Shelby Steele calls it *A Dream Deferred: The Second Betrayal of Black Freedom in America*. Racism is a relatively new term, one that is used in place of the older expressions of the 40s and 50s and 60s: discrimination and bigotry.

Chapter 11

The Corruption and Racism of Boss City Government:
The DFL Dumps a Black Mayor Who Favors Democracy

This chapter discusses the out-and-out corruption and racism in government that feeds into the greater society. By racism I mean simply that no Blacks need apply. The DFL had to dump its Black mayor, Sharon Sayles Belton, as their plan was to create Black ghettos with the redistricting of Minneapolis, which she would have opposed had she known of it, and, of course, none of us knew about it until *after* the elections. That is how clever they are.

Now, dear reader, if you conclude that I think of myself or of Blacks as victims, you are wrong. If you are asking do I think we are victimized, then of course the answer is yes. If you are asking is "victim" our identity, the answer is yes for some, no for others, which is why it is so hard to get solidarity among Black people (Chapter 14). My identity is that of Black, bold and beautiful. I am more than a survivor; I am a victor, a winner. What I am writing about here are the heroic efforts of those who have been victimized and then got up after being knocked down and who then continued forward, refusing to act as victims. Most of the Interludes bear testimony to Blacks being victimized and yet picking themselves up after being knocked down and moved on. As Sandy Stephens used to say, we may get bloodied, but we will not get bowed. In the meantime, as Nellie Stone Johnson used to emphasize, we go about living our daily lives just as anyone else does.

But there are those who do carry the identity of victims, seeking separate status, seeking benefits as an entitlement for victimhood, seeking protection from victimization, as they don't feel they can protect themselves. Many government programs treat Blacks this way, as separate, as having to be taken care of, as outside the mainstream and unable to enter it. This is seen especially when young Blacks are led to think by other Blacks that being smart and studying is being White, and that being promoted, in school or at work, should be automatically based on being Black victims, as a kind of reparation, rather than by studying and earning it. In Minneapolis politics, this has meant that Blacks buckle under to whatever the Democratic-Farmer-Labor Party says they have to do, for they need the DFL if they are to survive, as they don't think they can do it on their own. That is being a victim, not a victor.

As long as the Black leadership fixates on symbolic racism only, it plays into the hands of those who don't want Blacks to have political power or economic wealth. Yes, the racism continues, but it hasn't the power it had 50 or 100 years ago. As long as Blacks get conned into carrying the torch of such symbolic issues as hate-crime laws and opposing welfare reform and school vouchers, the real issues—education, housing, jobs and participation in the social economic and political mainstream—are ignored and our lack of participation in them is perpetuated. Think what could be done in these areas if the energy put into the symbolic areas was transferred. If Whites must still be racist, that is their problem. The Jim Crow laws are gone. The law is on our side (even if the judges and interpreters of it are not). We can't stop people from being racist, but we can stop being consumed by it. Let's invest our energy where it counts: in education, housing, and jobs, generating wealth and obtaining political power.

The DFL's interest in us is as voters for their candidates. And as a past leader in the Urban League, Civil Rights Commission, and the NAACP, I have tried, albeit too often unsuccessfully, to get these organizations to move from serving the DFL first, their organizations second, and the people last, to serving the people first.

Recall my discussion of the Kerner Commission's wrong-headed notion that we, as a country, were heading into two separate nations, one Black, one White, and that because history has changed, Blacks would not be able to improve and enter the economic mainstream as immigrants have done and thus the government would have to take care of them. Hence, the billions of dollars slated to Black support programs. Just as community organizers were co-opted with government jobs beginning in the 1960s, the major organizations like the NAACP and the Urban League began to be co-opted in the 1980s and 1990s. And thus the 21st century for Black Americans is a return to *de facto* segregation, this time self-imposed, as too many seek a kind of attached separatism, separate from the mainstream and yet attached for survival to the DFL in Minneapolis and the Democratic Party nationwide.

The story of Sharon Sayles Belton is the story of someone whose gender and race was no longer useful to the DFL. Her Blackness was no longer needed or wanted. Indeed, if the DFL had its way, there would not be one Black person on the City Council today. That there is one, Natalie Johnson-Lee, a Green Party member, is because the DFL's attempt to force an elected official out through gerrymandering chicanery failed (Chapters 13 and 14).

Belton was a Council Member from the former 5th ward, was City Council President for several years, and then was Mayor for two terms (8 years). In all, she gave of herself to the city and community for 18 years, a strong person who impacted positively on the lives of all people regardless of their race, age, or gender.

Belton was the first African-American woman elected Mayor of a major U.S. city. She was known for her energy and for the innovation she brought to her duties. She took her job seriously. She served everyone, the well-off and the poor, the underserved and the over-served, majority and minority alike. I am proud to have been involved with her while she was at City Hall, to have supported her, and to call her my friend.

But she ran afoul of the gentrification mess. The White Tenant Rights groups, who were opposed to her, took her on. They wanted funds for White gentrification, not Black low and moderate-income housing, so they attacked her. They were part of the housing activities of former Council President Jackie Cherryhomes (Chapter 8). But Sharon and Jackie were both DFL, had been through a lot together, and so Sharon, acting out of a sense of loyalty, could not bring herself to break the ties with Jackie or to confront Jackie.

A year before the election, I told Sharon that Jackie was killing her, that Jackie's housing thing (Chapter 8) would wind up helping to bring her down. Sharon's problem was that she had too many White advisors, who kept telling her the way to campaign. Despite her years of success and achievement, they still treated her as a Black woman who needed to do as they said. They didn't ask what they could do to help her but what she could do to follow them. There is nothing wrong with having White advisors, but when the DFL provides mostly White advisors in a city that is one-third Black, that is not a good sign. Any non-White politician in the midst of racist people with a plantation mentality also needs non-Whites just to keep things honest.

So, with the approach of the elections, things were happening that needed to be dealt with. Belton's staff got angry and upset. Along with the DFL, they had destroyed all the institutions that could have provided help for her, directly or indirectly.

Belton was a popular, twice-elected mayor, who was a 100%-loyal DFLer. The national Democratic Party could count on her, and she could count on them. She was considered mayor of a city that the Democrats, whether Bill Clinton or Al Gore, could count on. But as loyal as she was to the local DFL, it turned out in the long run that she herself could not count on them. I realized that she was not going to win, and I had a conversation with several friends and we all saw the same thing: she would get pushed out and lose. Some of her staff could not see it. Other key staffers had already switched to the DFL side against her. The DFL withdrew its support, subtly. just enough to ensure that she would not receive the party's endorsement. Can you imagine a party not endorsing its own popular incumbent? Sharon knew this, and yet, like a loyal trooper, played her role out to the end. The DFL made sure that their own Black mayor would find it impossible to win.

Sharon's story is also the story of how R.T. Rybak became mayor. Rybak is a weak mayor, a front man, who puts Sharon down in his constant comparison of how much better things are with him as mayor. The DFL and Republicans divided up the territory, giving the DFL the suburbs and the Republicans downtown. They needed to get rid of their own twice-elected mayor and install a weak person who would not contest the redistricting (let alone understand it), and they had to redistrict the downtown into its own district so the neighborhood people could not bother them.

So the decision-makers made it clear that Sharon needed to be defeated and embarrassed. Once Sharon knew she couldn't win, she really should not have run in the primary. The county commissioner, Mark Stenglein, created the African-American Men's Project to give himself a power base on the North Side. People convinced him that if he did this, he could pull votes away from Sharon and be the next Mayor of Minneapolis. He had visions of grandeur and, as a county commissioner of the county that includes most of Minneapolis, he had the name recognition. So he ran for Mayor. It should be noted that Stenglein, as I write this, runs an all-White operation: He has no Blacks in his office and none are affiliated with his election campaign.

Another player was City Council Member Lisa McDonald, who also thought she could beat Sharon. And she was right except for one thing: The power brokers of downtown Minneapolis, who turned their backs on Sharon even though Sharon had worked out the development plans that enabled them to go forward with construction downtown, didn't want her either. They wanted Rybak because they could control him. It became important for them to have Sharon, Rybak, and McDonald all fight each other in the primary. There was only one person who could have defeated Rybak: Lisa McDonald. Anybody in Minneapolis politics knew that, so it became important for Belton and Stenglein to defeat McDonald, and they did. It didn't matter who beat McDonald and came in second for the run-off. All that was important was that there would be no run-off between McDonald and Rybak.

Both McDonald and Stenglein would have taken the job of Mayor seriously, and that would have put the behind the scenes DFL players in second place. Just as Irv Dirksen was said to have been unhappy that Eisenhower won, because then Irv was no longer the most powerful person in his party, so too the party bosses today feel they are more important than the elected officials. They prefer to control things behind the scenes. This used to be a more visible rule in U.S. Cities (Tammany Hall in New York, Pendergast in Kansas City). They keep it less visible today. That is why it is up to the citizens of each city to maintain vigilance. To keep a strong person like Lisa out, the DFL power brokers lured another strong person like Mark to run, leading him to believe that he could win. Capitalizing on anti-Black sentiments, they split the White vote, leaving Sharon the winner. RT could beat anyone but Lisa. Mark helped take out Lisa. That just left Sharon. Sharon would lose. The DFL party regulars would now be in charge again.

In a similar act, they convinced Sandra Miller, a Black American, to drop out of the School Board and run for Council against Councilman Brian Herron, who they knew was under indictment and would not run again. Herron and others had been wire tapped since 1998, so a lot more people will go down even though they were doing what the bosses wanted. They don't realize that the bosses can do it legally, and so when they try to cut themselves in on some of the take, through bribes and fixes, which is not legal, they get caught and sent to jail, even though they take very little compared to how much the bosses take legally (Chapter 8).

The DFL knew the wiretaps would bring evidence for this. Sandra was much more malleable as a house Negro than Brian, who, like Sharon, agonized over the compromises he had to make to accomplish anything for the people of his Ward. But after Herron resigned and pleaded guilty because of the scandal, his council assistant, Vicki Ann Brock, ran, won the sympathy vote, and Sandra lost. The deal cut was to offer her a new district. That would put the two field hands, Natalie Johnson-Lee and Brother Shane Price, in the 4th Ward where they would split the vote and both disappear. But the backlash caused by the Black community when they saw that the NAACP and Urban League were in cahoots to boot out the only elected African-American Council Member, led to their leaving Natalie in her 5th Ward.

Rybak, who defeated Belton and went on to win as Mayor, is weak and will be easy to control. His resume shows that he has rarely completed a job he has started. The political powers wanted this novice they could control. Part of this was because, as we now know, but did not know then, they were already planning to put Downtown under one Ward and wanted an easy guy to control who wouldn't investigate or stop it. And as we shall see in Chapters 12-13, despite being told everything about the fraudulent redistricting, let alone the stolen files, Rybak hasn't lifted a finger. The powers have achieved what they wanted: all of Downtown in one district and the control they could not get while Belton was mayor. The key to all of this, as we saw in Chapter 2, is that it is legal. Not fair, but legal. Not just, but legal.

Their plans were all thrown off-course when Johnson-Lee beat Cherryhomes, so then they had to try to get rid of Natalie (Chapter 12).

What had them scared was that their calculations would be thrown off by what had happened in the African-American vote of 2000, which led to the post-election redistricting plan geared to reduce if not eliminate the possibility of any challenge from the Blacks of Minneapolis. For those who don't know, let me let you in on why they ran scared: the African-American voter turn-out in Minneapolis in 2000 had been huge. 45,000 newly registered voters, the largest percentage of newly registered voters in the United States in 2000. The large majority of those new voters were African-Americans. Minneapolis had the highest voter turnout in the entire country in 2000, with 82% of the registered voters in Minneapolis turning out. Al Gore won Minneapolis and he won Minneapolis with the African-American vote. And because of the African-American vote, Mark Dayton, of the famous retail store chain family, which includes Target stores, won the first election he ever ran for, that of U.S. Senator. He would have lost had it not been for those 45,000 newly registered voters. As it turned out, the DFL didn't need to worry. Blacks reverted to form: demoralized by what they considered a stolen election in Florida, they did not turn out nearly as well in 2001, although they did turn out in Ward 5 to elect Johnson-Lee and defeat Cherryhomes in the biggest upset and political victory in the history of Minneapolis politics. The DFL reaction to Johnson-Lee since that election has been to make sure the Blacks of Minneapolis were shorn as much as possible of any influence or power. It is my hope that after reading about the Minneapolis Story, the Blacks of Minneapolis will be encouraged to stand up for themselves and seek the influence that is ours for the taking by virtue of making up 35% of Minneapolis, so we can change the direction of the Minneapolis ship of state in terms of education, housing, jobs, and Blacks entering the social, economic and political mainstream.

Interlude 11

Congressman Adam Clayton Powell: *Keep the Faith, Baby*
(Showtime Movie*)*
What A Black Leader Can Do Who Doesn't See Himself As a Victim:

Adam Clayton Powell, Jr., was one of the 20th century's most powerful and influential Black politicians. He laid the foundation upon which both Martin Luther King, Jr., and Malcolm X later built. He began as a pastor in the Harlem Abyssinian Baptist Church of his father. Active in his community, he organized rent strikes and bus boycotts before running and serving on the New York City Council (the first Black man ever to do so). He ran for Congress, becoming the second Black ever elected to the U.S. House of Representatives. He is less well known today than Martin Luther King, probably because he didn't hide his private side. In addition to being a Congressman, preacher, and civil rights leader, he was also a flamboyant, audacious, drinking playboy. These and other scandals would eventually give his enemies the ammunition they needed to undo him.

He is another man whom young Black men need to learn about to see what one man can do. He is featured in the movie *Keep The Faith, Baby,* first shown in February of 2002 on Showtime. Powell first entered the House of Representatives in 1945. Because of the racism of many members of the House, then all White, he was immediately disliked. But all of them had to sit together in chambers. One so disliked the idea of sitting next to a Black man that he immediately got up and left. Powell immediately followed him to sit down next to him each time that he got up to get away from Powell. Powell let it be known that although he knew they hated his color, he would not be intimidated. So, despite the slurs and name-calling, he kept his head high and worked hard to learn the system and become one of the most powerful, productive members of Congress, causing him to be hated even more. And even though it was common practice then to misuse travel vouchers and to put relatives on the payroll, his hypocritical brethren used their own practices against him, calling his doing so ethical infractions, and expelled him, just as Luther Darville was punished at the University of Minnesota for doing what others did (Chapter 10). Powell made a point of being no better than his peers but was open about it where they were secretive.   And they, of course, define who is and isn't ethical or scandalous.

Nonetheless, he was a trailblazer on many fronts, not the least being getting African-Americans accepted into society. He fought openly against segregation. He became Chair of the House Education and Labor Committee, a chairmanship he arranged with John F. Kennedy in exchange for Powell amassing Black voters to support JFK's bid for the Presidency in 1960. The chairmanship gave him unprecedented power for a politician, White or Black, but especially so as he was Black, for he had control of the committee that controlled 40% of the domestic budget of the United States. After he left, the Democratic leadership dismantled the committee to make sure no Black could be in such a position to do that again.

Powell helped create landmark programs such as Medicare, Medicaid, and Head Start, and he contributed to the Civil Rights Act of 1964. Under his leadership, the Committee approved over 50 measures authorizing Federal programs for minimum wage increases, antipoverty measures, education and training for the deaf, school lunches, manpower and vocational training, student loans, and standards for wages and work hours (equal work for equal pay) as well as Federal aid to elementary and secondary education and public libraries, and the National Endowment for the Arts.

He made it possible for Blacks to become teachers and to hold positions unavailable until then.

As a young man, he was encouraged at first to avoid Whites. He refused. As he said: ""In order to put out fires, you've got to deal with the people who own the water." As a young man, before holding office, he showed his willingness to learn and act. He started a church-sponsored relief program providing food, clothing, and temporary jobs for thousands of Harlem's homeless and unemployed.

When he went to Congress, Blacks were not allowed in the Congressional Dining Room except as waiters and bus boys. Powell ignored this, walked in, sat down, ordered lunch, and just like that it was an integrated dining room. It is often just a little audacious behavior that is delivered with courage that can break down barriers that are held up only by unchallenged fear.

On the other hand, as he became more powerful, he lost his ear for the people. He dismissed the civil rights activists, including Martin Luther King, Jr., as amateurs, and threatened to call him names. As a result, he was not invited to speak at the March on Washington, of which he said dismissively: "Anybody can have a dream. My speech would have been: 'I have a plan.'" However the two did join together in 1965 for the greater cause they both served.

Chapter 12

The Corruption and Racism of Boss City Government: Gerrymandering Ward Redistricting

Abraham Lincoln, in his famous June 17, 1858 "House Divided" Speech (Springfield, Illinois, at the close of the Republican State Convention, in the Hall of the House of Representatives) talked about how sneaky the pro-slavery forces were and how they worked behind the scenes to sustain the Dred Scott decision (Interlude 6). I maintain that this is the same kind of behind the scenes manipulation done in Minneapolis by the DFL, which is essentially pro-White and anti-inner city Black. Here is how Lincoln put it:

> We cannot absolutely know that all these exact adaptations are the result of preconcert. But when we see a lot of framed timbers, different portions of which we know have been gotten out at different times and places and by different workmen—Stephen, Franklin, Roger and James, for instance—and when we see these timbers joined together, and see they exactly make the frame of a house or a mill, all the tenons and mortises exactly fitting, and all the lengths and proportions of the different pieces exactly adapted to their respective places, and not a piece too many or too few,—not omitting even scaffolding,—or, if a single piece be lacking, we see the place in the frame exactly fitted and prepared yet to bring such piece in,—in such a case, we find it impossible not to believe that Stephen and Franklin and Roger and James all understood one another from the beginning, and all worked upon a common plan or draft drawn up before the first blow was struck....

Lincoln is saying that the various anti-Black, pro-slavery forces worked behind the scenes ("preconcert") to sustain the Dred Scott decision and to work to allow slavery in the territories. I maintain that the same kind of behind-the-scenes activity took place with redistricting, as the powers that be in Minneapolis worked in "preconcert" with their own "lumber" to construct a down-town district of wealth and a shanty-town district of poverty in the 5th Ward. Lincoln saw it being done to the nation. I see it being done to Minneapolis. If you look carefully, you will see it too. The power of Lincoln's speech is that he points out that this was not done out of blindness or mistake or by not seeing something different, but by forethought followed by direct and deliberate plan, and action. I am saying that is the same in Minneapolis. Lincoln was appalled and fought it. I am appalled by it in Minneapolis and fight it here too. As you learn more about what is going on in Minneapolis, I'm sure you are appalled as well. I invite you to join in the fight against it.

Redistricting is done after every ten-year national census to ensure that each state has the number of representatives its population allows and that each congressional district has the number of voters as set by the Constitution. This is then also applied to city wards. When those in power (whether Democrats or Republicans) try to rig the lines of the district by gerrymandering them (Interlude 12), some strange-shaped districts result. This gerrymandering is to achieve an advantage, be it by party or race (both heavily influenced also by class). Unfairness and injustice becomes the result. There are two types of gerrymandering: partisan/political, and racial. According to the political science web site, http://www.fairvote.org/redistricting/legality.htm, "political gerrymandering is the drawing of electoral district lines in a manner that discriminates against a political party. When used to insure party success, political gerrymandering is usually legal but can be contested. At this time it is legal to draw district lines to protect incumbents of both parties."

"**Racial gerrymandering**" originally referred to manipulating legislative district lines to under-represent racial minorities. Tactics such as **packing** Black voters into a single district or **cracking** them to make Black voters a minority in all districts can be illegal. This sort of gerrymandering was first used in the South after the Civil War to dilute the Black vote. Then in 1982, the Voting Rights Act was amended to require many political jurisdictions to create **majority-minority** districts (drawing the lines to ensure that districts had a majority of non-White voters) in order to allow more racial minorities to elect candidates of their choice. After the 1990 census, the Supreme Court invalidated several such redistricting plans as unconstitutionally race-conscious," signaling that it would be okay to pack and crack again.

http://www.senate.leg.state.mn.us/departments/scr/redist/red2000/ch5parti.htm,   a government web site, states that the judiciary has treated this age-old practice either as "a skeleton in the family closet—always there yet never directly addressed in polite company, or as a political question, and therefore not proper for the Court to determine ('nonjusticiable')."

As citizens, we have the right to challenge any gerrymandering, especially on fairness and justice grounds. The U.S. Supreme Court, in *Davis v. Bandemer*, only went so far as to declare *partisan* gerrymandering justiciable (proper for the court to determine). *Bandemer* created a standard for finding as unacceptably partisan any gerrymander that the plurality admitted was "difficult of application." That difficulty resulted in relatively little litigation in this area during the 1990s that shed new light on the issue. The standard created in *Bandemer* requires proof of both discriminatory intent and effect (my emphasis). The latter is found when the redistricting "consistently degrade[s] a voter's or a group of voters' influence on the political process as a whole." In this chapter, we shall see how the Minneapolis redistricting openly and intentionally achieved that degradation of fairness and dilution of the Black vote.

This is my point: that the first redistricting map that literally drew both candidates Natalie Johnson-Lee and Brother Shane Price (both are from the Green party) out of their wards (5 and 3, respectively), and put them both in Ward 4 (pitting these two Green Party members against each other, which would have greatly diminished each of their chances) was intentionally done to degrade and dilute the Black vote and any non-DFL (read Green) vote. The Minneapolis City Council was all DFL. No Republicans. No Independents. This plan was clearly to eliminate the remaining party, the Green Party. The plan then was to hold new elections, resulting in neither getting elected. This was proposed in the state legislature by the DFL representative Len Biernet, whose brother is DFL Council Member Joe Biernet, under investigation for collusion regarding work with and money received from a plumbers' union official. Joe would have also benefited from the new election.

Due to the uproar, that first map was changed, and the final submission left both Johnson-Lee and Price in their respective Wards. But Ward 5 was shorn of its downtown section, degrading its economic base, removing it from economic development grants, and turning it into a poverty zone. The Minneapolis branches of the Urban League and the NAACP participated in and acquiesced to all of this. Neither stood up for the Black community. In a twist of the old Western, racist echo that "the only good Indian is a dead Indian," for them "the only good Black is a Democrat." And if these Blacks were going to be Greens, they had to be eliminated.

In the meantime, creating a downtown ward of just the Downtown was creating a super sub-city within the city, making the Downtown Ward Council Member the Mayor of Downtown and putting the bulk of economic approval and taxpayer development money in the jurisdiction of just one Council Member. The Minneapolis *Star Tribune* listed all of the projects being worth close to $200 million. My point is that this is bigger than just the 5th Ward and minorities. This should concern all of us, Black and White, in all the wards. We can't let our guard down or be asleep at the switch. Ward 5, now represented by a Black woman, has been stripped and degraded of all of its downtown influence and of the economic programs that could have brought investment and development to the people of Ward 5.

As I have noted before, and as I will show you below, just because you don't read of this in the *Minneapolis Star Tribune* doesn't mean it isn't being covered. All of this gets reported, but not to any extent in the major papers. To get all the news of your city, read or subscribe to the Black newspaper. In Minneapolis, that newspaper is the *Minnesota Spokesman-Recorder*, whose article I include below. Indeed, in any urban setting, if you want the truth in terms of front-page news, read your Black newspaper. The other excellent alternative newspaper in Minneapolis is City Pages (also online at www.citypages.com).

Here is the set-up: The DFL appoints the Charter Commission. The Charter Commission appoints the Redistricting Commission. The Redistricting Commission thus follows the wishes of the DFL, two steps removed. That, in a sense, is how the DFL launders the decision. So you don't think this is just me, I will quote the story in the *Minnesota Spokesman-Recorder,* a story that you didn't and won't get in the *Star Tribune.* It should be noted that there was no response, no denial, not even coverage of it by the *Star Tribune* that came anywhere close to that of the *Spokesman-Recorder.* The city's power brokers considered themselves so immune to challenge that they just sat back and watched and laughed and carried on as if nothing unusual was happening. And why shouldn't they when their dirty water is also being carried by the Urban League and the NAACP. They had told Cherryhomes that they could deliver the 5th Ward Black vote for her. They failed and Natalie Johnson-Lee was elected instead. Trying to help Cherryhomes get back in by trying to freeze out Johnson-Lee, they worked hand in hand with the DFL and the Redistricting Commission to perpetuate this travesty on the concepts of equal access and equal opportunity, not to mention perpetuating a travesty on the concepts of justice and fairness.

This is from the *Minnesota Spokesman-Recorder* of April 11-17, 2002 (pp. 1 & 14, by Jerry Freeman (**emphasis** is mine):

Headline: **City's lone Black council member under siege**

Subhead: **Embattled Johnson-Lee faces new threats from redistricting plans**

Large letterbox: "It does seem like I should be able to concentrate on working on behalf of those who elected me to office without constantly having to watch my back"   [-- Natalie Johnson-Lee].

Text of article:

It's beginning to look like Minneapolis' Fifth Ward City Council Member Natalie Johnson Lee just can't get a break. In fact, it's beginning to look like the **city's power_brokers** are determined to **undermine or terminate her** political career before it ever really gets started—**by any means necessary.**

In her successful bid for office last fall, Johnson-Lee faced tough odds against three-term DFL-endorsed incumbent Jackie Cherryhomes. After an *exhausting grassroots campaign on the Green Party ticket earned her an upset victory, she came to City Hall in January only to find most of the Ward's records mysteriously missing. All the background information she needed to pick up where her predecessor left off was, well, gone. Lost? Shredded? Stolen? No one seems to know.*

Now, just three months into her term, Johnson-Lee finds herself blindsided by two redistricting proposals that would either strip away much of her leverage as a council member, or draw the new political boundaries in such a way as to **gerrymander her right out of her own** *(for the moment) Fifth Ward.*

The Redistricting Commission Proposal

The proposal **to disempower Johnson-Lee** *and her ward comes from the nine-member Redistricting Commission, eight of whom represent their respective parties – three DFLers, two Republicans, two Independence Party members, one Green Party member – and one member having no party affiliation. Only one of the commission members is a person of color, this in a city that is nearly one-third non-White.*

This group is as political as a body can be, its mission being to carve up the city map into voting units – the 13 wards. The district map is revised every decade or so to adapt to changing demographics so that, among other considerations, the numbers of potential voters in the wards remain roughly equal. The Commission first unveiled its proposed new boundaries last Tuesday, April 2. It will approve a final plan on Friday, April 12, **allowing all of <u>nine</u> days for public review***.*

The Commission's proposal **would remove the Fifth Ward areas of Downtown that have long strengthened the power base for the rest of that ward's constituents***. Downtown commercial development, and the fact that Downtown contributes 46% of the city's tax base, give the ward's council member leverage to benefit other ward residents who may not otherwise have much bargaining power – poor and working class people and people of color.*

Instead of sharing this development leverage with wards like the Fifth containing large numbers of low-income people*, the new commission plan would group Downtown as a unit with neighborhoods to the southwest like Kenwood, Bryn Mawr, and the million-dollar homes clustered around Lake of the Isles and Cedar Lake. It looks like* **rich folks gain and poor folks lose again – a new version of the Hollman Consent Decree, the gentrification project that cleared public housing residents off of lucrative real estate near Downtown.**

The NAACP/Urban League proposal

The proposal that would render Johnson-Lee ineligible to serve as *the Fifth Ward's council member – because she would no longer live in the ward – comes from an alternative* **plan offered jointly by the Minneapolis NAACP and the Urban League**. *One strength of this plan is that it maintains the Fifth Ward's Downtown constituency. However, it does so* **by drawing the boundary line a block from incumbent Johnson-Lee's home**, *thereby forcing her to run a new campaign in another ward if she wants to get back on the council. A recent "Insight" article touting the advantages of the NAACP/Urban League plan failed to mention this little glitch.*

That plan would free up the Fifth Ward's council seat – a ward still retaining the new upscale Hollman development and Downtown – for somebody else to run. Might that not tempt the recently defeated Jackie Cherryhomes to try again for a fourth term? **Cherryhomes' residence remains comfortably within the proposed ward boundaries.**

Missed by one block – doesn't it seem like good common sense to draw that line a block further and include the new council member in her own ward? Especially when the plan's architects are the city's most eminent civil rights organizations dedicated to advancing the interests of people of color? Especially when the disenfranchised council member is Natalie Johnson-Lee, the only person of color currently on the city council? What's wrong with this picture?

Some are saying the exclusion of Johnson-Lee from the NAACP/Urban League's proposed Fifth Ward was a mistake and not intentional. If it was a mistake, it was a grievous, devising mistake that must be rectified quickly to avoid disastrous consequences for public confidence in these institutions.

Traditionally, redistricting is done so as not to cause undue hardship to those currently in office. Tradition similarly dictates that an outgoing officeholder does not foul up the transition for his or her successor. **It's beginning to look like these traditions of respect have been suspended in Johnson-Lee's case**.

Redistricting dirty tricks

There is also a tradition of dirty tricks behind the redistricting process. Only a decade ago, a similar commission gerrymandered City Hall into the Fifth Ward to add a few more minorities to the count – the prisoners in the city jail. According to a recent Skyway News article, "A cynic might note that the prisoners boosted minority 'opportunity' but never voted in the 5th ward because they didn't live there – or were ineligible because of past *felony convictions." **Cynicism is hardly necessary to smell the stink on that one.***

One requirement of redistricting is the creation of several "minority enterprise" wards where people of color are sufficiently represented to have a fair chance of electing one of their own to office. Without such a requirement it is possible to draw ward boundaries that "divide and conquer," splitting people of color to dilute their voting clout. The requirement is also meant to prevent "packing" people of color into a few wards, thus limiting their overall influence on the council. The new Fifth Ward, if the Commission has its way, would be 83 percent people of color. If that's not "packed," then common sense no longer applies to politics in this city.

Guess who will be counted as "minority" residents of the proposed new Downtown Ward: residents of homeless shelters, residents of the Salivation Army, residents of Copeland's Caring and Sharing Hands, prisoners in the city and county jails, even long-term residents of Hennepin County Medical Center. *Since these are people who often do not, or cannot, vote, their influence would be negligible beside that of Downtown businesses, penthouse millionaires, and Lake of the Isles dwellers.*

The rush to approve

The Commission appears to be in a great hurry to get its plan finalized. *For citizens to receive this information, digest it, discuss it, understand its implications and how it affects their long-term interests, **the Commission has allowed – this demands repeating – nine days!***

*Although Commission members apparently feel they have been unprecedentedly open and accessible this time around, that only testifies to the pitiful lack of public participation in previous redistrictings. **Last week the "Spokesman-Recorder" reported the frustration of participants in the March 28 NAACP/Urban League-sponsored forum on redistricting due to the absence of proposed maps for people to examine – no one but the Green Party offered a clue as to their [NAACP/Urban League] plans.*** *A few participants thought it might be an early April Fool's joke, but no, the Commissioners are dead serious about their secrecy.*

Although tentative plans have been "floated" around elite circles, neither the Commission nor the NAACP/Urban League's proposals were disclosed to the public until April 2. A public hearing is scheduled for April 11. The Commission will approve a final plan at noon the next day, April 12. And that's it, folks. That's all the say you get.

Apparently the modus operandi of both the Commission and the NAACP/Urban League is to hold their secret plans close to the chest until the last possible minute, then quickly announce them, rush through an obligatory public hearing, approve a final plan and go home without too much chance for messy democracy to interfere.

Says Johnson-Lee of this latest development, "One of the things that's reinforced is that there will always be a battle. It does seem like I should be able to concentrate on working on behalf of those who elected me to office without constantly having to watch my back. However, I will always keep fighting for the rights of others, even when I also have to fight against those who avowedly protect the rights of others but have chosen not to do so."

Adding insult to injury

It gets worse. A month before the redistricting plans were revealed, three DFL state legislators – including North Minneapolis' Gregory Gray – introduced a House bill, HF 2593, that would require holding new city elections in 2002 and 2003 in wards with population changes greater than five percent. This would prevent Johnson-Lee from serving out even the four-year term to which she was duly elected.

It's beginning to look like the DFL just can't wait to get this Green Party upstart out of the way.

And although it was a small story buried in the Minneapolis *Star Tribune*, the *Spokesman-Recorder* continued to made it the subject of the next week's lead articles as well (April 18-24, 2000) as we see in these three front-page *Spokesman-Recorder* story headlines:

"Commission ignores public outcry: Hearing participants found commissioners elitist, arrogant, rude."

"Fifth Ward Incumbent's exclusion 'honest mistake'."

"Hearing Coverage Exposes Media Bias.

Here are excerpts from the first story, by Kimani Jefferson:

"It's been published as best we know how. It happens every 10 years in the year ending in two." This is what Rev. Parker Trostel, the very rude and inept chair of the Redistricting Commission, stated on Thursday, April

11, at City Hall when asked why other meetings haven't taken place regarding restructuring Minneapolis' wards.   She was correct in her answer.

Or was she? I was at the last meeting on March 28. I remember there being less than a handful of commission members present. I also clearly remember there being no tentative plan.

...

*What happened in Minneapolis [was not "Democracy in Action" but] instead was political inaction characterized by deliverable procrastination on the part of the Commission. **The Commission waited until there was no time legally to change the larger problems in their plan and then declared themselves finished.***

What was the cost? The people most vocal in their objections to the Commission's plan got, as one citizen commented, "raped."

...

Some of the 200 citizens in attendance lashed out at the Commission. ...Gerrymandering...[does not] represent people of color...called the Commission elitist and arrogant.

They had good cause. There was a distinct difference in the way people of color were treated when they spoke. Many were interrupted before completing their statements; and to add insult to injury, the chair kept the time running and smugly held the timer to her microphone when the period elapsed, beeping yet another interruption into the ears of taxpaying citizens.

...

*Even though the public was raw on Thursday, **there was something even darker and uglier going on in the commission seats.** One resident asked the Commission one simple question: **"What is a minority?" The Commission didn't know** [despite their being] eager to create up to six "minority opportunity wards."*

[When asked about] voting age population considerations, they responded by saying ... we cannot take voting age population into account when developing a redistricting plan." [This]} is dead wrong.

...

*...**at least we know of one issue Democrats and Republicans have a bipartisan agreement on: keeping all other parties out of the loop and practicing "politics without principle."***

The second story is an attempt by the NAACP and Urban League to deny any wrongdoing or undermining of Natalie Johnson-Lee, calling it all an "honest mistake." This, of course, is not true. Indeed, the State NAACP, the Sunday before, had passed a resolution congratulating the Minneapolis NAACP for its work, even after I had personally informed them of what had happened. They were not prepared for the voters to rise up and no longer do their bidding.

And if you think my statements of media bias and purposeful non-coverage and suppression of the news are made up, here again is the *Minnesota Spokesman-Recorder*, read these excerpts from the third front page story, "**Hearing coverage exposes media bias**" by Jerry Freeman:

> *It's often not so much what is said that reveals the bias in media; it's what is left out. The "Star Tribune" coverage of the April 11 Redistricting Commission public hearing is a revealing case in point. The article, "Tentative redistricting map draws criticism in Minneapolis," published the day following the hearing, managed to ignore just about everything of importance that occurred – particularly with respect to race and class.*
>
> *Bad enough that this story,* **concerning a process that will lock the city's voters into new wards for the next decade, was buried deep in Friday's [Star Tribune] newspaper**, *on the last page of the Metro/State section. The dominant front-page article in that section featured some corporate executives who played principal for a day in the St. Paul public schools.*
>
> **As anyone can attest who attended the hearing or watched it live on cable TV...four prominent issues were raised:**
> - *The commission's racial and cultural imbalance and its apparent ignorance of, or disinterest in, the racial and cultural implications of its work;*
> - *The capture of the entire Downtown and all its economic clout by the Seventh Ward;*
> - *The possible gerrymandering of Fifth Ward Council Member Natalie Johnson-Lee out of her ward; and*
> - *The splitting of the Little Earth housing complex and its Native-American community into two separate wards.*
>
> *Of these four very serious issues, the "Star Tribune" article mentioned one: Downtown.*
>
> *There was no mention of several overt challenges...*
>
> *There was no mention of the numerous supporters of Fifth Ward Council Member Natalie Johnson-Lee...*
>
> *There was no reference whatever to the Native Americans who spoke...*
>
> **This coverage was, in plain and simple terms, a total Whitewash of the public hearing on city ward boundaries** *with a proposed map that has occurred for 10 years, and that will not occur again until the year 2012.*

Nor was it just the "Star Tribune" -- **to our knowledge, _no_ major TV or radio stations covered the event.**

No better argument is possible for a strong, independent, fearless alternative media in this city to fill in the huge blanks.

And that independent, fearless alternative media, as in newspapers, in Minneapolis are the *Minnesota Spokesman-Recorder* and *City Pages*.

How much more evidence does a person need? I have personally been involved in many of the meetings and with many of the people involved. In Chapter 13, I give my summary and my recommendations for how to clean up the mess. I also worked with another group of concerned citizens, in the meantime, to create a web page to address this, and helped draft the materials sent to the Honorables: the two Minnesota Senate candidates (Democrat Paul Wellstone and Republican Norm Coleman), David M. Mason, the head of the Federal Election Commission, R.T. Rybak, Mayor of Minneapolis, and the heads of the national offices of the NAACP (Kweisi Mfume) and the Urban League (Hugh B. Price). None of these Honorables responded. If the reader is moved to respond to them, I encourage you to do so. Their addresses/emails/faxes are below.

Now as you read this, you are probably wondering if it could get worse. And the answer is: of course it can; this is Minneapolis. It was the attempt to prevent things from getting worse that led to the web page. To repeat: despite the several messages sent, none of the Honorables responded. They didn't even have the courtesy to have a staff person respond.

And two of these addressees are the national heads of the NAACP and the Urban League. Here are the two pieces put out by these community people from their web page, http://www.citizensforfairnessandjustice.com. They were sent to them, via Email (and two by fax):

The first piece sent to them, beginning on the next page, was an open letter about our concerns.

This open letter is on the website http://www.citizensforfairnessandjustice.com.

An open letter from Citizens for Fairness and Justice in Voting to:

The Honorable Paul Wellstone   The Honorable Norm Coleman
The Honorable David M. Mason   The Honorable R.T. Rybak
The Honorable Kweisi Mfume   The Honorable Hugh B. Price

Dear Honorables,   April 10, 2002

The **Citizens for Fairness and Justice in Voting** request that you take action to prevent any redrawing of the Minneapolis Ward Districts until the current issues have been resolved.

The irregularities in the plan proposed last week by the Minneapolis Redistricting Commission, the body that realigns the city's 13 wards, are not only unfair and unjust, they may also be **illegal**. The circumstances leave citizens no choice but to seek action to bring about fairness and justice. We are asking you to investigate this situation and to consider our recommended solution.

The situation:

> 1. The proposed redistricting plan for Minneapolis' 13 wards that has been submitted by the Minneapolis Redistricting Commission is gerrymandering at its worst, and is wrong. Period.

> 2. Re-elected Councilman Joe Biernet (under investigation by the FBI for irregularities and abuse of office) would benefit by the proposal of his brother Len (in the State legislature) that new elections be held after the new ward plans are approved, a proposal we also submit is wrong. Period.

> 3. The proposed redistricting plan is an attempt to disenfranchise the residents of the 5th Ward as citizens of the United States by moving their newly elected 5th Ward Councilwoman, Natalie Johnson-Lee, outside of their Ward. This proposal would also unjustly separate downtown from the near North side, the closest residential neighborhood to downtown.

> 4. The plan is a clear sign of the lack of respect shown by the Minneapolis Redistricting Commission for the wishes of the voters of the 5th Ward of Minneapolis.

> 5. The Minneapolis Redistricting Commission sought and received the blessings of the leaders of the local DFL political party. The local NAACP and the local Urban League have a separate proposal that is also wrong. All three groups have stepped beyond their authority by blessing proposals redistricting plan for Minneapolis' 13 wards that are unfair and unjust, about which their members were not given full details.

> 6. Defeated City Council President Jackie Cherryhomes (who took out of her office the files covering her 12 years in office; she has, to date, refused to

turn over the files) would benefit from the newly assigned district in which Natalie Johnson-Lee, who defeated her, would be redrawn outside into another ward.

The proposed fair and just solution that we recommend is that the redistricting plan be placed on hold until separate investigations can be conducted by you and your offices. Here are the recommendations we ask you to consider:

1. We ask you to get an explanation from the Minneapolis Redistricting Commission as to why they proposed the plan they submitted and to list which individuals and organizations helped them in the re-drawing of the proposed new Ward boundaries.

2. Because of the voting irregularities the plan represents, the Director of the Federal Commission on Elections should inquire and investigate the process and system and results of the actions of the Minneapolis Redistricting Commission.

3. Specifically, nothing should be done until the FBI investigation assures **you** that Minneapolis City Councilman Joe Biernet is not guilty of any irregularities, and that he has not been involved in the plan of the Minneapolis Redistricting Commission.

4. Specifically, nothing should be done until the missing files that Natalie Johnson-Lee's predecessor, former City Council President Jackie Cherryhomes, took from the office, are returned.

5. We hope that after your review you will agree and use your influence to see that a re-alignment is achieved that is fair and just.

To make it easier for you to pass this request on to others with whom you must work as you carry on your independent investigations, we have conveniently placed this letter on our Web site, http://www.CitizensForFairnessAndJustice.com.

Members of the Citizens For Fairness and Justice in Voting
A committee of the Community Advocates Bakers grassroots movement

We can be reached at: info@CitizensForFairnessAndJustice.com

Contact information: see next page

The Honorable Paul Wellstone
U.S. Senator, Minnesota 136 Hart Senate
Office Building Washington, D.C. 20510

Email:
http://wellstone.senate.gov/webform.html
Phone: 202-224-5641 Fax: 202-224-8438

The Honorable David M. Mason
Chairman, Federal Election Commission
999 E Street, NW
Washington, DC 20463
Email: commissionermason@FEC.gov,
http://www.fec.gov/
Phone: (800) 424-9530 Phone In
Washington (202) 694-1100

The Honorable Kweisi Mfume
President and CEO, NAACP
4805 Mt. Hope Drive
Baltimore, MD 21215
Email: Phone: 410-580-5600
http://www.naacp.org/
Phone: 410-580-5600
Toll Free: (877) NAACP-98
NAACP 24 Hour Hotline: 410-521-4939
Fax: 410-486-9255

The Honorable Norm Coleman
Republican Candidate for the U.S. Senate, M
Energy Park Plaza

1410 Energy Park Drive #11
Saint Paul, MN 55108
Email: info@colemanforsenate.com
http://www.colemanforsenate.com
Phone: 651-645-0766 Fax: 651-646-1387

The Honorable R.T. Rybak
Mayor, Minneapolis, Minnesota
331 City Hall
350 South 5th Street
Minneapolis, MN 55415
Email: mayor@ci.minneapolis.mn.us
http://www.ci.minneapolis.mn.us/citywork/
mayor
Phone: 612-673-2100 Fax: 612-673-2305

The Honorable Hugh B. Price
CEO/President, National Urban League
120 Wall Street
New York, NY 10005
Email: info@nul.org
http://www.nul.org
Phone: 212-558-5300 Fax: 212-344-5188

Here is the second piece that was sent to "The Honorables," which also was not acknowledged or responded to. It was sent by Email, and two by fax. It too is on the http://www.citizensforfairnessandjustice.com web page. In this piece we showed the redistricting map and the results of the redistricting:

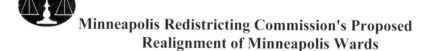

Citizens for Fairness and Justice in Voting

Minneapolis Redistricting Commission's Proposed Realignment of Minneapolis Wards

This map shows the new boundary lines adopted by the Minneapolis Redistricting Commission for the 13 Wards of Minneapolis at their April 12, 2002 meeting. Note the highlight of the new boundary lines for Wards 5 and 7. The red-tinted section is the downtown part of Ward 5 that was taken away from Ward 5 and given to Ward 7.

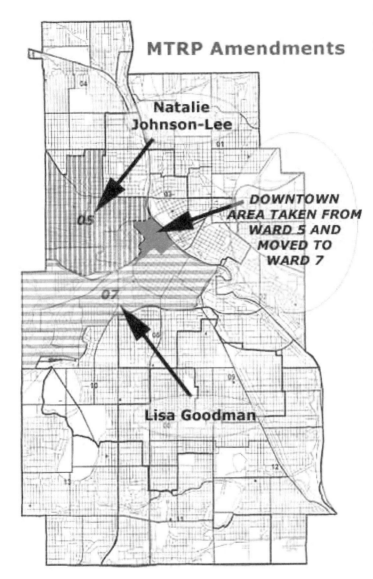

There are some things we are pleased with and some things that we are not pleased with:

We ARE pleased with:

1. Natalie Johnson-Lee was reinstated to her Ward 5.

2. The support that came out in support of Natalie Johnson-Lee demonstrates that when "we the people" wish to act we can have power and authority, meaning we can do even more in the future.

3. The Senate voted down 2002 re-elections in the Wards.

We are NOT pleased with:

1. The fact that the 5th Ward has had the downtown part of it eliminated, which is unfair, unjust, and wrong. Losing downtown will have a negative economic impact on the Wards losing their part of downtown.

2. The fact that the redistricting commission brought to Minneapolis gerrymandering, which has proven throughout the country to be an unfair, unjust, and destructive social force.

3. The fact that the entire downtown has been placed into one Ward rather than the three as before, making that Council Member the *de facto* Mayor of Downtown, which is unfair, unjust, and wrong.

4. The fact that the NAACP made a proposal and tried to withdraw it under fire, all done while overstepping their bounds and making false claims of representing and knowing what is best for the African-American community, which is patently false.

5. The fact that the benefits of the several hundred million dollars of improvements and economic development that went to Downtown between 1992 and 2000 will now fall to one ward under one person, who will now represent one special interest, not the "we the people" of Minneapolis, which is unfair, unjust, and wrong.

Interlude 12

The History of Redistricting Gerrymandering as Vote Swaps
from Internet Research
"Racial Gerrymandering: Enfranchisement or Political Apartheid"
By Maraleen D. Shields
http://www.drury.edu/ess/irconf/MShields.html

What is gerrymandering?
Gerrymandering is a term that describes the deliberate rearrangement of
the boundaries of congressional districts to influence the outcome of
elections.

Where did gerrymandering come from?
The original gerrymander was created in 1812 by Massachusetts
governor Elbridge **Gerry**, who crafted a district for political purposes
that looked like a **salamander**.

What is the purpose of gerrymandering?
The purpose of gerrymandering is to either concentrate opposition votes
into a few districts to gain more seats for the majority in surrounding
districts (called packing), or to diffuse minority strength across many
districts (called dilution).

How has Congress regulated redistricting?
In 1967, Congress passed a law requiring all U.S. representatives to be
elected from single member districts—the system we use today. All
other redistricting regulations comes from the states or the courts.

Copyright © 1999 The Center for Voting and Democracy
http://www.fairvote.org/redistricting/gerrymandering.htm

Today, the major issue does not concern black suffrage, but that even with the right
to vote blacks are not able to ensure adequate representation. Block voting from
blacks in most districts will not even ensure that blacks receive a representative of

their choice. To guarantee some type of representation for blacks as well as other minorities, legislatures began to deliberately create majority-minority districts. This controversial method of districting has received a great deal of attention as a result of the Supreme Court case of Shaw v. Reno.

Cracking, packing and stacking are three methods of districting that can be used to dilute the black vote. **Cracking** involves taking a large group of black voters and splitting them between several mostly White districts. **Packing** occurs when a large number of Blacks are placed in a small number of districts. While blacks will have political success in a small number of districts, they will have lost political influence in the state at large. Finally, **stacking** involves placing Black population in a majority-white district. Whites who still did not want Blacks to vote were able to find loopholes in the system to ensure that Blacks could not exercise their right to vote.

Where Things Began

The election of representatives was not always done via the district system that we know so well today. Nowhere in the Constitution did our founders articulate a manner in which representatives were to be chosen. In some ways this explains the roots of the controversy today. Each state receives a number of seats in the House of Representatives based solely upon the increase or decrease of the state's population. This is called apportionment and occurs every ten years after a Federal census is taken. Until the inception of the Apportionment Act of 1842, states elected representatives in at-large (statewide) elections. However, this process is unfair to the losing party as the winning party is able to control the whole state leaving members of the losing party with without representation. For example, take a historically Republican state. In an at-large election Democrats (up to 49 percent) could potentially not be represented in the legislature. And if it was the reverse (Republicans with up to 49%), then they potentially could also be prevented from having representation in the legislature.

The Apportionment Act of 1842, had, in effect, the had the same goal as the creation of majority-minority districts today, greater representation. The Apportionment Act required states to divide the state into districts equal in number to seats in the house the state is given, thus allowing an opportunity for more than one party to have control in the state. The district system that stems from the Apportionment Act was put in place solely to increase representation of minority views. Majority-minority districts, which are now at issue, are also aimed at increased representation and protection of minority interests. Tyranny of the majority or having a ruling group that is able to make decisions for the whole was as much an issue in 1842 as it is in 1998.

Chapter 13

Redistricting: Themes, Conclusions, and Recommended Remedies

For The Corruption and Racism of Boss City Government: 6 Overall Themes and 5 Major Conclusions, All Reflecting 25 On-Going Points To Ponder, Followed by 5 Recommended Remedies

The Truth Behind The Redistricting Plan

6 Overall Themes

1. The racist and oppressive politics of the Minneapolis DFL.
2. Political dynasties attempting plantation politics of bossism..
3. The iceberg tip of politics is no longer all that shows:
   The whole iceberg is being lifted out of the water by the DFL's over confidence and their "no one can do anything about it" attitude (seen in their using a fake map with the public and then not using the real redistricting map until the last week prior to submission, and then submitting it at submission time, reflecting their true agenda).
4. Bossist manipulation of DFL by political families: Biernet, Dziedzic, Ostrow, Rainville, just like the Southern Plantation families.
5. Use of twin swords of racism and established power bases for families seeking political dynasties and setting themselves up as rulers over their own personal territories.
6. The racism of the DFL, seen in its treatment of Minnesota Blacks as field hands and the collusion with the DFL by the NAACP and Urban League to be the house Negroes over the field hands.

5 Major Conclusions

1. Oppressive and controlling politics of the Minneapolis DFL exclude other parties, using dynasties where possible for name recognition, doing so in part by treating specially selected Blacks to control other Blacks, which they treat as field hands, and which is questionable on corruption, justice and fairness grounds.

2. There is an obvious pass-through of directives from the DFL to the Charter Commission to the Redistricting Commission; again, this is questionable on corruption, justice, and fairness grounds.

3. The redistricting is obviously done to squash the Green Party and keep the DFL in control, which is questionable on corruption, justice and fairness grounds.

4. Downtown is being made into a powerful island unto itself at the expense of the other wards, which are thereby impoverished and disempowered, ensuring that minorities are kept out of planning, contracts, and other development, by redlining minorities out on maps [drawing lines for use in determining where they can't go or must stay] and using "Boot Hill" [dead voters' names] and other phantom voting methods to pretend they are counted, all of which are again questionable on corruption, justice, and fairness grounds.

5. The city and the media are covering up the Biernet investigation and the removal of files by Jackie Cherryhomes, which, if released or found, could shed light on most of these matters. These matters need to be investigated for their obvious illegality and fraud as arranged through gentlemen's agreements by the DFL bosses, practices that are questionable on legal, corruption, justice, and fairness grounds.

25 On-Going Points to Ponder About the Redistricting

1. The objectionable redistricting was put into action by the bossist act of the DFL manipulation by dictating to the Charter Commission what the redistricting should be.
2. The objectionable redistricting was also put into action by the bossist act of manipulation of the Charter Commission (chaired by Karen Dziedzic) dictating to the Redistricting Commission.
3. The objectionable redistricting was also put into action by the bossist act of manipulation of the Redistricting Commission drawing up new lines based on what they were told to do.
4. It is unfair and racist to remove the economic "gravy" of downtown from Ward 5.
5. The objectionable redistricting was also put into action by the bossist act of manipulatively using "Boot Hill voting" by counting inmates of jails, homeless shelters, and transition housing as resident voters, despite the fact that this is illegal.
6. The objectionable redistricting was also put into action by the bossist act of putting economic development areas in DFL-controlled wards so as to dcprive the others of tax-increment financing development and placing empowerment zone dollars into limbo.

7. The objectionable redistricting was also put into action by the bossist act of making sure all evidence of bossism manipulation that resided in the vast bulk of files taken by outgoing City Council President Jackie Cherryhomes would not be available to her democratically elected Ward 5 successor, Natalie Johnson-Lee, which neither the new mayor nor the city attorney have addressed.

8. The redrawing of Ward 3 made it favorable for Karen Dziedzic to run for City Council Member.

9. The redrawing of Ward 5 made it favorable for any one other than Natalie Johnson-Lee to represent the downtown.

10. The original redistricting map drew both Johnson-Lee's and Brother Shane Price's homes out of their respective wards into Ward 4, which, with the new election they wanted to hold, would have knocked out the Green party.

11. The language of Empowerment Zones is now Orwellian, as the words don't mean what they normally do, as instead of empowered they are disempowered and, from an economic development sense, financially disemboweled.

12. The concentration of poverty and city neglect in Ward 5 of Natalie Johnson-Lee sets up overwhelming work for the Ward 5 Council Member, essentially taking her out of the game with the rest of the council, using the map to segregate her from the rest of the White council's business and activities.

13. This redistricting ploy continues the tradition of excluding minorities by union towns and by unions.

14. This redistricting ploy continues the tradition of excluding minorities from unions and, thus, big construction jobs.

15. This redistricting ploy continues the tradition of the city using out-of-town contractors for exclusionary purposes (excluding local contractors with minority workers), especially for downtown.

16. This redistricting ploy was an unfair and racist attempt to move Natalie Johnson-Lee out of Ward 5.

17. This unfair and racist redistricting ploy was also an attempt to move Shane Price out of Ward 3.

18. This unfair and racist redistricting ploy was also an attempt to crush the nascent Green Party.

19. This unfair and racist redistricting ploy was also an attempt to disempower minorities by redistricting them out of development areas.

20. This unfair and racist redistricting ploy was also an attempt to put all of downtown under one Ward instead of several wards, as if it were done to set up the Ward 7 Council Member as the Downtown Mayor.

21. The corruption charge against Joe Biernet needs to be settled.

22. The attempt by City Council Member Joe Biernet's brother Len (a Minnesota legislator) to schedule an immediate new election to finish off Natalie needs to be addressed.
23. The Enron-like disappearance of Jackie Cherryhomes's office files needs to be addressed.
24. Neither the national head of the NAACP nor the national head of the Urban League replied to the letters sent to them from the Citizens Committee for Fairness and Justice in Voting.

The Whites did not respond to the Citizens Committee for Fairness and Justice in Voting either: not the new Mayor of Minneapolis nor the two candidates running for Senator, one a DFL, the other a Republican, nor the head of the Federal Election Commission.

7 Recommended Remedies:

1. That the information presented above be investigated for possible illegalities and corruption.
2. That the information presented above be investigated on justice and fairness grounds.
3. That the redistricting process be re-done.
4. That the submitted redistricting map list all assumptions used to develop the map, as well as empirical data backing these assumptions and their attendant influence on the re-drawn ward lines.
5. That the Redistricting Commission be reconstituted to include at least one person from each ward and reflect proportionally the results of the most recent election, now and for all future redistricting census reports.
6. That the corruption charges against Joe Biernet be made public.
7. That the City Attorney be instructed to report why no investigation has been conducted as to the missing Jackie Cherryhomes files and be instructed to immediately commence such an investigation.

Interlude 13

The 1921 Tulsa Race Riots
As Told To Me By My Grandfather

For those of us fortunate to have been able to spend time with our grandparents, we learned things from the past that gave us a greater appreciation of our present. Unlike many of the Interludes, the story of the Oklahoma Race Riots is unknown to most Whites. My dad was Alfred Edwards. His dad, my grandfather, was C.M. Edwards.

A self-educated man, my Grandfather Edwards fled home at the age of 16 after killing a White man for molesting his sister. He moved to Birmingham and then to New Orleans, until he ultimately got a job with the Pullman Company in Kansas City, Missouri. I used to visit him in his little two-room apartment, where he shared a bath with four others. In those days, there was little senior housing and certainly none for African-Americans. He lived to be 96. When I moved to Minneapolis at age 7, I would still visit him when I went back to Kansas City every summer, usually for 5-8 hours at a time.

I remember my Grandfather Edwards fondly. It was always he who came to look out for me when my parents could not. From our time together, I came to understand and appreciate the depth of his wisdom. He educated me about the Tulsa Race Riots when I was 17 years old, another influence on my decision to work as a community advocate. You can read about them in *Riot and Remembrance: The Tulsa Race War and Its Legacy* by James S. Hirsch (Houghton Mifflin Co, 2002) and in *Black Wall Street: From Riot to Renaissance in Tulsa's Historic Greenwood District* by Hannibal B. Johnson (Eakin Publications, 1998).

My grandfather went into more detail, and I have been able to corroborate what my grandfather said. The reason most Whites don't know the events of this shameful episode in American history is because Tulsa, both White and Black, tried to erase all mention of it, just as Duluth Whites and Blacks did of the lynching there (Interlude 15). But news of such murders will always get out. In addition to the mass lynching in the African-American Greenwood part of Tulsa, there was also the slaughter of over 200 Black women and children in the stockyards of Tulsa. Their bodies were left in the mud for the swine to feed on.

Hirsch also points out in his book that Tulsa tried to keep the news of the mass lynching from spreading. Any mention of the Greenwood affair was deleted from official documents. Innocent Black scapegoats were used. The Johnson book illustrates for young Blacks today that despite those times, the Greenwood Blacks were prosperous (which is why they burned Greenwood to the ground), and if we get back into that educated, entrepreneurial mind set, Blacks in the inner city who think things are hopeless can learn that they too can prosper.

My grandfather heard of the events from Blacks on trains that passed through Kansas City, and from telegraph messages (this was when Blacks were still allowed to be train engineers and telegraphers). He vividly recounted for me how in 1921, 200 armed young WWI Veterans from Chicago and another 200 from St. Louis, joined with 400 from Kansas City and Chicago, to go to Tulsa to try to stop the killing. Some came from Omaha, which was famous at the time for the local newspaper picture of the young African-American nailed to a cross made of two railroad ties, soaked in kerosene, and burned alive.

My grandfather told me that the postal train that had passed through Tulsa, with Black engineers and crew, reported that trouble was brewing, that lynching was possible, and many were surrounded and trapped. In telling the story, my grandfather always spoke with pride that despite the incidents of lynching and brutalities across the Midwest, that Kansas City was one of the few cities where no Negro was ever lynched.

On the second day, when the next postal train passed through, they learned of the atrocities. They also learned from hundreds of women and children who were on a special train that spirited them out to protect them. He reminded me that many of the Blacks who gathered to go to Tulsa were WWI veterans. Others were with Teddy Roosevelt in Cuba or were Buffalo Soldiers with experience settling the West. All had their own arms, and all wanted to go to protect those being slaughtered or being held in detention camps that became the models for the internment camps in California for Japanese-Americans during World War II.

This is another example of the kind of racial cleansing that had taken place 12 years earlier in the southern part of Missouri and in the Ozarks of Arkansas. Many who were killed had originally been granted safe conduct. Bi-planes were then used by the Oklahoma National Guard and Oklahoma militia to bomb and strafe Blacks with machine gun fire. When this ambush and killing was reported by the mail train and survivors on the special train on the second day used to get them away, the local militia organized to go to Tulsa. And although they commandeered a train to take them, the Feds impounded the train and they were forced to drive in caravans of trucks and cars. They arrived too late.

When the dust settled, here is what was left behind in Greenwood: one of the most horrible injustices and slaughters of Blacks in U.S. history. The entire prosperous Black town of Greenwood was torched: 1,256 homes, churches, stores, schools, hospitals and a library, all looted and burned to the ground. To me this is another case for reparations.

Then there was the lynching and slaughter in the stock yards. Others inside row houses were burned alive when their homes were set on fire. The incident ended with an additional 6,000 Blacks forced into detention centers at gunpoint. Tulsa then became a center for the Ku Klux Klan, as Whites worked to keep the Blacks from rebuilding Greenwood. This was the result of the *de facto* apartheid of the Jim Crow culture, a culture of violence that would be seen again in the 1960s in such cities as Selma, Birmingham, and Watts, to name but a few. It is events such as these that make it difficult to find common ground on the two polarizing issues of affirmative action and reparations.

I have discussed these events and these books on several programs of my TV show. I learned that Blacks have just as hard a time believing this story as Whites.

Don Ross, whom I had met at a meeting and who was elected to the Oklahoma legislature, told me that he too had learned of this from his parents and grandparents. He talked about how it was one of the best-kept secrets. Two years ago, Don Ross was instrumental in getting Oklahoma Governor Frank Keating to provide the funds for a special commission appointed to investigate this, to educate people about this, and to set up a reconciliation between Blacks and Whites.

The Economic Meaning of Stories Like Tulsa: Black's Can Be Prosperous

Tulsa, Greenwood, and what I've said about Minneapolis Black commerce in this books, is what John McWhorter would call "usable black history."

My goal with stories like Tulsa is not to horrify, although it horrifies. My goal is to point out that despite all that took place, Blacks carved out economic prosperity in times far worse than today, far worse. But as McWhorter points out, "a history of horrors cannot inspire." My concern is today's young Black men. They hear the horror stories but they don't hear the success stories. My goal has been to make my book a blend of the two, so they don't forget our shared glass half empty history but also that they can take inspiration from viewing it as a glass half full which they can work on to fill.

In his August 22, 2001 column, "A usable black history," Walter Williams echoes what McWhorter has written in discussing McWhorter's Summer 2001 City Journal article. We must avoid, at all costs, as painting all society as our enemy and lose hope. To succeed with good jobs and housing we must first gain knowledge through schooling and training and seek to become a part of the economic mainstream and not pull away into enclaves of helplessness as victims. These stories attest to the fact that successful economic communities can be built.

As Williams points out, and this is key for our young Black men to learn, focus on the reality of the incredible Black successes in the face of seemingly insurmountable odds. As Williams summarizes McWhorter:

> From the late 1800s to 1950, some black schools were models of academic achievement. Black students at Washington's Dunbar High School often outscored white students as early as 1899. Schools such as Frederick Douglas (Baltimore), Booker T. Washington (Atlanta), P.S. 91 (Brooklyn), McDonough 35 (New Orleans) and others operated at a similar level of excellence. These excelling students weren't solely members of the black elite; most had parents who were manual laborers, domestic servants, porters and maintenance men.
>
> Chicago's "Bronzeville" is a handy example. After 1875, blacks occupied a three by 15 block enclave on the South Side. During the early 1900s, Bronzeville was home to several black newspapers and 731 business establishments, by 1917 in 61 lines of work. The Binga Bank opened in 1908 by its founder Jesse Binga, who started out with a wagon selling coal and oil. By 1929, Bronzeville blacks had amassed $100 million in real-estate holdings.
>
> Chicago wasn't the only city where blacks established a significant business presence. Other cities would include New York; Philadelphia; Durham, N.C.; Atlanta and Washington, D.C. -- and Tulsa's Greenwood district, which was destroyed by rioting whites.

These successes were accomplished "in a harsh racial environment. No one can attribute their successes to SBA minority loans, business set-asides, affirmative action and measures deemed indispensable by today's race experts. It was accomplished through hard work, sacrifice and, as my father used to say, coming early and staying late."

Blacks have achieved before. We can again. We don't have to wait for permission or someone else's kindness. We just have to act. We should be very proud of the fact that Black Americans " have made the greatest gains, over some of the highest hurdles, in a shorter span of time than any other racial group in mankind's history. That speaks well of the intestinal fortitude of a people, and it also speaks well of a nation in which such gains were possible." Now we have to bring it to Minneapolis.

Chapter 14

The Role of Minneapolis Black Organizations In The Minneapolis Story

**Civil Rights Commission, Urban League, NAACP,
Churches/Synagogues/Mosques—
Being Part of the Problem Rather than the Solution,
As They Move Toward White-Like Black-Elite Rule,
For Spoils Not Principles
And Sell Out Inner city Black Community Interests:
Education, Housing, and Jobs, Dignity and Recognition**

The Civil Rights Commission, the NAACP, and Urban League were formed to achieve for the African-American the civil rights announced by the Declaration of Independence and the Constitution that were at first restricted essentially to White males.

This chapter discusses how the local Minneapolis branches of these time-honored Black organizations have turned from serving Blacks of the community to serving the DFL (Democratic-Farmer-Labor Party, the Minnesota state party of the National Democratic Party) giving in to selling out as they are herded by the DFL. These organizations used to do great things. Now they are contributing to the very problems they used to combat. In the beginning there was elite White rule. Now, among African-Americans, we have elite Black rule. These groups no longer serve the interests of inner city Blacks.

There should be no need for a Civil Rights Commission, an Urban League, or an NAACP. That they exist tells us that evil exists and that attempts to return to them exist as well. The worst thing these organizations can do is link up with those committing the evil they were founded to fight. That is the dilemma they find themselves in today. I've spent most of my adult life as a part of these organizations. I have always loved them, and still do, even if they have not always loved me for my criticism regarding what they have done or are doing. My positions with these organizations have included:

<u>Minneapolis Civil Rights Commission</u>

- Chairman 1979 – 1983
- Vice-Chairman 1967 – 1972
- Member 1968 – 1983

Minneapolis Branch of the Urban League

- President, Chairman 1978 – 1989 (longest of any of the 25 people who have served)
- Executive committee 1972 – 1989

Minneapolis Branch of the NAACP

- Executive Committee 1999 – 2002
- Housing chair 1999 – 2002
- Member, 1962 – Present

Minnesota-South Dakota NAACP

- Political Action Chair, 2002 – Present
- Education hair for the Minnesota-South Dakota NAACP, 1999 – Present
- Executive Committee, 1997 – Present

Other

- Spokesperson for the Black Police Officer's Association 1996 – Present.
- North Side Settlements 1975 – 1983
- Member, Pilot City Board of Directors 1971– 1979
- Pilot City Planning Committee 1967 – 1970

I love these organizations. But there comes a time when we have to confront those we love when they are not doing what they ought to be doing. It is said that doing the same thing over and over again yet expecting different results is a definition of insanity. It is also a characteristic of those more concerned with job security than organizational mission. If the inner cities of America are still the left behind areas of the country, there are only two reasons for it: either Blacks are too dumb and lazy or the organizations responsible have given up, for whatever reasons. Experience tells me the former is not true. Experience and observation tell me the latter has occurred, as the key organizations have settled for the grants and government monies that come with being lackeys for the Democrats. It is harsh to say but the results clearly show they have sold out. Too many solutions exist that work in too many places that these groups refuse to try or refuse to champion, especially in education, housing, and jobs. I invite all of you readers who are members of these organizations to give them your encouragement to change to marching again with their eye on the prize of freedom, not on the atta-boys and atta-girls from a favored political party.

<u>The NAACP</u> (The National Association for the Advancement of Colored People) was founded by Blacks but has always allowed Whites to join as well (this is very different from many White groups). Its <u>mission</u> (<u>www.naacp.org</u>):

> For more than 93 years, the NAACP has been built on the individual and collective courage of thousands of people. People of all races, nationalities and religious denominations, who were united on one premise—that all men and women are created equal.

However, the 10 initiatives for the next 10 years outlined by the NAACP on its web site are not community-oriented except in the sense of supporting government programs and initiatives tied closely to the Democratic Party. Its focus has changed from social justice issues to social services. It needs to refocus on social justice issues again as well as on Black economic empowerment and wealth generation.

The fact that the NAACP still calls itself the NAACP shows how out-of-touch and out-of-step it is. Few Blacks in America today call themselves a Negro or Colored, and certainly no one under 40 does. Only older elite Blacks think the NAACP is still something. It is not. The money they raise is to keep the organizations going; they serve little in the community except their own cliques. And they don't take a step back to look at who they really are and what they are really doing.

If the name the initials stand for don't mean anything real, how can the organization? The NAACP needs to rethink and reorganize and change its name from NAACP to NAAAP: The National Association of African-American People.

I personally prefer Black. But I am also African-American in the sense that my ancestors came from there. In another sense, African-Americans are probably the only true, real Americans, in that we are the only ones truly self-created here in America. Native Americans have morphed into a culture that is a pale reflection of who they were briefly between the time the Spaniards came and introduced horses to them and when the Whites came who took away their horses and mobilty. As Blacks, we were totally cut off from our people, our languages, our religions, our culture, our way of life. We were literally recreated as a people twice, first by the Mastuhs, as we played the public roles they expected, and secondly as our own people created by ourselves for our true selves when we were not with the Mastuhs. In that sense, we are Negro Americans, Americans created by Negroes. All other groups in America carry traditions and food and stories of "the old country" from which they immigrated.   The more immigrant groups as well as Native Americans become educated and assimilated into the mainstream culture and economy, the more they become the "American" to the right of their hyphens. I have heard some remark that American Indians are now the Native American Gamblers or the Gambling Indians. And when enough tribes have casinos, their heritage will be as picturesque and quaint as European Americans dressed in "native" old country clothing for dances no one else dances except as "ethnic festivals" (certainly their kids wouldn't be caught dead wearing them to school dances). Their past will recede as that of both the pre-Columbian and post-Columbian peoples.

The Urban League states as its mission (www.nul.org) that it is to

> [To] enable African-Americans to secure economic self-reliance, parity and power and civil rights.

Traditionally, the Urban League has sought

> [To] emphasize greater reliance on the unique resources and strengths of the African-American community to find solutions to its own problems.

The Urban League's three-pronged strategy for pursuing the mission is:

- **Education and Youth:** Ensuring that our children are well-educated and equipped for economic self-reliance in the 21st century

- **Economic Self Sufficiency:** Helping adults attain economic self-sufficiency through good jobs, homeownership, entrepreneurship and wealth accumulation.

- **Racial Inclusion:** Ensuring our civil rights by eradicating all barriers to equal participation in the economic political and social mainstream of America.

These are great goals, but in reality, the Urban League concentrates more on social services and policy analysis than on social justice issues and wealth generation that comes from "economic self-sufficiency." The Urban League needs to stand up for Black education, inclusion, and economic self-sufficiency in actual situations, and stop providing automatic votes for candidates of the Democratic Party, which seeks out Black votes but not Black participation nor Black economic empowerment and wealth generation.

To achieve this, and to suggest getting back to its roots, I suggest that the Urban League needs to enter into alliances with other groups, public and private and then change its name accordingly to "The Urban League of Alliances" or "The Urban Alliance."

The closest the Urban League got to these goals was during the tenure of Vernon Jordan. He very much tended to business, and was helpful to us when he was in town. Given his stature and credentials in this country, including being an advisor to Presidents and sitting on major corporate boards, he would meet directly with the leaders of the Minneapolis corporate community. He was aware of my presence because I would raise issues for the bosses in Minneapolis as well as at the annual Urban League meetings. Local Urban Leaguers brought their concerns about me in Minneapolis in the 1970s to Vernon Jordan. But it is frowned upon in the Urban League to criticize your board, especially just for personal reasons. I was the unpaid Chairman of the Board. Nonetheless, Gleason Glover, then the paid President of the Minneapolis Urban League, started doing so, especially about me. Vernon saw that regardless of whatever petty complaints those jealous of me that they had, he understood that under my leadership we enjoyed continued and expanded funding and growth. From mutual acquaintances in St. Louis and Kansas City, he found out about my pedigree through L. Virgil Miller, and although I was considered by some to be the Black sheep in our family, I was still the real deal.

In the mid-70s, I was the Manager of Environmental Affairs for NSP (Northern States Power), with a staff of over 20, which was prior to my becoming Manager of the Community Affairs Department. Bob Engles, then Chairman of NSP, who was interested in the environment. He served as a mentor to me. He was impressed with my work, and over objections of other company executives, he affirmed my recommendation that Vernon Jordan be the Keynote Speaker for an NSP-sponsored national conference on the environment and how it affects the community. Vernon is a Renaissance man. He had become well-versed in environmental issues, and after hearing him speak on it at an earlier Urban League gathering, I knew he was just the man for a national conference on the environment in Minneapolis. It was the first nation-wide conference on energy and the environment. Glover and others were upset that I was able, on my own and without them, to successfully invite Vernon to speak.

The national Urban League has a covenant with the United Way, as well as with other non-profit organizations, including the Boy Scouts and Girl Scouts, that in case there is a rebellion and the affiliates go against the wishes and interests of the national, the United Way will cut their funding. The national sends the board of the local branches a list of who is eligible to be considered for the paid position of branch head, which may or may not include a local. Part of the tightness of this control is the result of the time when the Black Panthers and similar groups began to move on these organizations back in the 60s. Most affiliates cave in to the wishes of the national. Unfortunately, despite the passing of that period, the structure remains in place, which leaves the locals too dependent on the national. But affiliates like Minneapolis, where we were getting significant funding from not only the United Way but also government and other sources, took a more independent stance. The national Urban League's largest programs were the Seniors Program and the Employment/Labor Program. The programs and locals were listed by priority, and at the time of my leadership, we were in Category I in all of their programs.

Gleason Glover was eventually forced out and replaced by Gary Suddeth, who was later replaced by Clarence Hightower. After six years with The YMCA, Clarence joined City, Inc., which used to be the controversial non-profit Way organization. The Way was put out of business by the United Way. Paid Urban League Executive Directors became the paid President, and the previously unpaid President became the unpaid Chairman, as they changed terminology to parallel corporate structure better. Despite Hightower being under investigation at City Inc. for irregularities, behind-the-scenes maneuvering resulted in Hightower being elected President of the Urban League, providing the White bosses a person they wanted, as he is a person they can control.

The Civil Rights Commission, which was called the Fair Employment Practices Commission when it was started in 1946 in Minnesota, became the Human Rights Commission in 1964; in 1975 it became the Civil Rights Commission. The Commission is separate from the Civil Rights Department.

The Civil Rights *Department* is an administrative arm of the City, staffed with paid employees of the city; it investigates filed cases alleging civil rights violations. The Civil Rights *Commission* is a legislative arm that hears the cases brought by citizens.

All of us on the *Commission* were unpaid appointees. When I started, it had 15 members. But I was considered so tough to deal with that the City Council, in 1968, demanded and got to appoint another six. I guess that made them feel more comfortable. When they did that, I chuckled and said that was probably the right number so they could have enough to equal me. Since then, there have always been 21 members. Now the powers had to have the commission, but were not sure what it would do. Not trusting inner city people, they "of course" made sure that half of the members appointed were prominent people who lived outside the city. I guess they decided we inner city folks needed help from the good White folks in the suburbs to deal with the inner city. Nonetheless, we worked well together. We had very fine people. We had attorneys who went on to become excellent judges. It was a wonderful group of unpaid yet highly qualified professionals who all shared the same ideals, even if we didn't always share the "hows" to go along with our "what."

According to the web page of the City of Minneapolis, the mission (http://www.ci.minneapolis.mn.us/citywork/civil-rights/history.html#about) of the Civil Rights Commission is to

> implement the City's Civil Rights policies through public information, education, mediation, conciliation and enforcement as stated in the Minneapolis Code of Ordinances. The primary objective of the Commission is to promote and protect the civil rights of the citizens of Minneapolis.

During my time on the council, as noted below, none of our decisions were ever reversed.

The 1960s were a time of great promise, hope, and expectation. The 1980s were a time of reversing that promise. The last five years have, in some ways, taken us back in some ways to a climate in Minneapolis that is almost like the climate before the 1960s.

The 1960s

In the 1960s, I began my work as an unpaid community advocate. It was tougher then than it is now. As Minneapolis Mayor Arthur Naftalin stated in his inaugural message for his second term, July 1963:

> A fire of protest against indignity and denial is burning here as it is elsewhere. It will not be extinguished by promises or pledges that are not translated into action.

He pointed out the need for equal treatment by civic and public agencies and for equal opportunities for education, jobs and housing. Sadly, in terms of the inner city, of North Minneapolis, we are still at that point: the needs remain unfulfilled, now as then, because of "promises or pledges that are not translated into action." It is my contention that the powers that be in Minneapolis are no longer interested in even pretending: they will show the world how they keep the Black person in his or her place.

Mayor Naftalin set up the Minneapolis Civil Rights Commission in 1968. I am proud that, as a result of my efforts in the community at the time, I was appointed by the Mayor when I was 28, to be one of the first group of 15 members. Our task was to work on fair employment practices, fair housing, and other anti-discrimination measures.

The 1980s

During the 1980s, I began to formulate my idea that Minneapolis was becoming the great experiment of the last outpost to demonstrate how to keep Blacks where they "belong" began, as Minneapolis began to work toward a *de facto* reversal of the Civil Rights laws in Minneapolis just as the Jim Crow laws had achieved the *de facto* reversal of the 13th-15th Amendments in the Southern states. The 13th Amendment ended slavery and servitude. The 14th Amendment counts each citizen as a whole, not as a fraction, as Negroes were before. The 15th Amendment granted all citizens in all states the right to vote.

A major change in the 1980s came when civil rights was no longer interpreted in terms of race, which was to enable Blacks to better play catch-up after 300 years of slavery but instead began to be defined in terms of victim groups based on gender and sexual orientation. Thus, the Civil Rights Commission, which was traditionally against racial discrimination, is no longer about civil rights as that term was traditionally defined. It is now open to all kinds of new groups, now called "protected classes," which includes not only those of gender and sexual orientation, but the physically challenged (who used to be classified as "handicapped").

I'm not opposed to these groups working out how to obtain their rights as well, but it is not the same thing. The key is that most of these groups are White, which defeats and ignores the original purpose.

For instance, the number of White women who joined the police department in 1984 exceeded the number of black police officers, male and female, in the entire police department. And the number of female officers in the police and fire departments outnumbered all of the African-Americans. The trend in Minneapolis has been to hire fewer Black officers. And it is critically important to have Black police officers in the neighborhoods of a city that is over 30% Black, for all that inner city kids see today is White cops stopping Black kids, day after day. The message in their minds would be very different if it were Black cops stopping Black kids. Then drugs and guns would no longer be a Black thing to be defended against Whites but a neighborhood thing to be freed from. And yet, how can the police inspire the neighborhood when people feel subjected to endless daily harassment by them and their verbal drive-bys, shouting racist comments and giving them the finger. That is neither kind nor courteous nor civil. And I could also make the case that the situation resulting in the young White female police officer being killed by the Black woman in her 60s in August 2002 (Chapter 16) might not have happened had the police officer been Black.

With Civil Rights now being defined in other terms, such as gender, sexual orientation, and physical disabilities, the quotas become dramatically changed. For example, if the desire is to hire 24 fire fighters and 18 police officers, and that within these goals, 30% have to be minorities, and the latter is defined as 50% and within those 25% lesbians, that means that the African-American numbers shrink as it pertains to inclusion.

Now please, dear reader, do not say I am making a negative comment about the gays or women or what used to be called the handicapped. I am not. What I am saying is that no other group can claim equivalency with Blacks: not women, not gays, not the physically handicapped, not any group. They didn't endure slavery, Jim Crow laws, the Ku Klux Klan, and segregated lunch counters and practically segregated everything else. The difference between their experiences compared to those of Blacks is huge. Also, there are no inner city ghettoes of women or gays or the physically disabled.

This new reinterpretation enables other groups, and in Minneapolis the other group most benefiting is what is called the GLBT community (gay, lesbian, bi-sexual, transgendered), to take away from the Black community, especially in housing (Chapter 8). Women are not a statistical minority, yet for legal purposes are compared that way. They have the voting clout, as women make up over 50% of the population. Gays are a legitimate minority but want majority status and privileges. To appoint, as was done in 1984, a gay White woman as head of the City's Civil Rights Department, who was not even from Minneapolis, was to turn the whole Civil Rights Movement on its head. Women are not a legitimate minority, but have gotten proclaimed so nonetheless. Not that woman and gays and the physically challenged don't have their own grievances, but to lump them together is to trivialize and marginalize Blacks. That is what I'm opposed to. And let us be realistic. The 20th century wars slaughtered mostly young men, and indeed, the majority of the tens of millions killed in the 20th century were White males. So everyone has a grievance. But none like Black men and women with their history along with Federal policy based on the false notion that says they can't make it on their own, and are thus denied access to the economic mainstream given to others. That so many have succeeded anyway is a testament to the Black soul, not White support.

My protest against having a White woman as head of the Civil Rights Department in 1984 was not because she was White or gay , but because it solidified the further erosion and watering down of civil rights, giving non-Blacks equal if not greater weight than Jim Crowed Blacks. That Whites cannot understand the deep insult to and trivialization of Blacks that this represents is another example of their deep racism, even if they can't see it themselves. As various stories in the papers have noted, Blacks' issues are getting pushed aside in favor of "pornography and domestic partnership." These confrontations between White feminists and Blacks often make it seem as if White women don't care about women who are Black.

Civil Rights was, is, and should be about prejudice and discrimination based on race in jobs and housing. To add pornography and partnership issues as if they have suffered the same as Blacks in terms of discrimination in education, jobs and housing, is the equivalent of their turning their collective White backs on Blacks. This is what I fought. To ask for a conciliatory tone and approach from those who are being forcefully shoved aside on the Civil Rights agenda is to make a mockery of the terms "negotiate in good faith" or of "reconciliation" or "consensus," when the consensus of the majority is to boot out the concerns of Blacks. Women and gays and the handicapped have to understand that the kinds of devastation delivered to Blacks should and must take priority. I have never excluded women, gays, or the physically challenged. But I am not in favor of letting them replace Blacks or act as if there is an equivalency, when there decidedly is not.

You can also see this in the construction industry, where there are actually more White women on the construction sites of Minneapolis than there are Blacks.

For me, the 1980s ended when the Minneapolis Urban League tried to set me up in August 1989, when the national Urban League held its annual meeting in San Francisco. It was the first conference ever that Gleason Glover, the paid President of the Minneapolis Urban League, did not attend. He stayed back to help the Feds put together a late raid on the Urban League, in order to find evidence in the files against me. Of course there was none. There never is, because I have never done anything wrong with the Urban League or the NAACP or the Civil Rights Commission, or any other group, now or in the past.

While I was in San Francisco, Glover was telling people that the local stations, WCCO radio and WCCO-TV, would be breaking a major story about a civil rights leader who was fooling around. Me. Well, that, of course was not true.

They were out to get me because Minneapolis Mayor Don Frasier felt I had stepped over the bounds in regards to Sales Seron Scott, shot and killed by White Minneapolis police, when I got the case reopened because of my relationship with a good friend who had a very good relationship with then U.S. Attorney General Edwin Meese. And Glover had his own reasons. He was compromising staff for personal favors in order for them to maintain their employment and was supported by what I consider a bunch of thugs. WCCO even had the title of the story they planned to run before they went out to investigate, they were so sure of themselves: "Betrayal of Trust: The Shame of a Civil Rights Leader."

Glover and others has guaranteed WCCO that they would get the goods on Ron Edwards, and they would be able to "destroy the phony loudmouthed hypocritical SOB." Truth may set you free. But not everyone wants the truth to be told, and not being able to hide it can make people angry. My understanding of the WCCO plotting came from Isaiah "Ike" Watkins. He wanted me to tell this story some day. That day has come. This is another story I never told before. Ike was a great guy. His father and grandfather were born in southwest Minnesota. Indeed, we think that the Black guy in the story of *Little House on the Prairie* in Walnut Grove was probably his father. Ike was born in Denver, and then moved to Minneapolis in the 1950s. Ike was one of my great friends. Ike had six daughters, one of whom was a TV/News anchor in NewYork City. She had a highly placed White friend at WCCO who told her father that WCCO had spent $75,000 to send their investigative reporter Al Austin and others out to San Francisco to investigate me, an investigation that turned up nothing on me. I was my usual hard-working self, attending all working sessions. They bugged my room, tapped my phone, followed me with hidden cameras, and still came up with nothing.

Now understand what is so unique here: Glover for years had always gone to the annual conference two days early for the Presidents' meetings with the national leaders. We usually sent 12-18 people, including at least 5 board members and at least 5 staff members.

Glover told CCO that they could get me with women and drugs in San Francisco. Now, first off, that was never my scene. But, again, people accuse you of things they do, as many people assume what they do is natural and therefore others must be doing it too. Of course Glover couldn't do this on his own. He was controllable, just doing the bidding of the Mastuhs. This whole plan was actually masterminded by Mayor Don Fraser and his Police Chief Tony Bosa.

On a day early in the conference, after the sessions, a couple of us went to a party hosted by the NAACP. There were lots of women, but no Urban Leaguers. And we saw what looked like undercover cops as well as a camera discreetly placed, which I would not have noticed if it if it hadn't been for its red light. When someone sat down next to us and poured some white powder on the glass coffee table, I knew it was time to leave. We immediately said that because we were taking Nellie Stone Johnson (Interlude 3) out for dinner, which, in fact we were, we had to leave, and then promptly did so. It was a set-up, and I was just beginning to develop an understanding of the magnitude of it, the full ramifications of which would not hit home until after we returned after the conference.

The next day I was cool about it, as I watched the scene carefully to check out the heavy stuff in play. Our Minnesota State Human Rights Director, Linda Johnson, was there, walking hand in hand with her man, whom she had made Assistant Commissioner. We chatted briefly and then headed for the escalator. I looked up and saw five individuals, one holding a video camera. The call letters were taped over on the camera. As I looked more closely I saw a guy who had been watching me on the airplane on the flight out four days earlier. So I turned my back on them, put my hand behind my back as if to scratch it, waved at them. Those who saw this incident still laugh when they think or talk about it. And then at the bottom of the escalator I ran into Linda Johnson.

Poor Linda. WCCO, having made a big deal about their pending exposé, couldn't come back empty-handed. While we were out there, they had already begun to run teasers: "CCO's investigative team with Al Austin taking a look at civil rights leaders who don't serve their people." We heard about the teasers in San Francisco and so the parlor game for us was to try to guess who. We had no idea who in particular the were referring to. Because they were running teasers about facts they allegedly had, and as I hadn't done anything, I didn't think it could be. That didn't explain the behavior I saw but I didn't put them together until after I got back. Four days after we got back, we were glued to the TV to see the report. They showed the Urban League convention with words of what its expectation were, along with file footage, and finally said: "During CCO's investigation of those who have betrayed the trust, we followed," and then they focused on Commissioner Linda Johnson. As I looked at the footage, I saw that it was the same as when I was there. Then they showed the scene of her and her man and me talking at the escalator, but with no mention of me. What I learned later is that by Day 4, Al Austen had called back to say Ron Edwards was only attending sessions. The general manager of CCO, who had never forgiven me for being a Black militant years before, was now finally going to get me for running my mouth for 20 years. They had hired six deputies for their protection, "just in case," as I was considered a "bad Negro." So the WCCO expose turned out to be about Linda and her man. They told the governor's office. She was then told to submit her expense account within 48 hours of returning. She didn't see it coming. She padded it, of course, to cover the expenses of her man. Nothing about human rights or race relations, but a tawdry little expense account scandal was all they could show. She was forced to resign.

Two weeks after we returned from San Francisco, another play was made on me when the Urban League was raided. We were at the office of John Derus, the County Chairman, on the 24th floor. Gary Suddeth was called out of the meeting and then returned to tell us that the police, with warrants, were raiding the Urban League, and that it was about me. The raid was led by David Neber, my arch enemy, as described in Chapter 3. They took out thousands of documents. And of course they had the media there. And the reporters were shouting: "What do you have to say about the allegations that you have been involved in the theft of $5,000 and other money?" I told them I knew nothing about it.

We went to Glover's office where he had the cameras and reporters waiting. I was told I had forged a check and that I had forced the White controller to go along with it. Of course I had done no such thing. Which was what the Grand Jury decided also after hearing the evidence or, more properly phrased, lackiing any evidence. They saw it all as nonsense, and dismissed it and declined to indict me.

Another accusation was the use of long-distance calls from the Urban League (they even had wiretaps of calls made from the Urban League). It was true that I made calls but they were for Urban League business. They were not personal. . And where were these calls made to? South Africa. And not just me. They involved calls made that included a number of us Board members, together on the speaker phone, including Nellie Stone Johnson, in calls to Bishop Desmond Tutu of South Africa, and to the journalist Erich Duma. After the dust settled this too was all seen to be proper and above board. We had called Bishop Desmond Tutu of South Africa. Erich Duma, a journalist in South Africa, had come to me about the Sullivan principles (explained beginning in he next paragraph below) and Apartheid and the boycott, as the University of Minnesota Board of Governors had refused to apply sanctions to companies dealing with South Africa. South Africa was also tapping Duma's phone. He had been arrested in South Africa and tortured in the 1970s, during which time they cut off two of his fingers.

Rev. Leon Sullivan, who has been called by some the most influential man of his time, was raised in a shanty off a dirt alley in abject poverty. He rose to become a member of the Board of Directors of General Motors, and from that position, waged a humanitarian battle for those who lived in the poverty he knew only so well when he was growing up. He loved to tell inner city Black kids his story, and that even though they were poor, they still had pride. He used to say, if you want to excel in this world: "STAND UP, STAND UP, STAND UP."

Sullivan's humanitarian work has had a global influence, especially in South Africa, where he was instrumental in getting companies to fight apartheid in their plants and in the communities surrounding their plants. He was also instrumental in helping get Nelson Mandela freed from prison, who had been incarcerated for 28 years for his active protest of apartheid three decades earlier. His message then is still valid today, as he urged kids to dedicate themselves to learning, working hard and believing in themselves. " He told these eager faces that they were like balloons, and that "It's not your color that makes you rise or fall, but what's inside of you. Believe you can be anything you want."

When he died a few years ago he was on his latest mission, which was to revitalize all of Africa. His goal was to encourage foreign investment, build 1,000 new schools and modernize medical facilities on the continent. His goal had been to encourage investment, build schools and hospitals and strengthen democratic institutions. America and Africa lost a lot when he died. Indeed, his work in Liberia was cut short by his death in his late 70s in the late 90s. It may be that had he lived, Liberia would not have descended into the Civil War that so devastated it. As the co-producer of a film on his life said, he was "a man who fights without fists ... a man who is not blind to injustice but is blinded by a fury to right the scales."

In the early 1960s, Sullivan led a Philadelphia-wide boycott of Philadelphia companies that would not hire Blacks, using the mantra, "Don't buy where you don't work." *Life* magazine named him one of the country's 100 leading citizens and described him as an invigorating presence because of his dedication to the public good (learn more about Leon Sullivan in his book, *Moving Mountains,* and on the web site of http://www.horizonmag.com/8/leon-sullivan.asp). You can read of his Six Principles at http://www.horizonmag.com/8/principles.asp. But Minneapolis was not interested in the Sullivan Principles. In general, from his position on the GM board, he called on American multinationals to pay all people equally, train non-Whites for professional jobs and create an overall atmosphere of tolerance. "Every business, large and small, can find a way to improve the standard of life for poor people who need help in America and in the world." Yes, but not in Minneapolis. GM said it would disinvest in South Africa if they didn't end apartheid. Sullivan's Opportunities Industrialization Centers is what the Urban League should be backing.

Nellie and I and the rest enjoyed our conversations with Bishop Tutu and were excited about the possibility of his coming to the University of Minnesota. But his phones in South Africa were tapped too. The Apartheid South African government called the U.S. The Feds in turn contacted Minneapolis. We were going to bring Bishop Tutu to the University for a lecture. Local officials, public and private, didn't want Bishop Tutu brought to the University because of the disinvestments issue according to the Sullivan principles. They didn't want a campus movement in favor of disinvestments when the University had already determined it would not divest nor favor divestment. I have explained how powerful the University is (Chapter 10).

So once again, their effort to discredit me failed. But that did not stop them from trying again.

The Urban League tried to damage me again during the investigation of Luther Darville and the University of Minnesota (Chapter 10).   I spoke often by Bob Minnix, the chief investigative reporter for the NCAA.   I was the only one to testify for Luther at the trial (Chapter 10).   They had hoped to also disgrace me for perjury for what I said on the witness stand that I had talked to Minnix a number of times and was familiar with the charges.   Glover had said I had only talked to Minnix once, hence the perjury.   He was wrong but didn't know it.   But by this time Nellie and I had already been kicked out of the Urban League.   Nonetheless they kept trying.

So the City officials called Minnix and, not realizing he was Black, told him that they were investigating Rod Edwards for committing perjury at the Luther Darville trial. He heard them say, "We want to nail the bastard, that Black SOB."   There were six individuals in the room tape-recording their call to Minnix, gleeful that they were now going to "get" me.

Glover was protected from his shenanigans by cooperating so they didn't go after him for his Urban League activities.   Instead of downsizing the staff, Glover began selling off Urban League properties purchased by the League during my long tenure as Vice Chairman and Chairman, which had been part of my drive toward self-sufficiency.   Together, these properties were worth $3.5 million.   He impoverished the League.   He was also involved in the same kind of activity, as Linda Johnson had been caught for.   But the Mastuhs would let him be if he would help "get" me.

And so, despite setting up two grand juries, all White, to try to find me guilty of something so they, in their minds, would no longer have to deal with the notorious Ron Edwards, their efforts were futile, as I was never part of anything improper.   As always, I decline to be hung out to dry.   The ones who do little for our people and lots for themselves, like Glover and Hightower, get off, because the bosses don't want them doing anything for our people.   And they like to hold their inappropriate activities over their heads to keep them in line.

They asked Minnix if he knew me.   He said yes.   They did not know that his office was in Shawnee Mission, Kansas, not far from my mother's home in Kansas City. They asked him if he had ever talked to me.   He said yes.   They asked him how many times.   He said that, over the last several months, as he investigated the University, he had talked to me over 200 times, including face-to-face meetings in Kansas.   He confirmed my testimony.   That ended yet another attempt to "get" me.

It should be noted that after the Urban League had double-crossed Nellie Stone Johnson as well as me, Governor Rudy Perpich was no longer available to meet with their leaders.   As Rudy put it, he wasn't interested in talking with any organization that did not have room for a Ron Edwards or a Nellie Stone Johnson.

Some final thoughts on my tenure as Civil Rights Commission Chairman

I was last involved with the Civil Rights Commission in 1983 and the Urban League in 1989. My concern today is about the redistricting and the continuing destruction of the futures of young Black males in Minneapolis. Nonetheless, because many don't know about the work done back then, I want to list some key statements about the work we did. It was important then. It is important now. I could write many chapters on the work we did; instead, I want to just clarify for the record the work these 21 people did together, year-in and year-out (although it was never the same 21 each year). I played key roles from 1967 – 1983. But I was not alone. It couldn't have been done without these superb people. Here is what is important to know about the work of these people during that period:

- We were _never_ reversed (very few such commissions in other states can say that).
- We were an effective commission.
- The record clearly shows we took on _all issues_ of _all classes._
- We were _never_ frivolous.
- We _never_ gave the opposition (Conservatives) fuel to burn us: We _always_ followed the rules and we _never_ opened ourselves up to be seen as irresponsible.
- We rejected the "entertain us but don't represent us" mentality.
- We had some of the best legal minds available to us. I want to especially mention attorneys Pam Alexander, Michael Davis, and Lajune Lang, whom I encouraged to monitor us closely so we were always on the straight and narrow. **Again: we were _never_ reversed**.

To add to my last bullet point: Pam Alexander, Michael Davis and Lajune Lang all became good friends and all went on to become outstanding judges, Michael as a Federal Judge and Pam and Lajune as State District Judges. It is because of them that we were considered one of the best Civil Rights Commissions in the country.

One of my favorite newspaper stories of the time was in the November 18, 1982 Twin Cities Courier, with the heading "Edwards' rejection could now awaken the 'Sleeping giant'," which discussed how my reappointment to the Minneapolis Civil Rights Commission for another three-year term had been rejected by the City Council on a 7-6 vote (I was reinstated later when then Mayor Fraser vetoed them).

Now we all hope our government leaders are grown-ups and will not act like pouting little kids in the play yard, as far greater things are at stake than personal likes and dislikes.

As the City Council couldn't come out and say they were opposed to Black progress they could go after the guy promoting it. And when they are quoted in the papers, the best they could do was accuse me of not having enough "Minnesota Nice," which is more important to many than is justice. They were reduced to not attacking what I stood for or my goals but me personally:

- "personal grievances against the man's attitude"
- he "made us look small"
- his "style and attitude was that of the sixties, not the eighties"

Note, the grievances of the City Council were not substantive, and had nothing to do with civil rights. They were all personal. They wanted a Minnesota nice boy to go along with their continued blockage of Civil Rights progress. Here is what my supporters on the Council said about the value of my work and legacy:

- "What you are saying to every minority in the city is, be careful, because if you stand up and speak out, the Liberals on the city council will put you back where you belong."
- "The liberals went against Edwards because he had been outspoken, and for no other good reason."

My leadership was missed. Indeed, two years later, three of the commission members resigned. Here is what various City Council members said later:

- "I regret taking Ron out of the Chairmanship [with my deciding vote]. I wouldn't have done it if I had known it would be two years of hell [without Ron as Chairman]."
- "Black racism is alive and well in this city among people who call themselves Black leaders."
- "It will deter civil rights in the city with Edwards out as chairman."
- "Edwards' supporters felt the organization went downhill in his absence."

Some of my detractors also accused me of being mainly concerned about discrimination against Black males. In truth, I included all classes with grievances. I was all in favor of including everyone but **not** at the expense of Blacks in general and certainly **not** at the expense of the group with the largest grievances, young Black males.

And what was the result of putting Mary Emma Hixson, a gay white woman, in as Director of the Civil Rights Department? As reported in 1987, in the minds of

Blacks, under Director Hixson, the office demonstrated an anti-Black and anti-male bias, as the power and emphasis shifted from Blacks to White feminists.

The Last Five Years

Some have called me a Jeremiah after the Old Testament prophet who was constantly railing at the Israelites to obey God. I take that as a compliment. I continue to rail against the Urban League and NAACP for not following their own stated missions, for not putting inner city Blacks first, for seeking primarily personal or institutional survival, and for turning away from saying to the bosses, as Moses once said: "Let my people go."

As I noted earlier, when I say "corrupt" I mean it in a moral sense. Too many Black leaders today are deluded, mesmerized by decades of government help and support, and unwilling or unable to stand up against such obvious miscarriages of justice with Blacks, as when $1 billion is used to tear down our homes and replace them with only 52 units (Chapter 8). Or standing by while our kids are not taught to read or write (Chapter 7). Or standing by while our young Black men are sent to jail rather than provided jobs (Chapter 9). Talking about it won't help. Without providing solutions, what is the point other than to make the White man feel good that so many so-called "good" Blacks are talking about it, showing everyone how well Blacks and Whites agree that it is a sad state of affairs, and that nothing can be done about it.

I completely reject that. When people say society isn't ready, it is because too many Blacks have sold out. We didn't in the 50s and 60s. Black leaders today have too many Blacks thinking they can't make it without them. And if Blacks don't think they can why would Whites attempt to help us too? People need to admit that they are afraid yet still committed. Its not like walking into lunch counters and risking getting beaten for sitting there or risking getting beaten for crossing the Edmund Pettus bridge in Selma in a march to the Alabama capital in Montgomery.

The White Citizens' Council of the 50s and 60s had one strategy: delay, delay, delay. Why now do the local Minneapolis chapters of the Urban League and the NAACP do the delaying for the Whites? We were once prepared to direct our future, to create our own lives, and then we faltered. Can we do it by ourselves? When you look at the advancement made by Blacks against all that is arrayed against us, the answer can only be: "you bet we can." Can we do it with each other's help? Absolutely. So lets help each other. And let us direct the government on how they can help us, not the other way around.

We need to return to the days when Clarence Mitchell, head of the NAACP's Washington Bureau, walked the halls of Congress in the 1950s and 60s, taking the case to legislators to make the Constitution a reality for Blacks as well. His influence case to legislators to make the Constitution a reality for Blacks as well. His influence was substantial. He was called the 101st Senator. He walked fast, he went to every Senator's and Congressman's office, and those offices that did not throw him out bodily he took as favorable (some Senators refused to meet with "the Ni**er"). He didn't pause for lunch or for a drink in the afternoon. Day after day, week after week, month after month, year after year. It was said of Clarence he didn't rest, didn't eat, didn't drink, just got called names and kept on working. He didn't take his eyes off the prize.

I was on the Pilot City Planning Committee in the late 60s. What a wonderful facility Pilot City is today. And yet if you visit, you'll find many white bureaucrats using it for their offices. Indeed, the Whites of Hennepin County, who supply 64% of its budget, want to shut it down as a community center. And what is needed to keep it going? A few dollars. When Jawanza Kunjufu (educational consultant, www.AfricanAmerianImages.com) spoke at Pilot City on November 1, 2001, he pointed out that all that was needed was $1.5 million. He made the point that when you take care of your own, you don't need to march or be on welfare. All that was required to provide the $1.5 million for the budget, Kunjufu said, was for 1,500 Blacks in the Twin Cities to give $100 each, to keep Pilot City free of Hennepin County. And yet we are so addicted to government funds that that idea didn't fly. And why not, when Blacks are sitting there saying Hennepin County has the money, for after all they have no problem funding the $7 million cost-overrun on the prison. But the latter is being built by Whites to house Blacks. Some say it's not fair. They willwait until Hennepin County does the right thing. No. The real issue is that we take care of business and not wait for others to do it for us. We need to do the right thing and handle it ourselves. If 1,500 of us can't come up with $100, we have a much deeper problem. And, with 150,000 Blacks in Minneapolis, $10 from 1,500 would also do it. Are they right, we need Whitey's help? What are we willing to do for ourselves?

And as for you Whites who want to blame everything on one or two Whites to get the rest of you off the hook, I remind you of the real truth of the matter, as spoken by Martin Luther King Jr.:

> I'm here to tell you that the businessmen, the mayor of this city, and every-body in the White power structure of this city must take responsibility for everything [any white official or company] does in the community.

But he had a word for Blacks as well, assessing their role in the misfortune that happens to Blacks, when we:

Passively accept the evils of segregation and stand on the sidelines in the struggle for justice. ...we must work unrelentingly to make the American dream a reality.

Why the continued request from Whites for us to wait and to cool off? We need to remember the message James Farmer sent to Bobby Kennedy in 1961. Bobby Kennedy asked Martin Luther King, Jr., to intercede with James Farmer of CORE (Congress of Racial Equality), in 1961, to halt the Freedom Ride, an interracial group riding on busses going through the deep South, duplicating the 1947 Freedom Ride through the upper South, in order to enable a cooling-off. Farmer sent back word that Blacks had been waiting 350 years and that if they cooled off any more they'd be in a deep freeze.

Black Like Us? Only if they treat us as equals.

When Maya Angelou called Bill Clinton "the first Black President," I knew we were in for more trouble. Clinton is not to blame for her saying it but he is to blame for basking in it. His apologies to Blacks in Africa for slavery were as wrong as it could get. He should have been apologizing to Blacks in America for what the Democratic Party has done to them, and he should have been attempting to make things right in terms of the land and wealth stolen from Blacks (Interlude 8), in this country (not to mention the theft of so many generations' education, housing, and jobs).

White people thinking they know Blacks and thinking that they are like Blacks, as in Angelou's first Black President comment, was a foreshadowing of the March 17, 1999, *City Pages* article, "Black Like Us," featuring the faces of Dee Long, Phyllis Kahn, Don Fraser, and his wife Arvonne Fraser, all of whom are White. When I saw that, I also knew we were in trouble. I quote from this article not because it provides anything new, as it will sound repetitive, but because it supports my arguments and provides the evidence some will claim should be here in case my eyewitness accounts are not enough.

When the South Minneapolis Sabathani Community Center opened its doors on January 9, 1999, for the election of officers for the local chapter of the NAACP, we saw a long line of people waiting to vote, **most** of whom were White. At stake, as The City Pages article points out, were "costly, long-term city and state projects." They wanted the "right" Blacks in charge. Leola Seals, President of the local NAACP branch, had questioned some of these projects, especially the Hollman public housing lawsuit handling and the racist nature of the Minneapolis Police Department's CODE4, which was the code for stopping Blacks.

They did not want Ms. Seals in charge. Because of her background, they viewed her as a field hand who didn't mix with the high falutin' elitist house Negroes. As the article pointed out, "At public functions Seals is rarely as well-dressed or as smoothly spoken as the people who last summer started organizing her ouster." When she was elected, "she promised to tackle a series of issues on which the NAACP had been silent or tactfully low-key."

This line-up of Whites trying to influence the outcome of the election was not new. In the 1964 election, Thomas Johnson II seemed a shoo-in, but he had radical views. So on the morning of the 1964 election, "several school buses packed with 'little old white ladies" clutching brand-new NAACP membership cards pulled up at the polling place." Where did they come from? As the article points out, they were "recruited by the DFL."

This episode shows how far off-track the NAACP has become from its original mission. Recall its proud history, as it evolved from fighting discrimination in the workplace in the 1930s and 1940s to fighting segregation in housing and local businesses in the 1950s and 1960s, and finally, the greatest of their battles, the battle against segregated public education. This meant taking on the massive public education system and all its supporters, mostly White.

We thought we were on the right course, fighting segregated housing, that forced Blacks into bad housing and segregated schools that forced Blacks into poor schools. But of course many Whites didn't see it that way. When a Federal judge sided with the Minneapolis NAACP in 1973 and ordered the integration of public schools, all hell broke loose. We won the battle but it was a costly victory, as it has kept us from winning the war. Whites, who made up 80% of the public schools of Minneapolis, voted with their feet. Between 1974 and 1989 the number of public school students dropped from 55,000 to 40,000, of which now only 50% were White. And in some schools, the percentage of minority students climbed to 95%. And it has gotten worse since then.

We lost the war because by 1995, minority students were concentrated in the inner city in inferior and inadequate schools getting an inferior and inadequate education. Bill Davis, then President of the local NAACP, filed suit against the state of Minnesota for "failing in its constitutional duty to provide an adequate education for all children." When Leola took over in 1996, she focused it even further: demanding that school officials improve test scores of minority and low-income children. Why? Because when it came to the state's basic-skills test, 95% of Black students failed. She also focused on the fact that the city, state, and federal governments, through their handling of the Hollman housing issue, had created a segregated public housing district in the near North side. This was another battle won that didn't win the war, as all that was accomplished was the demolition of the housing of Blacks in North Minneapolis with few units being put up in return (Chapter 8). She also fought the idea of the money going to the city's handpicked White developers.

To the Whites, this uppity Black had to go. Whites particularly looked for new members to help vote their way. I cannot be called impartial, as I was also running for election, for the Executive Committee, on the Leola Seales slate. And so, in the early hours of the voting at the polling place, the ratio of Whites to Blacks was 3 to 1 (late in the day that reversed). Our slate lost. And so Whites turned out to determine the election results of a minority's advocacy group's volunteer officers. The Whites won. We lost by 16 votes, 218-202. However, 22 votes were challenged, 18 were not counted, and 3 were "lost." As we lost by 16 votes, these votes could have given us the win.

The Whites succeeded in making our NAACP Branch into an arm of the city's DFL. They succeeded in driving a wedge between the in-crowd of Black NAACP members and the low-income and poverty-level Blacks whom the NAACP is supposed to support but does not. One of the first things the Black slate elected by the Whites did was to drop the lawsuit against the White state regarding the poor education of Black kids.

2001-2002

The most recent attempt to silence me came this year. On the following pages are copies of the following documents:

1. The April 5, 2002 NAACP letter I received telling me to step down from my position of Chairman of the Minneapolis Branch NAACP Housing Committee
2. My April 7, 2002 reply to the Director of National Field Operations, National NAACP
3. My April 9, 2002 Complaint brief submitted to the National NAACP
4. The Minutes of the April 1, 2002 meeting of the local NAACP Executive Committee Meeting
5. Excerpt from the Constitution and By-Laws of the Minneapolis NAACP

Here is the problem. It is 2002, and yet neither the NAACP nor the Urban League want to rock the boat. They also don't want the truth to come out. So after my decades of service, of trying to get them to focus on the community and the poor, they attempted to boot me out over a procedural issue, saying I had not handed in monthly written reports. On paper, this is true. But in practice, few at the Branch ever do, including those who are accusing me. We are volunteers. We are unpaid.

So most of us report orally, rather than in writing, to those staffers who are paid. After years and years of loyal service, they have come at me hiding behind unconstitutional organizational nonsense, as you will see in the following copies of our correspondence and the copy of the grievance that I filed.

Why have they done this? The simple answer is: because they can, because the law means nothing more to them than it seems to mean to anyone else in high visibility lately, including Presidents, Vice Presidents, CEOs and auditors. We seem to be living in a time when it's not about the law but how to get around the law and, more importantly to write laws to allow taking advantage of the system in unjust ways. In other words, people in the headlines seem to have stopped concentrating on principles and are concentrating on spoils. The same is true with the Urban League and the NAACP.

Note: below and on the following seven pages, the emphases, of **bold** and underlined, are mine.

True Copy of Letter from the Minneapolis NAACP to Ron Edwards   (my emphasis added)

MINNEAPOLIS BRACH NAACP
NATIONAL ASSOCIATION FOR THE ADVANCEMENT OF COLORED PEOPLE
310 East 38th Street, Suite 136, Minneapolis, Minnesota 55408, 612-822-8205

April 5, 2002

Shalia M. Lindsey
PRESIDENT

Darrell Graham
FIRST VICE PRESIDENT

Tony Byers
SECOND VICE PRESIDENT

Brett Buckner

Mr. Ron Edwards
P.O. Box 11363-55411
Minneapolis, MN 55411

Dear Mr. Edwards:

I want to thank you for your service and commitment to the Minneapolis Branch as its Housing Chair. At times your **breadth of knowledge on housing issues, among other topics,** assisted the Branch in devising a strategy in addressing housing issues. Nonetheless, I am writing to inform you that I have made a decision to

THIRD VICE PRESIDENT

Barbara Beaman
SECRETARY

Andy Martin
ASSISTANT SECRETARY

Samuel Richardson
INTERIM TREASURER

relieve you of your duties as the Housing Chair immediately.

As of November 2001, I specifically mandated that all members of the Executive Committee turn in month written reports as stated in Article IV, Section 2b and Article IV, Section 5s of the NAACP By-laws. Your duty as an executive Committee member, as it relates to **written reports**, was further reiterated at the State Conference Training in Rochester. To date I have not received a formal written report from you as Housing Chair, nor do I recall receiving a written report at any time during my tenure as Branch President.

Your recent testimony before the City of Minneapolis Redistricting Commission caused great concern at the Branch. I have independent verification that you made comments as the MN-Dakota State Political Action Chair, on municipal redistricting matters that undermined the **authority of the Branch** and confused the Commission members as to whether the State Conference or the local Branch had the authority to discuss issues surrounding the municipal redistricting process. The testimony you provided was both misleading and confusing. Your testimony served to undermine and hinder the efforts of the local Branch to effectively work within its jurisdiction on these types of matters.

I am further disappointed in your use of confidential Branch information on your television show. I have not authorized any public comments relative to the Hollman Lawsuit nor the status of documentation regarding the lawsuit contained in the Branch, Regional, and National offices. Again, your statements could only serve to undermine and hinder the efforts of the Branch.

Based on the above, not only have your actions and comments been unfavorable to the Branch, they may have caused irreparable **harm to the organization**, something **I am sworn to prevent**. Your conduct is inimical to the NAACP. I have serious doubts that your continued duties as the Housing Chair will be constructive or productive in the long run as I attempt to steward the Branch into the future.

As President, **I do not condone your behavior and therefore am relieving you** of your duties as an Executive Committee chair.

I hope you will continue your participation in the Branch as a general body member. Your wisdom and knowledge can be useful in that capacity.
Sincerely,

Shalia M. Lindsey
President

Cc: ExecutiveCommittee Members, Minneapolis Branch
      Claudie Washington, MN-Dakota State Conf. Pres.
      Rev. Gil Ford, Region IV Director

TRUE COPY (EMPHASIS ADDED) **of** my (Ron Edwards) Letter of response to the Minneapolis NAACP. I received **no response** to this letter from the NAACP, national or local.

Ronald A. Edwards
Chair, Minneapolis NAACP Housing Committee
Political Action Chair, Minnesota — Dakota Conference of NAACP

P.O. Box 11363–55411,
Minneapolis, MN 55411
Phone 612–715–0269

Date: April 7, 2002

Director of National Field Operations
Nelson Rivers
NAACP
4805 Mt. Hope Drive
Baltimore, Maryland 21215

Dear Sirs/Madams:

Enclosed please find a petition of utmost urgency. **My petition to you involves actions and <u>collusion</u> between members of the <u>Minneapolis NAACP</u>, their Executive Committee and the <u>Minneapolis Urban League</u> Branch in violation of the NAACP's constitution and bylaws.** This combined action is an attempt by these bodies **to influence redistricting in the City of Minneapolis to defeat the only Minneapolis African-American Council member in future elections.**

Most recently, the chair of the Minneapolis NAACP, Shalia Lindsey, in a letter to me dated April 5, 2001, demanded my removal from the Housing Committee and the Executive Board of the Minneapolis NAACP. Her action is clearly **retaliation against me for strong advocacy for African-American residents and plaintiffs in the Hollman lawsuit** and as expressed in my December 15, 2001 report to Lindsey and the NAACP. The result of these actions is **an attempt to intentionally denigrate and defame my reputation** as a member of the Minneapolis Branch and as political chair of the Minnesota – Dakota Conference of the NAACP. I intend to address the latter defamation in the very near future.

Since this colluded and illegal redistricting action has moved past the recommendation stage and will be considered and acted on in a few days by the Minneapolis Redistricting Commission, it is **imperative that your body takes action on my petition at deliberate speed** to prevent harm to this elected official and to my reputation and standing in the community. If you choose not to proceed in a timely manner, I will have no other choice but to bring an action in court asking for the rescission of the recent action as violate of the Constitution and Bylaws of the NAACP.

All relevant materials including my petition are attached.

I will expect your inquiry and response shortly.

Sincerely,

Ronald A. Edwards
Minneapolis NAACP Executive Committee

Cc: Kweisi Mfume, President
       Julian Bond, Chairman

<u>**True Copy of April 1, 2002 Minneapolis NAACP Minutes**</u>   [**Emphasis** added]

Minneapolis Branch NAACP
Minutes of Special Executive Meeting 4/1/02

Purpose of Meeting: Approve Branch's Proposed Redistricting Plan

Members present: Brent Buckner, Silas Houston, Shalia Lindsey, Sandra
Miller, and Stephanie Watts.

The minutes were recorded by President Lindsey.
The discussion started at 6:25 pm.

Third Vice President Buckner presented the Branch's proposed redistricting plan. See attached packet of information which includes: **Redistricting Principles, Map #1**, Population Summary Report, Minority Report–Total Population, Minority Report–Voting Age Population, and Map #2.

This plan was **a collective effort of the Branch, Minneapolis Urban League**, Council on Black Minnesotans, Rep. Neva Walker, Mathea Little Smith (Black State Political Action), and Vic Thorson.

The Branch's proposed plans offer greater compactness, increases the likelihood of minority election to city council, treats the Mississippi River as a natural boundary, maintains neighborhoods, and **does not take into account incumbency nor residence of current council members**. The proposed **plan creates six (6) "minority opportunity districts." Therefore, six minority candidates could potentially become elected to office**.

Third Vice President Buckner also presented maps proposed by the following parties: DFL, Republican, and Green/Independent. None of the aforementioned maps offered the exact number of "minority opportunity districts" nor seemed to reflect the best interest of communities of color.

As a result, the members present **unanimously supported Map** #1 (proposed by Vice President Buckner and Political Action Chair, Gaskins) as our first option and Map #2 as our back up option.

The discussion ended at approximately 7:30 PM.

Grievance submitted by Ron Edwards to national NAACP re: the Minneapolis NAACP [emphasis added]

1	NAACP Board of Directors
2	Director of National Field Operations
3	**Petition of Ronald A. Edwards**
	P.O. Box 11363–55411
4	Minneapolis, MN 55411
5	
6	In Re: Ronald A. Edwards
7	Petitioner
8	vs.
9	Minneapolis NAACP, its Executive Committee, and the Individual Members of its Executive Committee
10	
11	Respondents
12	
13	Ronald A. Edwards (Petitioner) brings this petition requesting investigation,
14	remedial action and appropriate sanctions against the above-named respondents
15	for **intentional violations** of the NAACP's Constitution and Bylaws.
16	
17	Petitioner has standing to bring this petition for Investigation. He is a member in
18	good standing of the NAACP, the Minneapolis branch NAACP, the Executive
19	Committee of the Minneapolis NAACP, the Minnesota – Dakota Conference of
20	the NAACP, and the national NAACP.
21	
22	Petitioner is well known in the state of Minnesota and the metropolitan area of
23	Minneapolis/St. Paul as **a long-time advocate for civil and human rights**.

24 | Petitioner has a reputation for defending and advocating for the rights of the

25 | people of color and specifically for African Americans in these communities.

Summary of Petition – 1

1 |

2 | In April 2002, Petitioner received documentation showing that the Executive

3 | Committee of the Minneapolis NAACP presented a written proposal and

4 | recommendations to the City of Minneapolis Redistricting Commission. Said

5 | **recommendations proposed changing the fourth and fifth ward boundary**

6 | **lines** in **a** manner that would **effectively remove the incumbent African**

7 | **American** City Council member, Natalie Johnson-Lee **out of her current**

8 | **constituent fifth ward** and place her into a new fourth ward comprised largely of

9 | residents who had not participated in the recent election of Johnson-Lee. The

10 | proposed new fourth ward is comprised of a significantly lower ratio of African

11 | American voters than is the current fifth ward in which Johnson-Lee was recently

12 | elected as Council member. **Certain members of the NAACP Executive**

13 | **Board in fact bragged about "cutting out"the incumbent African American**
Council member.

14 |

15 | The respondents were under no legal requirement to present these recommendations

16 | to the Redistricting Commission.

17 |

18 | The probability is greater than not that should **the NAACP–Urban League**

19 | **redistricting recommendation** be accepted by the City of Minneapolis, that the

20   only African American City Council member will be adversely affected and

21   irreparably harmed in her future attempts to retain her seat on the Minnesota City.

22   Council.

23   Respondent, in violation of NAACP Bylaws and Constitution, **failed and refused**

24   **to give notice of a special or general membership** meeting to Petitioner or to the

25   general membership **for the purpose of considering their intent** to recommend

Summary of Petition – 2

1   redistricting to the Minneapolis Redistricting Commission. The Constitution and

2   Bylaws of the NAACP branches, **Article VI Meetings**, state in relevant part,

3   **"Section 4 Special Meetings:** Special meetings may be called at any time and

4   place and on **three days' written notice** to all members by direction of the

5   President, or any three members of the Executive Committee... **The notice must state the purpose** for which

6   the meeting is called. Section 4 Meetings of the Executive Committee states:

7   ...Special meetings of the Executive Committee may be called by the President,

8   Secretary or by two members of the Committee on three days' written notice."

9

10   Petitioner to date has **not received notice of the special called meetings as**

11   **required** by the above provisions of the NAACP Constitution and Bylaws.

12

13   The above cited actions of the Respondent NAACP are **in opposition to the**

14   **desires** and wishes of the Petitioner, the majority **of the residents of the fifth ward, and of the**

15   **general membership of the NAACP.** The actions and recommendations of the NAACP

16   and Urban League concerning the redistricting recommendations have become

17	public and well known throughout the Minneapolis–St. Paul metro area and beyond.
18	The actions and recommendations of the Minneapolis NAACP and its Executive
19	Committee, of which Petitioner is a member, **holds that committee and its**
20	**members up to scorn in the African American and other communities.** The actions
21	of the NAACP and its Executive Committee are viewed by Minneapolis citizens
22	as **undermining the political representation of African Americans in Minneapolis.** The
23	actions of the Respondents are, by association, seen as those of Petitioner and
24	therefore **hold the Petitioner up to the ridicule and scorn** of the community, and
25	**make it appear Petitioner advocates against the interests of the African American**

Summary of Petition – 3

1	community. **Petitioner's reputation and character** as a supporter and advocate
2	for the African American community have been and will continue to be
3	**impugned and maligned by the illegal actions of the Respondent** and its
4	Executive Committee.
5	To date Respondent has not presented a formal legal retraction of its
6	discriminatory redistricting recommendation to the Redistricting Committee.
7	
8	**Petitioner requests an immediate action by the NAACP to correct these illegal and**
9	**violate actions by the Minneapolis NAACP Executive Committee.** Absent
10	the NAACP's immediate intervention, Petitioner requests the authority to proceed with an
11	external legal action to prevent harm to the interest of the African American

12   community and the sole African American Council member in Minneapolis.

13

14

15

16

                              Dated this 9th day of April, 2002

                              By
                                        Ronald A. Edwards
18   Petitioner

19

20

21

22

Summary of Petition – 4

Excerpt from Constitution and By-Laws for Branches

ARTICLE VI
MEETINGS

Section 4   Special meetings may be called at any time
Special   and place and on three days' written notice
Meetings   to members by direction of the President,
                    or any three members of the Executive
Committee, or on failure of these to act, by any ten members
of the Branch. This notice must state the purpose for which
the meeting is called.

If, after reading the above, I sound hardhitting on this, I say thank you. I'm trying to be. Not because I want to but because I don't see any other choice. There is no greater sign of how well certain aspects of Black-White relationships have become integrated than when the so-called Black leadership has gotten into the corrupt bed of their White Mastuhs, in this case, the DFL. The DFL agenda is probably 90% against Black people, especially those Blacks in poor communities like North Minneapolis. The anger of Humphrey and Mondale over losing the Presidential races of 1968 and 1984, falsely blaming the riots of Blacks, still smolders in the DFL in Minnesota. My response to the DFL is: "grow up." Many of those riots were due to Democrat/DFL policies. And even though it is true that the Democratic Party in Minnesota has abandoned the inner city Blacks, they need to do a historic reality check regarding how much they have abandoned the principles of freedom and liberty for Blacks for two centuries.

Despite the Democratic Jim Crow laws in the South, it was Blacks who gave the Democrats their moral mantle as a result of the Civil Rights Movement beginning in the 1950s and Anti-War Movement beginning in the 60s (Northern Democrats; Southern Democrats and too many Republicans opposed both movements). In response, Blacks have received nothing but disdain, disrespect, and mistreatment as if they were all "boys" or "farm hands." We gave the Democrats the moral mantle to make up for their shameless treatment of us during the slave period, during the Reconstruction period, during the Jim Crow period, and since then. Their thanks have been to treat us as suckers and to attempt to fool us into thinking they support us when in truth they want us back as lackeys, as Jim Crow dummies, the way Democrats, especially Southern Democrats, have always treated us.

From John F. Kennedy to Hubert H. Humphrey to George McGovern to Jimmy Carter to Walter Mondale to Bill Clinton to Al Gore, they have acted as plantation Mastuhs, getting to office on the backs of Black voters while leaving them in their political shanties, using house Negroes in government jobs (national, state, local) and on government commissions and boards, to keep us imprisoned in the ghetto with a focus on anything but that which would give us wealth and power.

Even the Congressional Black Caucus has always been a Democratic Party Black Caucus. So when asked what kind of Democrat I am, I reply: a "Nellie Stone Johnson Democrat" (Interlude 3).

In the Old Testament story of the Israelites wandering in the wilderness for 40 years, it is said that God didn't want people with a slave mentality to enter the Promised Land, for they would not handle it well. So he had them wander until new generations without the slave mentality took their place. Blacks after the Civil War wanted to be free. They started businesses, were elected to office. Then came the end of Reconstruction and the beginning of the Jim Crow laws when the Democrats gave the Presidency to the Republicans in 1876 in exchange for having the Federal troops removed and Reconstruction ended. The NAACP and the Urban League were founded in order to battle Jim Crow. Since then, the Urban League and NAACP have returned to a slave mentality of servitude to the Mastuhs. Maybe it will take Blacks joining another political party, like the Green Party to shed their slave, "yassah DFL boss" mentality. But until that is done, we will continue to wander in the wilderness.

The evidence for this is plentiful. I'm willing to bet that much of it is in the missing files Jackie Cherryhomes took from her office, when she was defeated in November 2001. Whether she shredded them or just spirited them away for the time when she hopes to triumphantly return from her exile in Elba, the fact remains: the evidence is gone. Rather than be on Elba, Cherryhomes should probably be in jail. Neither the local NAACP nor the Urban League protested her actions, although the *Minnesota Spokesman-Recorder* did. Nor did these groups protest the redistricting. Indeed, they helped perpetrate that fraud on the Black community (Chapters 13 and 14).

So what is the NAACP? They say: "The National Association for the Advancement of Colored People." But more and more they have become The National Association for the Advancement of Corrupt People. If that doesn't suit your fancy, try The National Association for the Advancement of Cowed People. Finally, a very descriptive name: The National Association for the Advancement of Corrupt Plantations, the latter referring to the DFL.

These local branch Urban League and NAACP leaders have lost their sense of village and community and retained only the sense of being chiefs and rulers. And so slavery enters in again, a slavery of the mind and soul, as those who should be serving the community have become enslaved to the appetite for more power and wealth, regardless of how that hurts the community. If they want to pursue power and wealth, then they need to do so outside the NAACP and outside the Urban League. These are supposed to be organizations for the people, not for the self-aggrandizement of their leaders. It helps them but not our people in the inner city.

Many of the NAACP and Urban League leaders as well as others deeply involved with the City Council are ministers of the Gospel of Jesus Christ, which is what makes this such a scandal, that some of those representing the virtues of love and service and care and help for the poor, have become turncoats who seek instead to be treated as demi-gods served by the people, not serving the people.

I was in a group of over 40 people who met with Mayor-elect R.T. Rybak after his election in November 2001. All that transpired was an example of corrupt leadership: The group talked of themselves, not of the people they serve. They talked about what they could get rather than ask tough questions of how to provide despite the cuts. They talked about the state's billion-dollar shortfall as well as the shortfall for Minneapolis rather than talk about Black employment preservation or the preservation of others. 41% of those jettisoned in the cuts, those laid off, were African-American.

As I am the spokesman for the Black Police organization, I asked the new mayor, R.T. Rybak, why, in the current class of police officers, there were *no* African-Americans. He expressed hurt and said my remarks were "mean spirited regarding the cuts. And yet, only the African-Americans were jettisoned, including the department of Labor Relations, with two officers, headed by a Black.

How do these Black organizations of Minneapolis react? In silence. Silence regarding these cuts and silence regarding these cuts and elimination of jobs of African-Americans, as they do the bidding of their DFL Mastuhs.

During the 1960s, when I was at Syracuse University studying community organizing, we often wondered how a country of such ideals could treat Blacks the way it did. I had a hard time then, and I have a hard time now, understanding both the intellectual confusion and corruption (slavery being seen as good because it "protected" and "cared" for Blacks, as if liberty and freedom were only for White), and the moral confusion and corruption (holding states' higher than human rights, forcibly separating families and legally keeping whole generations of Blacks uneducated and poor), all expressed in the kind of 1984 language of George Orwell, that this was a "good" for all involved. No matter how you define it, those were all acts of evil. We find Black organizations slipping into that as well.

There will be readers who will wince at my use of the term evil. But what else can we call it? One may have a different opinion of how to go about doing something, but the results I have reported cannot be debated. They just are. So how do we deal with evil that most people seem to want to deny exists? I agree that evil is a mystery. But what else would you call the events in my Interludes? If slavery, lynching, burning entire towns down, murdering women and children, and stealing a people's land and wealth are not evil, then there are no absolutes and nothing is wrong, so the only goal is to obtain power and used it however one wants against others.

The problem comes when people attempt to establish as absolute that which is not. For instance, the Constitution was used to suggest slavery was an absolute, followed by the Missouri Compromise stating the same absolute (thus for every free state admitted to the Union a slave state had to be admitted too, in order to maintain balance). The Democrats traded the Presidency in 1876, in exchange for the

Republican promise to rcmove Federal troops from the South, essentially ending Reconstruction and allowing Democrats to enact Jim Crow laws that created a *de facto* American Apartheid, for which the foundational idea was continued by the Democrats in their Kerner Commission Report in 1968, which concluded that Blacks couldn't make it by themselves and needed to be cared for by the State. The consequence of this idea is to educate us a little, give us poor housing, and do little to enable us to engage in personal wealth building.

With the exchange in 1876, both the Democratic and Republican parties essentially rejected Lincoln's notion of "4 score and 7 years ago...all...created equal... of the people, by the people, for the people, shall not perish from the earth." The 4 score and 7 years ago referred not to the Constitution, which allowed slavery, but to the Declaration of Independence, which declared that all were created equal.

Whether or not Reconstruction was on its way out anyway, the fact remains that Jim Crow laws were then instituted immediately, the Ku Klux Klan was formed to implement them, and to terrorize Blacks so they would not enter the social, political, and economic mainstream. The Black progress achieved by that time was stripped from Blacks.

And, lest we forget, it was then Democratic Governor, Fritz Hollings (now Senator), who raised the Confederate Flag over the capital dome of South Carolina. It was the Democratic President Jimmy Carter who blocked making Martin Luther King's birthday a national holiday, which didn't come to be until a Republican President, Ronald Reagan, signed it into law what Carter refused to sign.

This is not to beat up unnecessarily on Democrats. Republicans don't fight for us either, as they believe in self-reliance, not reliance on government. They advocate boot strapping and refuse to recognize their role is making sure Blacks have few boots and thus few straps. I agree that we need to be self-reliant. But when the chessboard is set up so that Blacks are pawns and Whites get to be King and Queen served by Rooks and Bishops and Knights, pawns don't have a chance.

Put another way, in Walter Karp's apt phrase and book title, Democrats and Republicans are *Indispensable Enemies* who have combined to short-change Blacks. Now I know there are Democrats and DFLers who will be angry about what I'm writing, some because they don't believe it and others because they see no reason to upset a perfectly good electoral apple cart that works in their favor. You can read the history of how both parties, and especially Democrats, have badly treated Blacks in Congress as well as Blacks in general, in *Just Permanent Interests: Black Americans in Congress, 1870-1992* by William L. Clay (Amistad Publishers, New York, 1993).

In the 19th-century's Gilded Age, it is said that the political parties were in a quest for spoils, not principles. That is what I see again today: a quest for spoils, not principles. My plea is that we get back to principles.

Please note that there are no Republicans on the Minneapolis City Council. Just as in 1876, it appears that the DFL and the Republicans have cut a deal to divide the area, giving Minneapolis to the DFL and the Minneapolis suburbs to the Republicans. Each party is so confident in their ability to run their worlds that they have no qualms about doing the illegal, unjust, and unfair, knowing they can get away with it. The Black organizations in town understand this. But instead of fighting it, they have sold out to the DFL so that their leaders can get their small piece of the pie, even if it means selling out those they claim to represent. They have become sell-outs to the DFL in order to make deals for themselves and their friends. And I understand why they sell out. They have bought into the idea that Blacks are victims and can't make it without government and outside help. The media support this notion as does the National Democratic Party and the Minnesota/Minneapolis DFL bosses. My chapters on education (7), housing (8), and jobs (9), demonstrate this.

They Mastuhs don't want people to know that Blacks were more economically engaged in Minneapolis business before 1950 than since 1950.

When Julian Bond, Chairman of the national NAACP, says that the NAACP is "immensely bureaucratic," he is explaining why he can't do what he wants to: shift the NAACP focus from providing social services to pushing for social justice. He is exposing the power of the bureaucracy (which is the same for all bureaucracies, Black or White, corporate or government, religious or non-religious non-profit) and his lack of personal persuasiveness to get them to change course, just as with any large organization. He can push for social justice but he can't will it. Instead of saying the NAACP is going to do so, he expresses it as a hope. This is another example of how individual leadership is often co-opted by bureaucracy, again: whether national or local, whether Black or White, whether private sector or public sector. However, the market quickly punishes corporations for that, whereas government agencies, schools, and non-profit organizations just keep on doing it, asking for more and more money to do less and less.

Two things stand in the way of the NAACP and the Urban League doing what they should be doing. First, their unwillingness to stop being arms of the Democratic Party, and giving up their dependence on the great sums of money that come from government programs for Blacks. They are not about to bite the hands that feed them. Secondly, their unwillingness to connect with the poor directly. They are comprised, as are so many do-good agencies, Black and White, of primarily middle class government bureaucrats. Look at all of the NAACP and Urban League leaders, national and local, and look how many are affiliated with the Democratic party, with governments and agencies, are or were office holders, are or were working for the government at some level, whether Federal, state, local, and look at how many work in their city's agencies or community's non-profit organizations. This is why, even though they have agency jobs, they also have time for these other organizations: their Urban League and the NAACP roles are part of their agency jobs.

Now ask this key question: when, in the last 10 years, have you heardd of these dual-track individuals doing anything for poor communities? As you can see from Chapters 7-13, they have hurt, not helped, the poor of the communities of Minneapolis.

How else can you explain why Black organizations like the NAACP and the Urban League do nothing when the Whites take away their housing, the education of their children, their jobs, opportunities for economic development? Why do they respond like lambs to the lies in the media and not feel outrage and stand up and say it's wrong? Why do they seem to just say: "well, if the bosses want it, then it is OK," even when time and again the bosses' decisions work against the poor of the inner city? Why? Because they are being paid to, one way or another.

These local Black leaders have thus gone along with the White interpretation of the Civil Rights laws in order to protect their organizations, not their people. They impede Black progress and racial healing in order to keep their paid representative positions. We must get beyond work that promotes adversarial approaches trying to make Whites feel guilty and helpless so Blacks can feel self-righteous. In the meantime, nothing changes in terms of education, housing, jobs, participation in politics and the economic main-stream for those left behind. More importantly, nothing happens to help build Black political power and Black personal wealth.

In his piece "Still Stuck On the (Now Integrated) Plantation," Kwame JC McDonald, in the *Minnesota Spokesman-Recorder* (April 4-10, 2002), writes how we:

> sometimes find ourselves endorsing programs, projects and/or people that we know are less than perfect, at best.

It gets worse. He goes on to write that:

> We often sanction activities, statements and actions that are questionable. In fact, we often find ourselves doing things that we later either question, reject, or downright deny.

The Civil Rights Movement is full of those kinds of inconsistencies, misappropriation of energy and time. There are, for instance, many who question the advisability of continuing to fight for integration, desegregation and assimilation.

He concludes his column by saying that we spend so much money that we have become slaves to debt, making us more enslaved now than at any previous period in the history of the United States. We are stuck on the plantation.

What I find interesting here is that he correctly brings it back to the individual rather than leaving it with the institutions. We need to stop looking to institutions to take care of us and instead find those who will help us take care of ourselves. We need to stop beating up on ourselves and start beating up on the institutions that claim to represent us and that instead enrich their leaders who then turn around and blame us. I submit this is so because we have just as many Black elitists as the White folks do.

Indeed, Black friends of mine who mingle with the Black elite of this town have been asked why they associate with Ron Edwards, as he is not really one of them. He is a porter's son. He is poor. He doesn't drive a new car. So instead of saying: "Hey man, that's cool," they condemn me. Instead of saying that Ron Edward is one of the guys who never took his eye off the prize and has always worked for equal access and equal opportunity and never for an organization, they condemn me for not having made money off any of these organizations as some of them have. Put another way, they ask this as plantation house Negroes looking down on the poor Black boy. And then they wonder why integration, desegregation, and assimilation haven't worked as well as we would have liked. They have gone along with the DFL and its policies to prevent integration, desegregation, and assimilation, the very things they should have been fighting for.

A clear sign of how the question: "who will lead" is confusing things is the disturbing conflict between the traditional organizations and their clergy, both Christian and Islam. So who will lead? Allah or Jesus? It is precisely the failure of Christian clergy and churches and traditional organizations like the NAACP and the Urban League that have led to the rise and success of our nation's inside Black nation, the Nation of Islam. Here we have a nation, the U.S., that has locked out Black Americans. So some have created their own nation within our nation, and called it just that, as in the case of the Nation of Islam, essentially rejecting everything on which the United States is based.

The rhetoric of the Nation of Islam, its fierce racism, its fierce hatred, its totalitarian structure have not helped (which is why it could not stand an independent Malcolm X and thus assassinated him). But their Us vs. Them attitudes, their hierarchy of leaders dictating to their followers, they learned in this country, as the Nation of Islam leaders became plantation bosses of their Black nation. And although the NAACP and the Urban League have a more benign type of leadership structure, they have the same plantation mentality, wanting all Blacks to do as they say. I find that these three organizations, today, do far more harm to our struggle than all the Whites put together. All the Whites have to do is sit back while we tear each other apart and keep each other down.

The racist Kerner Commission of 1968 said we couldn't take care of ourselves so the government would have to do it for us. The government then co-opted our leadership by buying them off with programs paid with mostly Federal funds. Thus, a number of the Black middle class have gained control of massive budgets dedicated to social welfare policy, housing, education, and government jobs. The Black elite misrepresent non-elite Blacks by using the co-opting money from Whites to keep the non-elite Blacks of the inner city down. This too has been the Minneapolis story.

And where is the proof of all of the corruption in development dollars handed out by the city? My guess is that much of it is in the missing files Jackie Cherryhomes took from her office. What has preoccupied too many of our leaders: opportunities for self-enrichment. My claim is that the leadership of the NAACP and the Urban League as well as other Black organizations needs to concentrate on confronting teachers' unions for not teaching minorities and confront civil rights leaders for caving in to the teachers' unions, and confront everyone else, including legislators, mayors, and City Council Members, who have and still have a hand in the failure to educate minority kids, steal their housing and property, not employ Blacks or use Black organizations and contractors, what is their value?

We know the only way out of poverty is education and learning. The way to develop prosperity is to learn both skills and discipline to get and hold jobs that pay. Yet too many Black leaders go along with the poor results as long as they get theirs. These Blacks are worse that the White Mastuhs, because it is our own Black kids whom they are sacrificing, who aren't learning in school, and who aren't learning skills and discipline for the rigors of life. Put simply, until Black leaders stop using race-conscious diversity politics to enrich themselves, they will continue to sabotage our dream by colluding with federal, state and local governments that look the other way because they have created an intellectual plantation on which the politically correct Mastuhs are in charge, on which the only agendas accepted are those of race, gender, ethnicity, sexual orientation, and environment rather than the agenda of equal access and equal opportunity in education, housing, jobs, and political and economic participation. As long as Blacks can be hustled to chase those ghosts, which takes their eye off the prize, the real focus which leads to the prize is ignored, as the prize is left unfocussed. Hence, we have participated in disenfranchising ourselves and have done so without shame. Places where this comes together like in no other are in education and housing and jobs (Chapters 7 - 9).

And the latest is Hennepin County's African-American Men's Project. A most incredible line, showing the County really wants servitude from Blacks, not initiative, is in the application list of those who are to serve on its African American Men Advisory Commission. Applicants:

> must be committed to the implementation of the recommendations in the African American Men Project report.

In other words, the project, funded by Hennepin County, established an advisory commission to advise the county and the City of Minneapolis on something it had already pre-conceived, pre-established, and pre-determined. Again, those who are eligible to serve must "first be committed to the implementation of the recommendations in the African American Men project report." In others words, they must do as the White Mastuhs say.

Where do the NAACP and the Urban League stand today?

At its annual convention in July 2002 in Houston, Texas, the NAACP President, Kweisi Mfume, a former Congressman, stressed patriotism and solidarity between the races, as he denounced "black bigotry" and called for members to stand against injustice from the "far, far left" as well as the "far, far right."

This was in contrast to what Jesse Jackson and NAACP Chairman Julian Bond had said, as they gave more fiery convention remarks. As Mfume said: "The mad men of today's world, much like the racists that dot our 93-year NAACP history, use terrorism to intimidate and lies to deceive." And although I don't agree with everything Mfume says, I do agree with his denouncing "sexism, racism, anti-Semitism" and "immigrant-bashing and union-bashing and gay-bashing and city-bashing." He said: "We must speak out not just against injustice to ourselves but against injustice to everyone." I agree.

I just wish he had included education, housing, jobs, and political and economic participation. In the 1950s and 1960s, White segregationist governors stood at Southern schoolhouse doors blocking entrance to Black students. Now the NAACP stands at the doors of the worst schools in the country, urban schools filled with

Black youngsters, blocking them from leaving, unwilling to let them out, as they serve their Democratic Mastuhs who continue their same poor education policies for Black inner cities, just as they did throughout the Jim Crow South.

Interlude 14

Lest We Forget A Common Heritage for All: Slave Ancestry

What has been called the "peculiar institution" of slavery was not always peculiar. Indeed, it was once universal. It is as old as humankind. It was not until the 19th century that slavery was abolished in most of the world, beginning with Britain in 1806. The U.S. did not outlaw it until it passed the 13th Amendment to the Constitution in 1865 (following Lincoln's Emancipation Proclamation of 1863). Different countries claim credit for being first, as Denmark does. The key fact is not who was first but the truth that it wasn't outlawed anywhere in the world, including in Africa, until the 19th century.

Records going back 5,000 years, before Biblical times, show slavery as a recognized institution. Besides those enslaved as a result of losing a battle or invasion, there were those reduced to slavery as punishment for certain offenses. Most were of the same race and culture. Men were allowed to sell their children or their entire family to pay off debts (for various time frames). Slaves were branded like any other chattel. Thus, the forces of slavery and oppression have been unrelenting for thousands of years. Archeological evidence shows how widespread slavery was.

Though not officially slaves, women of tribes were often treated as slaves as they were considered property owned by their father, husband, or brother. Slavery has been seen as natural for thousands of years. Most of us would be absolutely opposed to slavery if we had to be a slave, and others of us might not hesitate to support it if given the opportunity to own some. If we all go far enough back in our family histories, we will find slaves or serfs or peasants or dirt farmers. For Blacks, we don't have to go back very far at all. Indeed, most people of my generation know some grandparent or great-grandparent who either was a slave or knew slaves.

Slavery existed in Africa before the Americas were discovered. One tribe would enslave another tribe. This was before outsiders came and discovered what they called the Dark Continent. Then came the exporting of African slaves, first to Arabs, then to Europe, and then to the Americas. But the U.S. didn't start the traffic in African slaves to the Americas. That "honor" goes to Portugal. Indeed, Portugal and Spain began the African slave trade in the 15th century, with Arab and Black tribes as partners, long before the Pilgrims landed, joined by England in the 16th century. It was not until the early 17th century that North America got involved, a century that also saw France, Sweden, and Denmark involved in the slave business. And the carving up of Africa into colonial Africa was done without any participation by the United States. Africa was carved up by the colonial empires of Europe at the all-

European gathering at the Berlin Conference of 1884-85. Many Black Americans don't realize that most slaves from Africa went to South America, Central America, Mexico, and the islands of the Caribbean, not to North America. Whether in Europe or Asia or South and Central America, most people in most places were in some kind of bondage or servitude long before America was founded. And in the beginning of slavery in America, there were also a few Black slaveholders.

The first recorded word for freedom was found in 2350 B.C. Sumer, the result of a struggle between the ruler with his bureaucracy and the people, and also the struggle between the temple and the palace (what might be called church and state). We continue that struggle today. Don't forget that ancient Greece's 200-year experiment with democracy was conducted, when in fact 80% of the population were slaves.

Many of us, Black and White, have slaves in our family background. Not all of you think that way. You need to think again. Except for 20th-century immigrants from Africa, if you are Black and in America, it is quite likely that your ancestors were brought here in slave ships. If you are White, your ancestors were more than likely either serfs or bond servants, or runaway outcasts from persecution, whether religious or political, where they were treated as slaves and from which they fled to this country to be free. Sadly, some people become what they hate, and thus some went from hating being slaves to becoming slave Masters.

It is important to remember for both Blacks and Whites what I noted above: that for most Blacks over 50 years of age, we remember grandfathers or great-grandfathers who knew relatives who were slaves. Many Whites don't want to admit the historical reality that although Negroes in America were first slaves simply because they were sold a slaves, the notion changed, especially as the abolitionist movement grew to a more universal rationale that justified holding on to Blacks as slaves: they were slave because they were Black. This was based on everything from purposefully misinterpreting the Bible to declare that the Mark of Cain given by God was being Black-skinned, or using the story of Noah to say that because the one son looked on his father Noah's naked body he was sent to Africa and told by God that he and his son would forever serve his brothers. The slave states developed these and other theological arguments justifying slavery as being ordained by God. Others said that Blacks should be slaves because they were like monkeys, and thus not fully human.

Too many people still believe Blacks should be slaves or at least servants. That was the basis of Apartheid in South Africa, Jim Crow laws in the United States after Reconstruction to the 1960s, and the plantation attitude in Minneapolis today, and now the 21st century actions discussed in this book, all part of the unspoken plan reflecting the desire to keep Blacks in their place. We know the excuses before the 21th century. What is Minneapolis' excuse now?

Chapter 15

The Story of Punting the Minnesota Vikings.
Say Goodbye to The Vikings, They are Leaving,
Say Goodbye to The Vikings, They Are Our Loss.
That is the Plan.

Part of the title of this chapter may come as a shock to the reader, so it bears repeating:

Say Goodbye to The Vikings, They are Leaving

Say Goodbye to The Vikings, They Are Our Loss

What I will walk you through in this chapter is the plan of the movers and shakers of Minneapolis to move the Vikings out of Minnesota. At the same time, the story of the Vikings' departure is another look at the same dynamics we have witnessed about the character of Minneapolis.

Now you may ask why I would write with such an eloquent plea for equal access and equal opportunity in education, housing, and economic development, and then include a piece on a sports team?

For four reasons. First, it shows that if you take away the name Vikings and insert any other, you'll have the Minneapolis story as seen through your eyes as well. The sadness is that this is something about which most Minnesotans agree: they love their Vikings. They probably have more passion than most cities. They have sold out every game the past four years. But that doesn't matter. They don't fit The Plan.

Second, plain and simple, because I am a sports fan. Any sports fan will understand. I played football in high school. Everyone I know who has played the game, at whatever level, is always very interested. So, writing about the Vikings or any of the athletic teams is to also write about the Minneapolis story.

Third, sports stay with us all of our lives and impacts us in ways we often are not aware of, whether we played or cheered from the sidelines. When I sat down to begin this book, the first story I talked about centered on my high school football team. I talked about it for over two hours before I could begin to talk about my community advocacy work. And I find this is even true for some women who remember Friday night high school football games as well. It is a part of our social fabric, which makes it doubly difficult to imagine Minneapolis without the Vikings.

They have been a part of our social fabric for over 40 years. And now they will be ripped out of our lives.

Fourth, part of what I have been talking about is Black economic development, wealth and prosperity. For the longest time professional athletes were not paid the kind of money that is paid today. Now that they are, I often wonder what the White power structure of wealth thinks about having five dozen highly paid Blacks in town and playing on their golf courses. From my perspective, it could give a real boost to developing Black wealth in Minneapolis. On the other hand, the fear of that could be a reason why the wealthy Whites don't want them here in White Scandinavia land.

It sounds strange to think of Minneapolis without their Vikings. So ask yourself this question: can you imagine Chicago without their Bears or Bulls or Cubs or White Sox or Blackhawks as an integral part of their social fabric? Can you imagine Detroit without the Lions, the Pistons, the Tigers, and the Redwings all of whom are considered an integral part of their social fabric (Detroit just built two new stadiums, one for the NFL Lions and one for the MLB Tigers? Can you imagine New York City without their Yankees, Mets, Giants, Jets, Knicks, Islanders or Rangers? Can you imagine other cities without their teams, which are also considered part of their social fabric?

Can you imagine Minneapolis without the Twins or Timberwolves or Wild, and especially without the Vikings? Neither can I. But soon we will. The powers that be in Minnesota want the Twins, so they are safe. The cities choose to be on the hook for the arenas of the Timberwolves and Wild, so they are safe These powers don't want the Vikings, so they have created the false notion that the Twin Cities can't support four teams. As you will see, they don't want to. So they have made sure that the Vikings are leaving. I will show you how they did it. It will be our loss. But the powers do love the University of Minnesota Gophers, so they will be the ones to get a new stadium. The Twins will get a renovated Metrodome.

How is it that the powers in Minnesota not only imagine it but want it, encourage it, and have set the process in motion to kick the Vikings out, not caring about the role the team plays in the state's social fabric and the hearts of its people? I will connect the dots foryou. The powers have answered no to the question: To Keep or Not to Keep the Vikings. The people say keep the Vikings, but the wealthy who control, who could make it happen, say no. So the Vikings are leaving. Our loss.

Let's look at The Plan in the early 1950s. That version of The Plan was very Minnesotan, very bold, very gutsy, very "can do." In his book *Stadium Games: Fifty Years of Big League Greed and Bush League Boondoggles* (University of Minnesota Press, Minneapolis, 2000), the reporter Jay Weiner writes:

It was 1952. The Twin Cities were prairie towns seeking to compete with Milwaukee and Kansas City. The political and economic foundations for Minnesota's first major-league stadium were laid by a community—workers, captains of industry, and politicians—that wanted pro sports, that felt a team and a ballpark would gather them together, not tear them apart. Major-league sports would put Minnesota on the map. Getting teams was the cause; major-league sports would allow this overlooked section of the nation to, literally, play with the big boys. The symbol of arrival…a stadium (p. xxiii).

Getting teams was the cause; major-league sports would allow this overlooked section of the nation to, literally, play with the big boys. The symbol of arrival…a stadium (p. xxiii).

In 1990, The *Mpls.St.Paul* magazine wrote:

…the Twins won the World Series. As pennant fever mounted during those magical weeks of fall 1987, Minnesotans came together in an outpouring of excitement, joy and gratitude never before equaled in this state. Sports frenzy continues today, finding an outlet not only in the … Twins but in the Vikings, Gophers, North Stars and Timberwolves as well.

Then came the beginning of a loss of nerve; the "can do" attitude became a "won't do" attitude. The bosses decided they would not support luxury boxes for four major league teams. This is why Former Metropolitan Sports Facility Commission chairman Henry Savelkoul frequently trumpeted the bosses' line, masking it by saying that four teams could not "flourish." But note that the teams have plenty of attendance. The fans are there. But the lazy wealthy, with the money, didn't want four sets of luxury boxes. Weiner says the same thing in his book. Professional sports today has become an industry supported by taxpayers **and** by wealthy individuals or corporations, the latter paying big bucks for luxury seats or boxes, costs that which can range from $40,000 a year to $250,000 a year, but not in Minneapolis where major corporations are **not** sponsors.

The plan is to support two major teams, the Twins and the Gophers, at the expense of the most popular team, The Vikings. Sell the team to an outsider who would move the team, leaving the Metrodome to the Twins and a new on-campus outdoor football stadium for the Gophers. That is The Plan. As far as I can tell, that plan still holds.

The problem with The Plan is that the goal of being Big League will be sacrificed. There is only one sport in America today that is truly the American pastime, if not obsession, and that is football. Baseball has been in decline for a number of years. It may retain the name of American pastime, but it is football that is The American Passion. Only football holds the imagination of America, every Friday night at high schools, every Saturday for colleges, and every Sunday for the NFL. When the Vikings leave, Minneapolis will no longer be considered in the first tier of major league cities.

Now I know that by now, dear reader, you are wondering how can all this be? How come, you ask, you haven't read it in the press? If this is true, why hasn't it been in the newspapers and on TV? Good questions. But it has been. And if, dear reader, you ask where, then I know you don't read the Black newspaper, *The Minnesota Spokesman and Recorder*, and I know that you don't listen to the Black news on TV station KMOJ, nor, for that matter, my TV program. For several years we have all carried the story. In fairness, the White papers have carried it as a joke or in snippets, but not enough to upset anyone, for they know the Vikings are not to be saved. And they know Whites are not reading the Black newspaper, so they have nothing to fear. But I read both. I know. But you want proof. Here it is from the July 12-18, 2001 *Minnesota Spokesman and Recorder*, and with a story title that says it all: "**Conspiracy of Silence**" by Larry Fitzgerald:

> The Vikings are now the NFL's most popular team. They have the two most popular players in the league in Daunte Culpepper and Randy Moss. In the three years that [Red] McCombs has owned the team he's made $15 million, while Jerry Jones has made $165 million directly from his stadium. When the business community decided to build Xcel Energy Center in St. Paul and bring the NHL back, they chose hockey over the Vikings. NHL players are 98 percent White, while NFL players and the Vikings are 80 percent Black. The Vikings have the worst stadium agreement in sports. Nobody is happy with the Dome; the Twins want out, the Gophers [and] the Vikings [want out too], yet nothing is getting done.

Fitzgerald concluded by predicting that the Vikings will move to Los Angeles, the Twins will stay in a renovated dome, and the Gopher football team will get its own stadium on its campus. Has anything changed since last summer? Here is Fitzgerald again, in August 2002, not only answering this question but also pointing out the unheralded but necessary reading of the Black independent newspapers in this country:

Twins Aren't Leaving, Vikings Are

Once the Vikings are out of the picture and are sold to a Los Angeles-based ownership, it will become very clear that the Twins are going to accept a renovated Metrodome. And the new University of Minnesota President—whoever he or she is—will lead the way along with the new athletic director to build a smaller version of an on-campus football stadium for Gophers.

With the merged departments, it is imperative that the football program starts to carry the weight of generating the kind of revenue needed to support the athletic budget. Remember I told you months ago that Gov. Jesse Ventura would not seek reelection. I have a solid overview of the lay of the land.

Larry Fitzgerald, *Minnesota Spokesman-Recorder*, July 25, 2002
http://www.channel4000.com/msp/sports/stories/sports-157742020020725-120732.html

And thus we can figure out the answer to the question as to why none of the Fortune 500 companies of the Twin Cities are sponsors of the Vikings: They understand The Plan. This also lets us interpret why the previous owners refused to sell to a local person who wanted to buy the team but instead sold to an outsider, despite the well-known stadium issue: because they wanted the new buyer to move the team.

Not coincidentally, the same group of 1950's men who brought the Twins are big Gopher fans who have contributed significantly to the University. As I noted earlier, the Gophers are the only Big Ten Team that has to share its fans with a professional team. As Minnesota Governor John Pillsbury said of the University, in 1889, "when I am dead and gone, this institution shall be kept for all time, broad in its scope, <u>powerful in its influence</u>" (emphasis added). Not once has the university said: yes, let's do it, to the proposed joint Vikings-Gopher stadium. Recall that the University of Miami was able to keep the first attempt of pro football out of Miami. The first team that attempted to do so wound up in Buffalo.

Fitzgerald fixes the blame on a lack of vision that is not only less than the vision of the 1950s, but a vision that remains White at the exclusion of non-white, which the series in the *Star Tribune* in 1990 and the two cover stories of *Mlps.St.Paul* magazine in 1990 and 2001 support (Interludes 2 and 10). Regardless of whether the Vikings are moved by Red or sold by Red and moved by the new owner, Red McCombs will wrongly get the blame. The blame will reside with the previous owners who passed up the local buyer for the out-of-town guy with the understanding that the team would be moved.

Fans will be even more enraged when they learn that some of those who voted to sell the Vikings to Red McCombs and make big buck returns didn't invest much in the first place. They borrowed their investment money, and then had their loan payments paid out of ticket sales and TV revenue. The return they received when they sold to Red was pure gravy, a value they didn't create, a value that was created by the fans. They then paid off their loans from receipts rather than pursuing free agents ("Vikings are Going, Going, Gone!" Larry Fitzgerald, *Spokesman-Recorder*, May 8-14, 1997). In other words, do the math, connect the dots: rich guy borrowed money to buy the Vikings and then used Vikings revenues to pay off their loans rather than go after free agents. Why? To set them up to leave.

And given the many ways to finance a stadium and the many ways to generate revenue, we are left with the realization that Fitzgerald and Wiener are correct, that the former owners don't want to put in the work and time needed to select among the many solutions available because they had already decided they wanted the Vikings to move. These former Vikings owners are emotionally tied to the Twins and Gophers. They view the non-Scandinavian Vikings (Black) as expendable and desirably so. They obviously don't see things through my eyes nor the eyes of the vast majority of Minnesotans who love their Vikings.

The fans' rage will be even greater at the reality of how these wealthy owners went along with the use of outside money to ship out the people's Vikings, as reported in *USA Today* (August 6, 2002): the NFL gave or loaned Red McCombs $100 million to help him buy the team to ensure that it would be shipped out. No one knew this before. This was the first time this news leaked out, meaning it had been a secret for five years. Note: you did not read this in the *Star Tribune*. But it was in *USA Today*, and it was featured in Larry Fitzgerald's column in the *Spokesman Recorder* and on his "Fitz Beat" on www.Channel4000.com of August 27, 2002: "McCombs Looking To Sell Team."

This proves two things: (1) the fix was in to move the Vikings, and (2) to make sure that the outside guy could outbid the local guy, the NFL loaned the outside guy $100 million, so he could bid $250 million (his first bid was $150 million). Then the outside guy would be set to sell the team to buyers in Los Angeles.

The Plan called for the Vikings to move. And the NFL wants a team in Los Angeles. A match made n heaven. Fitzgerald continues:

> **The big business community sold out Minneapolis.** Headrick, who was not a favorite with many local media, never believed he could beat Taylor in a financial round to buy the Vikings.
>
> Why didn't the league want Headrick to have the team? After all, he was a local guy and was team president.

Now the dots are connected for you: the power boys don't want the team in Minneapolis and the NFL wants a team in Los Angeles. Still want more proof, dear reader? Here it is:

Former Vikings Chairman John Skoglund hinted in 1997 that the team would be forced to move without a new stadium (Pioneer Press, April 10, 1997). So, this is not new, and is not about Red. It's about a group of leaders who turned their backs on the people of Minnesota. The former owners made this same argument in their presentation before the Sports Facility Commission in December 19, 1996, as did NFL Commissioner Paul Tagliabue in his statement before the Advisory Task Force on Professional Sports in Minnesota, September 25, 1995: no stadium, the team moves. They have positioned Red and the legislature to be the scapegoats.

Want more proof? Here it is: Henry Savelkoul, former Metropolitan Sports Facility Commission chairman, prior to the sale to Red and since has maintained, falsely in my view, that the four teams cannot flourish, that one has to go. He stated this in his "The Viability of Four Major Sports Teams in Minnesota," which he concluded was not viable (pp. 421-422 of Weiner book). Indeed, Weiner writes, after interviewing legislators, corporation executives, government leaders, that "In the end, I believe we in Minnesota can' afford four major league teams (p. 467). That is the single real purpose of his book, in my view: to sell the idea there is no room for the Vikings.

Weiner then goes on to say that four teams can't stay and that "triage" has to be exercised, and although he says the state has to decide (blames the legislators, get it?), he clearly believes it is the Vikings that have to go because they play only 10 plus games a year vs. the 81 a year the Twins play, which fits the tourist and travel industry schedules much better. Minneapolis weather is like Bismarck, South Dakota, not like Milwaukee or Chicago. Can you imagine a World Series outdoors in Minnesota in October?

If the Twins were really going to go, they would have been sold and moved. There exists no known official document of any kind suggesting the Twins would be contracted. It was all talk, designed to get people eager to keep the team and to set them up for paying for the Metrodome renovation once the Vikings are gone.

The legislature appointed a task force. They were provided with ten models and 8 different ways to finance new stadiums without new taxes, and they never contacted the person submitting these models, even though he gave them to not only the task force but also to key legislators, the governor, the Twins, and the Vikings, paper copies as well as a web site in which all were listed for easy access. Not one person from any of these entities contacted him. When the individual went to Minneapolis and walked in to meet with the Vikings administrative vice president, he was told they didn't nccd any of the models as they had a deal in the legislature and a deal with the university. Why did he say that? Because it ended the conversation in typical Minneapolis nice fashion for ending them: lie so people will go away.

Remember the Minnesota Northstars National Hockey League team? Norm Green was promised the new area where Target Center now is upon the completion of the Mall of America, as well as that he would get a piece of the action for the Mall's Phase II. Curt Carlson and others were against Green's development.

But the Northstars' owner outfoxed the bosses. They thought Norm would heel and do as he was told. Doesn't everyone? But he wasn't from Minnesota. He didn't know he was to genuflect and obey. So he left Minnesota, taking the Northstars with him, leaving Minnesota, producer of more American-born hockey players than any other state and home of the Hockey Hall of Fame, without a hockey team. Yet when it came time for the NHL to expand, Minnesota got a team. So you see, dear reader, when the Bosses want something to happen, the bosses can make it happen.

The bosses wanted the Met Center land for the Mall of America. The Mall was needed for travel packages for Minneapolis-headquartered Northwest Airlines as well as for Japan Airlines and Korean Airlines. And in all of this, under the capable eye of Bloomington's Mayor James Laughinghouse (Bloomington is the town adjacent to Minneapolis where the Mall of America is and where the old stadiums for the Vikings and Twins and Northstars used to be). In all of this, there was not one role for any minority. These travel packages, by the way, are also why the Twins needed a covered stadium, or dome. Rainouts and cold are death to travel packages; playing indoors makes it controllable, all orderly. They built it and people came.

The movers and shakers believe that the community prefers Gophers football because it is what *they* prefer, but attendance records show the opposite. The preference is for the Vikings, but facts have never gotten in the way of men used to getting their way and who have already made up their minds.

How can the bosses kick out a team that is so loved by Minnesotans? Because they can (like 800-pound guerillas who feel they don't have to follow either the people or democracy). No one will stand up to them. Minnesotans drive in the lambs' lane. They follow. Even though the bosses have the economic muscle and the financial and development models to use to profitably purchase the team and keep it in Minnesota, and keep it profitable, they won't do so. Why? What other conclusion is there than that they want the Vikings out of town, which follows their Plan?

I've read so many stories in the Minneapolis *Star Tribune* that it is hard to keep track of them all. But Vikings owner Red McCombs has gotten older (don't we all). He is in his mid-70s or more. He has slowed down. From the papers it looks to me like the younger Gary Woods (the team President who made promises to the city businessmen that Red decided for a while not to follow) and the much younger saboteurs at Winter Park (see the many stories in the *Star Tribune* in November and December 2001), apparently found it easy to manipulate him. To prepare the team to move, they must have concluded that it would be best to have a White administration. So they plotted to get rid of the Black coach, even though he had the best active record in the NFL for the past 9 years and the 8th best in overall NFL history. That didn't matter. They had to clean up the team. Of 13 coaches and staff who were let go, 12 were Black. The one strong voice in the community for the Vikings was gone. The blond Vikings were back in charge. And now they could more easily ready the team for sale.

So you see, the Vikings are just a foil, a diversion for the real winner in the stadium derby, the baseball Twins, who will get a renovated Metrodome, and the University of Minnesota Gophers, who will get a new stadium. The City of St. Paul chose to support a mostly White team and the city of Minneapolis chose to support the small number of Blacks on the basketball team. That leaves the choice for the third spot between the Twins and the Vikings. As we have already seen, the Twins fit into their plan; the Vikings do not. Therefore, bye-bye, Vikings. The Gophers will get their stadium and not have to share football fans with a pro team. What better way for the Gophers to increase their attendance to a self-supporting level than to get the Vikings fans to do it for them once the Vikings are out of town? The University is King.

Now despite what the sports writers have written in the Minneapolis *Star Tribune*, the Metrodome was built for baseball. I can hear the regulars who read the sports pages crying out: "wait a minute, the papers are always writing about how the compromises made favored the Vikings, so it is a football stadium." There, you see? Note there is nothing about the compromises made by baseball. They didn't need to make any. The compromises were made for the team that was shortchanged by the original design: football. The dome was built for baseball. Baseball in Minneapolis in April, not to mention sometimes in May, September, October and, for the first time last year, November, is in weather that is uncomfortable and uncontrollable. And the powers that be want to control everything, even the weather. Minneapolis weather, except for June, July, and August, is unpredictable except for the reality of the bad weather of these months, which would then cause weather delays or postponements, etc., as in "the good old days." The powers that be can't have tour charters, team charters, and individual tourists come to town and then be rained out. No month is invulnerable to this. Thus, the Dome stays.

This has long been a nightmare for schedulers in the league just as it is for vacationers, tourists, and the industries that cater to them. The Dome was built to defy the weather. So the Dome will stay. It won't be demolished. Minneapolis gains from the national events held there and it would be stupid to turn down the revenue and the free publicity and exposure gained from the telecasts of these various events, many of which are beamed worldwide. Tearing it down would hurt business, it would hurt tourism, and it would hurt the University. Do the math. The Dome stays. And the Twins stay in it. The Vikings will leave town. And then the University will get its on-campus stadium.

Society needs visionaries. Looking back, you cannot help but be proud of those in the 1950s and 1960s who brought professional sports to Minnesota, trying hard and steadily, through many disappointments, to finally succeed. They are a model of perseverance for all of us. But their vision did not include Blacks.

When you look at the I-694/I-494 circle of commerce, the great ribbon of concrete that encircles Minneapolis and St. Paul, the transportation highway of the area, notice the highway bisecting both cities, I-94 and I-394, as well as the North-South split of Highway I-35 through Minneapolis with I-35W and St. Paul with I-35E. You can't help but be in awe of the men and women who thought the great thoughts, had the grand visions, who invested their time and talent and treasuries to make the Twin Cities the unique area that it is, one of the most livable areas in the country, not to mention in the world.

How did The Plan, the grand vision, get so distorted that the Vikings became expendable to the Mastuhs? How did the planners of the 1950s do so much with far fewer resources, whereas today, with the far greater wealth and resources, with billionaires and millionaires, with over a dozen headquarters of the Fortune 500, with a Federal Reserve Bank, all of a sudden they talk as if they have been struck by "poverty" (Twins owner Carl Pohlad received $1 billion for the sale of his banks) and that there is no such money in the Twin Cities? Minnesota was proud of the fact that it didn't support stadiums with public dollars but rather provided financing that was paid back. Why now is the conversation about paying for them, not financing them? Why have they gone from self-reliance to a demand for corporate welfare? Because Minnesota won't pay, and thus "force" the team to leave.

Economic data demonstrate that all four teams can be supported. Projected demographic data regarding the population growth over the coming years demonstrate that such an argument will be made more moot for all but the most rabid detractors of professional sports, as the area will experience great population growth. Regardless, all the signs add up to a development scheme that started out to be inclusive and that now is exclusive, willing to sacrifice the peoples' team in this new version of The Plan. How did Minnesota leaders get to the place where they are no longer into "the vision thing?" Why cede them power to claim to represent the people when what they have been about is to chase the people's team out of town?

"In the beginning," there were two cities, always feuding. They were divided between those who felt that the center of the universe was in Minneapolis and those who felt the center of the universe was in St. Paul. Neither view turned out to be correct. The center of the local universe turned out to be between the two downtowns, the nexus of the airport and Bloomington. This became clear n the post-war years (late 1940s and early 1950s), with the first significant developments, in which major moves centered on this real estate crown jewel of the region.

The powers of that generation had vision and wrapped their two towns into a unifying area distinguished by a single, shared beltway called 694/494. Many of the Minneapolis power brokers live on the west side near Lake Minnetonka. Interstate 94 came in from the East through the two cities and then went north. Interstate 394 picked up the westerly direction, giving the powers on the west side a quick way to get into either downtown, just as 494 whisked them to Bloomington and the airport.

Thus, there are **two Golden Triangles.** *The first* is formed by the three points of the airport/Bloomington, downtown Minneapolis, and downtown St. Paul, with the University of Minnesota and the Metrodome on the line between the two downtowns. *The second* is larger, with the central point still Bloomington and the airport. The other two points are St. Paul and Wayzata, with Minneapolis, the Metrodome, and the University of Minnesota on the line between St. Paul and Wayzata.

All of this talk about the Vikings leaving helps support my contention that we need to recognize that, in fact, the specter of racism is not a specter. It is very real. Much of it is the closet kind that hangs in the shadows and works its discrimination in quiet and out of sight. Indeed, the Minneapolis *Star Tribune* ran a huge series on the topic (Interludes 2 and 10). It opened with how race affects everyone "from birth to death" and that it "sets our agenda for life." It is now setting the agenda for the Vikings.

The lead story on p. 33 of the *Star Tribune* series is headlined: "Few people of color shape policy in the state." And the seeds of the drive to rid the Twin Cities of the Vikings can be seen in the headline: "Sports teams are slow to reach out to minority fans." Despite having a Black basketball coach, the paper noted that "the Gopher program has ignored the contributions of the minority community." The Vikings "are viewed from a distance." And the Twins organization itself "is burdened by a history of racism." The hockey team assumed "that if there are no minority athletes, there will likely be no minority fans," which is certainly a racist comment.

Finally, recall Interlude 10 and its report on the January 1990 issue of the *Mpls.St.Paul* magazine cover story "I'm Not Racist, But...," and then sub-headed with "'Nice' Minnesotans don't talk about it, but the ugly fact is that racism is alive—and growing—in the Twin Cities." The author also wrote a cover story in October 2001 and, for maybe the first time since the magazine's cover story on racism in 1990, admitted that in that 2001 piece one of the problems is that the closet racism is still "operating in one of the nation's Whitest metropolitan areas," casting "a shadow" under which I as a Black man, and all other Blacks in Minneapolis must live.

I only see one thing that could save the Vikings: if the younger generation of the White wealthy families stood up to their fathers and said it is their future now, and that they want the Vikings, and that they will do what is necessary to keep them. All the ways for doing so are outlined on the web site referenced earlier. But I won't hold my breath, for the young heirs, as we have seen, were de-powered long ago and just don't seem to have the fortitude to stand up on their own.

And so the 15-25 families who make up the power base of this town, the Mastuhs, the "Families," view the Minneapolis story through a different lens of perception than I do. Most of them know of The Plan. They will cry crocodile tears when the Vikings leave, but they will be tears of joy. But it doesn't matter. Say goodbye to the Vikings, they are leaving; say good-bye as that is our loss. Why? Because that is The Plan.

Postscript of October 5, 2002: more disinformation

One of the famous lines of the presidential debate of 1980 was: "There you go again." And here we go again. This article, "Vikings owner denies rumor of sale" (*Star Tribune,* October 5, 2002), continues the same pattern as 1998 when the former owners sold the team. Do you remember, dear reader, as I do, all of the press in the Twin Cities regarding the same kind of information about Glenn Taylor and Tom Clancy, the well planted disinformation, lies, deception, and playing Minneapolis people like chumps? Here we go again. I'm just as convinced now that Glenn Taylor is a stalking horse for Red's sale just as I was that he was a stalking horse for the sale to Red in 1998 to bid up the price. It is all part of the plan. It shows how little respect, the bosses have for the people of Minneapolis. The real issue is the fact, as the article points out, that Red loses his tax write off after this year. He buys and then sells athletic teams after the tax write off period ends. And by making all of the moves necessary to ensure an 0-4 start, the scene is set for people to be so mad they won't care until after the moving trucks have left town, after which it will be too late. And so, dear reader, unless someone steps forward to thwart The Plan, the plan remains: The Vikings leave. The Twins just moved on in the playoffs. Does anyone seriously think they could have played outdoors in this series or the ones coming up?

Interlude 15

Lynching: Duluth, 1921
Assassination: Martin Luther King, 1968

Despite the attempts to hide the truth of the 10,000 Duluth Whites who lynched three young Black youths on June 15, 1920, I learned of it in 1955, 1967, 1969, and again in 1975. I remember the dates, as the story is so terrible and vivid.

I first learned about it in 1955, on a train trip to Kansas City for Christmas (a trip I made every year for 40 years). On this trip, I sat down next to a tall young man like myself who happened to be from Duluth. We both played sports and when we introduced ourselves we recognized each other's names. Somehow the discussion turned to what he had learned from his uncles, who had lived in Duluth since 1916 or 1917 and who had just told him about the 1921 Duluth lynching. We shuddered and dropped the topic.

The second time was in 1967, when I started to work for the gas company. After I had been there a couple of months, I was elected Union Steward. There were 19 of us in the shop, including two other Blacks. After a few months, one of the old White guys on the evening shift told me he was from Duluth. And he finally told me that he had been a 14-year old at the Duluth lynching. He obviously left out details about what his role was. He became very emotional. He broke down and cried as he talked of the brutality. He was most agitated by the fact that even though there was a mob of 10,000, his father insisted on taking him up close to the front so he actually saw the bodies. Of course, I was so angry, I just didn't know what to do. I just listened quietly. We never spoke of it again.

The third time I heard of it was two years later when, as a young community activist, I visited Duluth and asked about the lynching. Most would not talk about it, as Black and White alike conspired to cover it up. But one Black did talk about it with me, in detail.

The fourth time was when I mentioned it on my radio show in 1975. Some callers told me to get it off the air. But others told me they had papers and documents about the lynching.

I tried to get the Minnesota legislature to put up a memorial. It took 20 years. And finally, last year, there was a service at the First Lutheran Church in Duluth. Over 500 White folks came. The Minnesota Historical Society Press published a book on it in 2000, *The Lynchings in Duluth*, by Michael Fedo. There is also a permanent pictorial record of lynching in America, including the one in Duluth, at the Allen-Littlefield Collection at Emory University in Atlanta.

Lynching used to be a time-honored practice in America. The NAACP reported 3,436 people lynched between 1889 and 1922. And this does not include the hundreds killed in Tulsa, Oklahoma, that I discussed in Interlude 13, in which hundreds of Blacks were murdered by thousands of Whites, nor the carnage in Rosewood, Florida, where the whole town was wiped out by Klan vigilantes, who burned Rosewood to the ground, killing at least 200 Black men, women and children. This story was recently told in the motion picture, *Rosewood,* by John Singleton. During those peak lynching years, Black men accused of offenses ranging from murder and rape to not stepping off the sidewalk to let a White person pass were lynched. It was not a strictly Southern practice, occurring from Gadsden, Alabama to Duluth, Minnesota, to the Hanging Tree in Helena, Montana. And in most cases, someone with a camera was there. Some of these pictures of lynching, with happy White men, women, and children smiling as they stood or sat next to the corpses, were turned into postcards until the postcard practice was outlawed by the Postal Service in 1909.

This was a period when mobs dragged Black men out of jails or off the streets and hanged them from the nearest tree, post, telephone pole, or bridge. Sometimes they burned them alive on crosses and at stakes. Sometimes they put their heads on poles. Most of the time, those lynched were landowners whose land was then seized. Again: a case for reparations.

In Duluth, in 1921, a White girl said she had been raped. Twenty young Blacks were rounded up. Three were identified. Later she admitted she had lied, but by then it was too late. The crowd was worked up. 10,000 Whites stormed the jail. They beat them savagely, almost castrated them, and then hung them in downtown Duluth.

Fathers were heard to tell their sons that: "It's not the same, son. It's not the same. They're not like us. They're not men. They're not human." Well, now you're talking about propping up a guy's ego. And it goes back to what William Buford Hughes wrote in his book, <u>Black Like Me</u>: when you start talking about, you know, "goddammit, if I'm not as good as a Negro, then what am I as good as?" So these kinds of things were being played out in 1919, 1920, 1921, and it led to the kind of conflict that brought about acts of unthinkable and abhorrent brutality and terror.

Of course, I wasn't there. But television brought many of us there during the Civil Rights battles in the South. And radio and TV took us there the afternoon Martin Luther King, Jr. was assassinated. That brings up the question I've raised earlier regarding non-violence. Recall the riots that were held across this country when Dr.

King was murdered. I don't know if a lot of people truly understand the kind of impact his assassination had on so many of us young Blacks and what happened inside many of us. Of course many could see the riots on their TV. Recall that many young Black men carried weapons for protection, usually in their cars.

I can tell you from conversations that many a young Black man trembled with anger upon hearing that Dr. King had been killed. I myself heard about it over my car radio when that news bulletin came on: Flash! Memphis, TN. Martin Luther King, Jr. has been assassinated. It is difficult, even today, to describe the anger that swept across me. It continues to motivate my work.

The anger at King's assassination was expressed with riots across the country. Some old me that their rage was so great it was all they could do to keep from getting a gun and killing White people. But that would have made us like the good White people of the South and Duluth. So they took it out on objects, on buildings, on cars, on buses, on taxicabs, and on storefronts.

I was able to channel my own anger into committing myself even more deeply to the cause Dr. King died for. He said we would overcome if we did it non-violently. I'm not about being violent. I don't want to relieve any White person of any guilt they feel. I want people to say: "Hey, enough is enough." Let's all work for justice and fairness for all. Let's all get along and work together to make Dr. King's dream a reality.

Postscript of October 3, 2000: My thoughts after the October 3 City Council meeting regarding the Civil Rights Department and its responsibilities regarding (1) hiring compliance; (2) CRB, and (3) potential future quarantining

Chapter 16 talks about the problems if we insist on a future consisting of repeating the past. Chapter 17 talks about positive possibilities for the future. We are at a pivotal time in our history. We really do have people out there who want to see us eliminated. How we handle this, as with all major situations, will determine what America is like after the threat is passed and this war joins its place on the bookshelves of history with all the others.

There are two issues, both of which were poorly addressed October 3rd. The first is the **CRA, the Civilian Review Authority** (budget severely cut, rarely sustains complaints, without authority to discipline, virtually no impact on policy, folded into Civil Rights Department, losing its independence), and the **quarantining** if we are hit with biological warfare and maybe chemical ones too.

As usually, you won't find the news in the establishment papers, but do check the *Spokesman-Recorder* and *City Pages*. I was at the meetings. These papers were represented and they said they would be providing full coverage.

The Civil Rights Department continues to do everything but civil rights work. So far it has done nothing to obtain subpoena power, so how will it get information it needs? It won't, of course.

The Department was asked to provide a report on the compliance of construction sites regarding Black contractors and Black workman on the sites. We have been asking for this information for over a year. Finally, because we have a Council member not in league with the Mastuhs, Natalie Johnson-Lee, they were forced to come to the meeting by Johnson-Lee to report, in writing. They reported that they didn't have the information and asked for a month to generate it. Is there any wonder you don't see Black contractors or Black workman, when the compliance office discreetly ignores it so the White contracting/worker system can go on without being bothered by Blacks?

The Department could also not answer how the Civilian Review Board responsibilities were going to be integrated into the department after the City Council shifted them from their independent status to the Department last month.

During the national police chief convention in town, the Somalis demonstrated because of the lack of jobs for Blacks.

I then raised the question of the Quarantine Plan. This is part of a bill the Minnesota Legislature marked up in February as part of the House Crime Prevention Bill. This bill authorizes **detention camps** be set up in state parks. The plan also calls for making anyone quarantine to pay back the state for any expenses of the quarantine. So if there is a biological attack, those quarantined could possibly lose their houses if they have to repay the state. They all denied knowing anything about it, and yet I knew from the February meeting at the capital that the Mayor and Police Chief knew. Any attack would obviously be centered on the city as opposed to the suburbs or rural areas. That means Blacks in the inner city forced to repay the city and state for quarantine costs would be fully and completely impoverished.

What kind of city and what kind of state would treat its people like medieval serfs made to pay the castle baron for him to protect them? That is what we do with our taxes. Now they want to take individuals' personal monies. This will create undue hardship on the poor. But what, my dear White friends who live in the city, do you think of you having to pay this bill, should it come to be? And what other "expenses" are they planning to hit us with as hidden taxes?

Chapter 16

The Status Quo Future: Same ol' Same ol'.
Is August-September, 2002 a Preview of the Status Quo Future?

August-October 2002 Proves the Points
of *The Minneapolis Story Through My Eyes*

**Will The Beacon Continue to Shine Brilliantly to Lead the Way,
And will the drum beat for freedom continue to beat?**

**Or Will the Beacon's Switch Be Turned Off,
And the drum sticks set down,
Leaving No Path to Create or Sound to Follow?
Can We Get Away From the Need to Checkmate Each Other?
Can We Stop Long Enough to Talk About How We Can Just Get Along?**

By serving each other we become free.
Inscription on the table used by
The Knights of the Round Table

**Even a dog knows the difference between when he's been
stumbled over and kicked.**
Oliver Wendal Holmes
U.S. Supreme Court Chief Justice
On law codes and evidence

**It is "not that [we] may have been complicit in the vices of
capitalism, but that [we] are today insufficiently complicit in the
virtues of democracy."**
Benjamin Barber

Headlines

From the Minneapolis, *Star Tribune*, August 2002, That Show That "United We
Stand, Divided We Fall"

- **Police shooting leads to violent protest**

- **Yea, though I walk in the valley of double standards**

- **God called on to help ease tension in North Minneapolis**

- **Editorial: Take a breath / Cops, community still must work together**

And how does Minneapolis react? By stalling and avoiding:

- **Federal mediation of Minneapolis police relations on hold**

And it is not just Minneapolis, as these headlines from the *New York Times* demonstrate:

- **A Melee in an Upstate City Is a Sign of Urban Despair**

- **Secrecy Is Our Enemy**

Viktor Frankl wrote of his experiences in Nazi concentration camps during World War II, in his book, *Man's Search For Meaning,* published in 1959. In 1991, The Library of Congress named it one of the most influential books in America. For a later edition, Frankl wrote what he called his "Postscript 1984," entitled "The Case for a Tragic Optimism." I accept his notion that "life is potentially meaningful under any conditions," as the history of Blacks in America has shown beyond a shadow of a doubt. The actions of the police during August 2002 brings all of this into sharp focus.

This chapter is a kind of postscript about August - October 2002 in Minneapolis and about moving beyond it for a meaningful life for all. Frankl ended his postscript with:

So, let us be alert—alert in a twofold sense:

Since Auschwitz we know what man is capable of.

Since Hiroshima we know what is at stake.

Before we look more closely at how August – October 2002 in Minneapolis provides up to the minute proof of my thesis let us add these words to introduce Minneapolis in August 2002:

> The big secret that all Black people know is that the machinery of our country's operations are to keep the Ni**er in his place.
>
> James Baldwin

> Segregation and poverty have created in the racial ghetto a destructive environment totally unknown to most white Americans. What white Americans have never fully understood - but what the Negro can never forget - is that white society is deeply implicated in the ghetto. White institutions created it, white institutions maintain it, and white society condones it.
>
> The National Commission on Civil Disorders in 1968
(Often referred to simply as The Kerner Report)

> The Southerner rebelliously clings to what seems to him the hard core of truth in this whole controversy. *Here and now*, in his own communities, in the mid-1960s, the Negro race, as a race, plainly is not equal to the white race, as a race; nor, for that matter, in the wider world beyond, by the accepted judgment of ten thousand years, has the Negro race, as a race, *ever* been the cultural or intellectual equal of the white race, as a race.
>
> This we take to be a plain statement of fact, and if we are not amazed that our Northern antagonists do not accept it as such, we are resentful that they will not even look at the proposition, or hear of it, or inquire into it.
>
> "On Behalf of the South"
James Jackson Kilpatrick, 1962
An excerpt from *The Southern Case for School Segregation*

The nobility of America's civil rights struggle comes through with the directness and strength of a spiritual.

> The New York Times
> Cover page quote for *Eyes on the Prize: America's
> Civil Rights Years, 1954-1965,* by Juan Williams,
> The Companion Volume to the PBS TV series

Is this not the crux of the problem? Kilpatrick was then editor of *The News Leader* in Richmond, Virginia. He later became a contributing editor of William Buckley's *National Review* and a frequent commentator on national television and radio programs (*Eyes on the Prize,* p. 28). This is where Republicans and sometimes Libertarians have gone wrong and why Blacks support Democrats: the belief that states' rights have sovereignty over the Federal Constitution. We Blacks are not stupid. We know that Democrats have created a great system of patronage for us, in exchange for our vote, a system that although it is racist, with patterns resulting in Blacks being relegated to the cities (hence the Democratic advantage in the city blue zones on the political maps over the suburban and rural red zones of the Republicans, which we'll see a lot of as we enter another election season), the patronage is nonetheless still there. And some believe that something is better than nothing. But now that system too has to go. We must return to the words of the dream of Martin Luther King, Jr. (excerpts in Interlude 4), and follow only that, and not a specific party. Whichever party offers to follow that dream is the one we should follow, be it Democrat, Republican, Green, or Independent. In the best of all possible worlds, all parties would attempt to realize the dream of Martin Luther King, Jr., a dream for everyone. Whoever does, actually, really, is who we should vote for.

In what direction will the Minneapolis story turn? Do you read this as a wakeup call or a story to be suppressed?

As I was finishing up this book, I again came to face to face with why all of this is important, for it is, for some, a matter of life or death. What will guide us? The Beacon on the hill, shining brilliantly on the roads before us, showing us our choices, or will the switch be turned off, by Whites or Blacks, who fear choice, who fear the co-mingling of people and ideas, who would prefer to keep people in the dark so they will follow them, as they provide leadership from what one popular movie series would call The Dark Side? Or will the Whites simply clear the board and holler "check mate" to the Blacks, treating them worse than pawns?

It remains a choice for Blacks and Whites. Together we can keep the light burning. Or we can turn it off and descend into the hells of our individual and group darkness. Here are three more sets of headlines, with story excerpts, from August 2002, for us to ponder. How we deal with the stories will tell the future of the Minneapolis story:

Police shooting leads to violent protest

By   Brandt   Williams
Minnesota   Public   Radio
August 23, 2002

Minneapolis officials and leaders of a north Minneapolis neighborhood urged peace and calm Friday, following an incident Thursday night that resulted in one wounded boy and assaults on several reporters. What began as a drug raid escalated into a riot, when a bullet fired by an officer at a pit bull dog either ricocheted or dislodged concrete that hit the boy in the forearm. People upset by the injury to the boy yelled at police and hurled rocks and bottles. They also took out their anger on several news reporters and their vehicles by setting one on fire and breaking out windows in others.

Syl Jones: Yea, though I walk in valley of double standards

Syl Jones
Star Tribune
http://www.startribune.com/stories/1519/3163834.html
Published Aug 18, 2002

See, a few weeks ago, a crazy, drunken woman named Martha Donald, who happens to be an African-American, apparently pulled a gun and shot a police officer named Melissa Schmidt. A double killing involving two women is rare anywhere, Lord. But the worst part -- if you can believe this -- is what happened after they died.

After these two women were killed in what can only be described as a horrible chain of events, Minneapolis City Council Member Natalie Johnson-Lee wrote a letter to her constituents in north Minneapolis. In the letter she praised the policewoman, saying, "Officer Schmidt gave meaning to the words 'community policing.' Her responses to our calls for help transcended racial and economic lines . . . ." Johnson-Lee then went on to acknowledge Donald's death by saying: "On this day of mourning, we pause to reflect on the untimely deaths of two fellow citizens -- two fellow human beings."

Lord, you might have thought that Johnson-Lee had cursed Officer Schmidt instead of praising her. The Police Officers Federation of Minneapolis angrily denounced Johnson-Lee and called for her resignation. Letters castigating her appeared in the newspaper for days. Local talk radio lit up with hatred from the good folks who were apoplectic at the unfair juxtaposition of these two deaths. People couldn't stop talking about how indignant they were that the alleged murderer Donald could in any way be considered a victim.

Please note, dear reader, that what is left out of this story of the "melee" of Thursday, August 22nd, is the fact that the police were firing MP5 sub-machine guns. And what is the Mayor's response? None. None, that is, until the news came in that five White journalists had been beaten (with one disappearing for a while). Two were from the *Star Tribune*, one from the *St. Paul Dispatch*, and two from WCCO. KMSP-TV Channel 9's van was burned up. A number of news vehicles were stoned and rocked. A separate bus was also pelted with rocks. Needless to say, as it was journalists that were injured, the news media sensationalized it in a way they don't when police pick up kids on profiling pickups—picked up because they are black— not because of any charges, and beat them up before turning them over to the juvenile authorities. The broadcast news came on with sensationalized bulletins every seven or eight minutes in terms of the "disturbances" in North Minneapolis. Here journalists were finally not just bystanders but the subjects of their reports. That's heady stuff. Their compatriots across the country saw them as heroes and picked it up for national reporting that otherwise would have been ignored. And what pictures did they show? Sensational ones: police officers with automatic weapons silhouetted against a burning truck.

What they didn't report is that the police withdrew and left the media in the middle of the melee because they had not deployed enough police officers. At 9:45 pm, Spike Moss tried to defuse things, but was unsuccessful. Around 11:15 the Mayor made a call to Natalie Johnson-Lee. He is petrified, as he is getting calls from the White community with visions of Blacks racing through their communities (after the shootings of Officer Schmidt and Mrs. Donald, the only racing done was done by White police up and down the streets of North Minneapolis with their lights flashing and sirens wailing). At 11:20 pm I called Jesse Taylor in Chicago, the Regional Director of the Human Relations Divisions, the mediators of the U.S. Department of Justice. Then the State Highway Patrol sent in helicopters, which introduced another medium of sensationalism. Around midnight Brother Shane Price entered the area, and spent 40 minutes. I then talked with some of them, but by then the melee was over (it had started around 7:45 pm), as everyone was hungry, tired, and spent, after four hours. And although White vigilantes showed up to support the police, it was all kept under control.

Needless to say, it then became time for the White politics to start. I called Jesse at approximately 6:25 am Friday morning. He asked me for an assessment, as we had been talking all week about the Minneapolis issues. And indeed, on Wednesday, 28 hours before the melee began, I had sent him a letter asking for Federal intervention here. By Friday, everyone was concentrating on Spike Moss and Shane Price, praising them for ending the violence, even though they didn't. I was at City Hall Friday for a meeting with Council Member Dean Zimmerman and the lawyers for the group I helped put together, The Committee United Against Police Brutality. City Hall was abuzz. The Mayor was about to have a nervous breakdown. The Chief of Police did not return until Friday morning. City Hall was in a state of near panic, while they praised Spike and others. I continued to go into the area as I had each evening.

The Mayor and the rest tried to suppress any help from outside. In the meantime, I was looking forward to the arrival of Patricia Glenn, the Federal mediator. While waiting, I worked with the attorneys to help get the release of the Grandmother of one of the families that was involved, a nice woman of the neighborhood whom I had known I've known for years. Her mistake was to utter the statement: "No justice, no peace." She became the only one they arrested.

The Justice Department made an inquiry from another direction, as they saw the political value too: the Democrats in Minneapolis can't control their coloreds, providing a story to help their candidate for Senate, Norm Coleman, to surge to the top on White fears.

Patricia Campbell Glenn, of the Justice Department's Human Relations Division, was ordered into Minneapolis. She arrived at 5:30 pm Friday. We arranged a meeting at 6:30 pm, at a downtown location, with the committee's two attorneys, Council Member Natalie Johnson-Lee, and me. We were surprised to be joined by the U.S. Attorney for the Federal District of Minnesota, Todd Hefelfinger. We met for two and a half hours. I've known Ms. Glenn for several years. She is a top mediator. She then met at 8:30 pm with Clarence Hightower of the Urban League because the Mayor and his people were trying to position the Urban League as a prime player, even though they had no personnel on the street Thursday night. She met with him for a couple of hours and outlined her plan for mediation.

About 11 pm Friday night, she went back into the neighborhood. She met with residents, accompanied by fellow African-American woman, Natalie Johnson-Lee. At 11:15 pm they ran into Spike Moss. He didn't know who Ms. Glenn was. He went off looking for a White guy in a suit. Ms. Glenn continued to meet with people in the neighborhood, and then returned to her hotel.

On Saturday morning, around 8:30 am, she began a series of meetings with the Mayor and the Chief of Police and at least five Council members. The mayor indicated continued resistance to meeting with her. They met until 10:20 am. She then went to other meetings, one of which was another group I'm working with that is dealing with construction jobs: the lack of African-Americans in construction jobs in Minneapolis, which is part of what has contributed to much of the tension in the neighborhood. The mayor came to that meeting and indicated he was leaning toward Federal mediation. Ms. Glenn left Sunday, and then returned Thursday to receive the Council's decision. After she left, the Mayor gives off signals that he is opposed.

It became our fervent belief that we needed an independent, objective, non-biased mediator to help bring peace between the city and the police or, more accurately, the Blacks of North Minneapolis and the Police. It boiled down to a conflict: the community wanted it but the Mayor and Council resisted it and turned away from it. They wanted a biased, non-objective private mediator whom they would hire and thus control the outcome.

For several days before the meeting with the City Council, the papers were full of the incident in the Jordan neighborhood. And although the papers praised Spike Moss, the Jordan community questioned the use of Spike Moss. The angle of the Moss group's proposed solution was training money and jobs to be given to them. On Tuesday, August 27th, the *Star Tribune* ran a story saying the Chief agreed to fund patrols of Spike Moss after the "melee." Moss was paid $6,000 to provide patrols for the area, and was to sign a contract locking them in as informants for the police, which greatly angered the community. Spike and the Chief had actually agreed to this on August 13th, after another police shooting. This is in all probability why Spike and his people, on Sunday, August 28th, began to say that they wanted a private mediator, like the Mayor, and didn't want a Federal one. They also talked of their love for the Chief of Police, which was probably too much for someone who then leaked the fact of the $6,000 paid to Moss. Interestingly, on Thursday, Doug Grow, in his column, asked who the real Spike Moss was and stopped just short of calling him a police informant.

All of this is backdrop to the public hearing at City Hall, Thursday night, 5-7 pm, August 29, 2002. Ms. Glenn returned, met with various groups, and prepared to meet with the Council. The numbers that showed up shocked the Council. It was unheard of: estimates put the turnout between 400 – 500 citizens (a number which the media refused to mention in its reports). The Council took 90 minutes of testimony, running about 20-1 in favor of Federal mediation, which neither the Mayor nor the Chief of Police wanted.

Please note that there were only 12 Council Members at the meeting. It is important to note that this was not a meeting called at the last minute. It had been called three weeks before for the purpose of voting on where they would put the police Civilian Review Authority; they wanted to transfer it to the Civil Rights Department where they would have better control over it. The CRA is to investigate police brutality complaints. Previously it had been an independent agency. Now it will be run by the city, which means police. Putting the fox in charge of the hen house does not foster trust in the community.

So the meeting was on everyone's calendar, made all the more important by the incidents discussed in the headlines at the beginning of this chapter. And obviously the issue of police-citizen relations was not new. It has been simmering for a long time and, indeed, the history of the CRA shows this has been a constant for years. This meeting was for the Council to decide to transfer the CRA into the Civil Rights Department. They then opened up the meeting to public comment. I was the second speaker. I spoke not only in my role as a community advocate, but also in my role as the spokesman for the Black Police Officers Association, and talked in terms of how they were treated and disrespected during this period by the city and the department.

I then handed over to the Clerk a packet for each member of the Council, the Mayor, and Ms. Glenn, a packet that showed the history of the tension between the department and its Black officers as well as the battle carried on by the Black Police Officers Association to deal with the steadily shrinking number of African-Americans in the police department. Others followed, with testimony after testimony after testimony. I discovered the next day that the packets I had submitted had gotten "lost," adding further to the delay in getting all of the relevant information before these august decision makers.

Instead of receiving Ms. Glenn and hearing her statement and recommendations, the Council reconvened as the City Council (prior to that they met as "The Committee Of The Whole") to deal with the CRA placement. Now despite this meeting having been on their agendas for three weeks, they began to leave. First to go was Council President Ostrow. Natalie Johnson-Lee then asked that Ms. Glenn be heard. Ms Glenn went to the podium and outlined her concerns. As she spoke, another council member, Colvan-Roy, departed. And then, Council Member Schiff announced that he wanted to make a motion to direct the City Attorney to begin to draft a contract between the Department of Justice and the City of Minneapolis for mediation. At that point Council Members Benson and Biernet, and the Mayor, all got up and left. And then Jellnick. That left the council with only 7 members. Gary Schiff made the motion, and it was seconded. Barb Johnson, Council Member for the 4th Ward, five blocks from where the melee happened, then got up and very theatrically exited the chamber. At that moment, Council Member Zirby continued the game and asked if there was a quorum. The City Attorney ruled that the quorum must be present (some say that once attained it stays until adjournment, even if people leave). With this ruling, they could not take a vote. With the exception of Natalie Johnson-Lee, most of the rest then got up and left, leaving Ms. Glenn and over 400 citizens behind alone in their chamber. The few council members left asked Ms Glenn if she could come back on September 12, be questioned more, after which they would decide what to do.

Ms. Glenn and I just looked at each other. We realized what had happened. They contributed to creating even more tension in the community, tension they claimed they wanted to defuse. But their actions showed their true intent. Blacks showed up to express support for the Council to resolve the issues for their neighborhood. The Whites on the Council don't want outsiders. When the council members left they not only showed their contempt for the neighbors at the meeting, they showed that when it came to the concerns of the Black neighborhoods, they were going to do as little as possible, and if the neighborhood went up in flames, so be it, that would be, at a minimum, the price they were willing to pay and, at a maximum, would be what moved the Blacks out faster.

The crowd was incensed.   The Council Members, in their inimitable arrogant fashion, killed the quorum in their own inimitable hypocritical fashion.   Citizens were there seeking their help, asking the City to protect their citizenship franchise, their rights, under the law.   The mayor and council not only turned their backs on these citizens, they told the Black government official to cool her heels for two weeks.   This is their business as usual, proving once again the truth of what I have written in this book, that from Whites there is little citizenship franchise for Blacks.

One reason given by Council Member Zirby was a concern about the Ashcroft Justice Department.   Yet the council, in its turn, then use the same tactics themselves that they claim not to like in the Patriots act and the President's new voluntary snitch program, ratcheting up their hypocrisy even more.   As Ms. Glenn explained to the Council, the Community Relations Division is independent to the Justice Department as it pertains to the sharing of information, as backed by Supreme Court rulings.   But they didn't want to hear that.   In the newspaper accounts not one of those who left early to kill the quorum was interviewed.   A number of constitutional attorneys called the *Star Tribune* and bitterly complained that the Tribune reporters had not sought out those who had abandoned the governmental process.   You see, there are also Whites in this town who are concerned about the imperial path this new Council seems to have set for itself.

This Council meeting was also televised; live, so that tens of thousands at home were just as flabbergasted as we were, trying to figure out what had happened.   So the Council members obviously met in advance, in their own little conspiracy, to thwart the system and undermine those in attendance and the neighborhoods they represent. These liberals may decry what they call the Imperial Presidency but are just as eager to be Imperial themselves.

Because it was prior to the Labor Day weekend, most of them had plans to be out of town the next day, Friday, and they all knew when they got up to leave they would not be in City Hall on Friday to take any heat.   Council Member Dean Zimmerman is a White Council Member sympathetic to our concerns and, indeed, marched with us in the 60s.   The bottom line is that the Council delayed the action on mediation between the police and the community, made no move to get help, and shifted the review of civilian complaints about the police to the Civil Rights Department under their control.   Imperial indeed.   The people reached out in desperation to their Mayor and City Council and they turned their backs on them, and left them turned for the long weekend, which for them was four days. In the meantime, for the past three nights at the juvenile facility, young Blacks were being picked up on sweeps and beaten up before being checked in. The police were out of control. And the Council was out of control. With this kind of reaction from the police and the Council, it is only a matter of time before the police feel free to notch another shooting.

On Friday the 13th, the Mayor was quoted in the paper as saying no Federal mediation was needed, that it could be done with private mediation. But that raised the question of who would do it and what they would be paid (if the Federal mediator does it, there is no cost to the City). And it raises the question of whether a private mediator, paid by the City, would be impartial or, worse, be paid not to be.

Some thought this was an act of cowardice by the Council. I don't. I saw it as a bold and deliberate attempt to avoid the issue, keep outsiders out, embarrass Ms. Glenn, and signal that nothing was really going to be done about it, postponing the vote two weeks in the hopes that the interest would subside in the meantime. This was a power play. This was an Imperial City Council. This was a mind-boggling demonstration of contempt for the Black community. History says their method of operation is to delay and hope things go away. So who will stop them? I, for one, will try to do so. Now, to add to my claim that what is happening to the Blacks of the Minneapolis inner city is happening across the country, let's sample the *New York Times* and two articles it ran, on September 2 and August 26, 2002.

Minneapolis likes to operate in secrecy. Minneapolis offers no checks and balances. And like Connecticut, Minnesota is mostly white. So we are not alone. Let's turn to three other examples, one in New York State and the other in Connecticut, before returning to the Council chambers for their September 12 consideration whether to use mediation and if so, how: Federal or private. Here are excerpts from three *New York Times* articles:

A Melee in an Upstate City Is a Sign of Urban Despair

New York Times
Newburgh, New York
September 2, 2002

The fracas began, the police said, when someone threw a bottle or a brick at a car.

It escalated after driver, a 33-year-old woman, got out to confront her attackers.

By the time officers arrived, an estimated 150-200 people were battling with sticks, knives and bottles.

Few in this declining city on the west bank of the Hudson expressed surprise at the outbreak of violence.

Factories in the area have closed, with thousands of jobs lost. And as unemployment and crime have mounted, so has apathy among youths.

They're unemployed or underemployed, and they seem resolved to destitution. They see no future for themselves.

Secrecy Is Our Enemy, by Bob Herbert

[President] John Adams, nearly two centuries ago, said, "Liberty cannot be preserved without a general knowledge among the people." And in a letter to Thomas Jefferson in 1816, Adams said, "Power must never be trusted without a check."

...unanimous ruling that...excessive secrecy compromised the very principles of free and open government that the fight against terror is meant to protect.

Democracies die behind closed doors.

A government operating in the shadow of secrecy stands in complete opposition to the society envisioned by the framers of our Constitution.

The government "absolutely" had an obligation to "vigorously" fight terrorism. But excessive secrecy [is] intolerable.

The essence of the [secrecy] ruling was the reaffirmation of the importance of our nation's system of checks and balances.

Poverty in a Land of Plenty: Can Hartford Ever Recover?

Hartford, once the richest cities in the nation is now one of the poorest, the most destitute 17 square miles in the nation's wealthiest state...30% of its residents live in poverty (2nd highest percentage in the nation, behind Brownsville, Texas).

Connecticut, affluent suburbs and almost universally floundering cities. Central question for all of America's troubled cities: What role, if any, should their wealthy suburbs and state governments play in their recovery?

Lousy City Hall leadership, regressive tax policies, racially antagonistic relationship with its White suburbs. Its 32 public schools are 95% Black and Hispanic and among the worse performing in the nation, in a state that is 86% White.

...so dramatically segregated by class and race that it is no longer viable economically...racial Balkanization.

To mediate conflict resolution and serve the people, or ignore them and not serve them? That is the Question!

To mediate conflict resolution and serve the people is our goal. The City's goal is continue its self-appointed path since the last election of ghettoizing and containing the Black community (Chapter 12) so they can get on with the important work of the White community. As noted above, when it came time to vote for a constructive process to mediate the tension between the police and the community, the Council Members got up and left, one by one, until a quorum was no longer possible.

Imagine, we were over 400 citizens who came to voice our concerns and exercise our citizenship franchise, filling the Council chamber and overflowing into the hallways, and they showed us their backsides. And how did the Council react to this overwhelming number of Black citizens? By essentially telling us that we really don't have a citizenship franchise. It was if they meant to say, "hey, we are in charge here, we're leaving, and you can't do anything about it." This is the Minneapolis way. That is what I am calling the Minneapolis story. History says their method is to delay and hope things go away so they won't have to do anything, leaving the status quo, meaning leaving us in our place. With no one to stop them, they demonstrated a mind-boggling contempt for the Black community. They were showing that they refuse to be held accountable, that they are not responsible, and that the poor Black neighborhoods can continue to fend for themselves.

The history of the intersection in North Minneapolis of Knox and 26th Avenues in the Jordan neighborhood where the follow-up shooting took place illustrates the Minneapolis approach of containment, not solution. This crossroads, along with a six-block stretch on 26th Avenue (about which the police received 605 calls from August 2001 to August 2002) is an example of the problem and the system. Here we have some obvious inner city activity we wish was not going on, including drug dealing, shootings, fights, robberies (1/3 of the city's burglaries are in this area), which the citizens, often Black, call the police about. The police response is a good example of how the system is not broken down at all, but rather is purposefully allowing this to happen.

The routine is always the same: the police receive calls daily all year, and yet nothing is done other than sending police to search kids, enter homes with warrants, fire their weapons, make arrests, and move on. **Doug Grow** of the *Minneapolis Tribune* has probably given the best explanation of this ritual:

> My simple answer for all of this is that Minneapolis leaders have failed—and continue to fail—to create any sense of trust between civic institutions, especially the Police Department, and large numbers of blacks in inner city neighborhoods.

Note the past and present tense, "have failed—and continue to fail," which means the future is already set: same ol' same ol': just continue the same dance. Same song, new verse. And so we see the two goals: the city wants only to contain the area so it can ignore it, whereas the residents are trying to solve the problems, to make things work. The City only allows daily continuation of repeating the same ol, same ol. And what was the new White mayor's response after a recent blowup in the Jordan neighborhood involving his citizens and his police, in which a number of residents went on a rampage to protest how the police handled the situation? Was he willing to meet with members of the community who were involved? No. Was he willing to support our call for Federal mediation? No. He said he expected us to follow the city's official complaint process, as if we were dealing with a library card that was sent to us but that got lost in the mail, requiring us to fill out a missing card form and submit it for processing.   That is White Liberal Plantation leadership, but it is not community leadership.

It should also be noted that during the police skirmishes with the police over the shooting of Blacks by police in August 2002, the White mayor extolled the virtues of the White indicted Council Member Joe Biernet, who is still in his job despite being under Federal indictment on extortion charges.   When Black Council Member Brian Herron was indicted for extortion, he was forced to resign and sent to prison.   White Biernet is still on the council.   How else is the Black community to interpret this other than it is one more example of the inequity and racism of the Minneapolis System in general and this particular Mayor and most of the City Council in particular, including those who claim to be liberals?

In the words of *City Pages*, August 28, 2002, "When it comes to police brutality, the mayor is all talk" (http://www.citypages.com/databank/23/1134/article10665.asp). As the article reported, "Tensions between the Minneapolis Police Department and city residents were already sizzling when the summer started, especially in neighborhoods like North's Jordan and South's Phillips, where cops pound the pavement with all the subtlety of a jackhammer."   And yet the mayor's response is to take the only agency that deals with police issue complaints, the Civilian Police Review Authority (CRA), and fold it into the City's Civil Rights Department.   This would render the CRA, with its "the power to call witnesses, render objective decisions (for and against the police), and dole out punishment," far less effective and able to meet its mission.   Which is what the Mayor and the City Council want.

You see, dear reader, the White Council members wanted no part of a Black-initiated process.   Forget the fact that they didn't have one.   They don't want one.   We had contacted the Chicago office of the Justice Department's Community Relations Service.   Patricia Campbell Glenn, who is a senior mediator with the office, and whom I have known for many years, came to Minneapolis.   I walked around with her to the key neighborhoods of concern.   She met and talked with residents.   She also held a meeting at City Hall.   So when they kept her waiting at the Council meeting on August 30th, it was intentional, and their walking out was intentional.   That is the Minneapolis way.   That is, indeed, the Minneapolis story.

But we see another way: education, jobs, hope, and enfranchisement.   Those are the choices.   The beacon that is this book illuminates not only the need for jobs and hope and education and enfranchisement, but also shows how too often those people who call themselves leaders, both White and Black, make choices which make that impossible.   That is why I consistently pound the drum beat for freedom for the people of the inner city of Minneapolis.

The pastors' call for help from God reminds me of the Old Testament prophet Daniel, who, in captivity, did not give up hope. Daniel decided against mediocre living despite the surrounding the settling done by his friends who were content with the status quo, even though they were captured and made slaves. Daniel was able to find and create meaning in his life because he made three decisions I encourage all of us to make, Black or White, for the good of ourselves and for the good of our community. Echoing Martin Luther King, Jr., Daniel chose character over comfort. Echoing the great leaders of history, he chose discipline over disorder. And echoing the Golden Rule, he chose to live in love and service.

That is not easy, given the grievances that we have. That is why we need mediation, and why, given that the grievances are all "home grown," we sought Federal mediation. I met with the different groups attempting to address this issue. One of the groups consists of 300 African American Northside residents who have formed what they call the Northside Information Exchange (NIE). They held a meeting on August 27, 2002. They sent their concerns to the Minnesota Attorney General, the Federal General Accounting Office, the Department of Justice, the U.S. Department of Education, Minnesota Senators Wellstone and Dayton, and the ACLU. And once again, as I write this Chapter in September 2002, not one response.

My thoughts after the 8-29-02 Council walk out: Federal mediation is the best next step to take

To show our concerns and to demonstrate our desire for a Federal mediator, we held a rally on Monday, September 9, 2002. Our concern was not the police per se, for after all, we did not want gangs and drugs and shooting in our neighborhoods any more than anyone else. And they don't have Black officers for the neighborhoods. Instead, they send in White officers who profile, meaning if they see a Black youth they pick him up, and if they see a Black they feel should not be in a White neighborhood, they stop him. This is why the City doesn't want Federal mediation: they would have to listen to us and install real solutions, not the phony displays for which they are so famous.

We sought Federal mediation because we believe it is inherently fair. We need someone who is experienced, not to tell us what to do, but to mediate, or "referee" between us and the city and its police. A Federal mediator gives no orders, but helps the opposing sides come to an agreement and then monitors the agreement, not to enforce it but to remind each side what they have agreed to. At no point does the government take the community to court if one or both sides don't cooperate with each other or do as they agreed to do. Whatever comes out of mediation is entirely up to the community.

And although any Federal mediator would do, we preferred Patricia Campbell Glenn because not only does she have the expertise gained in over 30 years experience mediating in cities all over the country, but because she was here during our happenings, walked the neighborhoods, talked to the neighbors, and then met with city officials, and thus had an "on the ground" experience no one else had.

No one has given a good reason not to be confident in the Federal process in general or in Patricia Glenn in particular. That is not the case with the Mayor's private mediator proposal. First, it will take tax dollars for a budget already taking cuts that hurt.   Secondly, this Council has not shown any willingness other than the willingness to manipulate and delay. Private mediators obey whoever pays them. There is no incentive for the City to cooperate, as it already knows it can stonewall us and we can do nothing about it. Those in favor of a private mediator, including the Mayor and the police, do so because they don't want anything changed.

This is why I conclude that this is not an example of a city without a system or process, but rather a city that *has* a system, a process, of *containment*, willing to pay the price of unrest to avoid hiring Blacks, to avoid educating Blacks, to avoid providing Housing Blacks, all in order to keep us in our place.

My thoughts after the 9-12-02 Council Turn-Down of Federal mediation: We need outside help: Federal mediation

First let us look at what the two major newspapers said about the Council decision, then let's discuss what actually took place.

The Minneapolis *Star Tribune* downplayed the walk-out and its significance. I must admit that the St. Paul *Pioneer Dispatch* was more accurate in its reporting. The most accurate reports you'll get is from the Minnesota *Spokesman-Recorder* and from *The City Pages,* when they write their stories. But I can assure you that their stories will be far more detailed and accurate than either of the White papers. My report that I give to you here is from my usual front row seat. The New York Knicks have Spike Lee in their front row. The L.A. Lakers have Jack Nicholson in their front row. Minneapolis has Ron Edwards in its front row, front row center, on the spot, on the scene, sitting in the front row at the Council Meeting of Thursday, September 12, 2002, seeing the dynamics, and shaking my head at how unbelievable they are, and yet maintaining hope, for the prize of freedom is worth whatever wait one must endure.

Bottom line: the Council refused mediation 8-5. What happened, again, is that the Liberals pulled another of their double crosses. Only three members expressed support for Federal Mediation: Natalie Johnson-Lee, Gary Schiff, and Dean Zimmermann.

Thus the council has caused tensions to run very high in the streets. So, despite at the meeting admitting that Minneapolis has "deep, deep problems revolving around race relations in the city," they still refused to deal with that reality. When one citizen in attendance objected, and reported something had to be done, as her "child had been run over by a police car" leading to the *Star Tribune* then reporting that "Police Chief Robert Olson later encouraged her to file a complaint" with no comment nor follow-up, demonstrating again how cold the police and the media are toward Blacks in the community. Your kid is hit by a police car. And they respond: file a complaint. That was probably the best sound-bite about the police: file a complaint.

Gary Schiff had put the motion forward on August 29th to direct contract negotiations and the signing of the contract. That is when Council Member Barb Johnson walked out and broke the quorum. Schiff made the same kind of motion September 12th. Then council Vice President Robert Lilligren, Democrat and Liberal, of the 8th Ward, which is a significant ward of color, put a counter-proposal on the table: to send it back to committee. That put Natalie Johnson-Lee on the spot, as it sent it back to her Health and Human Services committee and to the Public Safety and Regulatory Services committee, which is chaired by Joe Biernet, who is currently under indictment, with the directive to examine what is going on, appointing a committee of city officials to look at mediation and the ground rules. The vote passed, 8-5, essentially killing mediation.

The day before, on Wednesday, September 11th, Patricia Glenn, the 61 year old Black mediator with 30 year experienced mediator, met with the Council, who put her through the washer, the dryer, and the ringer in their interrogation of her. Rest assured, as I reported on my subsequent TV show, that had she been White she would not have been treated that way. Their favorite straw man was the question of Attorney General Ashcroft and the Justice Department. Natalie Johnson-Lee then laid it out on the table for all of them: that her colleagues had been saying behind Patricia Glenn's back that she was nothing more than a spy for Ashcroft, and despite their attempt to make fun of that, Johnson-Lee nailed it squarely on the head. And as the mediators don't blame nor investigate, but just get people to talk, what are they hiding that they are afraid of such non-binding talk?

In this process, the City has raised the question of the right people being at the table, insisting that they be allowed to choose who is involved. In other words, they, the foxes, want to be in charge of the hen house. In the final analysis, it was the Liberals who killed mediation. The resolution by Lillegram talks in terms of a process that is unending—they can run it in perpetuity and never make a decision. He hid behind the Liberal pretext of needing more dialogue and getting the issues defined and sharpened, and then maybe after that ask for some mediation. At least Councilman Gary Schiff had the decency and courtesy to put a time frame on his motion to have it finalized and ready to go.

The major difference between Federal and private mediation is that the feds develop agreements that include a mechanism for self-enforcement, so that if one party doesn't follow through, mediation would be reconvened. There is no such provision with private mediation, as it would be just what the council wants to pay for. The hypocrisy and deception was even further demonstrated when Council Member Paul Zerby raised his concern about Ashcroft's "readiness to erode our civil liberties" and then turned around to back the Lilligram motion which did exactly that to us Blacks.

Then the Mayor, to cover all of his bases, once it was clear the Council would defeat any motion for Federal mediation by using the Lilligram motion to gut it, then talked out of the other side mouth, saying he was in favor of Federal mediation. The *Star Tribune* unknowingly caught him in that lie when it reported that what the Mayor and Council Vice President Robert Lilligren want is a Community Police Relations Policy Action Group which would regularly to hash out problems. That would be fine as an internal working group. But that would not be mediation with a community. It would be dictating to it.

This again proves the point that they keep playing games. The citizens present were not happy about this. They grumbled. This scared the Council and made them nervous, as the Star Tribune reported on September 14. They had called the police and had them on alert downstairs to stand by, just in case. And yet, if they put the process in place, that tension would dissipate and there would be no need for the police to stand by.

Their favorite method of choice is to try to co-opt the Black community and buy off its leaders, which has been very successful in the past. Too many Blacks go along with this and act worse than the DFL itself. Three things to note:

(1) the emerging new generations of Black leadership have tired of and are rebelling against those who rest on their laurels as civil rights leaders of the 60s and 70s. As written in the Northeast Information Exchange E-zine, "many emerging black leaders who say they appreciate the wisdom

and work of their elders, but find themselves stifled by outdated strategies and little trust in their ideas and abilities."

(2) Just when ideas to fit the times are needed, the "old guard," who have conveniently developed amnesia on the point that they **all** started out young too, are now telling the young they have to come to them for permission first. Its hard for the elders to let go, just like the old wealthy yet greedy White guys in their corporate sand boxes. Indeed, Spike Moss exemplifies this when he says the emerging black voices lack the dedication and passion of his generation. He forgot he started young too. Now he says that because the original civil rights advocates were too caught up in the movement to mold the next soldiers, that they must now come to be molded. He stated on the radio recently that the young ones must come to he and the elders to get permission to do what they want. There are three Blacks running for Governorships in the United States this election season. One is in Minnesota, Booker Hodges. But he is young. And the "wise old elders" of the NAACP refused to invite him to a candidate's forum. He explained in an open letter "I was told that I should have asked a certain group of individuals for permission to run for office."

(3) It is difficult to develop confidence when the old guard continually reverts to the old standby procedures of getting paid. Most people are loyal to their paymasters. Hennepin County Commissioner Mark Stenglein gave $25,000 to Spike Moss to hire $7/hour young workers to provide patrols in the Jordan neighborhoods. Needless to say, this made the residents of Jordan very angry. They were not only being ignored, but they were being sent watchdogs from other neighborhoods who are Black and on the payroll of the very people the police report to about which they are upset and seek Federal mediation. Now I am not opposed to funding programs of effective leaders. Now Spike Moss and the rest of the self-appointed Black leaders have gotten lots of press and funding. But ask yourself this question: when was the last time they delivered a winner?

My thoughts after the September 22, 2002 Minneapolis Civil Rights Commission Vote to Ask for Federal Mediation Was Turned Down by the City Council

The City of Minneapolis purposefully turned its back on us. But we are a great nation with a great system. We have checks and balances to counter the attempted tyranny of leaders. It was clear to me that with the Mayor and his allies on the City

Council, tyranny over citizenship was their game. There was one hope left: the city's own Civil Rights Commission. Recall that I was a member beginning in 1968, was Vice Chair 1967-1972, and Chairman from 1979-1983. I was always proud of the commission and our record (Chapter 14). I knew if there was any organization that could help, it was the Civil Rights Commission. I went to their meeting September 22 (their last regular meeting was August 19th, prior to this recent debate regarding Federal mediation. They graciously allowed me to present the case for it. They voted 17-2 to seek Federal mediation. Those words echoed again in my ears: "of the people, by the people, for the people." For a detailed account of the meeting and the thoughtfulness that went into the resolution, read *The City Pages* (www.citypages.com). This is democracy in action. Once again, behind the scenes, I was glad to be able to contribute my small part to the tending of freedom in the liberty garden, which the Mayor and City Council have chosen not to tend, not to water, not to nourish.

I am reminded of the famous phrase "Those who cannot remember the past are condemned to repeat it." Many misunderstand this statement by the philosopher George Santayana, when he says "cannot," not "won't." I have come to the conclusion that what is happening in Minneapolis is that the past is not only *very* much remembered, it is being repeated on purpose. It is not that Minneapolis can't. It is that Minneapolis won't, because her "ideals" do not include Blacks. The only other conclusion possible is that the political and economic powers are the stupidest people on the face of the earth. As they are clearly not that, it has to be on purpose. Let's look at what "the past" is. I only thought of this after the Civil Rights Commission session, as I struggled again to do what I do best: connect the dots. The past is simple. It consists of what underlies the current tension in Minneapolis, which the past tells us will get worse unless the purpose of repeating it is reversed by the political and economic powers.

There were two famous studies of the urban disturbances of the 60s, one being the Federal study by the Kerner Commission after the 1968 riots (which was good descriptively but wrong with its prescription), and California's McCone Report, after the 1965 Watts Riots. The problems they highlighted are the very same ones I've written about in this book (http://www-lib.usc.edu/~anthonya/la/reb/causes.htm).

The Watts Riot of 1965 resulted in 34 deaths, 856 injuries, and 4,000 arrests.

Between then and 1968, there were 300 riots. Whites blamed them on criminals, communists. Half of Blacks thought they were due to a lack of education, jobs and housing, while only 7% of Blacks thought they happened because of police brutality. http://www.independent.org/tii/media/pdf/tir52bean.pdf

The McCone commission, headed by John A. McCone, conducted "a sweeping survey of life in Watts and Los Angeles," and found that the causes of the disturbances were (emphasis added):

- A scarcity of **employment**;

- A scarcity of **education** designed to meet the special needs of disadvantaged Negro children; and

- A resentment, even hatred, of the **police** as the symbol of authority.

Their big three were: "employment, education, and law enforcement-community relations," which, in no surprise to the readers of this book, "were the most critical to improving life in the impacted areas." Their recommendation regarding community-police relations was:

> That law enforcement agencies place greater emphasis on their responsibilities for crime prevention and that they institute improved means of handling citizen complaints and developing community relationships.

This is all that we ask for. This is what the new White mayor and mostly new City Council are denying us, with the support of the DFL, beginning with its redistricting plan and continuing on through its walking out on the citizens on September 12, 2002.

The lessons of Watts were ignored in the nation. And thus the riots of 1967, especially in Newark and Detroit. In its investigation, the Kerner Commission, studying it nationwide, found that an "explosive mixture" existed in American cities, fed by:

- Pervasive discrimination and **segregation in employment, education and housing**;

- Black in-migration and white exodus, which had provided a growing crisis of deteriorating facilities and services and unmet human needs;

- The black ghettos, where segregation and poverty **converged on the young to destroy opportunity and enforce failure.**

The Kerner Commission found 12 "deeply held grievances" in the communities it studied. In descending order of intensity, those grievances were, with **police practices** heading the list:

1) police practices

2) police practices unemployment and under-employment

3) low quality housing

4) not enough housing

5) poor recreation facilities and programs

6) ineffectiveness of the political structure and grievance mechanisms

7) disrespectful white attitudes

8) discriminatory administration of justice

9) inadequacy of federal programs

10) inadequacy of municipal services

11) discriminatory consumer and credit practices

12) inadequate welfare programs

And so what did **both** commissions conclude? That:

> **poverty**, **segregation**, lack of **educational** and **employment opportunities**, widespread **perceptions of police abuse**, and unequal consumer services as the principal grievances which led to the civil disturbances of the 1960's.

Nothing changed much. And then in March of 1991, an amateur cameraman caught on videotape the arrest and vicious beating of Rodney King, a Black man, by four L.A. Police officers. When the for went on trial, and were acquitted, demonstrators gathered at police headquarters with signs that said "No Justice, No Peace." And the the City of Los Angeles erupted into violence and flames. Over a three day reign of terror and destruction, 50 were left dead, countless numbers injured, and $750 million worth of property had been damaged or destroyed.

The Minneapolis story bears witness to the fact that despite these reports in L.A. and the nation, little has changed. Why? What other conclusion can there be than because Minneapolis doesn't want it to. The plan now is to run Blacks out (gentrification, Chapter 8), disempower the inner city Black neighborhoods (redistricting, Chapter 12), keep the next generation in its place (Chapter 7), and remove as many high profile successful Black "heroes" of Black youth (Chapter 15), which fits into the general war on young Black men (Chapter 9). The plan is to achieve this through the coordination a racist government (Chapter 12), a racist DFL (Chapter 11), a racist judiciary (Chapter 3), a racist university (Chapter 10), and through the sabotage by and co-opting of the so-called Black leadership who have opted for the Booker T. Washington approach to race relations, a "separate but equal" mentality (Chapter 14, Interlude 4). In other words, they want to perpetuate poor education, eliminate job opportunities, segregate, impoverish, and hope they'll get the message and leave town.

I maintain instead the approach of W.E.B. DuBois, which is to work for equality now, and to push steadily for its attainment (Interludes 3, 4, 6, 9 11). My path to Minneapolis (Chapter 2) still keeps me on my mission. I will continue to work for the people of Minneapolis, especially the poor and forgotten Blacks of the inner city. I will strive to be a beacon on the hill (Chapter 1, Interlude 1), shedding light on the situation, seeking justice and fairness for all (Chapter 5), working to bring out the best and suppress the worst characteristics of Minneapolis (Chapter 6), so that the negatives are no longer here, there, or anywhere (Chapter 4). Much has been done to the Black person in America that is shameful (Interludes 2, 8, 10, 12-15), and yet we still have good news to report regarding the great progress we have made since the Civil War and especially over the last 40 and 10 year periods (Interludes 5, 7), because we are dedicated to the belief that we shall overcome. Hence I will continue to beat the drum of freedom (Chapters 5 and 17).

So I am bullish on Minneapolis. I keep my eye on the prize of freedom. I believe it can be a city on the hill for all people, not just White people. The City of Minneapolis over the years has had some great City Fathers. They have grown old. Their time has passed. Their sons can raise Minneapolis to another level or circle the wagons around their wealth and falsely claim they have what they have due to their own good works. They have the power to enable Minneapolis to achieve the YESes or condemn her to eternal NOs until the riots of the 1960s repeat themselves.

I offer some guidance on becoming a city of light shining a beacon on the hill fostering equal access and equal opportunity for all (Chapters 5, 17), and some values around which we can all gather to make it so (Chapter 17). The choice is ours, both wealthy White and Black poor. I choose to continue to work toward equal access and equal opportunity for all. And I hold these positions despite what has taken place in the neighborhoods and community following the redistricting assault on the wards and the harassment by police.

Bottom line, we need to get along. Neither side has figured out a way to find the common ground. That is why, in this chapter, I have concluded that we need outside help, Federal mediation, to help us get to where we can sit at the table as equal citizens and find that common ground on which we can all stand and on which we can all work together to get along together. The prize is in sight. I remain hopeful.

Back to the thought about repeating history if we can't remember it. The past occurred a day at a time. So does the present. And the future unfolds that way too. The philosopher who said that was actually trying to draw the same conclusion: that we are not like infants who cannot remember. We actually can remember the past. We have experience and education and what we have learned to draw upon. Thus a major issue deals with the "ideal" in our minds (what some call ideology). "The American Dilemma" remains: what to do with Black people (Chapter 1). If our ideal is still to have separatism, if our ideal is to have segregation and not integration, if our ideal is to keep certain others always in an inferior state, if the ideal is to keep the Negro in his place, then Minneapolis is saying that it is willing to pay the price to achieve that. And here is the crux of the issue: this means that cities like Minneapolis are willing to entertain riots and disturbances if that is the price to pay to, in James Baldwin's phrase, keep the Negro in his place.

Most people in Minneapolis, from newspaper columnists (except those for the *Spokesman-Recorder* and *The City Pages*) to TV commentators and to the blue-collar worker and white-collar worker, don't realize that this is the plan. I lay it out, after 40 years of watching it, to remind everyone, Black and White, that this is still the shortsighted choice being made. A great deal of emotion and energy is expended by the political Left and Right over the issue of *choice* as it applies to births. But freedom says we need choice in many areas: the choice of the individual to exercise options enabling access and opportunity in education, housing, jobs, economic development, and participation in terms of the social, political and economic mainstreams.

Blacks are denied Choice. *That* is the battle for choice that liberals ought to be engaged in. But as long as the culture wars can be made a part of the front and center political debates, White liberals and conservatives can enjoy their spats and fights while ignoring Blacks as well as poor Whites, using the culture wars as a way to resolve "The American Dilemma" by returniing to a situation where Blacks can be kept separate from Whites.

My goal is that this book serve as a beacon and a drum: to illuminate the path we take together as follow the drum beat of freedom. We can learn from it and make better choices along the path to the future. Or we can turn it off and go where the darkness makes us stumble around. I urge you to use The Minneapolis story as a light for yourself and for your community. The stakes are not unlike those Viktor Frankl lists at the end of his 1984 postscript to the reissue of his 1959 book, *Man's Search for Meaning*. He ends with: "So, let us be alert—alert in a twofold sense:

> Since Auschwitz we know what man is capable of.

> Since Hiroshima we know what is at stake.

And so, the Minneapolis story reminds us to be alert in a twofold sense as well:

> Since slavery, Jim Crow, Tulsa, Rosewood, Duluth and Hollman and August 2002 in Minneapolis, and the racism of Interludes 2, 6, 9-15, we know what man is capable of.

> Since the Civil War, Dred Scott, Martin Luther King, Jr., the land and wealth takings of Interlude 8, the attempts to bring Jim Crow back and the current problems in the inner cities in terms of education, housing, jobs, and equal access/opportunity, we know what is at stake.

Interlude 16

Calculating A Better Future For All

**From "The Valley of the Fallen" To The "Mountain of the Risen:"
A Parable of Calculating Actions and Laws
For Their Attendant Pain and Meaning,
To Better Envision A World Integrating All People
into the Mainstream of Equal Access and Equal Opportunity**

I believe our new, smaller government must work in an old-fashioned American way, together with all of our citizens through state and local governments, in the workplace, in religious, charitable and civic associations. Our goal must be to enable all our people to make the most of their own lives -- with stronger families, more educational opportunity, economic security, safer streets, a cleaner environment in a safer world.

President Bill Clinton, State of the Union Message, 1996

The era of big government is over. But we cannot go back to the time when our citizens were left to fend for themselves. We must go forward as one America, one nation working together to meet the challenges together. Self-reliance and teamwork are not opposing virtues; we must have both.

From *Pyramids of Sacrifice: Political Ethics and Social Change* (Basic Books, NY, NY, 1974), Peter L. Berger:

Thesis #11: We must seek solutions to our problems that accept *neither* hunger *nor terror.*

Thesis #15: Those who are the objects of policy should have the opportunity to participate not only in specific decisions but in the definitions of the situation on which these decisions are based.

Thesis #22: A key area for such institutional innovation will be in the creation of *intermediate structures*—intermediate, that is, between the modern state and the undifferentiated mass of uprooted individuals typical of modern societies. This policy imperative cuts across the capitalist/socialist dichotomy.

Peter Berger ends his 1972 book Pyramids of Sacrifice: Political Ethics and Social Change with the story of the Spanish Civil War. It was filled with moral ambiguity and unspeakable brutality on both sides, with the Nationalists, the *Falange,* attempting to "hold at bay the forces of modernity, to turn Spain back to the virtues of an earlier age," as they fought against the Republican ideals of modern democracy and revolutionary salvation. Both were "historically specific conservatives."

Spain's monument to this conflict, near the Valley of the Fallen, was dug out of a mountain, where thousands from both sides are buried, with the inscription: "to die for God and Spain." Berger's chilling statement is: *And the Spain that is now emerging has nothing to do with what either side fought and died for.* This can be said also about the Civil Rights movement as it applies to Blacks in the inner city.

Few historical actions lead to intended consequences, whereas many lead to unintended consequences. So good intentions are not enough. We need a way to evaluate both our policies and our deeds. I have suggested one approach with my YESes and NOs of Chapters 5 that are repeated in Chapter 17.

Since then, Berger has developed another way of helping us understand social dynamics by casting aside the model of Left and Right, Liberal and Conservative. He notes how we are all conservative, in that once we get our way, we want to keep it that way. In other words, the basic difference between political Left and Right is in what they want to conserve. For those on the political far Left, the ideal is an imagined utopian future that they want to put in place, often through revolutionary means, and once established, conserve it by freezing it in place, and accept no more change. The model usually includes some component of socialism. This, in my view, is the essence of the 20th-century's socialist totalitarian societies. For those on the political Right, the ideal is an imagined golden age that they wish to resurrect from the past, often through armed means, and once established, conserve it and freeze it in place, and accept no more change. Both are "historically <u>specific</u> conservatives." An alternative is what Berger calls "historically <u>nonspecific</u> conservatives," those who recognize that no matter what one tries to freeze in place, there will still be change, both unpredicted and unintended, and therefore one need "make haste slowly." He discusses this in his 1991 essay "Capitalism and the Disorders of Modernity," in the journal *First Things.* One way to tell the difference is to ask if anyone is being asked to be saddled or assumed to be naturally saddled, and are others saying they were born to ride them?

If we agree that no solution should be accepted that accepts hunger or terror, and that those who must live under policies should have the opportunity to participate in the policy decisions, especially in intermediate institutions of community, neighborhoods, churches, and voluntary organizations, then we must include an acceptance of the phrase "preferential option for the poor," especially in terms of education, jobs, and housing.

To integrate everyone into the social and political mainstream means they have to have equal access and opportunity in the economic mainstream. Many theories have been proposed for how to do so. Only one system has proven to bring more people out of poverty than any other: capitalism, a market economy, and only one system has proven to offer more freedom and liberty than any other: democracy, with its emphasis on equal law and private property. Some might call it democratic capitalism (because dictatorships also use capitalism). In other words, you can have capitalism without democracy, but you cannot have democracy without capitalism. Many think the Scandinavian countries are socialist. They are not. Their socialist-style welfare programs have been supported by economies that are capitalist.

Throughout, I have held that "equal opportunity" does <u>not</u> mean "equal results". That is foolish. Many think Lyndon Johnson's worst deed was the Vietnam War. Certainly I was no fan of the war. It may not have been necessary. It surely wasn't executed right. But as Gorbachev later said it helped bankrupt the Soviet Union, we may have to begrudgingly admit it helped end the Cold War. And his Great Society was well intended (we were all in favor of ending poverty even as we disagreed on the means to do so). His worst deed was how he defined the goal of the Great Society. The reason the Republicans were so horrified by the Great Society is because they correctly interpreted his Left, Socialist goal as being unintentionally totalitarian. The goal, as LBJ stated it, was:

> not just equality as a right and a theory but equality as a fact and as a result.

To achieve "equality of result" in terms of equal access and equal opportunity is one thing. To expect, as many on the Left pushed for, equal results and the redistribution of property and wealth, would require absolute state coercion at every level, including the redistribution of private property, and telling everyone what they could become in society, as if they were potted plants to place in a socially engineered garden, which is the opposite of what most of us mean by freedom and liberty.

Here is where the Democrats really went wrong, set an impossible goal, and caused many needless debates, not to mention programs doomed before they started. It is a beautiful, poetic statement albeit a wrong and deadly one. I still wonder today if Johnson really understood it or if it was just another of the many speeches he saw for the first time when he read it. We all know that human beings are, by nature, unequal, whether we are playing in the Super Bowl or on Jeopardy. What I have been talking about is that Blacks haven't been allowed to participate in the game.

Equality of result is decidedly not what I mean. And I don't think LBJ did either. But many programs since then have been run as if they can have equal results. To me, equal results can only be understood in terms of equal access and equal opportunity in education, jobs, affordable housing, and the option to participate in the social, political and economic opportunities of our society.

The political Right gives lip service to "equality of opportunity." It doesn't want it because it either views some as not worthy or because it doesn't want the government to have the coercive power to make it happen. In other words, if it requires government regulation to give the poor and minorities a chance, they are opposed to it, although they lap up the regulations that allow those at the other end of the social spectrum to enrich themselves, as in the 80s and the 90s.

The political Left, on the other hand, gives lip service to "equality of results," for that policy clearly favors them and would give them the great coercive power of the government to enforce it, as they don't believe everyone will try unless they are prodded. But it is a mask: they only want it for themselves as leaders over their subservient followers. And if some were to overdo it and get too much result, the Left stands at the ready to take it from them. So the real issue for both the Right and Left, as I see it, is power, not fairness or justice, even if the words "fairness" and "justice" are used to justify the taking of freedoms and liberty. But as we saw from Chapter 2, "law" by itself is not enough if it isn't exercised equally: we want total impartiality in the application of law. And as we have seen in Interlude 8, this has clearly and purposefully been denied to Blacks.

It is time that all Blacks be included at the table. One of the great tools offered citizens by the United States is the mechanism of asset management that most take for granted. It allows assets to become liquid and turned into something else, such as investment money from the mortgage on a home or building or cash for your kid's education. But to have investment income one needs a living wage with some discretionary money left over to invest. To make asset management work means having not only laws that enforce private property rights but also laws that prevent its theft, whether stolen by the private sector or public sector. Much inequality is not due to capitalism, but due to many being forced out of it, whether forcibly (see Interlude 8) or through benign neglect (Chapters 7-9). Education is the key for all in our modern society. When we offer public education to the poor and inner city that does not teach the key tools of reading and writing, or when housing is kept out of reach by depressing wages below livable levels that don't allow making mortgage payments combined with practices that deny mortgages to minorities, then we have said you are not welcome at the table.

Ancient King Solomon asked for wisdom to discern what to do. The facts of this book can give us the wisdom to know what can probably work and in all probability what will not work. In his *Pyramids of Sacrifice,* Peter Berger gives us a "recipe for discerning whether what we are doing is wise or not, by giving us a calculus to use, one of meaning and one of pain. I have attempted to use this recipe in our accepted YESes and common NOs of Chapter 5. This book has addressed the "calculus of pain" of racism and Jim Crowism in terms of the immense human costs borne by those who did not request or conceive the projects but were forced to live under them. Public policy needs modesty. Public policy needs wisdom. Imaginations are still needed. But so too is the wisdom with which to use them and wisdom with which to judge the consequences of those policies. Hence the YESSES and NOs, the ultimate contest of ideas, a "contestation" between our ideals and an examination of them in both economical and ideological terms. The Senator who tried to have family live a week on the minimum wage was a good start. Every legislator, Federal and State and City, should attempt to live on the minimum wage for at least a week (although a month would be more of a learning experience). Then we could really get serious in talking about positive future possibilities.

Chapter 17

The Positive Future Possibilities for Minneapolis:
Envisioning the Dream, Sustaining the Vision:
Not Asking Permission, Making No Apologies For Being Free

As Martin Luther King, Jr., said at the Lincoln Memorial in Washington, D.C., in 1963, in his "I Have a Dream Speech:"

> I say to you today, my friends, that in spite of the difficulties and frustrations of the moment, I still have a dream. It is a dream deeply rooted in the American dream.

> It would be fatal for the nation to overlook the urgency of the moment and to underestimate the determination of the Negro. This sweltering summer of the Negro's legitimate discontent will not pass until there is an invigorating autumn of freedom and equality.

> In the process of gaining our rightful place we must not be guilty of wrongful deeds. Let us not seek to satisfy our thirst for freedom by drinking from the cup of bitterness and hatred.

> I have a dream that my four children will one day live in a nation where they will not be judged by the color of their skin but by the content of their character. I have a dream today.

> I have a dream that one day this nation will rise up and live out the true meaning of its creed: "We hold these truths to be self-evident: that all men are created equal."

This can be also be done by the YESes and NOs wanted and not wanted. My goal is a set of YESes and NOs that provides equal access and equal opportunity for all. We need to combine our reason and our resources to calculate what happens with our policies and actions, to ensure there is more meaning than pain resulting from them, and to regularly evaluate results on this basis, making changes when the balance tips toward more pain than meaning. We need to work together to develop a calculus that will enable us to judge whether or not public and private policies are facilitating equal access and equal opportunity in education, housing, political participation and economic development (jobs, living wages, and entrepreneurial growth across racial and gender lines), within the context of freedom and liberty for all.

That is the Minneapolis story I want to see in the near future. It is the Minneapolis story I want to see become the story of everyone, a story seen not just through my eyes but seen through the eyes of everyone else and experienced in their lives everyday.

Finally, let us revisit the notion of "talking the walk" and "walking the talk." What is the "talk" to be walked? This is not a "how to" book. But I have listed a number of things that can be used to evaluate any existing or proposed "how to" in order to better evaluate whether to continue or terminate a program, whether to start or re-work a program before beginning it. Walking the talk also means evaluating whether the results of programs in education, housing, and jobs, among others, are working. For those who want to maintain the status quo, the YESes and NOs would be reversed. For those who want to change the status quo in directions I have outlined in this book, then the YESes and NOs are, as we used to say, "right on." I have suggested several in my book that I believe should be applied in Minneapolis (but elsewhere also, as in here, there, and everywhere). Here are the major ones:

Chapter 5 suggests the policies for a "To Do" **list of YESes** and NOs for the future that everyone can work together to bring about. The first set of YESSES, simply put, centers on policies that would result in positive outcomes regarding education, children, and families:

- YES to a better quality of life for ALL citizens
- YES to a better quality education for all students; higher graduation rates for all schools
- YES to a first-rate health care
- YES to wider home ownership

Next are those policies that would result in positive outcomes for transportation, energy, and the environment:

- YES to abundant natural resources, including clean water and clean air
- YES to highways that keep up with the increase in cars
- YES to energy policies that prevent a California in Minnesota

Finally, these policies would result in positive outcomes for the economy, jobs, wages, and business:

- YES to low unemployment and wages that let full-time workers support their families
- YES to contractors who do business with the City to hire minority workers (preferably all businesses, but at least those doing business with the City).
- YES to business-friendly environment
- YES to world-class corporate research and world-class university research
- YES to rural-metro partnerships, not needless competition
- YES to tax breaks for individuals and for companies
- YES to a respect for property and laws and access to both for all
- YES to equality of opportunity for all races, especially in terms of education and job training

- YES to keeping our place among the top five states in income per capita in the USA
- YES to keeping Fortune 500 Companies headquarters
- YES to once again earning the "Most Livable State" award

Chapter 5 also has a corresponding list to consider for **our collective NOs**. The first set of NOs centers on policies that say NO to those outcomes that are negative for education, children, and families:

- NO to only 17% of our African-American male high school students graduating
- NO to 25% of 4th graders today being unable to read at 4th-grade level (of which the percentage rises to over 50% for Hispanics and over 60% for Blacks)
- NO to minority students being kept in school systems where they are provided far fewer resources and score much lower than White students. They are our friends and our neighbors, and they too will join us as part of tomorrow's work force. They should have the same opportunities.
- NO to hunger and children living in garbage

Then there are policies to say NO to that result in negative outcomes for transportation, energy, and the environment:

- NO to highway construction that does not keep up with the increase in cars
- NO to an energy policy that is not adequate for the future

Finally, there are policies to say NO to that result in negative outcomes for the economy, jobs, wages, and business:

- NO to having people work full time for wages that won't support their families
- NO to 25% of our citizens not being able to afford to own their own homes
- NO to companies contracting to government agencies who don't hire minorities
- NO to maintaining a conflict between rural and metro areas, and instead form partnerships
- NO to doing nothing to keep companies and their jobs from leaving Minnesota
- NO to our taxes becoming too high for the return we get in services
- NO to terror and totalitarianism
- NO to not being willing to evaluate programs for their true consequences, so that we can be prepared to change policies that result in high pain and low meaning, whether for individuals, schools, or companies

Finally, let us revisit the notion of "talking the walk" and "walking the talk." What is the "talk" to be walked? Several outlines have been suggested. Here I put them all together.

Interlude 8 suggests that A **National Commission of Reconciliation and Reparations** should be established to investigate and work out the payments that would be involved for the land and wealth stolen from Blacks. This basis for reparations is also stated in Chapters 9, 12, 13, 16, 17, and the Preface.

Chapter 9 offers a **list of steps** to take **to correct oppression of Black people** in going before various official bodies, agencies, and investigations:

1. Certainly try to get the numbers, but have them certified; don't take their word for it.
2. Join with those who would unite and demand a Federal grand jury investigation.
3. Present the wealth of information already available to City Hall to let them know you know what you are talking about.
4. Demand, politely or through legal injunction, to get the city to state why they allow projects to continue that are not in compliance.
5. Demand, politely or through legal injunction, to get the city to state why they hire contractors with records of not being in compliance.
6. Continue to hold public forums.
7. Continue to come up with plans of action to foster success.
8. Continue to agree on who will carry out the various steps of the plan and then do so.
9. Stop being patient with practices that have gone on since the 1960s.

The end of **Chapter 12 suggests 7 remedies for the redistricting problem**.

1. That the information presented [in Chapters 12 and 13] be investigated for possible illegalities and corruption.
2. That the information presented [in Chapters 12 and 13] by investigated on justice and fairness grounds.
3. That the redistricting process be re-done.
4. That the submitted redistricting map list all assumptions used to develop the map, as well as empirical data backing these assumptions and their attendant influence on the re-drawn ward lines.
5. That the Redistricting Commission be reconstituted to include at least one person from each ward and reflect proportionally the results of the most recent election, now and for all future redistricting following census reports.
6. That the corruption charges against Joe Biernet be made public.

7.   That the City Attorney be instructed to report why no investigation has been conducted on the missing Jackie Cherryhomes files and be instructed to commence immediately upon such an investigation.

8.   How will you, dear reader, use the information in this book? Will your children and grandchildren tell you how proud they are of your having done something about what you read here or that they are ashamed of you for not doing anything about it?

From **Chapter 14:** develop a set of **"Sullivan Principles for Minneapolis."** Hold a series of Black on Black and Black on White discussions on just how such principles should read.

Chapter 16, and **Interlude 16,** as well as **Chapter 17** and this **Conclusion,** all open with propositions and theses of Peter Berger which should also be part of our calculus of deciding what public policies to advocate and support.

Chapter 16 also lists the three things to avoid, according to the McCone Commission, after the Watts Riots in L.A., if urban unrest is to be avoided:

- A scarcity of **employment**;
- A scarcity of **education** designed to meet the special needs of disadvantaged Negro children; and
- A resentment, even hatred, of the **police** as the symbol of authority.

Chapter 16 also has a list of things to avoid, taken from the Kerner Commission after the riots of 1968:

- Pervasive discrimination and **segregation in employment, education and housing**;
- Black in-migration and white exodus, which had provided a growing crisis of deteriorating facilities and services and unmet human needs;
- The black ghettos, where segregation and poverty **converged on the young to destroy opportunity and enforce failure.**

Both commissions concluded

> **poverty, segregation**, lack of **educational** and **employment opportunities**, widespread **perceptions of police abuse**, and unequal consumer services as the principal grievances which led to the civil disturbances of the 1960's.

What is needed to fix the broken wheels of Minneapolis? Let me offer my constant refrain as a suggestion and reminder: Society's stability depends on accessible and accountable government and the rule of law applied evenly to all.

Prosperity depends on a market economy that encourages private enterprise (incentives) and that allows for private property. Thus, continuity with the best of the past and present combined with recipes and plans for the future offers a chance at security for the future. We know that order (stability) is the fundamental mandate of human societies, no matter how small or large, and that it is helped by regularity (schedules). Isn't our task to achieve order (the great political science question) that allows the sovereignty of both state and people (the great question of liberty)? To achieve this, more power must devolve to individuals, not just to states and cities.

Despite much that has happened that has not been good for Blacks in this country (all Interludes except 5 and 7), much good has happened to many Blacks in this country (Interludes 5 and 7). But remember my goal: equal access, equal opportunity for all, not just those in power. The inner city has intentionally been left behind. We still have much work to do for those in the inner city. Our individual and collective futures depend on it.

Many work full time in low paying jobs in the United States that still translate as poverty. This raises the question of the minimum wage and what is now called the "living wage." The Republican Eisenhower administration in the 1950s pushed for the first minimum wage on moral grounds, that no one working should have to earn less than what it cost to raise a family in this country. It passed, but was awfully low. It was the Republican President Nixon who proposed a floor below which no family would be allowed to fall, but the Democrats defeated it. These were not bad ideas, as they were considered "good for the economy." But Democrats, who controlled Congress, voted against these measures for the working poor, meaning people who are poor even though they were working. I now believe they did so because they wanted Blacks beholden to them, having convinced Blacks that only government run by Democrats would provide more for them, and would if they would just vote for Democrats. The evidence shows otherwise.

In my view, there is something wrong with a system that has people working full-time at wages that will not sustain a family; I don't mind the rich getting rich but not on the backs of their workers. And I also mind when they don't pay a living wage. Certainly, no one can make a moral argument for the pay and life style of the CEOs who took millions in value while collapsing their employees' pension funds, laying them off from work, and keeping the wages low of those left with a job. That is not capitalism. That is robber baronism. Capitalism is supposed to be about incentives. To pay senior executives bonuses and stock options when their company loses money is merely exercising the power of robber baron pirates. To hold people accountable (checks and balances) and to provide incentives is the American Way. To have no accountability and to have legislative-established loopholes for campaign contributors to enable them to enrich themselves at the expense of their companies, shareholders, and employees, and tax receipts is just as heinous as violent crime. Calling it "white collar" crime makes it sound benign. But it is malignant to our economy and society and should be labeled for the evil it is and punished for the evil that it is.

This does more than raise the philosophical question of fairness, as it points up the significance and importance of the "ladder of mobility" for those not fortunate enough to be born rich, and the question of whether people in poverty will be allowed to climb up or purposefully be "kept in their place." It has been my contention that Minneapolis has consciously, intentionally, and purposefully prevented people when they tried, and thus they have slowly killed the incentive of many young Black men in the inner city to try, and thus preventing them from succeeding, hoping they'll descend into drugs and crime so they can be jailed and their inner city space be made available to the White gentrifiers. This is being aided and abetted by the partnership of the DFL and the Black organizations that sold out their memberships, the local branches of the NAACP and the Urban League (Chapter 14).

The ladder of social mobility contains five rungs, three traditional ones, and two new to modern times. The traditional ways of getting out of or avoiding poverty were through marriage, being born into a powerful family, or through military conquest or service. The two new modern ones are education, and learning how to present oneself in different personal and professional situations.

In terms of education, think of our earlier discussion of high-tech immigrants from poor countries being hired for our high-tech companies because we are not turning out enough of our own. And of course we are not. How could we when so many of our 4th graders, especially minority 4th graders, are unable to read? It is no wonder we have to import talent. The only possible conclusion, as Democrats and teachers' unions control education in this country, is that when push comes to shove, they care more about their jobs and retirement than they do about the learning of the students, coming up with many excuses as to why it's the students' or the parents' fault. And as Blacks vote for Democrats anyway, there is no incentive for the Democrats to do anything for minorities in the inner cities. This holds especially true for Minneapolis.

It is not possible for a family of four to live on today's minimum wage. And it is not possible to earn more than minimum wage without an education and without knowing how to comport oneself.

Now I admit that fairness is a tough issue. But let us look at the facts. They will help us deal better with our negative or false emotions. Many successful young people of the past two decades have succeeded because of what an article several years ago called "The Yuppies' Dirty Little Secret," which is that they had parents with enough extra money that they could help them out. This "dirty little secret" reflects more than the difference between the rich and the poor. It is the difference between the poor and any who have discretionary income, and thus the yuppies' dirty little secret is that their parents are affluent enough or that they have parents who, though not quite affluent, used what extra they had to help them. The kids of all of these thus had and have access to money of their parents that many workers do not have, especially the poor. Also, their parents were able to live in good neighborhoods that had good schools so that these kids would get the best education available that wasn't in a private school.   That secret enabled them to go to the right schools, have the right experiences, meet the right people, and get the right training and contacts.   Their key was the money of their parents, not their own, and the money the taxpayers spent on their schools and their opportunities, schools and opportunities not available to the poor in general and in particular poor Blacks.   It is difficult for Blacks to accumulate wealth in this fashion when they are subjected to the treatment reported in the Interludes.

This has been going on for a number of generations, certainly since World War II. For this reason, it is said, depending upon who you read, that the current group of Baby Boomers will inherit somewhere between 3 and 7 trillion dollars, most of it in homes, but some, of course, in stocks and bonds and money market accounts, and other instruments.   This is what separates the Blacks from the Whites.   There will be no such handing over of property and negotiables worth trillions to Blacks. Remember how the Whites have taken the wealth and property of Blacks (see Interlude 8).   In other words, the poor minorities trapped in the inner cities don't have parental affluence to back them up.   When Jane Fonda told her gym floor cleaner she should exercise and get in shape, she was told: "Miz Fonda, if you had two jobs like mine and kids to raise with no help, you'd look like me too."

A U.S. Senator in the mid-1960s attempted to live with his family of four for a week at the poverty level and could not, although that did not change anything.   In the late-1960s, Dillon Ripley, then Secretary of the Smithsonian, wanted, during Dr. King's poverty march, to put a poverty village on the grounds of the Smithsonian on the Mall.   The Democrats who controlled Congress were appalled and vetoed it.   It would be too embarrassing to their policies.   But they haven't yet done much to allow real poor people to get a good education in order to get good jobs in order to earn money to preclude such poverty.

Minneapolis has to decide what it wants its story to be for the 21st century. I know what I want it to be, and I know what I will continue to work for.   In my eyes, people ought to have a living wage, an amount that allows them to support their family, a wage based on the moral high ground of Eisenhower and the Nixon floor below which they are not allowed to fall.

Establishing a livable wage would have a profound impact on welfare as well, as it would provide more than welfare pays without any of the strings, reducing both the impulse to go on welfare as well as encouraging parents making babies to stay together.   Thus, the living wage could be purposefully set above welfare levels as a further incentive.   The best minds in Minneapolis should look at the question with the intention of solving it, not just containing it.

It could cause an influx of people wanting to work for the higher wage, but these would all be self-selecting folks with skills and a work ethic, which would be good for Minneapolis.   But will the DFL and the Black organizations go along with it, as they seek not to empower and liberate people but to subjugate them so they will vote for them and leave them the luxury and splendor of being in charge? Bosses, regardless of race or ethnicity, love to be in charge. Power is a strong drug. Will Minneapolis citizens stand up for themselves or stand up for the bosses against the rest of the people? Will we have more acknowledgement of truth or more cover-up?

I agree with those who say that one of the great achievements of the United States is that it has gotten people from every area and country to join together to become one fantastic country, a country where the children of former slaves stand with children of former slave owners and sing "God Bless America." What clouds judgment and thinking in America today are those who think this happens everywhere. It does not. It is not true, for instance of any Arab country and true in very few European and Asian countries.

I have remained faithful to the dream. Many Blacks have remained faithful to the dream. We don't want to give up nor give in, although some do. There are still enough of us willing to do what it takes to overcome hardship and adversity, to achieve the triumph of our own human spirit. What we want now is to instill the dream of Martin Luther King, Jr. in both Liberal politics and Black organizational sell-outs that have caused it to be either driven out or seen as not achievable.

How long will the Black community put up with the DFL? Blacks automatically voting for the DFL is what helps keep Blacks on the short end of the economic stick. The local DFL, with state approval, because of their internal fight over judge nominations, has also set in motion the defeat of their own DFL Senator, Paul Wellstone, which could put the U.S. Senate back in the control of the Republicans. For the DFL, who does Wellstone think he is? He is just an elected Senator. The self-appointed DFL is convinced it knows better and wants the power, no matter who is sacrificed.

This is why the candidacy of Natalie Johnson-Lee of the Green Party is so important. The DFL is now causing people to think Green Party. As a result, the Green Party is now the second largest party in the state. I'm sure the DFL would love to fold the Green Party into itself, just as Nellie Stone Johnson's Farmer-Labor Party was. But then they double-crossed Nellie. Would they double cross the Green Party? Given the way they are currently acting and constituted, of course they would.

Our future in the inner city is now tied to the political fortunes of Natalie Johnson-Lee. She has the principles that enable her to stand up for the concern, rights, and fairness of the people, principles that should be exhibited by every elected official. She treats those who elected her as her purpose, not as her cannon fodder. She is one of the few elected officials capable of being a great Mayor of Minneapolis and a great Governor of Minnesota. She has the ability to get people to support her as she stands on the truth, stands for what is right, stands for fairness, and stands for what is best for the city as a whole and for the people who make up the city. Even though the odds are greatly against her, I am predicting that she will get stronger and stronger as time goes on, that the deals people have made will become unraveled, and that the Minneapolis Blacks who have customarily sold out their fellow Blacks will be on the run. Hopefully the days of the NAACP and Urban League helping them do their dirty work will soon come to an end as well, so that they will no longer be sell-outs and that once again they will return to an agenda for the whole community.

Hopefully, the future belongs to community groups too. We've come full circle. It is time for grass roots movements again. These provide hope because they show how to be successful in a positive way.

I have written about the Minneapolis story in the hopes that it will prod Minneapolis to the greatness that awaits her if all get equal opportunity and equal access. I have not asked permission to write this book and I make no excuses for writing it. I invite Black readers from other cities to write the story of their cities through their eyes as they view the fairness, or lack of fairness, and the involvement, or lack of involvement, of Blacks in the social and political and social mainstream of their cities. I will continue to live the Minneapolis story and comment on it. I urge readers to do the same, in whatever town and state you live in. I'll continue to add my comments on a regular basis on my web page, www.TheMinneapolisStory.com.

Will the Black community in Minneapolis continue to vote the DFL party line? They stopped this year in New York City when 25% of Blacks voted Republican in the Mayor's race, which put former Democrat Michael Bloomberg into office as the Republican Mayor. If the Black community will vote to support whoever will work for equal access and equal opportunity and end the plantation mentality in education, housing, and jobs, they will no longer be at the bottom in these areas. And if that means they vote Green or another party and the DFL becomes a minority party, well, that is what the DFL deserves for having openly betrayed the Black community in terms of access, opportunity, education, housing, jobs, and for having betrayed the ideals of Nellie Stone Johnson.

There is a real danger with racism and intolerance, and that is that it hinders participation in the economics and politics of this country. What is the "American creed" if not equality? The prize on which we all keep our eyes is the trinity of freedom and liberty and equality, using Lincoln's words for the first 3 entries below:

- "We hold these truths to be self-evident, that all men are created equal"
- "Fourscore and seven years ago our fathers brought forth on this continent a new nation, conceived in liberty and dedicated to the proposition that all men are created equal"
- "We the People of the United States, in Order to form a more perfect Union, establish Justice...and secure the Blessings of Liberty to ourselves and our Posterity"...
- "Principles of freedom, equality, justice, and humanity"
- "Indivisible, with liberty and justice for all"

This is the bedrock of liberty, and is still what fires the imagination of every group in America, and those around the world hoping to come to America. This has always been the vision of Blacks in America. It is the beacon that draws us, a beacon to which we must not close our eyes. The more we articulate that vision of equality of access and opportunity, the less we can grant special status to any group, Black or White, male or female, North or South, straight or gay.

In biology, it is said that each species reproduces itself, that, like produces like. So too, in my view, does society, that poverty breeds poverty just as wealth produces wealth. This is all the more reason to integrate Black and White poor into the economic mainstream. Racism and prejudice and segregation keep Blacks out of the economic game. Put more simply, there is a fear in Whites of how far Blacks will go if allowed to play on a level playing field. The truth is they will do the same as Whites: some will prosper greatly and some not so much. All will have a chance.

Would that we could all join in a shared quest to discover the common ground on which we can all stand as citizens of our great country, our great state, our great city. It is said that the world has changed far more in the last 100 years than any previous century. Naturally, there are those who believe this has happened because of their ideology or religion or economic system or just themselves alone. In reality, the great changes, be they in civil engineering or warfare, medicine or space flight, have been due to technology and capitalism. These two things have brought more people out of misery and poverty than anything else. And yet there are those who spurn it on religious grounds (especially Arab Islam) or who are unable to take advantage of it on political grounds (socialism, dictatorships).

There are also those, especially among the wealthy of Minneapolis, who believe they are self-made men or women. In truth, there is no such thing as a self-made man or woman. Scratch one and you will find someone helped them either with money, contacts, encouragement, marriage, birth or a combination of these. Blacks of the inner city need help too, not the least of which is being allowed to help each other.

My goal has been to expose for Minneapolis, in my own small way, the differences between the American ideal and the reality of discrimination and segregation that keeps too many Blacks out of the economic mainstream and, as a result, hurts the White community as well. It boils down not only to what is moral or right or even just. It boils down to what is legal. The redistricting we discussed earlier was legal, but it was not moral, right, or just, as it disempowered, disenfranchised, and ghettoized the people it stacked in the new Minneapolis 5th Ward.

So let's look at where we are:

- We are not educating our kids
- We are not enabling housing for all races

- We are not allowing participation in the economic and political processes for everyone
- We are not working toward full equal access and full equal opportunity in education, housing, and economic development.

Rather than hang its head in shame and say that's the way of the world, Minneapolis needs to raise its head and its eyes to take the steps needed to reverse these. In the meantime, we have created a moral crisis in the inner cities where young people believe that "anything goes." Free love/sex/disease/addiction have created terrible results for poor, inner city Black youth.

Some think I sound like a Conservative because I stress our community relationships more than I do so-called "rights," and that I stress economic self-sufficiency over government support. But how else can we inspire our youth to understand that Blacks not only can make and hold wealth and property, but that they have, and did so back when the climate for such success was far worse that it is today. We overcame then. We must get our youth to understand that we can overcome now. They must be made to see that they can overcome now, as so many Blacks before them, if we continue to accept them and push them to do so, using the dream of Martin Luther King, Jr. as a beacon, demonstrating to them that it is not government programs and subsidies that are needed long term, but that we need government protection and assurance to guarantee to equal access and equal opportunity.

And we need to emphasize and model the importance of relationships not only between parents and children but also between neighbors, both Black and White. We need to make heroes out of parents and those being responsible for nurturing the health of family units. American culture is more important than either White or Black culture. Needed is an emphasis on education and on personal morality that will enable equal participation in the social, political and economic mainstream of this country.

And before I get accused of being a Pollyanna and thus not capable of assessing the way the "real world" works, let me assure you that I recognize not everyone is salvageable, that Blacks have bad apples just as Whites do. What I am concerned about is that we are making bad apples out of good apples in the inner cities as we continue to accept, endorse, and implement quasi-apartheid policies. We need our own Sullivan Principles for our own inner cities. Until we stand up and say "no more" and work hard to obtain equal access and equal opportunity, how can we expect Black youth to accept us, follow us, or work hard to take advantages of opportunity if they see that their climb up the ladder of mobility is purposefully blocked?

I will work hard to support Natalie Johnson-Lee and help her against the DFLs attempts to block her. For many reasons, but most of all because she ran without asking their permission (which is why she ran as a Green Party candidate, not the DFL). They are picking on the wrong woman. She is not a house Negro sell-out.

She is a field hand. She works for all the people, White and Black, as she works for equal access and equal opportunity for all, regardless of color. That is why I can say that someday she will make a great Mayor, a great Governor. The DFL fears her future. They want to nip it in the bud right now. That is why they have turned to underhanded tactics to subvert the will of the people.

The Founding Fathers believed in what is called "natural rights." Political rights were needed to protect each person's "natural rights," and for human beings there were common natural ends that all sought. This was the basis of Thomas Jefferson's wonderful image of a "saddle on the backs" of the unfree and his image of tyrants being "booted and spurred" to ride those on whose backs they placed their saddles. In other words, by his words, he said it was not "natural" to consider some men born with saddles on their backs, while others were born booted and spurred to ride them.

As a young man, much earlier than 1776, Jefferson spoke up against slavery in Virginia. He nearly lost all he had from the opposition he ran into. He then remained silent on the issue. He stayed true to his ideals when he wrote the Declaration of Independence, but could not again bring himself to live those ideals personally, as he needed his 80 slaves to run his home at Monticello to free him to do the work he wanted to do. Our task is to do both: stay with the ideals and live them in our own lives as well, to walk the talk, not just talk the walk. Sadly, in terms of Blacks, as Wendy said in the movie 'Hook," to Peter Pan, "why Peter, you've become a pirate," so too could it be said to Jefferson and Southerners, in term of blacks and slavery, "why Thomas, you've become a tyrant." But that doesn't negate his words, which still fill the beacon of hope with light and still provide the drum beat of freedom with rhythm. His not freeing his slaves doesn't negate the idea of freeing slaves and treating all equally. We need to shine the light of his words on all of the remaining inner-city Monticellos, and then actually act on the words, not just mouth them, and support the drumbeat of freedom for everyone.

Jefferson's words still reverberate in me with excitement, that it is not natural to consider some men born with saddles on their backs, nor is it natural to consider others born booted and spurred to be ridden. And that is exactly what I have fought for these past 40 years: that people not be viewed as wearing saddles that others can then ride. The Minneapolis story is a story of the saddle. For some of the Minneapolis Mastuhs, the saddle is for everyone, and the saddle belongs on the back of the city, so that the city carries them. For other Minneapolis Mastuhs, the saddle was meant for individuals. Those holding this view also believe they were born booted and spurred to ride them. Either way, the most recent examples of this are the Redistricting of Minneapolis (Chapters 12-13), the Hollman housing project (Chapter 8) and the jail project (Chapter 9), all of which represent saddles on the backs of many young Minneapolis inner city Black men. Indeed, until we can demonstrate to the young Black men of the inner cities that they are not predestined to wear the saddle, we will not be able to address the inner city moral cries of drugs, gangs, single moms, and promiscuous sexual practices. Rights are important, but so too are responsibilities and personal achievement that transcend civil rights, and those are the rights of newborns to a united family and a safe community. We need to work with public officials, including the police, to get both Black and White bad apples out of our communities while also showing officials and the police that many whom they would harass and beat up are not bad apples and should not be treated as they are. We need to show them not the profile of being Black but the profile of being human, of achieving, and then providing the access and opportunities needed to move on up.

Lets work together to write a new story of Minneapolis, a positive one that provide hope and access and opportunity for all. I want to be part of those who serve as Beacon to help light a new path for the Minneapolis story, as those who provide a tempo for the drum beat for freedom. I don't want the living library that I represent that can help shed that light to disappear. I want to leave people, Black and White, armed with the kind o knowledge of how Minneapolis works so they can work together to make Minneapolis work better.

October postscript: remembering our grandchildren

Although I don't agree with everything in Bill Clinton's October 2nd speech, I enjoyed his close. It reminded me of the story that Israel's Menachim Begin was finally willing to make a deal with Egypt's Anwar Sadat (The Camp David Accords), when Jimmy Carter's secretary handed Begin a picture of his grandchildren and asked what he was willing to do for them. This part of what Clinton said goes for all of us too:

> I would like to close with this simple idea. All of the hopes that I have for my daughter's generation, for the grandchildren I hope to have, for all of you who are younger than me and, unlike me, still have most of your lives ahead of you, rest upon our ability to get the world to embrace a simple set of ideas, that we must move from interdependence to **integration** because our common humanity matters more than our interesting differences and makes the expression of those differences possible; because every child deserves a chance, every adult has a role to play and we all do better when we work together.

> That is why we must build the institutions that will help us to **integrate**, that is why we must stand against the threats, whether they are from weapons of mass destruction, terrorists, tyrants, Aids, climate change, poverty, ignorance and disease which would tatter this world and prevent us ever from coming together as one. [I would like all of us to go] beyond the exclusive claims of old opponents to a future we can all share; going beyond the fears and the grudges, the fights and the failures of yesterday's demons to a truth we can all embrace.

Conclusion

Not Losing Sight of the Prize of Equality's Freedom

Without economic participation and equal access and equal opportunity for prosperity, the past will continue to be repeated. Whites may be willing to pay that price. I am not. This is evidence from studies around the world, from Peter L. Berger, *The Capitalist Revolution: Fifty Propositions About Prosperity, Equality, & Liberty* (Basic Books, NY, NY, 1986, pp. 211-215:

Proposition #1: Industrial capitalism has generated the greatest productive power in human history

Proposition #5: Advanced industrial capitalism has generated, and continues to generate, the highest material standard of living for large masses of people in human history.

Proposition #12: In all advanced industrial societies education has become the single most important vehicle of upward mobility.

Proposition #16: Capitalism is a necessary but not sufficient condition of democracy.

Proposition #22: At least in Western societies, if not elsewhere as well, capitalism is the necessary but not sufficient condition of the continuing reality of individual autonomy.

Proposition #28: Capitalist development in Third World societies leading to rapid and labor-intensive economic growth is more likely to equalize income distribution than strategies of deliberate policies of income distribution.

Proposition #30: East Asia confirms the superior capacity of industrial capitalism in raising the material standard of living of large masses of people.

Proposition #40: The movements toward democracy and individuation in East Asia have been greatly strengthened by the adherence of these societies to an international capitalist system centered in the West.

Proposition #48: There can be no effective market economy without private ownership of the means of production.

The following seven commonly held values (pp. 218-221) are held by more people around the world than any others (regardless of what their political leaders may like or say or put forth in the contest over ideas and values that often keep their people from benefiting from these values). These seven values are far better fostered and far more greatly delivered by democratic capitalism than by socialism or "third way" approaches, and relate directly, in my mind, to the inner-city of Minneapolis:

1. The material well-being of people, especially of the poor
2. Equality (equity, equalities, reducing inequalities)
3. Political liberties and democracy (freedom)
4. Protection of human rights (civil, political, economic, cultural, religious), i.e., "protection of individuals and groups against the most common acts of tyranny (massive terror, arbitrary executions, torture, mass deportations, the forced separation of families," as well as "protection against economic misfortune" (the purpose of welfare)
5. Individual autonomy
6. Preservation of tradition
7. Community

I list the above for those still waffling between the left and right extremes and their agendas. We cannot understand the importance of education, housing, and jobs, without first keeping clear, that the **empirical** evidence shows that more people have been brought out of poverty by capitalism, and that "democratic regimes have the best record on the protection of human rights in *all* the categories employed by human rights theorists."

I list these for two simple reasons: first, less than 8% of small businesses in America are Black, and yet most jobs are created in small businesses. Secondly, minorities will not succeed in business unless they have the education to do so.

This has been *The Minneapolis Story Through My Eyes*. What will be The Minneapolis story over the next decade? What dreams will be envisioned? How will visions be sustained?

We have come a long way from the day when we had to ride in the back of the bus. We have come a long way since the time we weren't even allowed on the bus. Now we have come to the time where it is important that we also drive the bus.

We have just finished the 20th century, a century of many dreams, ranging from capitalism to socialism, from far Right to far Left, from Hitler and Franco and Mussolini to Lenin and Stalin and Mao. Their dreams, as we have seen, were very costly. Their visions were death traps. From the perspective of these men, it is wonderful for us that the 20th century is over. But what will we envision for the 21st? What will we dream for the next decade? How might what I have written about the Minneapolis story help with future visions, future dreams?

I won't lose sight of "freedom's unfinished business," of the prize of equality's freedom. Here are the words of Frederick Douglass, a free Negro, active prohibitionist, who also never took his eye off the prize. Hear him in 1852, prior to the Civil War:

> This, for the purpose of this celebration, is the 4th of July. It is the birthday of your National Independence, and of your political freedom. This, to you, is what the Passover was to the emancipated people of God.
>
> I have this day presented of the state of the nation, I do not despair of this country. There are forces in operation, which must inevitably work the downfall of slavery. "The arm of the Lord is not shortened," and the doom of slavery is certain. I, therefore, leave off where I began, with hope. While drawing encouragement from the Declaration of Independence, the great principles it contains, and the genius of American Institutions, ... the multitude walked on in mental darkness. .... Intelligence is penetrating the darkest corners of the globe. .... The fiat of the Almighty, "Let there be Light," has not yet spent its force. No abuse, no outrage whether in taste, sport or avarice, can now hide itself from the all-pervading light.

> Frederic Douglas
> "What to the Slave is the Fourth of July?" speech
> 5 July 1852, Rochester Ladies' Anti-Slavery Society
> Rochester Hall, Rochester, N.Y.
> Reminding his audience of liberty's unfinished business.

This legacy question is not as easy as it sounds. We all want to be remembered for our positive things, not our negative. A guiding light of mine is that you only pass this way once. And probably one of the greatest disservices that we can do to our legacies, to our souls, is to have passed this way and done nothing. And so, I'd like to be thought of as having done a number of things that helped others and maybe in some small way led to positive change. That basically is it. But what I seek is more than the final story of Ron Edwards. The real legacy that I want to keep alive is the legacy the struggle to keep the eye on the equality's prize of freedom. It is my hope, my intent, that this will be the legacy which all of us can lift up for the young Black men of our city.

I have spent 40 years as a community advocate in pursuit of fairness in the pursuit of justice. The pursuit of inclusion is not an easy road; it is not a part of Dorothy's yellow brick road, you know. You'd like to think that you're going to the Land of the Wizard of Oz, but for Black folk the Wizard meant something different. The

Wizard represents the Ku Klux Klan, if you will. And so, not all roads are paved with gold, but in our quest to move down those roads, we need successes to go along with the inevitable reversals. And because of who we are and what we are and where we are, we do not necessarily have the lives we want. But we can have the soul and attitude we want. And those are worth all the potential material comforts. I have the soul and the attitude I want.

Now don't get me wrong when I say what I'm about to say. I am a humble man. I live humbly. I speak humbly. But I don't rest on false humility either. Let me put it to you this way, as a friend told it to me. He said that I have a significant opportunity that puts me in the top one percentile of those who get an opportunity to tell their story and help others by doing so.

And I must be doing something right, as both White and Black organizations have tried to wipe me out, have fought me and tried to diminish me as a man and as a force for equal access and equal opportunity in the community, as an advocate of justice and fairness. At the same time, those who have opposed me as well as those in the media that cover these battles, have sought my comments, because whether they agree or disagree with me, they know I will give them the straight scoop (hence the many times I've been quoted in the newspaper (Interlude 1).

Now, dear reader, it is important to me that you understand that every morning when I wake up, I'm at peace with myself, with my being. Now that does not mean I don't have stressful days, for I do, especially when my day has been filled with civil and human rights battles, as I speak out in one forum or another. Nonetheless, at the end of the day and at the beginning of the morning, I am at peace with myself, knowing I did what it was that I needed to do not only for the cause of peace but to be at peace with myself, that I saw issues that needed to be addressed and that I attempted to make a difference. That is what is important.

I leave it to others to judge how well we have spoken on behalf of fairness and justice for everyone. Although at one time they did, it is certainly clear that for a while now the NAACP and Urban League don't as well as they used to (Chapter 14). But I don't represent them. I represent the poor, especially poor Black young men, and Black police officers, and any and all who are denied equal access and equal opportunity, a denial that today comes as much from so-called Black leaders as from White leaders. Thus I also feel for poor Whites in Appalachia, where in some counties only 50% of people 25 and over have a High School diploma, where unemployment in some counties is 12% higher than in others, and where the per capita income of some counties is 30% below the U.S. poverty rate of $16,036, and where in most counties the number of children living in poverty is 40% over the national average. So what I write applies to them too. But I don't live in Appalachia. They are welcome to my words. I invite everyone to write their story. But I live in Minneapolis, so I have addressed what is going on in Minneapolis.

What particularly pains me is the fact that many Black church leaders are accepting money from the government to co-opt real activity that might get real results for the poor. This is not Christian behavior. This is important to understand because not all religions have such an emphasis on caring for the poor as Christianity does. And yet despite the widespread poverty in the world, Christians, who are to have a special concern for the poor, that "preferential option for the poor," not only give less and less in their offering plates, they also neglect the poor through policies geared to achieve support for the wealthy. They are like the religious leaders in the parable of the Good Samaritan who "passed on the other side."

Caring for others is a main theme in the Bible, and yet any "preferential option for the poor" means doing more than preaching on hunger on World Hunger Sunday. But how many in the pews, White or Black, would be happy if their preachers talked this up from their pulpits? All that I ask for is justice for the poor. And justice means equal opportunity and equal access to education, housing, and jobs. This is what is denied the poor by keeping them under educated or not educated at all, paying "minimum" wages that are actually "below minimum," as earning the "minimum" for a full time job won't support a family, despite all the cries for family values from politicians. Minimum wage for a full time job is still not a living wage. The first and primary family value is the living wage. The bottom line is that any preacher or civil servant who doesn't advocate for those unable to advocate for themselves, and this includes teachers in the schools, are "passing on the other side" and are either actively participating in keeping the poor in their place or acquiescing to it by standing by silently and not saying anything about it. Too many, seemingly, are happy getting theirs (job security and retirement) and are not upset if others are denied an opportunity to get theirs even when they are working full time.

I am doing my best to speak on behalf of those without a voice. Now, some would argue, "man you've been forced out of the Urban League and they forced you off the radio station, ha, ha, ha," and the NAACP has just recently tried to silence you, you know, and so you have been capped." Maybe so, but I'm an intelligent enough person; I'm an insightful enough person to know what the true indicators are. These things happened as a part of the battle. The battle keeps me going. It provides the fire, if you will, that continues to burn within my soul that makes me know that I'm right, that I am contributing to the meaning in people's lives, and not adding to their pain. And so, that's the thing that's kept me going, and in many respects that's the thing that has provided me with the sense of youth and rejuvenation; that I can still make a difference with my life for those I advocate for in the community.

I want to maintain a good accounting or stewardship, if you will, of the gifts God has given me. God gave me a gift of recall, tremendous recall. I've always said this to myself, and maybe to a few others, that it must be in the genes of my body and soul, so that if we were to go back 500 to 1000 years to wherever it was in Africa that my ancestors came from, it would be my ancestor who was the village storyteller. And not just my village perhaps, but maybe also a wider area encompassing other villages as well, because I know that when you have a gift, God expects you to use it. And that is why I know that the Minneapolis story applies to inner cities across America as well.

We live in a wonderful, awesome universe. There is more to it than just the green grass, blue water, and the air that swirls above us. So I also think that whether physically or spiritually, it is important to understand that we are not here by ourselves in the universe. Think of the awesomeness of the explosion of a Nova, if you will, that may take the equivalent of 3-4000 years in our sense of time, and in some cases, millions of years to reach us. We have to understand how insignificant, in some respects we are as "species" and yet something very significant in terms of Creation and Life. So, I think about those kinds of things and that's a part of strengthening my belief in what we are as human beings, that we were put here to help each other.

You see it bothers me to see the mean-spirited conduct and attitudes that I witness in person, read about in the paper, or see on the news. How can you kill a child? If you can kill a child, and empathize with that, you can kill anyone. And we have had several instances over the past year of mothers killing their children. Now I know there are sick minds and sick people. We all have the little dark closets, you know. But how do you take a 4 year-old or 6 year-old child and how do you assault them and mutilate them, burn them, or drown them? How do you beat a child; how do you smother a 15 or 16-month old baby? How do you deny life? How do you take a newborn and toss it in a dumpster? How the hell do you do that? And even worse, how can you then write, as several women columnists have, that they "understand" the urge to kill their children? In the Middle East, we have a people willing to send their children in to kill themselves in order to kill other children. Former Israeli Prime Minister Golda Meir once said: "there will be no peace until they love their children more than they hate us." So, if we can say we understand how mothers can kill their own children, then we have to step back and see what else is at work that we as a society would step back and allow kids to be clubbed to academic death in schools, as baby seals, and condemned to a life of failure by being denied education and the jobs that come once they are educated. How can people say they "understand" and walk away and let the status quo kill the hope and promise of yet another Black generation?

So as you read about the Minneapolis story, use it as a base to discuss our cherished topics, topics such as freedom and liberty and equality. Ask yourself, are things in Minneapolis being done in the open or are they being done by guile and deception, as institutions are taken over silently? Which is your value? Openness or deception? How you answer will greatly influence how you interpret what I write for you in this book. Think of it this way. We are not talking about rocket science. We are talking about how to treat others. That which is right, we feel free to talk about clearly and in the open. But that which is not right, what is not OK, we tend not to discuss; instead, we tend to act in private, where many are not allowed to listen or participate. We need to talk about education, housing, jobs, and participating in the social, political and economic mainstream in the open as well.

Another way I "test" myself is to ask myself these four questions:

(1)   Am I dealing with virtuous people? I am if they view freedom as responsibility and restraint and not as license and selfishness.

(2)   Do they teach character the time-tested way of modeling it and demonstrating it in their actions and behaviors with others, as they walk the talk, or do they just talk the walk?

(3)   What values do they espouse and practice? Are they values related to power and money only or do they also include the virtues of morality (and are they even willing to discuss virtues and values and morality)?

(4)   What do I see when I watch people? a desire for control or a desire to help, a passion for self or compassion for others, more about money, perks, sex, and abuse and mistreatment of others or more about self-control and power control so that people in the community do well too?

And for all of these, I look to see what level of support they give to what I consider the common ground for everyone, the YESes and NOs outlined in Chapter 5 (and repeated in Chapter 17).

How do we get there?

Do we follow the modern response of tolerance that comes with pluralism or the intolerance that comes from one or more of the singular fundamentalisms, be it political or religious? Pluralism, the rule of the West, is under attack from the East, especially from Islam, because they have no concept of pluralism; thus, they can't think in terms of tolerance or more than one road to the truth of the transcendent, believing steadfastly that their way is the only way. In their mindset, they are willing to self-destruct as martyrs, en masse, if need be, in the attempt to eliminate us. They not only want to push Israel into the sea; they want to push us there as well. They can do no other. Indeed, their doctrine of *Taqlid,* that no truth exists beyond that of revealed in the Koran, means that they either have to continue until they self destruct or until they are saved the way the Roman Catholic church was saved, with a Reformation (which then impacted back upon the Roman Catholic Church with the counter-reformation, leading, in another unintended consequence, to most of the changes Martin Luther championed).

It is the reverse in Minneapolis: the *Taqlid* is about the White Way, as it is the inner city Blacks, especially the young Black men, who are singled out for martyrdom by White policies and practices that deny them the access and opportunity to move up and support themselves and their families and communities.   This is the fundamentalism of White racism.

Yet I still have hope. For what could me more awesome than coming into contact with other ways. And so, by seeing the other ways, we are confronted with the greatest and worst part of being modern: **choice**. Indeed, the word comes from the Greek verb *hairein,* from which we get our word **heresy.** Those who claim the choices of others are heresy make a claim of truth. So, whose truth? We can choose to follow the radical, murderous, intolerant and exclusive versions of our favorite historically specific religion/ideology/political/ truth system, or we can chose to follow the historically non-specific path of tolerance and inclusion, using a calculus of meaning and a calculus of pain to resolve the contests between the different world views before us from which we can choose. Capitalism and democracy are a choice for the historically non-specific. Others are a choice of the historically specific. And so, dear reader, what have you chosen? And if you haven't chosen, what will you choose?

We act in bad faith when we say we were born into hatred or a sense of superiority over others. We learned it. And thus at some point we have to face the reality that we know the difference and that where we stand is based on our choice. By what standard do we justify our choices if they have resulted in continued impoverishment of the poor and continued poor education for Blacks and other minorities? How do we justify our choices in light of these outcomes? How do we stand on the debate between individuals being sovereign or a people being sovereign, a question phrased this way in the New York Times on August 4, 2002, by Al Gore:

> There has always been a debate over the destiny of this nation between those who believed they were entitled to govern because of their station in life, and those who believed that the people were sovereign. That distinction remains as strong as ever today.

These are good words. We should all adhere to them. And thus each November (and in the primaries preceding them) we are all faced with a choice when we vote for candidates for public office. My choice is to vote for those who would devolve political power to the community so it can better achieve the YESes and turn back the NOs as the instruments of federal and state policy that, continuing from the above speech by Al Gore, are "used for the benefit of the many, rather than the few."

I will continue to advocate for my community. And I will continue to document the activities of Whites and Blacks as if I were a zoologist exploring the city streets and the halls of government agencies, observing the hops and swings and grunts of those I observe, as I attempt to interpret their sometimes hilarious enjoyment and sometimes angry reactions to exploring each other's ways. My preference is the twitches and sighs and laughter and tears of inner city people, as we all work together to achieve equal access and equal opportunity with fairness and justice for all. I will post these on my web site, www.TheMinneapolisStory.com.

Public policy must foster both the creation of business opportunities as well as the creation of jobs and social change to improve the quality of life for all, and it must foster an end to divisiveness of all kinds, in order to allow prosperity and a sense of solidarity for and among its citizens, enabling political democracy and individual autonomy to co-exist positively and happily together, all done with humility and wisdom and openness to changing policies if an evaluation of their consequences turns out to be negative. This can probably best be done by instituting a dialogue among all the public and private sector groups with a stake in what happens, following standard models of conflict resolution when needed.

I, Ron Edwards, reject the saddle and the spur. I will ride no one. And no one will ride me.

I, Ron Edwards, pledge to continue to support Natalie Johnson-Lee, and join with her in fighting for fair access and fair opportunities for all. Won't you join me? What choices, dear reader, will you make?

I invite all citizens and institutions of Minneapolis, public and private, itself, to take the steps needed to create a public discussion about the future. I believe that everyone in the city is crying out for just such a family meeting. And, as all such meetings need mediators and referees and umpires, I suggest that we call upon the Federal Community Relations department. Although this department is a part of the Justice Department, it is separate from it in that the Supreme Court has ruled it is not to share its information with the DOJ because of the privileged nature of the covenant between those working for Community Relations and the cities into which they bring their mediation expertise. Part of this "conversation" should involve developing "Sullivan Principles" for Minneapolis (Chapter 14).

324   The Minneapolis Story

The Stakes Are For All Of Us, Which is Why Hope Still Beats Eternal

As I draft this conclusion in the shadow of the anniversary of September 11, 2001 Terrorist attack on the United States, I am filled by optimism because Lincoln's Gettysburg Address, parts of which I quoted earlier, was used in New York City and around the country to commemorate that day that will live in infamy as only a few other dates in our history will. But when we look at Lincoln's words again, especially as it relates to the future of America and the future of Minneapolis, lets us recall the five times Lincoln used the word "dedicate" and to what he said we should be dedicating ourselves:

- to "liberty"
- to the Declaration's "all men are created equal."
- "to a portion of that field as a final resting place."
- "to the unfinished work"
- "to the great tasks remaining before us"

And so to, with the constantly evolving process of how we work together to create our City of Minneapolis, I call on all people to dedicate themselves to these same ideals and goals. We too have unfinished work in Minneapolis: to bring to fruition the YESes and to eliminate the NOs (Chapters 5, 17).

That is the great task before us, or how else will we secure freedom and equality for all? Teddy Roosevelt said, "Aggressive fighting for the right is the noblest sport the world affords." I will continue to be aggressive, in writing, on my TV show "Black Focus," on my web page, and in any other way I can as I renew my dedication to my goal of doing all that I can to get all of us engaged in that "sport," the fight for the right, the right of all to equal access and equal opportunity, and especially for the Blacks of the inner city.

May this book about Minneapolis be like a beacon on a hill, illuminating our way to finish our unfinished work, to complete the great task of providing a place for everyone at the Minneapolis table. May it offer a rhythm for the drum beat of freedom. We can learn from it and make better choices along our shared path to the future, or we can turn it off and go where the darkness allows us to stumble around. I urge you to use the Minneapolis Story as a light for yourself and for your community.

The stakes for all of us are the stakes of freedom.

The companion book to the PBS TV series *Eyes on the Prize* ends like this:

> The decade spanning the *Brown* decision of 1954 and the Voting Rights act of 1965 saw more social change, more court decisions, and more legislation in the name of civil rights than any decade in our nation's history. Those changes were forced by millions of Americans who, with a sense of service and justice, kept their eyes on the prize of freedom.

> "I know one thing we did right
> was the day we started to fight.
> Keep your eyes o the prize,
> hold on, hold on.

We too must hold on and not take our eyes off the prize of freedom. We need another decade of great progress in race relations. We need to stand up for the kind of social change needed to enable us to achieve the prize of freedom for everyone. As I began this Postscript, doing so in the sense of the postscript Viktor Frankl wrote in his book, I again turn to how he ended his postscript, which provides the perfect recipe for ending mine:

So, let us be alert—alert in a twofold sense:

> Since Auschwitz we know what man is capable of.
> Since Hiroshima we know what is at stake.

And so, the Minneapolis story calls us to be alert in a twofold sense as well:

> Since slavery, Jim Crow, Tulsa, Rosewood, Duluth, Hollman and August 2002 in Minneapolis, and the racism, violence, and White terrorism described in Interludes 2, 6, 9-15, we know what man is capable of.

> Since the Civil War, Dred Scott, Martin Luther King, Jr., the land-takings and wealth-takings from Blacks, the attempts to bring Jim Crow back and the current problems in the inner cities in terms of education, housing, jobs, and equal access/opportunity, the Watts Riots of 1965, the urban riots of 1967, and the latest unrest in Minneapolis in 2002, we know what is at stake.

To Engage Ron Edwards as a speaker, contact:

Ron Edwards
Suite 900 -- PMB 107
505 Vicksburg Lane, No.
Plymouth, MN   55447

OR THROUGH

Beacon On The Hill Press
Suite 119 -- PMB 258
9220 Barber Blvd.
Portland, OR   97219

OR THROUGH

www.TheMinneapolisStory.com

To order copies of this book, go to:

www.TheMinneapolisStory.com

OR REQUEST A COPY
AT YOUR LOCAL BOOKSTORE

If they are out, they or you can order it through
www.TheMinneapolisStory.com

Or from the publisher, Beacon On The Hill Press
www.BeaconOnTheHill.com